Markku Peltonen examines humanist and republican themes in English political thinking between the mid sixteenth century and the Civil War. He challenges the dominant view that humanism fizzled out in the middle of the sixteenth century only to reemerge during the 1650s in the writings of such classical republicans as James Harrington and John Milton. The English never lost sight of humanism as a political discourse. They continued to use such deeply entrenched notions of the humanist tradition as the virtuous civic life and *vera nobilitas* throughout the period to portray themselves as citizens and to characterize their life as one of active participation rather than subjection.

In addition, early modern Englishmen resorted to more openly republican themes. They often argued that a republican form of government implemented in a highly successful manner the idea of meritocracy. The classical idea of a mixed constitution also exerted a profound influence on English political thought. Most importantly, some theorists felt no qualms about employing the central notion of republicanism – that governors should be elected rather than hereditary. As well as excavating humanist and republican themes, the study aims at locating their uses in their proper historical circumstances.

IDEAS IN CONTEXT

CLASSICAL HUMANISM AND REPUBLICANISM IN ENGLISH POLITICAL THOUGHT

1570–1640

IDEAS IN CONTEXT

Edited by Quentin Skinner (*General Editor*), Lorraine Daston, Wolf Lepenies, Richard Rorty and J. B. Schneewind

The books in this series will discuss the emergence of intellectual traditions and of related new disciplines. The procedures, aims and vocabularies that were generated will be set in the context of the alternatives available within the contemporary frameworks of ideas and institutions. Through detailed studies of the evolution of such traditions, and their modification by different audiences, it is hoped that a new picture will form of the development of ideas in their concrete contexts. By this means, artificial distinctions between the history of philosophy, of the various sciences, of society and politics, and of literature may be seen to dissolve.

The series is published with the support of the Exxon Foundation

A list of books in the series will be found at the end of the volume.

CLASSICAL HUMANISM AND REPUBLICANISM IN ENGLISH POLITICAL THOUGHT 1570–1640

MARKKU PELTONEN
University of Helsinki

CAMBRIDGE
UNIVERSITY PRESS

Published by the Press Syndicate of the University of Cambridge
The Pitt Building, Trumpington Street, Cambridge CB2 IRP
40 West 20th Street, New York, NY 10011–4211, USA
10 Stamford Road, Oakleigh, Melbourne 3166, Australia

First published 1995

A catalogue record for this book is available from the British Library

Library of Congress cataloguing in publication data

Peltonen, Markku.
Classical humanism and republicanism in English political thought,
1570–1640 / Markku Peltonen.
p.   cm. – (Ideas in context; 36)
Includes bibliographical references.
ISBN 0 521 49695 0
1. Political science–Great Britain–History.   2. Humanism–Great
Britain–History.   3. Republicanism–Great Britain–History.
I. Title.   II. Series.
JA84.G7P44 1995
320'.0941–dc20   94-44775   CIP

ISBN 0 521 49695 0 hardback

Transferred to digital printing 2003

Contents

Note on text

Original spelling has been retained throughout (except i/j and u/v in quotations), with the exception of those editions I have used where spelling has been modernized.

The year is taken to begin on 1 January.

The absence of any reference to women is, of course, due to the fact there were no such references: all treatises cited were written by and for an audience of men.

Acknowledgements

I have immensely enjoyed writing this book, so it is a real pleasure to acknowledge the debts of gratitude which I have contracted in the process. First of all, I am deeply grateful to Erkki Kouri whose help, especially in the later stages of the project, has been most invaluable. I owe much to his academic advice and personal support. I should also like to thank Pekka Suvanto and Matti Viikari. Pekka Suvanto guided my early tentative ventures into the field of historical scholarship; Matti Viikari has always been an uncompromising but kind reader of my writings.

My greatest debt is to Quentin Skinner. He first took interest in my writings when they were hardly worthy of critical reaction and has found the time to read them ever since. He originally suggested the topic of this book and has read and commented on its several earlier versions. His ever-instructive judgement and unfailing kindness have been a constant support and inspiration.

I am also indebted to Stuart Clark and Johann Sommerville for their early words of encouragement, to David Armitage and Brian Vickers for their later help and to Pirkko Haapanen for numerous discussions on republicanism. Thanks also go to John Calton, who corrected the language of the Introduction, Epilogue and Chapter 3. As for the rest of the work, I profited immensely from the help of my friends, Anne Finell, Walter Johnson and, above all, Ad Putter.

Margaret Grover has been my indefatigable guide as to the intricacies of 'Englishness'. Of the numerous friends with whom I have shared the enjoyment of scholarship, it would be churlish of me not to mention Anne Finell, Walter Johnson, M. Grazia Lolla, Ville Lukkarinen, Eero Palmujoki, Ad Putter, Ilkka Teerijoki and Jukka Vuori.

I am grateful to the Consistory of Helsinki University for granting me the Herman Rosenberg Travel Grant. The Academy of Finland made it possible for me to study at Cambridge University. The timely financial support of the Emil Aaltonen Foundation and especially that of Hämäläisosakunta enabled me to complete the manuscript. A part of Chapter 2 has appeared in *The History of Political Thought* and another version of Chapter 4 in *The Historical Journal*.

I should not have embarked on a project such as this without the moral support of Soili Paananen, much less carried it out without her and Frans's stalwart encouragement.

Abbreviations

Bacon, *Essayes*	Francis Bacon, *Essayes* (1625), ed. Michael Kiernan (Oxford English Texts, 1985).
Bacon, *Letters*	Francis Bacon, *The letters and life*, 7 vols., ed. James Spedding (London: Longman & Co., 1862–74).
Bacon, *Works*	Francis Bacon, *The works*, 7 vols., ed. James Spedding et al. (London: Longman & Co, 1857–9).
CD1628	*Commons debates 1628*, 4 vols., ed. Robert C. Johnson et al. (New Haven: Yale University Press, 1977–8).
CSPI	*Calendar of state papers relating to Ireland, 1586–96* (London, 1877–85).
Greville, *The prose works*	Fulke Greville, *The prose works of Fulke Greville, Lord Brooke*, ed. John Gouws (Oxford English Texts, 1986).
Greville, *The remains*	Fulke Greville, *The remains of Fulke Greville*, ed. G. A. Wilkes (Oxford: Zondervan, 1965).
PD1610	*Parliamentary debates in 1610*, ed. S. R. Gardiner, Camden Society, LXXXI (1862).
PPEI	*Proceedings in the parliaments of Elizabeth I*, vol. 1 1558–1581, ed. T. E. Hartley (Leicester University Press, 1981).
PP1610	*Proceedings in parliament 1610*, 2 vols., ed. E. R. Foster (New Haven: Yale University Press, 1966).
PP1626	*Proceedings in parliament 1626*, vol. 1 House of Lords, ed. William B. Bidwell and Maija Jansson (New Haven: Yale University Press, 1991).

Ralegh, *Works*   Walter Ralegh, *Works*, 8 vols., ed. W. Oldys
                           (Oxford University Press, 1829).

Somers tracts   Walter Scott (ed.), *A collection of scarce and
                           valuable tracts*, 13 vols. (London, 1809–15).

Spenser, *Poetical works* Edmund Spenser, *Poetical works*, ed. J. C.
                           Smith and E. de Selincourt (Oxford
                           University Press, 1912).

State trials   *A complete collection of State trials*, vol. II, ed.
                           T. B. Howell (London, 1816).

TGKB   Francis Bacon, 'Of the true greatness of the
                           kingdom of Britain', in *Works*, VII, pp. 45–64.

Introduction: classical humanism and republicanism in England before the Civil War

I

The Civil War and the Interregnum hold a prime place in the history of English political thought. There is a high degree of unanimity amongst historians that English political discourse faced an abrupt and total turning point in the 1640s and that the period between 1640 and 1660 gave rise to an exceptionally diverse body of political understanding and interpretation. One of the most significant and far-reaching traditions to emerge upon the stage of English political thinking was republicanism, in the writings of such men as John Milton, Marchamont Nedham, James Harrington and Algernon Sidney. Whilst scholars have long been aware of the great importance of these theorists, they have been keen to emphasize two issues in so far as the moment of the emergence of republicanism is concerned.

In the first place, they have pointed out that distinctively republican themes were discussed in a comprehensive manner relatively late. During the Civil War the idea of kingship was tenaciously held, and republicanism only gained currency for the first time after the regicide, as a device to legitimate the foundation of the republic. Secondly, and closely related to this, scholars have stressed even more strongly that before the Civil War there were no discernible signs of republicanism. That is to say, the republican strand of political discourse only appeared in England after the collapse of the traditional frames of reference. Before this there was simply 'no room for republican notions'; the dominant modes of discourse stressing eternal unity, harmony and hierarchy effectively inhibited the emergence of republican modes of thinking.[1]

---

[1] E.g. Zagorin 1954, pp. 146–9, quotation p. 146; Rawson 1969, pp. 187–8; Worden 1990, pp. 225–6; Worden 1991a, pp. 443–5; Wootton 1986, pp. 70–1. Cf., however, Worden 1981, pp. 182, 185–90, which depicts some family contacts; Scott 1988, pp. 18, 48–58. For the abrupt

The republicanism of the 1650s is often referred to as classical republicanism because of its obvious intellectual debt to classical Greek and especially Roman sources. It conceived of men as citizens rather than subjects; they were characterized not so much by obedience to the king as by active participation in the political life of their community through counselling and the law-making process. The citizens' participatory role was chiefly based on their virtuous characters, which enabled them to promote the public good. The term 'classical republicanism' thus embraces a cluster of themes concerning citizenship, public virtue and true nobility. But it also refers to a more specific constitutional stance. Virtue was closely linked with the distinctively *republican* character of classical republicanism: to ensure that the most virtuous men governed the commonwealth and to control corruption, magistracy should be elected rather than inherited. In this sense republicanism (in the narrow sense of a constitution without a king) could be an anti-monarchical goal: civic values required concomitant republican institutions, but monarchical arrangements were said to suppress these. Arrangements usually favoured by classical republicans were those of the mixed constitution, and the term republic was also used in the wider and more general sense of referring to a good and just constitution.[2]

If historians have concurred that classical republicanism only emerged in England during the 1650s, their unanimity further extends to its wider ideological background. They agree, in other words, that the broader political vocabulary which to a great extent underlay this form of republicanism – classical humanism – was also absent from English political debate between the mid sixteenth and mid seventeenth centuries. It is commonly assumed that classical humanism appeared twice in England. In its original form it reached England in the late fourteenth century and flourished during the early part of the sixteenth. It fizzled out, however, in the middle of the century to re-emerge transformed in the 1650s. Most accounts of the role of humanism in English political thought break off at the middle of the

change, see also Eccleshall 1978, pp. 153, 2; Sharpe 1989, p. 18; Salmon 1959, p. 12. See also Sommerville 1986, p. 58, for the absence of republicanism before the Civil War. Sommerville, however, maintains that the Civil War 'was no great watershed in English political thinking', p. 238.

2   For an excellent definition of the terminology, to which I am particularly indebted, see Goldsmith 1987, pp. 226–30. For suggestive remarks, see Worden 1991b, pp. 249–53; Mendle 1989a, pp. 116–17. See also Fink 1945; Worden 1981; Worden 1990; Scott 1988; and more generally Nippel 1988.

sixteenth century;[3] Lawrence Humphrey's treatise *The nobles or of nobilitye* (1560 in Latin, 1563 in English) was already 'a belated Humanist treatise'.[4] It has often been suggested that humanism must have had a considerable impact on Elizabethan and Jacobean statesmen, but this suggestion has never been fully explored.[5] By and large, scholars have moved directly to the mid seventeenth century. A case in point is Zera Fink who, having discussed the mid-sixteenth-century upholders of the mixed constitution, almost immediately shifts his attention to James Harrington and John Milton, hence skipping almost a century.[6] Likewise, Donald W. Hanson claims that pre-Civil War England was completely dominated by the concept of 'double majesty', whether in its medieval form of *dominium politicum et regale* or in its early-seventeenth-century form of *dominium regale et legale*. It was only during the mid-century upheavals that 'civic consciousness', a 'loyalty to abstract principles of government, justified in the name of concern for the public good', emerged. This new concept is exemplified by Milton's insistence that 'the task was "to place every one his private welfare and happiness in the public peace, liberty, and safety" '.[7]

Historians of English political thinking in the late sixteenth and early seventeenth centuries have mainly been concerned with the question of whether there existed any profound ideological disagreement. Whilst a number of scholars still maintain that the political thought of the period can be inclusively described as the common theory of Tudor monarchy – a theory of order and the rule of law[8] – recent scholarship has stressed that other political vocabularies – absolutism, the ancient constitution, contractarian theories, including even some forms of resistance theories – were in fact employed in political arguments of the day and that 'there was a variety of political viewpoints in early Stuart England'.[9] A common characteristic of all these accounts, however, is that they all ignore the humanist tradition. Scholars, irrespective of

---

[3]   E.g. Bush 1939, pp. 69–100; Ferguson 1965; McConica 1965; Dowling 1986, Fox and Guy 1986; Schoek 1988; Elton 1990; Guy 1988, pp. 408–13.

[4]   Morris 1953, pp. 21–6, 143–4

[5]   Caspari 1954, pp. 157, 207–8; Hill 1965, pp. 266–8; Rabb 1981, pp. 72–3; Ferguson 1986, pp. 89–92, 112–25; Charlton 1965, pp. 41–85; Skinner 1988, pp. 445–6; Worden 1991a, p. 444; Guy 1993, pp. 14–15.

[6]   Fink 1945. See also Rawson 1969, pp. 186–201; Mendle 1985.

[7]   Hanson 1970, especially pp. 42, 248, 254, 287–90, 310, 333.

[8]   Raab 1964; Smith 1973; Mendle 1973; Weston and Greenberg 1981; Sharpe 1985, pp. 14–18, 28–31; Russell 1990, pp. 131–60; Collins 1989.

[9]   Sommerville 1991, p. 70; Peck 1993b; Sommerville 1986; Sommerville 1989; Eccleshall 1978; Bowler 1981; Bowler 1984; Collinson 1987; Cust 1987, pp. 176–85. See also Allen 1938, Judson 1949; Greenleaf 1964.

their general predilection, seem to concur that humanism had no perceptible impact on the political discourse of the late sixteenth and early seventeenth centuries.[10] It is scarcely any exaggeration to say that there is a scholarly gap between the mid sixteenth and the mid seventeenth centuries in so far as the role of the classical humanist tradition in English political discourse is concerned.

The most forceful and dominant account of these issues has been offered by J. G. A. Pocock. In his study of the classical republican tradition, *The Machiavellian moment*, Pocock has put forward an argument as to why themes of citizenship and the republic did not gain ground in Elizabethan and early Stuart England. His point of departure, which he broadly speaking shares with other scholars, is that the emergence of republican and 'civic humanist' themes was effectively hindered by other modes of thought and that their real development in England only became possible after the collapse of older viewpoints in the wake of the traumatic experiences of the Civil War and the Interregnum. So although Pocock shares with other scholars the assumption that the Civil War entailed a total and abrupt change in habits of thought, he does not commit himself to the somewhat simplistic idea of the 'Elizabethan world picture' but offers an ingenious account of the roles of different political vocabularies in thwarting as well as paving the way for the development of the ideas of citizenship and republic.[11]

According to Pocock, the political vocabulary of the early-sixteenth-century humanists offered a way in which the English could develop civic awareness by projecting the image of the humanist as a counsellor to his prince. In this role the humanist possessed skills which the prince was lacking and he was, therefore, 'contributing to an association a virtue of his own, an individual capacity for participation in rule, and had then taken a step in the direction of the Aristotelian image of the citizen'. Pocock accepts, however, the idea that English humanism declined in the mid sixteenth century and that its intellectual inheritors, if it had any, were the Tacitean courtiers in whom we encounter the first signs of a fully fledged conception of a political community as an association of active participants. Even though the Tudor notion of descending authority was incompatible with a theory of mixed government, there were indications of republican vocabulary in imperfectly

[10] See, however, Sommerville 1986, pp. 81, n.1, 245.
[11] Cf., however, Pocock 1966, especially pp. 266–7, 270, where he accepts to an extent Raab's simplistic account of the political thought of Tudor England.

legitimized situations. In these situations there was more room for independent choices and decisions. 'It was consequently', Pocock declares, 'in the study of statecraft that Jacobean intellects were most likely to lay hold upon these elements of the republican tradition which ascribed distinctive characteristics – interests, humors, *particulari* – to kings, nobilities and peoples, and considered how these might conflict or be reconciled.'[12]

For Pocock, the idea of order and all that went with it was only one way of conceptualizing the political universe before the Civil War. There were other theoretical standpoints which offered directions for the early modern Englishman to develop an understanding of the political world, and which in their own ways developed into modes of civic consciousness but at the same time effectively impeded evolving republican and 'civic humanist' conceptions. Amongst these were the medieval vocabulary of *jurisdiction* and *gubernaculum*, the theory of ancient constitution, the doctrine of the elect nation and the tradition of natural jurisprudence. All these traditions contributed ultimately to preventing Englishmen from conceiving themselves as active, participating citizens and of the commonwealth as a genuine republic.[13]

Although Pocock's thesis has met with wide acceptance, his arguments have failed to convince the entire scholarly community. Recently some historians have become increasingly aware that there is perhaps something lacking in his account. It has become clear that in parliamentary elections, for instance, a 'surprisingly large social group became involved in legitimate politics'.[14] And it has been suggested that during the early seventeenth century the concept of liberty became associated with 'an ideal of community and a sense of participation in its public business'.[15] David Norbrook has emphasized how 'the conscious intentions of some [Elizabethan and Jacobean] poets may in fact have been less conservative than has often been assumed'. He painstakingly excavates a number of radical implications from their works and convincingly argues that many of them were expressed in classical humanist vocabulary.[16] Linda Levy Peck has recently asserted

---

12 Pocock 1975b, pp. 338–9, 347, 350–7; Pocock 1966, p. 279.
13 Pocock 1966, pp. 278–9; Pocock 1975b, pp. 334–7, 340–7; Pocock 1977, p. 15; Pocock 1981a, pp. 54–6; Pocock 1981b, pp. 356–7; see in general also Pocock 1970; Pocock 1971; Pocock 1975a.
14 Hirst 1975, especially pp. 4, 6–7, 104–5, 152–3, 176–7, 191–3. Cf. Underdown 1985, pp. 106–45.
15 Sacks 1992, quotation from p. 110.
16 Norbrook 1984, especially pp. 12–16.

that the discourses of patronage and corruption were in large part classical humanist in character.[17] Mentions of the republican notion of liberty have lately been found in debates about the puritan colonies in America in the 1630s.[18]

More to the point, Patrick Collinson has called attention to the fact that the Englishman's horizon concerning his active and participatory role in the life of his commonwealth was perhaps not as limited as Pocock allows. Collinson does not argue for 'a continuous, coherent republican movement' nor even for 'the incipience in Elizabethan England of a kind of constitutional monarchy'. But referring on the theoretical level *inter alia* to 'the legacy of early-sixteenth-century humanism' and on the practical level to the Bond of Association, he points out that the English, whether in the upper or lower stratum of society, were able to respond 'resourcefully and intelligently to a most unusual [political] situation'. We must, therefore, be careful 'not to underestimate both the political sophistication and the political capacity of high Elizabethan society'.[19] According to Collinson, 'Pocock underestimated ... quasi-republican modes of political reflection and action within the intellectual and active reach of existing modes of consciousness and established constitutional parameters'; 'citizens', Collinson adds, 'were concealed within subjects'.[20]

There are two closely related problems in Pocock's interpretation which offer sufficient reason to re-evaluate his account. First, in treating the Civil War period as an absolute turning point, his interpretation, in accordance with other assessments of early modern English political thought, tends to make too sharp a division between the modes of political discourse before and after the 1640s. Secondly, although Pocock recognizes the role of humanism in the incipient development of civic consciousness, in assuming that it lost force in the mid sixteenth century, he unduly neglects its importance in the late sixteenth and early seventeenth centuries.[21] There is no reason to belittle the importance of the Civil War in the history of political thought, but it does not follow that Englishmen were completely incapable of developing a civic consciousness before that period. It is arguable that Pocock under-estimates the level of sophistication of pre-Civil War English political

---

[17]   Peck 1993a, p. 208 and in general pp. 161–207.
[18]   Kupperman 1989.
[19]   Collinson 1987, citations pp. 422, 408, 423, 402; see also pp. 406–7.
[20]   Collinson 1990, pp. 23–4, in general 22–34.
[21]   See, however, Pocock 1985b, p. 150.

writing. A partial embracing and employment of republican themes in England was not entirely dependent on a complete and dramatic change in the political context. Nor was a fully fledged republican theory obligatory for the development of civic consciousness. Englishmen were to an extent able both to embrace parts of the republican vocabulary in their own context and to articulate their civic consciousness without a full-scale republican theory.

The main aim of the present study is, accordingly, to examine the role of classical humanism in English political writing from the 1570s to 1640. It is hoped that this examination will throw light on a number of issues central to early modern political thinking. First, a study of classical humanism should enable us to consider civic consciousness and the idea of citizenship in pre-Civil War England. If we wish, in other words, to assess the nature and development of these issues properly, it is to a large extent the continuance of the classical humanist vocabulary that ought to serve as the focus of our attention. Moreover, this investigation will enable us to analyse the republican features of early modern English political thinking. It is again primarily the classical humanist tradition which should be examined in order to gauge the extent of republicanism before the Civil War.

II

Humanism is taken to include the conscious revival as well as the reinterpretation of classical Graeco-Roman history, literature and values and, in so far as political thinking is concerned, their effective application to the political problems of the contemporary world.[22] It follows that classical humanism was 'a mode of discourse' or 'a political vocabulary' rather than 'a programme'; it was a means of grasping and conceptualizing politics, rather than a monolithic and detailed plan or strategy.[23]

Whether as a scholarly movement or a mode of political thought, humanism emerged, it is widely agreed, relatively late in England. Its inception in the mid fifteenth century was due partly to Italian scholars who diffused humanist ideas in England and partly to those Englishmen who acquired a predilection for humanist studies in Italy.[24] It is still

[22] See e.g. Burke 1990, p. 2; Todd 1987, pp. 22–3; Ferguson 1965, pp. 162–3; Logan 1977; Trinkaus 1990, pp. 681–4; Fox and Guy 1986, pp. 31–3.

[23] See Pocock 1987b; Pocock 1985c, chapter 1; Pocock 1977, p. 15; Lockyer 1979.

[24] Weiss 1957. For a succinct account of the dissemination of Italian humanism, see Burke 1990. For the connections between England and the continent in the early sixteenth century, see e.g. Dowling 1986, pp. 140–75.

essentially correct, however, to follow Francis Bacon in dating the chief
period of humanism, or as Bacon put it in his succinct definition of the
scope of humanism, 'the admiration of ancient authors, the hate of the
schoolmen, the exact study of languages, and the efficacy of preaching',
to the period between Erasmus and Roger Ascham.[25]

Humanism as a vocabulary of political discourse had a similar
beginning in England. One of the first humanist political treatises in
English was produced by John Tiptoft, earl of Worcester, who
translated Cicero's *De amicitia* as well as Buonaccorso da Montemagna's
Controversia de nobilitate as early as the 1450s.[26] It grew into prominence
during the first part of the sixteenth century, when its most celebrated
treatises such as Thomas More's *Utopia* (1516), Thomas Elyot's *The boke
named the gouernour* (1531) and Thomas Starkey's *Dialogue between Pole and
Lupset* (c.1529–32) were composed alongside numerous less famous
treatises by such authors as Thomas Lupset, Richard Morison and
John Heywood. A little later, in the mid Tudor period, it found its
exponents in such men as Thomas Becon, Roger Ascham, Thomas
Smith and in the so-called 'Commonwealthmen' in general.[27]

English humanists, together with their North European contemporaries, inherited a somewhat equivocal legacy from the political vocabulary of Italian humanism. On the one hand, humanism had been used
to defend and characterize republican values, although it would be
highly misleading to equate republicanism with humanism, for, of
course, there had been pre-humanist republican arguments.[28] In the
course of the fifteenth century, however, strong princely rule emerged
in various Italian cities with the consequence that the humanist
tradition was used to eulogize princely rule. By and large, northern
humanists were more inclined to employ the values and beliefs of the
princely mode of Italian humanism. They were particularly reticent on
some of the two central issues of the republican tradition: liberty and
the citizens' army.[29] Instead, they were preoccupied with producing
treatises in the same genres as those Italian humanists who advocated
princely rule – educational treatises and advice-books for princes and

---

[25]   Bacon, *Advancement of learning*, in *Works*, III, pp. 283–4. See e.g. McConica 1965.
[26]   Mitchell 1938.
[27]   See e.g. McConica 1965; Caspari 1954; Zeeveld 1969; Ferguson 1963; Ferguson 1965;
        Berkowitz 1984; Elton 1979; Todd 1987; Fox and Guy 1986; Elton 1990. For More, see
        especially Skinner 1987; Bradshaw 1981. For Starkey, see Mayer 1985; Mayer 1986; Mayer
        1989. For Elyot, see e.g. Lehmberg 1960.
[28]   See e.g. Skinner 1990a; Nederman 1993.
[29]   Skinner 1978 I, p. 200.

their counsellors – and were disposed to endorse similar sets of values as their Italian predecessors: the commonwealth was in its best state when a prince with a full range of personal virtues ruled it.[30]

Nevertheless, it is of crucial importance to bear in mind that Italian republicanism also had from the very beginning a considerable impact on northern humanists.[31] Although English humanists took the princely context for granted, it did not prevent their adopting a number of 'civic' and republican themes in their writings. In this they partly drew on Italian republicanism, but their main source of inspiration was the Roman stoic authors, who were of vital importance in the formation of the humanist view of politics.[32]

The first way in which English humanists can be said to have followed Italian republicanism was in conceiving themselves as reformers of the commonwealth.[33] This issue appeared with vehemence in Thomas More's *Utopia* and was treated even more extensively by Thomas Starkey in his *Dialogue*. Robert Whittinton translated Cicero's *De officiis* partly to explain what engendered the 'encrease of commen welthes' and what was the 'cause of [their] ruyne and decaye'.[34] A more important point of contact with the tradition of republicanism was the discussion of the merits of the mixed constitution. As is well known, Thomas Starkey was fully convinced that 'a myxte state' was not merely the best form of government and 'most convenyent to conserve the hole out of tyranny'; it was also the most suitable for curing the diseases of the English body politic.[35] It is equally well known that John Ponet employed the same vocabulary in his argu-

[30] See e.g. Skinner 1978 I, pp. 118–28, 213–17, 222–3, 228–43; Skinner 1988, pp. 423–30, 443–5. For republican humanism, see e.g. Baron 1966; Bayley 1961; Bouwsma 1968. For a balanced survey, see Rabil 1988. Cf. however Grafton 1991.

[31] See in general Skinner 1978 I, pp. 215–42, and for a succinct account where this point is made with particular pertinence, see Skinner 1988, pp. 445–8. In my characterization of the impact of Italian republicanism on the early-sixteenth-century English humanists, I owe an obvious debt to this account. Cf. in general also Todd 1987, pp. 22–52; Caspari 1954; Ferguson 1965; Bradshaw 1991.

[32] For the centrality of Roman stoicism for the development of the humanist political vocabulary, see Skinner 1978 I, p. xiv; Todd 1987, pp. 22–3, 27–9; Kristeller 1988, pp. 279, 285; Skinner 1990a, especially pp. 122–3; Tuck 1990.

[33] Cf. Todd 1987, p. 23; Bradshaw 1991, pp. 100, 130.

[34] *The thre bookes of Tullyes offyces*, translated by Robert Whittinton (London, 1534), 'An exhortacyon', sigs. b4ʳ–5ʳ; Anon., *The prayse and commendacion of suche as sought comen welthes* (London, n.d. [1549]). See also e.g. Robert Crowley, *The way to wealth, wherein is plainly taught a most present remedy for sedicion* (n.p. [London], 1550), especially sigs. A3ʳ⁻ᵛ, B8ᵛ; [Humfrey Braham], *The institucion of a gentleman* (London, 1555), sig. *6ʳ⁻ᵛ.

[35] Thomas Starkey, *A dialogue between Pole and Lupset*, ed. T. F. Mayer, Camden 4th ser., XXXVII, 1989, pp. 36–40, 67–73, 111–13, 119–23. Cf. e.g. Nippel 1980 pp. 183–9.

ments against Mary Tudor and that John Aylmer used it in his defence
of her half-sister Elizabeth.[36]

The belief in their own capacity to bring up and tackle the pressing
problems of the commonwealth increased, as Ferguson and Pocock have
pointed out, English humanists' 'self-image' and their understanding of
their own active political role.[37] It also led them to discard the Italian
princely humanists' predilection for the *vita contemplativa* and to embrace
instead the Ciceronian and republican conviction that the *vita activa* was
the highest form of life. *Otium* – learning – was, however, accommodated
to this conception as a necessary requirement for achieving the true ideal
of *negotium*. An active member of the commonwealth was something akin
to the Ciceronian ideal of a rhetorician: he joined learning (philosophy)
with the active life (eloquence). This was one of the topics which engaged
Hythlodaeus and More in *Utopia*,[38] and it was a governing theme of
Thomas Elyot's *The boke named the governour*. It was also the topic with
which Starkey opened his *Dialogue*, where Lupset persuaded Pole to
believe that 'al men are borne & of nature brought forth, to commyn
such gyftys as be to them gyven, ychone to the profyt of other, in perfayt
cyvylyte, & not to lyve to theyr owne plesure'. This was the true end of
'cyvyle lyfe', as Starkey termed it in true humanist fashion.[39] This
essentially Ciceronian doctrine of the great importance of the *vita activa*
was repeated in numerous lesser known humanist tracts, and it is scarcely
an exaggeration to state that it became a hallmark of the English
humanists.[40] The chief ways in which a man could offer his services to
the commonwealth were either to act as a counsellor or more indirectly
to submit written advice. An increasingly important role, however, was
attached to parliament and its law-making function, which was in some
ways becoming central to the English *vita activa*.[41]

Another closely related topic which gained currency amongst

[36] J[ohn] P[onet], *A shorte treatise of politike power* (n.p. [Strasburg?], 1556), sigs. A4ᵛ–B5ᵛ; cf.
Peardon 1982. [John Aylmer], *An harborowe for faithfull and trew subiectes* (Strasburg, 1559), sigs.
H2ᵛ–I3ᵛ, Q4ᵛ.

[37] Ferguson 1965; Pocock 1975b, pp. 339–40.

[38] Skinner 1987, pp. 128–35; Skinner 1988, pp. 449–50; Fox and Guy 1986, pp. 40–1.

[39] Starkey, *A dialogue*, pp. 1–6, cf. p. 142.

[40] Ferguson 1986, pp. 57–8; Kelso 1929, pp. 39–40. See e.g. 'An exhortacyon', *The thre bookes of
Tullyes offyces*, sigs. a5ʳ, b2ʳ, b4ʳ; *Marcvs Tullius Ciceroes thre bokes of duties to marcus his sonne*,
translated by Nicolas Grimalde (London, 1556), sig. c8ᵛ. [Braham], *The institucion*, sig. D6ʳ, see
in general sigs. D5ᵛ-6ᵛ, A2ᵛ, C4ʳ G6ʳ. See also e.g. [Leonard Cox], *The arte or crafte of rhethoryke*
(London, n.d. [1532?]), sig. B7ʳ; [Josse Clichtove], *The boke of noblenes: that sheweth how many sortes
and kyndes there is*, translated from French by John Larke (n.p. [London], n.d. [1550?]), sig. G1ᵛ–
2ʳ.

[41] Ferguson 1965, pp. 146–52; Pocock 1975b, pp. 339–40.

English humanists was the issue of true nobility.[42] The idea that only virtue constituted true nobility had, of course, been stated by Roman moralists and historians and their authority was used with vehemence by Italian republican humanists to mount an attack against their scholastic rivals. Likewise, Thomas More arranged some of the most important parts of *Utopia* around this theme, and it was an equally central topic in Thomas Elyot's and Thomas Starkey's writings. But the most extensive treatment of this theme appeared in treatises specifically devoted to the question of what constituted a true gentleman. The earliest treatise in English in this tradition was of course John Tiptoft's translation of Buonaccorsa de Montenagna's *Controversia de nobilitate* and a similar range of topics was later discussed in such well-known indigenous treatises as John Heywood's *Of gentylnesse & nobylyte* (c. 1525) and Humfrey Braham's *The institucion of a gentleman* (1555). Braham promised to 'describe such a man as may be worthelye called master, not leaving undeclared the blindnes of those which thincke theimselves Gentlemen, onely because their fathers & auctoures did discend of noble houses'. He invoked Cicero in declaring that 'those men maye worthely bee called honourable whom vertue hath avaunced and reysed them to dignitie'.[43] Together with the idea of the *vita activa*, this notion could lead to the conclusion that there was an intimate connection between virtue and citizenship. It was only by a relentless pursuit of civic virtues that a man could serve the commonwealth and become a truly noble citizen.

III

In this study I am particularly concerned with examining the continuity, development and re-evaluation of this cluster of closely related themes in early modern English political thought. I wish to challenge the assumption that they were completely replaced by other political vocabularies after the mid sixteenth century. I shall endeavour to indicate the remarkable extent to which Elizabethan and Jacobean writers maintained these values. More particularly, I seek to emphasize that, far from being completely absent, classical republicanism (as a

[42] For an interesting and perceptive discussion of the concept of honour in early modern England, see James 1986, pp. 308–415.

[43] [Braham], *The institucion*, sigs. *7^r, c5^{r-v}. See also for example [Clichtove], *The boke of noblenes*, passim; *The thre bookes of Tullyes offyces* (1534), sig. b1^r–2^r, b7^r; *Ciceroes thre bookes of duties* (1556), sig. c3^r, c8^v. See Zeeveld 1969, pp. 204–11; James 1986, pp. 376–9.

constitutional stance) had a limited but undoubted impact on English political thought in the late sixteenth and early seventeenth centuries. There is a caveat here; it is important not to exaggerate the positive role of republican vocabulary in pre-Civil War England. In a famous passage Thomas Hobbes could claim that it was mainly the influence of classical authors that was to be blamed for the Civil War. But Englishmen were, of course, aware of this danger in the early seventeenth century, as attested, for instance, by Fulke Greville.[44] An education in the classics was not 'a road to republicanism' willy-nilly.[45] An unmixed republic was hardly a practical option in England before the Civil War, and we do not, it ought to be emphasized, encounter a coherent republican movement. But it does not follow that there were no discernible signs of republican themes. Some of the most celebrated classical and Italian texts of the republican tradition were translated into English during this period, and traces of this vocabulary are to be found in texts composed by Englishmen.

The second, more important, argument concerns the idea of citizenship. Although classical republicanism as a constitutional goal was not fully developed in early modern England, a theory of citizenship, public virtue and true nobility based essentially on the classical humanist and republican traditions, was taken up, studied and fully endorsed throughout the period. Amongst historians who place the beginning of civic consciousness in the period before the Civil War, the widest conviction is that this trend owed its impetus and theoretical underpinning to puritanism. In political thought as in social theory, puritans are seen as in the vanguard of new trends. According to Michael Walzer, 'it was the Calvinists who first switched the emphasis of political thought from the prince to the saint ... and then constructed a theoretical justification for independent political action. What Calvinists said of the saint, other men would later say of the citizen: the same sense of civic virtue, of discipline and duty, lies behind the two names.'[46]

---

44 Thomas Hobbes *Leviathan* (1651), ed. C. B. Macpherson (Harmondsworth: Penguin, 1968), pp. 267–8. For some elaboration, see Norbrook 1994, pp. 57–8. Fulke Greville, *A treatise of monarchy*, stanza 641, in *The remains*, p. 196. Cf. e.g. Thomas Gibson, *The blessing of a good king: deliuered in eight sermons* (London, 1614), sig. Aa3ᵛ-4ʳ.

45 Cf. Sharpe 1985, p. 30; Worden 1981, p. 183.

46 Walzer 1965, pp. 2, 18, 181–2; also pp. 255–67, 277–90. Cf. e.g. Hill 1986a, 250–6; Hill 1986b, pp. 212–50; Hill 1972, pp. 47–8; Curtis 1962; Pocock 1975b, pp. 336–8, 345–8; Stone 1986, p. 99; James 1986, pp. 330–1, 403–4; Cust and Hughes 1989, pp. 21–2; Hughes 1991, pp. 87, 89, 102, 105–6, 114–15. Cf. Eccleshall 1978, pp. 59–75, 97–121, who relates the development of the idea of citizenship mainly to the continuance of medieval Aristotelianism.

The ideological novelty of Calvinism has recently come under close scrutiny and its position as precursor of political and social thought has proved untenable. Scholars have become increasingly aware that several modes of thought previously ascribed to Calvinists had no peculiarly Calvinist elements at all: Quentin Skinner has shown that the theory of resistance developed by Calvinists did not have any specifically Calvinist features, but was taken up almost directly from their catholic adversaries;[47] Margo Todd has recently established that rather than deriving the inspiration for their social ideas exclusively from the Calvinist theology, puritans owed an obvious debt to Christian humanism in their social thinking.[48]

It is a central thesis of the present study that in tracing the notions of civic consciousness and the theory of citizenship in early modern England, we should not look at expressly puritan or Calvinist modes of argument. On the contrary, we should place the development of these features in the continuance of classical humanism. The arguments and notions which were used in articulating the idea of citizenship and the active life did not embody any particularly Calvinist traits at all, but were instead expressed in a distinctively humanist vocabulary.[49]

There are two further points to be made about religion in general and puritanism in particular. First, although many mid- and late-seventeenth-century classical republicans were anti-Calvinists,[50] it has been argued that in the late sixteenth and early seventeenth centuries there were close links between strong protestantism or puritanism and humanist political parlance.[51] To some extent this seems to be the case. Puritan attitudes towards plays and maypoles, church ales and football could be described as 'Stoicall'.[52] We shall encounter important new connections between strong protestantism and humanism, most conspicuously in the writings of John Barston and Thomas Scott. It is no news that Thomas Scott exhibited strong features of puritanism in his pamphlet campaign in the early 1620s. But what is less often appreciated is the fact that he coupled his puritanism with a theory of citizenship and the commonwealth which owed its main intellectual allegiance to classical humanism and republicanism. Nonetheless, it

---

[47] Skinner 1978 I, pp. xiv–xv, II, p. 323.
[48] Todd 1987, pp. 8, 16, 17, see also especially pp. 94–5. Cf. Larmine 1982; Adams 1989; Adams 1990.
[49] Collinson 1990, p. 26.
[50] Worden 1981, p. 195; Worden 1991b, p. 252.
[51] Norbrook 1984.
[52] Philip Stubbes, *The anatomie of abuses* (London 1583), sig. L2ᵛ.

should be emphasized even more strongly that it would be grossly misleading to claim that the vocabulary of classical humanism was the exclusive domain of puritans. Many of the authors who loom large in this book (Richard Beacon and Francis Bacon are good examples) cannot be classified as puritans.

This leads me to the other general point I wish to make about religion. Since I am concerned with the humanist and republican aspects of the authors examined, other aspects of their writings receive far less attention. This should not be taken to mean that I want to belittle their significance and this applies above all to the role of religion. By focusing my attention on their humanist and republican notions and by not expounding religion and other facets of their thought more fully, I do not imply that the authors examined were thoroughly secular thinkers, nor that the other features of their writings are somehow less important or less worthy of analysis. What I wish to argue is that most of the theorists studied here held deep religious convictions, which did not inhibit them from deriving political concepts from Roman stoic sources.[53]

The argument that in tracing the theory of citizenship in early modern England we should study the humanist tradition receives further incentive from recent studies of education in early modern England. According to the standard interpretation, the humanist university curriculum of the mid sixteenth century was replaced by a return to the scholastic one at the end of the century.[54] But, as Margo Todd has convincingly argued, after its introduction to the universities in the early sixteenth century the humanist curriculum dominated well into the middle of the seventeenth century.[55] This means, of course, that when the gentry increasingly sought access to education in the grammar schools as well as in the universities they received an essentially humanist education which thus became 'the common possession of the whole governing class'.[56] It is perhaps then not exceptionally surprising to endeavour to seek humanist traits in the

[53] Omitting 'the wisdome which is Divine and Metaphysicall' from his 'handfull of Morality', John Hitchcock formed an exception rather than a rule, *A sanctuary for honest men: or an abstract of humane wisdome* (London, 1617), pp. 3–4, sig. A3ʳ.

[54] Kearney 1970, pp. 77–90; Costello, 1958.

[55] Todd 1987, pp. 53–94; cf. Schmitt 1983, pp. 17–29,,. For the,, introduction of humanism into English universities, see e.g. Dowling 1986, pp. 23–33, 75–107; McConica 1965, pp. 76–105; Todd 1987, pp. 43–52; Curtis 1959, pp. 70–2, 81–2, 94–6; Simon 1966, pp. 63–123, 148–62, 197–214.

[56] James 1986, p. 270; see also Hexter 1950; Caspari 1954, pp. 132–56; Stone 1964, especially pp. 68–80; Simon 1966, pp. 291–8, 333–68.

political discourse of Elizabethan and Jacobean England. On the contrary, this is exactly what we should expect to find.

It should be pointed out that by using the term 'tradition' I do not mean to imply that there was a self-conscious and sustained tradition in which different periods were linked by continuity of generic concerns. The authors examined did not consciously participate in an ongoing conversation, if by this we mean that they referred to authors of previous periods (with the important exception of Francis Bacon). Rather, the term 'tradition' refers to a complex of three issues: theorists addressed similar questions of citizenship, corruption, reformation, greatness of states and the well-being of the commonwealth; they did this with similar humanist and republican vocabularies; and they employed the same Roman stoic and earlier renaissance sources in so doing.

As well as seeking to show the presence of humanism and some features of republicanism in English political thought from the 1570s to the 1630s, I am concerned with the more particular historical circumstances in which these arguments emerged. I ask how this vocabulary was used and what kind of points were put forward by those who employed it. For my contention is that a more historical interpretation of political texts is achieved if we endeavour to find out what the authors were attempting when they composed their works. Although there was neither a dramatic nor pervasive change in the political framework, in writing their tracts or translating foreign treatises, early modern Englishmen were not so much seeking to answer timeless questions as responding to contemporary problems and issues.

In addition to these somewhat programmatic claims, there are a number of smaller points which I should like to make in the course of this study. Although there is a noticeable shift of emphasis of interest from Cicero to Tacitus at the turn of the century, it is misleading to describe this shift, as many scholars have done, as a complete change from a Ciceronian humanism to a Tacitean one. During the Jacobean period, as I hope to show, we still meet with an essentially Ciceronian assessment of the commonwealth. This also leads us to re-examine some of the generally accepted notions regarding Jacobean political thought. It is commonly claimed that Jacobean political discourse is exhaustively treated as soon as a proper account of absolutism and especially of the interpretations of the ancient constitution have been provided. But, it is argued below, this gives us an overly simplistic view of the depth and scope of political thought during James I's reign.

Recently historians have been more willing to undermine the once popular idea of the insularity (or more accurately parochialism) of Jacobean political thinking and to admit that Englishmen were perfectly familiar with theoretical traditions other than their indigenous ancient constitution.[57] The unearthing of the classical humanist vocabulary in Jacobean England elucidates not only the development of the theory of citizenship in England but also, and more particularly, the full range of political thinking of the period.

Furthermore, an attempt is made here to seek and establish an ideological context for Francis Bacon's political writings. Scholars commonly assume that this is to be found in his scientific pursuits – that he was carrying out a comprehensive single project including a reform of natural philosophy, a reform of law and a political programme of a similar nature.[58] I should like to argue, however, that the ideological context for Bacon's theoretical contributions to politics should be sought in classical humanist vocabulary. Some of his most important political writings were composed in the Machiavellian tradition and his ideas of politics in his more philosophical works carried characteristically humanist features.

Finally, an account of classical humanism and republicanism in English political thought before the Civil War must have an immediate bearing on the interpretation of the reception of Machiavelli's writings in England. The dominant interpretation of his impact on pre-Civil War English politics is congruent with some of the general accounts of the political thought of the period. Although Machiavelli was known in England at an early stage, his writings, the standard interpretation proclaims, met with a profound repugnance and dismay. This was so because the encounter of England and Machiavelli was an encounter between one dominated by 'an Augustinian universe' and another dominated by purely secular politics.[59] Machiavelli's writings, we have lately been told, constituted a grave threat to the 'Elizabethan world picture' since they 'not only challenged but subverted all the premises of the early modern English commonweal'.[60] Whatever can be said about the interpretations of Machiavelli himself in these accounts, it is clear that they leave something to be desired with regard to the

57   Sommerville 1986, pp. 57–85; Sommerville 1989; Sommerville 1991; Peck 1993b.
58   For documentation, see chapter 4 below.
59   Raab 1964 pp 30–106. See also Praz 1928; Beck 1935; Mosse 1957; Morris 1969. Cf. Shutte 1983.
60   Sharpe 1989, pp. 25–8; Sharpe 1985, p. 28. Cf. Collins 1989, especially pp. 110–11.

reception of his writing in England.[61] A comprehensive account of this reception is beyond the scope of this study, and I treat it only in so far as Machiavelli's republicanism is concerned.

It is to begin with completely unnecessary to presuppose that every sign of a 'secular' political outlook is also indicative of a debt to Machiavelli. Tudor and early Stuart Englishmen were entirely capable of treating politics as a separate field of enquiry without any necessary help from Machiavelli's works. The whole humanist tradition and especially classical authors themselves provided the Englishman with a massive body of 'secular' literature which enabled him to embrace 'secular' concepts of politics, whilst at the same time he of course retained his Christian outlook.[62] Terms like 'an Augustinian universe' or the order theory of the 'Elizabethan world picture' are perhaps not extremely helpful concepts, much less exhaustive ones, for describing the modes of political thought in early modern England.

Moreover, although it is clear that the bulk of the references to Machiavelli was closely connected with the dichotomy between religion and policy,[63] it is arguable that we should not focus our attention exclusively on these passages or more broadly on the mention of Machiavelli's name, but instead seek to place the reading of his writings in the proper context of the humanist political vocabulary in Tudor and early Stuart England. Machiavelli was scarcely only a theorist of 'policy' as against 'religion', neither was he only read as such. As we shall see, the most extensive usage of his republican writings in pre-Civil War England did not mention his name at all. And it was hardly a usage confined to the dichotomy of 'policy' and 'religion'.

[61] For detailed, pertinent criticism, see Anglo 1966. I am much indebted to Stuart Clark for drawing my attention to Anglo's work.

[62] Cf. e.g. Ferguson 1965, pp. 166–7.

[63] Raab's extensive list can in fact be enlarged considerably.

CHAPTER I

Classical humanism restated

Towards the end of the *Discourses concerning government* Algernon Sidney praised Henry V's government. Henry's main aim, Sidney said, had been 'the conquest of France' and he had, therefore, shown utmost care not 'to encroach upon the liberties of his subjects'. Since the only way to pursue glory and greatness was 'by the bravery of a free and well-satisfied people', Henry had instead maintained the 'courage, strength, and love' of his people. This willingness 'to preserve their subjects' liberty' had always been the chief characteristic of 'virtuous and brave' princes, who knew that this was the only means of encouraging 'the people's valour'. Although Henry had made an attempt to perpetuate his government and to discourage his successors from enslaving the people, he had not succeeded. On the contrary, Sidney was 'inclined to date the general impairing of our government' from Henry's death onwards. Princes had almost continuously attempted 'to advance their prerogative' at the cost of the people's liberty. The only exception had been Queen Elizabeth. Following Henry, she had not set 'about to mangle acts of parliament' but had maintained the virtuous nature of the people and thereby the principles of 'the mixed monarchies'.[1]

This chapter is concerned with the ways in which Elizabethans in the 1570s and 1580s were engaged in an attempt to perceive their commonwealth in terms of classical humanism and themselves as virtuous citizens devoted to the civic life and public service for the promotion of the common good. While it is often pointed out that authors such as Algernon Sidney's great-uncle, Philip Sidney, or Edmund Spenser, owe an obvious debt to this tradition, it has been argued, as we have seen, that humanism as a political vocabulary declined in the mid sixteenth century. The main aim of this chapter is to show the remarkable extent

[1] Algernon Sidney, *Discourses concerning government* (1698) ed. Thomas G. West (Indianapolis: Liberty Fund, 1990), pp. 575–8.

to which central humanist and even republican concepts and values were strenuously restated just at the time when they are said to have been replaced by the values of neo-medieval chivalric culture.[2]

Although the uninterrupted reprinting of some central humanist treatises (e.g. Cicero's *De officiis* seven times between 1558 and 1600, Elyot's *The gouernour* 1565, 1580, Castiglione's *The courtier* in English 1561, 1577, 1586, in Latin 1571, 1577, 1585) yields *prima facie* evidence for this contention, we need to consider two kinds of treatises in order to assess the ubiquity of humanist preoccupations. In the first place, traditional humanist values were upheld in the numerous translations of Italian and other continental humanist treatises, some of which had considerable republican leanings. Although some of these translations are well known, it is arguable that their importance in political thought has not been sufficiently recognized. Since reading is not a passive process, we cannot draw a clear distinction between the production of an original text and the translation of a foreign or classical one. It follows that translations should be understood as political and ethical comments on the contemporary world.[3] These translations of humanist treatises include Thomas Blundeville's translation of Federico Furió Ceriol's *A briefe treatise of counselers* (originally printed in 1559) from the Italian version of Alfonso d'Ulloa, Thomas Browne's translation of *A ritch storehouse or treasurie for nobilitye and gentleman* (1549) by the German humanist Johannes Sturm, both published in 1570, and John Charlton's translation of Cornelius Valerius' *Brevis et perspicua totius ethicae seu de moribus philosophiae descriptio* (1566) printed in 1571 with a typical humanist title *The casket of iewels*. These were followed in 1576 by Hieronymus Osorio's *A discourse of ciuill, and Christian nobilitie* translated by William Blandy and in 1581 by Stefano Guazzo's *The ciuile conuersation* (the first three books in 1581, the complete treatise in 1586).[4] However, the most remarkable of all these translations is an abbreviation of Franceso Patrizi's *De institutione reipublicae* rendered into English by Richard Robinson and published in 1576 under the ambiguous title *A moral methode of ciuill policie*. Closely related is the most famous translation of the whole period: Thomas North's translation of

---

[2] For a recent statement to this effect, see Smuts 1987, pp. 20–1. For a more balanced account, see Ferguson 1986.
[3] Boutcher 1991, pp. xii–xiii, 44, 46; in general pp. 45–67; Norbrook 1994, p. 46; Womersley 1991. The importance of translations in this period is acknowledged by Caspari 1954, pp. 152–5. See also e.g. Conley 1927; Matthiessen 1931; Lathrop 1933; Baldwin 1944.
[4] For Guazzo's impact on England, see Lievsay 1961.

Plutarch's *The lives of the noble Grecians and Romanes* first published in 1579 and reprinted four times before 1640.

By and large, a similar set of ideas was developed in a number of tracts composed by Englishmen themselves. Although the arguments of these English tracts converged, it is important to understand that they owed allegiance to two different intellectual traditions. First, there are Thomas Rogers's extensive *A philosophicall discourse entituled, the anatomie of the minde* published in 1576 and John Foord's compact *Synopsis politica* published in 1582,[5] which owe their closest allegiance to the Aristotelian theory of citizenship. Secondly, there are a number of writers whose arguments are essentially Ciceronian in character. Amongst these are the dialogue with the somewhat misleading title *The praise of solitarinesse* by Roger Baynes (who incidentally was soon to leave the country for his religion) published in 1577, John Lyly's *Euphues*, Thomas Pritchard's *The schoole of honest and vertuous lyfe* and an anonymous dialogue, entitled *Cyuile and vncyuile life* (reprinted in 1586 as *The English courtier, and the cuntrey-gentleman*), all published in 1579. One of the most centrally important of these treatises is Haly Heron's strongly Ciceronian *A newe discourse of morall philosophie*, also issued in 1579 and sometimes described as the first English collection of essays.[6] These were soon followed by such treatises as William Blandy's own tract *The castle: or picture of pollicy* (1581), Lodovick Bryskett's *A discovrse of civill life* (written in the early 1580s, but not published until 1606), based on G. B. Giraldi Cintio's *Dialoghi della vita civile*, and John Ferne's extensive and somewhat conservative *The blazon of gentrie* published in 1586. Some of the same themes were reiterated by John Rainolds in his lectures on Aristotle's *Rhetoric* delivered in the 1570s,[7] and by Philip Stubbes in *The anatomie of abuses* (1583).

Perhaps the most obvious point of contact between the earlier humanist tradition and these writers is the prominent place given to the unqualified endorsement of the benefits of the *vita activa*. The literary tactics often chosen were first to emphasize the theoretical excellence of the contemplative life, and then to show that in practice the civic life of *negotium* proved to be the most desirable. This arrangement appeared in

---

5   John Foord matriculated from St John's, Cambridge in Michaelmas 1572, obtained his BA 1576–7 and his MA in 1580. In 1584 he became rector of Goodnestone, Kent, Venn and Venn 1927 pt 1, vol. ii, p. 157; John Foord, *Synopsis politica* (London, 1582), sig. ¶4ᵛ; for his admiration for Ramus, see sig. ¶4ʳ. For Ramus, see e.g. Grafton and Jardine 1986, pp. 161–200. Foord's tract is mentioned but not discussed in Binns 1990, p. 517.

6   For Heron, see Heltzel 1952.

7   John Rainolds, *Oxford lectures on Aristotle's 'Rhetoric'*, ed. Lawrence D. Green (Newark: University of Delaware Press, 1986).

Patrizi's *A moral methode*. As Robinson rendered Patrizi's argument, 'there can be nothinge more sweeter or better to bee wyshed unto mortall men, then to leade a private lyfe'. But because of the nature of human things, the only way to avoid corruption was to organize a society as 'a Civill and well instituted common weale'.[8] A man ought to be a 'Civil man' – a man who was 'profitable to his common weale'; everyone should be willing 'to worke and traveile' in order 'to helpe the common weal'.[9] The same theme was even more central to Guazzo's *The ciuile conuersation*, which was organized as a defence of the civic life. Guazzo presented the conventional defence of the *vita contemplativa*, when he pointed out at the beginning of the first book that 'the solitary ... is whollye raised up to the contemplation of his originall and happie state'. It followed that a cloister was an appropriate place for a man and he should at all cost avoid 'the government of common weales'. The other interlocutor, Anniball, retorted that the solitary life was 'the forme of a beast'. Man was not born wholly for himself and, therefore, everyone should learn 'civile behaviour'. An immediate agreement was reached on this point, when Guazzo answered that it had not been his intention to praise those who 'do altogether withdrawe themselves into solitarie places', trying to escape the duties in the commonwealth, but simply to point out that man needed solitude in order to gain knowledge and learning.[10]

English authors not only expressed the same preference for an active life but some even adopted a strikingly similar argument. When Haly Heron began to discuss this issue, he exhorted men to be careful 'least [sic] by too muche contemplation, and desyre of knowledge, we be removed from al exercise & practise'. Although *otium* was excellent as such, it should only be taken as a means to *negotium*. 'Let us', Heron

---

8   Francesco Patrizi, *A moral methode of ciuile policie*, translated by Richard Robinson (London, 1576), fo.1ᵛ.
9   Ibid., fos. 48ᵛ–49ᵛ.
10 Stefano Guazzo, *The ciuile conuersation ... diuided into foure bookes*, the first three translated from French by G[eorge] Pettie, the fourth translated from Italian by Barth. Young (London, 1586), fos. 6ᵛ–7ʳ, 8ʳ–13ᵛ. See also Conrad Valerius, *The casket of iewels: contaynynge a playne description of morall philosophie*, translated by J[ohn] C[harlton] (London, 1571), sig. B4ᵛ; Joannes Sturmius, *A ritch storehouse or treasurie for nobilitye and gentleman, which in Latine is called nobilitas literata*, translated by T[homas] B[rowne] (London, 1570), fo. 19ᵛ; Jeronimo Osorio de Fonseca, *The fiue bookes ... contayninge a discourse of ciuill, and christian nobilitie*, translated by William Blandy (London, 1576), fos. 5ᵛ–6ʳ, 23ᵛ; Federico Furió [Ceriol], *A very briefe and profitable treatise declaring howe many counsells, and what maner of counselers a prince that will gouerne well ought to haue*, abridged and translated by Thomas Blundeville (London, 1570), sig. N4ʳ; cf. also e.g. Pierre de La Primaudaye, *The French academie*, translated by T. B[owes?] (London, 1586), pp. 74–5, 98–9, 369–70.

argued, 'say with Tully, that it is better to practise and doe advisedly, then to thinke and imagine never so wysely.'[11] Not surprisingly, Heron placed his chief emphasis on 'the true knowledge of duties, than the which nothing is more commendable in youth, nothing more profitable in a common welth, & nothing more acceptable unto God, which thing M. Cicero, the floare of eloquent Philosophers' had eminently showed in his 'large instructions of Duties'.[12]

According to Thomas Rogers, mankind could be divided into two. The first group consisted of those who forsook 'this world' and 'addicte them selves to the contemplation of celestiall thinges'. They imitated 'the divine & celestiall nature' and they were, therefore, called 'Contemplators'. Although there were 'infinite' arguments in support of their goal, Rogers dismissed them outright. 'Those contemplators', he argued, were 'not onely odious, but also ridiculous unto many'. Those who were called 'Civile' and whose chief end was 'a civile and active felicitie' formed the second group. Rogers gave several reasons for preferring this civil mode of life to the contemplative. On the one hand, was the argument based on the Aristotelian idea that man was 'called Animal sociale'. But the main argument Rogers put forward was that man was not born for himself, but partly for 'his friends' and mostly for 'his countrey'. A 'good man', therefore, was 'a civile man'.[13] John Lyly explained that there were both the 'active life', which was 'about civill function and administration of the common weale', and 'the contemplative life', which was 'continual meditation and studie'. As the former was 'an idle life' without the latter, so the latter was utterly 'unprofitable' without the former.[14]

As David Norbrook has emphasized, Philip Sidney's *Old Arcadia* not merely 'subverts the expectations aroused by its title and subjects the Italian courtly ideal of retirement, contemplation and love, to severe Protestant humanist scrutiny', it also calls into question the irresponsibility of an absolute ruler and seeks the ideal solution from the *vita activa*.[15]

---

[11] Haly Heron, *A newe discourse of morall philosophie, entituled the kayes of counsaile* (London, 1579), pp. 101–2, 109–10.

[12] Ibid., pp. 5–6.

[13] Thomas Rogers, *A philosophicall discourse, entituled, the anatomie of the minde* (London, 1576), fos. 81ᵛ–82ᵛ, 84ʳ–85ᵛ; see also fos. 68ᵛ–69ᵛ, sig. z3ᵛ–4ʳ, z5ʳ⁻ᵛ, z8ʳ⁻ᵛ. In the preface Rogers said that he had already written his treatise whilst he was a student, sig. [A3ᵛ–4ʳ]. Cf. in general e.g. Anon., *A discourse of the commonweal of this realm of England* (1581), ed. Mary Dewar (Charlottesville: University of Virginia Press, 1969), pp. 16–17.

[14] John Lyly, *Euphues: the anatomy of wit* (1579), ed. Edward Arber (London, 1868), p. 142, in general pp. 143, 154; cf. however pp. 148, 187–8.

[15] Norbrook 1984, pp. 92–7; Worden 1991b, pp. 244–5.

At the beginning of the *Old Arcadia* Basilius tries to avoid the future blows of fortune, forecast by the oracle, by resolving 'to retire himself with his wife and daughters into a solitary place'. Although Philanax makes the attempt to change Basilius' mind by calling forth virtuous action to overcome fortune, Basilius keeps his head. A similar discussion is repeated by Musidorus and Pyrocles, the former of whom impugns the contemplative life and 'solitariness', which 'doth most separate a man from well doing'. The latter retorts that solitariness and excellent contemplation go hand in hand. Moreover, the *vita contemplativa* receives fulsome praise in some of the eclogues of the *Old Arcadia*.[16] Later in the work, however, *negotium* gains the upper hand of *otium*. In the third book, Basilius regrets his embracement of 'this solitary life' and he feels 'inclined to return to his palace'. Euarchus agrees to help the Arcadians because it enables him 'to employ his old years in doing good, the only happy action of man's life'. Finally, Philanax receives his compensation when it is generally admitted that Basilius' 'solitary life' has not merely failed to bring the desired effect, but has exposed him 'to any traitorous attempt'.[17] In *The defence of poesie*, Sidney, of course, abandoned all this evocation and gave his unconditional preference for the active life.[18] 'But the truth is,' Fulke Greville described Sidney, 'his end was not writing even while he wrote, nor his knowledge moulded for tables or schools, but both his wit and understanding bent upon his heart to make himselfe and others, not in words or opinion, but in life and action, good and great.' Thomas Moffet agreed: Sidney esteemed 'the commonwealth before all things', being 'inspired by a certain heroic temper and very active virtue'.[19]

The question as to whether the contemplative or active life should be preferred forms a central theme in the anonymous *Cyuile and vncyuile life*. This is a dialogue between 'Vincent' and 'Vallentine', and the chief issue 'whyther it were better for the Gentlemen of Englande to make most abode in their Contrey houses, (as our English manner is,) or els ordinaryly to inhabite the Cittie and cheefe Townes, as in some

[16] Philip Sidney, *The Countess of Pembroke's Arcadia (The old Arcadia)*, ed. Katherine Duncan-Jones (Oxford University Press, 1985), pp. 5–9, 12–15, 76, 145–6.

[17] Sidney, *Old Arcadia*, pp. 156, 310, 334. See also Fulke Greville, *A dedication to Sir Philip Sidney*, in *The prose works*, pp. 8, 9–10.

[18] Philip Sidney, *The defence of poesie*, in *The complete works*, 4 vols., ed. Albert Feuillerat (Cambridge University Press, 1922–6), III, pp. 11–12. See e.g. Caspari 1954, pp. 161–5, 171; Lindebaum 1990.

[19] Greville, *A dedication to Sidney*, in *The prose works*, p. 12, cf. e.g. p. 25. Thomas Moffet, *Nobilis: or a view of the life and death of a Sidney* (1593), ed. and translated by Virgil B. Heltzel and Hoyt H. Hudson (San Marino: Huntington Library, 1940), p. 88, see also pp. 71, 76, 79, 80–1, 83.

forraine Nations is the custome'.[20] Vincent began by complaining of
the corruption which he believed he was witnessing in England.
Traditionally gentlemen lived in the country offering hospitality to
their equals and bestowing charity on their inferiors, but were not, as
Vincent carefully pointed out, 'called to attendance in our Princes
service'. Underlying this harmony was 'our care in education of
children', which made them 'honest and just, wise and welthy, obedient
and assured'. However, all this was placed in jeopardy by the new
fashion of living in towns and cities.[21] While Vallentine fully concurred
with his interlocutor that a good education was of crucial importance,
he could not accept the way of living it was meant to serve in Vincent's
vision. If the aim was 'to bring up your children in honesty, which is
vertue, and cheefely justice', it should be borne in mind 'what Tully
telleth you ... That men are not only borne to themselves.' It follows
that 'there bee persons prepared for sundry actions, not so much to
serve their owne turnes, as their Prince and Countrey'. And this kind of
life, according to Vallentine, was only possible in the court and city.[22]
Vallentine admitted that there was much wickedness and corruption in
these places but insisted that the best men were also to be found there
and that 'it is good, to know evill, not to use it, but to avoyd it'. Many
could indeed make their advancement in court 'by mere flattery' but it
was virtue which would carry the day: 'when occasion of service doth
happen, men of value & vertue bee those that shal stand their country
in steede, and honor them selves'.[23]

Some theorists did not feel any particular inclination to admit even
the theoretical excellence of contemplative life, but argued outright
that civic life should always be preferred. Thomas Pritchard based his
work on the virtuous life mainly on Cicero, calling him 'that gay
Gardener, and cunning Arborer' and 'a princely piller of Philosophie'.[24] Closely following his authority, Pritchard argued that 'all is
vaine' if 'Diligence' and 'Practice' were abandoned; a man ought to
'imitate the busie Bees', since 'Tullie saith in his *Offices*, that wee bee
borne partly to pleasure and profit our freendes, our Parentes, and
most of all, our native Countrey'.[25] When the herald, John Ferne,

20   Anon., *Cyuile and vncyuile life* (London, 1579), sig. A4ᵛ.
21   Ibid., sig. B1ʳ–B4ᵛ.
22   Ibid., sigs. B4ᵛ–C1ᵛ.
23   Ibid., sigs. C1ᵛ–2ʳ, D3ʳ.
24   Thomas Pritchard, *The schoole of honest and vertuous lyfe profitable and necessary for all estates and degrees* (London, n.d. [1579]), pp. 6, 9.
25   Ibid., pp. 15–16, 28, 30–1.

described how 'the grave authoritie of antiquitie' admonished everyone
to 'exercise and honest labor', it was chiefly 'publique' actions which he
had in mind.[26] Despite the fact that true felicity was found 'above the
stars', Lodovick Bryskett focused his attention on moral philosophy and
was convinced that it was above all this branch of learning which gave
men 'an active or practicke felicitie', since 'Tullie saith, and Plato
before him' that we have not been born for ourselves but for our
country.[27] John Rainolds justified his lectures on Aristotle's *Rhetoric* by
referring to Juan Luis Vives and Cicero, according to whom rhetoric
was immensely useful for 'public life' (*vita communis*). Similarly, Thomas
North pointed out in his translation of Plutarch's *Lives* that by reading
Plutarch Englishmen would 'be animated to the better service' of the
queen. Since Plutarch provided many examples of people who had
'strayned their wits, not regarded their states, ventured their persons,
cast away their lives, not onely for the honor and safetie, but also for
the pleasure of their Princes', his reader should be ready to do 'service'
for his prince and country both in war and peace.[28]

An equally unqualified endorsement of the priority of civic life was
given by John Foord. In his preface Foord wrote that Socrates had led
philosophy to 'civic life' (*vita civilis*) and that this tradition had
vigorously been maintained until it had degenerated into the barren
disputes of scholastic philosophy. Scholasticism had held sway until
Foord's own time when Socrates, Plato, Aristotle and Cicero were
rediscovered.[29] Having established this standard humanist view, Foord
proceeded in the main part of his tract to explain the contents of
philosophy and pointed out at the beginning that 'private utility should
be rather omitted, than the public good endangered'. He defined
'citizen' as 'an excellent man given to the commonwealth'.[30] Towards
the end of his tract Foord quoted Cicero as saying that 'a private
citizen' should be 'neither mean and contemptible nor enraging, but
live on equal and fair terms with the other citizens, and want such
things in the commonwealth which are quiet and honourable. Because
such, said Cicero, we are accustomed both to perceive and call a good

26 John Ferne, *The blazon of gentrie: deuided into two parts* (London, 1586), sig. A4ʳ
27 Lodovick Bryskett, *A discovrse of civill life: containing the ethike part of morall philosophie* (London, 1606), pp. 18–22. See also William Blandy, *The castle or picture of pollicy, shewing forth most liuely, the face, body and partes of a commonwealth* (London, 1581), fo. 8ᵛ.
28 Rainolds, *Oxford lectures*, pp. 95, 267; Plutarch, *The lives of the noble Grecians and Romanes*, translated from French by Thomas North (London, 1579), sig. *2ʳ⁻ᵛ.
29 John Foord, *Synopsis politica* (London, 1582), sig. ¶3ʳ⁻ᵛ.
30 Ibid., fos. 1ᵛ, 5ᵛ: 'privata potius utilitas est omittendo, quam communis perclitanda salus'. 'Civis est vir bonus civitate donatus.'

citizen.'[31] But Cicero had also argued, as Foord was careful to point out, that citizens should know how to obey in order to know how to rule.[32]

Reading Foord's tract, Gabriel Harvey fully concurred. *Negotium*, he commented both on the title-page and in the margins of Foord's tract, was far more important than *otium*, since 'all theory is puerile, without manly practice'.[33] A decade earlier Erasmus' *Parabolae* had occasioned Harvey to voice the same opinion; even most refined knowledge was mere vanity without private or public action.[34] In his *Ciceronianus* (1577) Harvey pointed out that Cicero was 'supreme in all pleadings, forensic and parliamentary [*senatoriis*], rustic and urban, oratorical and philosophical, jesting and serious, public and private'. But it was not merely Cicero's style and eloquence which aroused admiration; his subject matter inspired equal respect. Harvey explained that he had observed in Cicero 'not only the oratorical eloquence ... but also consular and senatorial wisdom'. Cicero had thus been a man of 'profound wisdom in thought' and a real 'statesman' (*politicum*). Beside many other things, Cicero taught how to be 'a highly respected citizen' and 'the possessor of a soul overflowing with the noblest virtues'.[35]

Philip Stubbes's *Anatomie of abuses* is, of course, permeated by puritan strictures on public morality, but every now and then Stubbes had recourse to classical and renaissance authors including Aristotle, Cicero and Sallust as well as Erasmus, Vives and Thomas Elyot. It should occasion little surprise, therefore, that he could write in his discussion of charity: 'And common reason advertiseth us, that wee are not borne for our selves onelie: for *Ortus nostri partem patria, partem amici, partem parentes vendicant,* Our Countrey challengeth a part of our byrth, our

---

[31]   Ibid., fo. 24ᵛ: 'Cicero primo officiorum privatum voluit, neque submissum and abiectum, neque se efferentem, sed aequo and pari cum civibus jure vivere: eaque in repub. velle, quae tranquilla and honesta sunt. Quia talem and sentire, inquit, and bonum civem dicere solemus.' Cicero, *De officiis*, 1.34.124.

[32]   Foord, *Synopsis politica*, fo. 24ᵛ: 'Idemque Cicero tertio de legibus, non solum ut tempore imperaturos. Nam qui modeste paret, inquit, videtur, qui aliquando imperet dignus esse.' Cicero, *De legibus*, III.2.5.

[33]   Gabriel Harvey, *Marginalia*, ed. G. C. Moore Smith (Stratford, 1913), p. 199; Stern 1979, p. 154.

[34]   Harvey, *Marginalia*, pp. 141–3.

[35]   Gabriel Harvey, *Ciceronianus* (1577), ed. Harold S. Wilson, translated by Clarence A. Forbes, University of Nebraska Studies in the Humanities, no. 4, 1945, pp. 49–51, 79, see also pp. 97, 101; idem, *The works*, ed. Alexander B. Grosart (London: Huth Library, 1884), 3 vols., I, pp. 136–7; idem, *Rhetor, vel duorum dierum oratio, de natura, arte, & exercitatione rhetorica* (London, 1577), sigs. E3ʳ, 11ᵛ

brethren and frendes require an other parte, and our parentes ... doe vendicate a third parte.'[36]

The longest and most thorough treatment of the respective merits of the contemplative and the active life appeared in Roger Baynes's dialogue *The praise of solitarinesse*. Its main topic was whether man 'ought rather to make choise of Solitarinesse or Societie'.[37] Eudoxus argued for the *vita contemplativa*, presenting most of the traditional arguments in support. He began by pointing out that the curing of the mind by the exercise of philosophy was possible only in complete solitude. It was in this state that we could reach 'the freenesse and libertie of our minde'. The majority of the people were corrupted, discarding true honesty and thinking that the things which were profitable were also honest. By reversing the order of these crucial concepts they abandoned all morality. It was impossible to try to cure them; a man could 'but little benefite the common wealth, nor doe good unto such, as will neyther take warning, nor can away to be controlled'. On the contrary, such company would also corrupt the wise man. The only way a man could safeguard himself from degeneration was to remain in a solitary state, to 'withdrawe him from the companie of such lewde disposed persons, retiring from thence into some solitarie corner'. The clearest instance of this prevailing degeneration and perverted order of values was the fact that 'small and petite robberies are severally punished, when great and horrible offences are praysed and commended'. Faced with such atrocities a wise man should 'patiently suffer, all adversities and mischaunces that shal hap to betide him' and instead 'enjoy a well settled minde'.

The contention of the advocates of the *vita activa* that man was born primarily for the commonwealth could easily be answered by pointing out that man was not merely a member of the particular common-wealth 'whereunto by birth we are privately allotted'. All men were also members of the universal commonwealth of mankind and it was 'more commendable' to pursue the good of this larger community. But this was not possible so long as a man was 'conversaunt abroade in any publike assembly, bycause in such places he can never be at quiet, but shall still be tormented and beaten with trouble'. To prove his point, Eudoxus resorted to the authority of religion and 'the auntient Philosophers' like Seneca and Plato. Although they had taught us 'to

---

[36] Stubbes, *The anatomie of abuses*, sig. B4^v.
[37] Roger Baynes, *The praise of solitarinesse, set down in the form of a dialogue, wherein is conteyned, a discourse philosophical, of the lyfe actiue and contemplatiue* (London, 1577), p. 1.

exercise pittie towards our parents, our friends, our countrey, and generally unto al men', their most important lesson was 'to have a continuall regarde to the due preservation of oure just and honest minds'. Most importantly 'Cicero himselfe' had agreed about this. Although Cicero had declared that 'the lyfe active' was 'more commodious' 'for the benefite of the common wealth', he had also confessed 'that the contemplative life, is more safe and easie both for the soule and bodie'. It was easy, therefore, to point at 'the leadable disposition of Cicero, or the excellencie of his glorious quietnesse'. Finally, Eudoxus gave a short exposition of both ways of living. Whereas man leading a *vita activa* was beset by troubles from the very beginning and was bound either to oppress 'the just & rightfull cause' or to uphold 'the wicked and unhonest pretence', solitary man had, as Eudoxus carefully pointed out, 'free choyce, either to staye at home, to walk abrode, or at libertie to go whersoever he lusteth', being 'without trouble or care of the worlde'; he could perfect himself in the 'fynding out and followyng of Truth'.[38]

Lysippus was the interlocutor who attempted to discharge Eudoxus' arguments and to uphold the values of an active life. He opened his case by ridiculing Eudoxus' entire stance. The most ideal life advocated by Eudoxus consisted of solitude where 'a man withdrawing himselfe from company, seeketh rather to live in the voide and desolate places of the earth, and there playing the Philosopher in the open wildernesse, doth seeme alone to contente hymselfe'. But the main way in which he sought to establish the superiority of the *vita activa* was by giving a Ciceronian account of the beginning of the commonwealth. Those who were accounted wise utterly condemned 'that uncivile kind of life, which ignorant people in the beginning of the world did brutishly leade, much after the manner of unreasonable beastes'. Lysippus described this original state of nature in most gloomy terms. Amongst these people 'there was neyther societie nor friendship maynteyned, no man living in the boundes of lawfull matrimony, no man certaine of his owne children, nor any law to distinguish the good from the evill mainteyned among them'. It was only when they were taught by reason that men began to organize themselves into commonwealths. This further taught man that it was 'his duetie, not onely to employ the best of his labour, but also to adventure the losse of hys life, for the better maintenance of the commen Wealth'. This straightforward

---

[38] Ibid., pp. 2–3, 7, 49–50, 52–5, 65–6, 75–6, 80; see especially also pp. 61–6, 73–84.

lesson could be gathered from Plato, but above all from Cicero. Cicero's true message had been that a man ought to avoid withdrawing himself 'unto Solitarinesse' and ought instead 'to stay in the Citie, and there to endevour as well as hee maye to doe that which is good'. The practical results of this lesson could be seen in innumerable instances amongst the Greeks and above all the Romans, but it was most readily to be seen in 'Tully, that great Prince of Eloquence ... who although sometimes', as Lysippus was willing to admit, 'seemed to command the Solitary life', had in fact been forced to do this and his real preference had always lain in 'the Citie, which he esteemd more pretious than any golde'.[39]

Despite their numerous convincing arguments, neither Eudoxus nor Lysippus could persuade the other to renounce his own conviction and accept the opposite. Although Eudoxus in particular showed some signs of giving in, admitting that 'manye things ... maye on both sides be spoken', in the end he remained 'fully perswaded, that more may be alleaged, in the commendation of Solitarinesse, than of Societie'.[40] The decision of the debate was, therefore, referred to Tales – the third interlocutor. At an earlier stage of the debate Tales had drawn attention to the rhetorical nature of the discussion by pointing out that 'this question may sufficiently be debated on both sides'.[41] When it fell to him to settle the debate, he began by showing similar hesitations; there was scarcely anything substantial to be added to Eudoxus' or Lysippus' arguments. Whether the preference was to be given to the contemplative or the active life depended partly on 'the time and the nature of eche man'.

At the beginning of his account Tales reminded his interlocutors that every living creature now and again needed solitude, and men also needed solitude of mind in order to be able to dwell by themselves and to converse with the wise. But the kind of solitude Eudoxus had in mind was suitable only for those who were capable of conferring 'wyth their bookes', since withdrawal 'wythoute learning is a very banishment, or rather a prison'. It was primarily this solitude that Eudoxus had been defending and it was essentially the same that underlay Cicero's rhetorical question: 'What is sweter than learned rest?' There

---

[39] Ibid., pp. 4–5, 56–9, 67, 69–71; see in general pp. 67–73. For a Ciceronian account of the birth of civil life, see also Heron, *A newe discourse*, pp. 37–8, and especially Blandy, *The castle*, fo. 13ᵛ.

[40] Baynes, *The praise of solitarinesse*, pp. 59, 73, 49.

[41] Ibid., p. 6.

was no doubt that the 'Solitarinesse of place' was 'to be preferred unto students, & to such only as are thought to be wise'. It was thus Eudoxus and the *otium* which seemed to carry the day.

But Tales went on to argue that although withdrawal ought to have preference for the sake of learning, learning itself should not be favoured for its own sake. Those who were inclined to solitude in order to achieve learning should always be ready, 'when neede shall require', to 'come abroade, refusing no peril, either for the safetie of their countrey, or for the savegarde of their friends'. Learning was but a means to the further end of the promotion of the commonwealth; life was given to man 'for the only use and behoofe of his countrey'. An active life for the good of his country was the true end of a man's life and it was the only way in which he could win 'fame and everlasting renowne' and not 'live in shame and reproche'. Tales' conclusion was thus that both the contemplative and the active life were required. 'A wise man therfore', he told his interlocutors, 'ought chiefly to knowe, howe beste to applye bothe time and place, aswell unto Solitarinesse as to Societie, following therin as nere as he may, the example of suches as in former time, have to his knowledge performed the like.' This was a conclusion which Eudoxus and Lysippus could readily accept.[42]

Before reaching this essentially Ciceronian conclusion, namely that a contemplative life of learning was invaluable, but only in so far as it served the ends of the active life, a question of crucial importance had to be settled. As Lysippus put it, 'we first define what vertue is: And after ... we wil further consider, whether Solitarinesse or societie may seme more convenient for the obteining therof'.[43] The point of departure of the treatise had been to explain 'first, what Vertue is, and whether a wise man that desireth to live vertuously ought rather to make choise of solitarinesse or Societie'.[44] The ensuing, somewhat ambivalent, discussion of virtue was opened by a brief description of the different classical schools of ethics excluding 'the Cinicke secte'. A strong case was presented for the superiority of the stoic definition. It was above all Cicero whose authority was employed in arguments against the role of the goods of body and fortune. Every day it was possible to encounter evidence 'that a noble & vertuous minde may possible lie hid under each kind of forme'. Along with physical beauty, physical strength and riches were regarded as 'indifferent things' in

---

[42] Ibid., pp. 84–6.
[43] Ibid., p. 7.
[44] Ibid., p. 1.

respect of the chief goodness.[45] The underlying stoicism also surfaced
in the treatment of the nature and contents of the concept of 'virtue'.
Tales in particular firmly held that although there were four main
virtues with different fields of application, each one of them was but a
part of a single whole and in this respect there was 'but one onely
vertue'.[46]

Eudoxus and Tales argued further the stoic idea that virtue consisted
in the avoidance of perturbation.[47] Although Lysippus was willing to
admit this, he also referred to Cicero's *Tusculan disputations* to point out
that few or no philosophers could lead a life 'as reason requireth'.
Furthermore, Cicero had taught that philosophy and wisdom was
'nothing except it be put in practise'. The chief characteristic of
philosophy was rather 'to make hir lovers to live wel in publique
conversation, than to speake & teach wel in private schooles' – a lesson
which was most obvious in Cicero's own life. Following 'the discipline
of Panetius the Stoike', Cicero had indeed set down 'the duetie of
eache manne exceedingly well' and he had even borne 'valiauntlye'
calamitous private and public perturbations, such as his daughter's
death or 'the Monarchie of Cesar oppressing the publike libertie'. But
it was sufficient neither to suppress perturbations nor to know virtue
and duty in detail. It was of overriding importance to be virtuous both
'in worde and deede'. As Tales put it later, only when a man combined
eloquence with wisdom, could he become 'a member very profitable,
both privately for hys friends, and generally for the whole estate'.[48]

This classical appreciation of the close connection between the active
life and virtues was also endorsed in other treatises which emphasized
the superiority of *negotium*. For Furió Ceriol one of the first things a
consummate counsellor ought to be familiar with was 'the ende and
true use of every vertue'.[49] According to Patrizi, those who held office
ought to retain virtues, and conversely, offices should be reserved for
the virtuous.[50] Cornelius Valerius argued that the only way men could
successfully pursue their chosen end was when 'vertue' was 'the guide'.
It was consequently impossible to govern 'a weale publike' if a man was
not 'informed with the rules of condicions and fashioned unto every

---

[45] Ibid., pp. 9–18; see also pp. 41–2.
[46] Ibid., pp. 40–1.
[47] Ibid., pp. 24–5, 26–7, 38, 39–40.
[48] Ibid., pp. 28–32, 42–3, 47–8.
[49] Furió [Ceriol], *A very briefe treatise*, sig. F3ʳ. Cf. in general e.g. Geffrey Fenton, *Golden epistles, conteyning varietie of discourse, both morall, philosophicall, and diuine* (London, 1577), sig. A2ʳ–3ʳ.
[50] Patrizi, *A moral methode*, fos. 4ᵛ, 21ʳ, 48ᵛ.

vertue'.[51] In defining the key concepts of his treatise, Guazzo emphasized that 'to live civillie, is not sayd in respect of the Citie, but of the
qualities of the minde'. 'To be short,' he specified, 'my meaning is, that
civile Conversation is an honest commendable, and vertuous kinde of
living in the world.'[52] Haly Heron agreed with Baynes that gifts of
fortune and nature – riches and health – were of no significance in
comparison with the 'quiet possession of vertues'. It followed that the
requirements of public duty hinged on virtues only.[53] According to
Bryskett, 'civill felicitie' was simply 'an inward reward for morall
vertues', and John Lyly, John Foord and Philip Sidney, as well as the
author of the *Cyuile and vncyuile life*, agreed.[54] When Thomas Rogers
defined a good man, who 'serveth God devoutly, and dealeth upright-
lye with all men', as a 'a civile man', he pointed out that such a man
was 'adorned with all vertues'; he 'embraceth vertue with all his hart'.
This was the chief quality which enabled him to promote the common
good.[55]

The underlying reason why virtues were given such a central place
in the pursuit of the common good was the particular assessment of
their intrinsic character. In truly Ciceronian fashion it was maintained
that the real cause of virtue demanded not just knowledge but practice.
In this account, as Baynes had declared, learning was valuable only in
so far as it was useful. Osorio argued that a learned man was not 'most
worthye & honourable', although he was furnished with 'rare and
singular vertues' and with 'profound knowledge in deepeste matters', as
long as he did not employ these qualities 'to the availe and commoditye
of the common wealth'. A man could be called 'a good and vertuous
man' when he was well instructed in the 'precepts of moralitie', but he
would win praise only when 'he applie them to the profite &
commoditie of the weale publique'.[56] The reason Heron exhorted his
readers to avoid 'too much contemplation' was that, as he paraphrased
Cicero, 'the chiefe praise of vertue consiste in Doing, and not in
Saying'. Those who 'spend their whole life in the curious studie of
Science, not regarding anye kinde of good practise' made a crucial

51 Valerius, *The casket of iewels*, sigs. c8ᵛ, D7ᵛ–8ʳ.
52 Guazzo, *The ciuile conuersation*, fos. 22ʳ⁻ᵛ 55ᵛ–56ʳ.
53 Heron, *A newe discourse*, pp. 4–5, 38–9. See also e.g. Pritchard, *The schoole of honest lyfe*, pp. 9–11,
    14–15; Bryskett, *A discourse of civill life*, pp. 155–6; Rogers, *A philosophicall discourse*, fos. 28ʳ⁻ᵛ,
    80ʳ–81ʳ, but see fos. 65ᵛ–66ʳ.
54 Bryskett, *A discovrse of civill life*, p. 41; Lyly, *Euphues*, pp. 183, 151, 153; Foord, *Synopsis politica*, fo.
    5ᵛ; Sidney, *Old Arcadia*, pp. 6, 8, 18, 20, 314.
55 Rogers, *A philosophicall discourse*, fos. 85ʳ⁻ᵛ, see also fos. 30ᵛ–31ʳ, 54ᵛ–55ʳ, 58ʳ⁻ᵛ.
56 Osorio, *The five bookes of nobilitie*, fos. 5ᵛ–6ʳ, 23ᵛ.

mistake, since the ultimate end of all learning was its virtuous application in practice.[57] Pritchard said: 'if diligence bee dismiste, and practice put aside, all is vaine, for the beeinge and continuance of Vertue, is in action and exercise'. Cicero had established this point not merely in his own life by being 'advaunced to dignitie and high calling among the Romaines', but also 'in his Rhetorickes' by writing 'that preceptes and rules of disciplines avayle nothinge, without daily diligence and paynefull practise therof'. 'The true tutche of vertue', Pritchard later added, 'doth not consist in the knowledge and science therof: but in exhibiting the same'; virtue 'consisteth in action, and daily deede of honesty'. In a well-known passage, Philip Sidney concurred: 'So that the ending end of all earthly learning, being vertuous action, those skils that most serve to bring forth that, have a most just title to be Princes over al the rest.'[58]

As well as discussing the nature of virtue, these authors treated the question of its particular qualities. First and foremost, as Baynes's *Tales* argued, the general virtue consisted in searching out 'the truth of eache matter' and especially in making 'choyce betweene profitable and unprofitable' – a quality which was called 'by the name of Prudence'. When the general virtue focused on 'the mayntayning of humayne Societye', it was called 'by the name of Justice'; when it exhibited itself in the 'valor of an unvincible harte', it was called courage or fortitude; and when it pertained to 'the orderly disposition of our sayings and doings', its name was 'Modestie' or temperance.[59] The same list of cardinal virtues (although hardly with such a close imitation of Cicero's actual choice of words) was prominent in Patrizi's description of the qualities of magistrates, in Furio Ceriól's account of the counsellor, in Osorio's account of nobility and in Valerius' treatment of moral philosophy, where the whole discussion was organized in accordance with it.[60] It occupied a scarcely less conspicuous place in the tracts composed by Englishmen. Although in the second part of *A discourse of civill life* Lodovick Bryskett drew the Aristotelian distinction between intellectual and moral virtues, later, when he defined the virtues 'appertaining to civill life', he maintained that they were four in

<hr>

[57] Heron, *A newe discourse*, pp. 101–2.
[58] Pritchard, *The schoole of honest lyfe*, pp. 15–17, 28; Sidney, *The defence of poesie*, in *Works*, III, p. 12.
[59] Baynes, *The praise of solitarinesse*, pp. 40–1.
[60] Patrizi, *A moral methode*, fos. 21^r–22^r, 50^v; cf. Richard Robinson, *The vineyarde of vertue collected, composed, and digested into a tripartite order* (London, n.d. [1579]), where the account was essentially Christian; Furió [Ceriol], *A briefe treatise*, sig. D3^v–4^r; Osorio, *The five bookes of nobilitie*, fos. 24^r–27^v; Valerius, *The casket of iewels*, sigs. D2^v–3^r, K7^r.

number: fortitude, temperance, justice and prudence.[61] The cardinal virtues were, according to John Ferne, 'the fountaynes, out of which al gentlenes, should and ought to streame'.[62] Thomas Pritchard opened his discussion of honest life by referring to Cicero who had 'grafted upon this Tree of vertue: foure brave branches: out of which, bud many springing sproutes, very necessary and spectant to perfection ... of mans life. That is, Prudence, Justice, Temperance, and Fortitude.'[63] Having pointed out that the only way of reaching the platform of 'civile man' was to embrace virtue, Thomas Rogers proceeded to 'declare what this vertue is, and of howe many partes it consisteth'. Faithful to his habits he began by presenting the different definitions of the ancient schools of moral philosophy. Aristotle, he wrote, divided virtues into intellectual and moral ones. 'But Plato best of all sayeth plainly, that vertue is divided into fowre parts' and it was this division which Rogers himself followed in the second part of his book which was devoted to a detailed explication of every virtue.[64]

Following their Roman authorities, humanists had argued that as well as advancing the good of the commonwealth the virtuous active life conferred honour and praise on the actors themselves. This conclusion was as strongly endorsed by the writers under discussion. Thus Baynes's *Tales* decided on the respective merits of the active and the contemplative life by reiterating that the former was the only way to win 'everlasting renowne'. 'Every man', as Richard Robinson rendered Patrizi's argument, 'laboureth for renowme, which when he shal se hymselfe prevented of, and that hee is frustrate of hope, he is never at quiet in hys mynde.'[65] As Guazzo maintained: 'when I sayde that ambition is the cause of manie abuses, I meant not those men, which knowing their owne valour, aspire to highe enterprises and honours, which by the instinct of Nature wee all covet: for that honour is the reward of vertue, and counted a divine thing.'[66]

The same argument was endorsed with equal vehemence by the English theorists. Haly Heron described the results of virtuous pursuits as 'the sweete Nectar & Heavenlye perpetuall flowing streames of

[61] Bryskett, *A discovrse of civill life*, pp. 120, 214–59; Foord, *Synopsis politica*, fos. 7ᵛ–11ᵛ.
[62] Ferne, *The blazon of gentrie*, 1, p. 30. See Blandy, *The castle*, fos. 9ᵛ–14ʳ.
[63] Pritchard, *The schoole of honest lyfe*, p. 6.
[64] Rogers, *A philosophicall discourse*, fos. 85ᵛ–87ʳ. For an endorsement of this and other traditional humanist values by John Dee, see Sherman 1990.
[65] Patrizi, *A moral methode*, fos. 5ᵛ–6ʳ, 3ᵛ, 88ʳ.
[66] Guazzo, *The ciuile conuersation*, fo. 44ʳ. See also Furió [Ceriol], *A very brief treatise*, sig. 13ᵛ–4ʳ. See also e.g. Valerius, *The casket of iewels*, sig. 12ʳ.

Fame'.[67] Bryskett went as far as to argue that, irrespective of whether a man was in public or in private, 'he never undertaketh any thing but that which carieth withall reputation, dignitie & honour'. A man, he added, ought 'to direct all his actions to the mark of honour, a thing esteemed ... among all others the greatest externall good'. It was, however, 'unfitting' to hold honour as the direct aim of one's actions; the only true aim was simply 'honorable and vertuous actions'.[68]

There was thus a dilemma: on the one hand, glory and honour were said to constitute the only true reward of man's action but, on the other hand, the unequivocal pursuit of these values was regarded as a distortion of their intrinsic nature. Nowhere is this dilemma presented with such acuteness as in Rogers's *A philosophicall discourse*. According to Rogers, ambition was 'an unmeasurable desire of glory' – 'the most daungerous thing in a common weale'. The proper quest for honour took place when man's behaviour was governed by the principles of wisdom and the ultimate aim of his action was the public good. To illustrate his point, Rogers referred to Tacitus and Cicero who had shown how ambition began to grow amongst the Romans, with the result of serious internal commotions and finally the tyrannies of Pompey and Caesar, who had not sought 'the profiting & commodity of their countrey, but their private commoditie'. But Rogers was most emphatic to stress that although glory 'ought not to be hunted after', it nonetheless followed 'good deedes' just 'as the shadowe doth followe the bodie'.[69]

These arguments that the virtuous *vita activa* would have favourable effects on the community at large and bring glory to the actor himself were almost invariably coupled with a closely related and equally central question of the classical republican tradition. This was the question of true citizenship: what were the necessary characteristics for a man to qualify as a truly noble citizen? Hence Patrizi treated in the sixth book of his treatise the issues of 'Nobilitie' and 'true citizens' and Osorio reiterated that 'I have thought it therefore must appertynent to my purpose, to search out diligently the nature, originall, right rule, and foundation of true Nobilitye.'[70] Hence, too, when Anniball suggested in Guazzo's *The ciuile conuersation* that they should 'speake of Gentlemen and Yeomen, betweene whom by reason of their difference and inequalitie,

---

67 Heron, *A newe discourse*, p. 46.
68 Bryskett, *A discovrse of civill life*, pp. 222, 231, 241–2, see also p. 76.
69 Rogers, *A philosophicall discourse*, fos. 10ᵛ–11ᵛ, 8ᵛ, 69ᵛ, 137ᵛ–138ᵛ. Cf. in general Ferne, *The blazon of gentrie*, sig. A3ᵛ. Blandy, *The castle*, fos. 7ᵛ, 10ʳ.
70 Osorio, *The five bookes of nobilitie*, fo. 2ᵛ.

there are diverse thinges to be observed in companie', Guazzo immediately requested Anniball to 'undo me the knot of this gentrie'.[71]

Again, the English authors agreed. Heron claimed that it 'hath beene a doubtfull question of long time amongst the learned, touchyng the firste cause and originall occasion of Gentrie',[72] whilst the chief issue John Ferne raised in his extensive treatise was 'what is civill nobilitie'.[73] The same task was undertaken by Richard Mulcaster in his educational treatise when he asked, 'what it is to be a gentleman or a nobleman, and what force the termes of nobilitie or gentrie do infer to be in the persons, to whom they are proper'.[74] Persons presented to the degree of MA in Oxford in 1583 were asked to dispute whether true nobility was achieved by one's own virtues or by those of one's forefathers.[75]

In seeking to answer this question, Patrizi referred to Cicero and argued that 'it is better, that I do florishe in mine owne actes that I have done, then to leane upon the reputacion of auncestrie'.[76] It followed that in the best commonwealth it was looked to that justice was done and that honour and nobility were conferred according to true merits of virtuous actions for the public good. The same idea had already occurred in the first book, where Patrizi gave a Ciceronian account of the origins of the civic society. One of the chief characteristics of a well-ordered society was that 'there were rewardes bestowed on them which excelled in any manner of vertue'.[77] Furió Ceriol suggested that the prince should establish a council devoted to advising him about the bestowal of rewards. Due to the lack of such councils, 'the vertuous sort which commonly be no cravers, are sildome or never considered, and such as least deserve, are alwayes best rewarded'.[78] The same idea was discussed even more fully in Osorio's treatise on nobility, according to which, virtue was 'worker and causer of so noble a qualitie' that it 'doth deserve greate honour and estimation'; nobility was 'a kindred excelling in more rare and principall vertues'.[79]

[71] Guazzo, *The ciuile conuersation,* fos. 81ᵛ–82ʳ.
[72] Heron, *A newe discourse,* p. 36.
[73] Ferne, *The blazon of gentrie,* I, p. 12.
[74] Richard Mulcaster, *Positions wherin those primitive circumstances be examined, which are necessarie for the training vp of children* (London 1581), p. 197.
[75] *Register of the University of Oxford,* vol. II (1571–1622), pt I, ed. Andrew Clark (Oxford University Press, 1887), p. 170; cf. 1587, p. 171.
[76] Patrizi, *A moral methode,* fos. 59ʳ⁻ᵛ.
[77] Ibid., fo. 3ᵛ.
[78] Furió [Ceriol], *A very brief treatise,* sig. c4ᵛ; see also sig. 13ᵛ–4ʳ.
[79] Osorio, *The five bookes of nobilitie,* fos. 22ᵛ, 23ᵛ, cf. sig. b3ʳ. See also La Primaudaye, *The French academie,* p. 254; Guazzo, *The ciuile conuersation,* fo. 84ʳ.

Thomas Rogers firmly held that those who were born of 'noble parentage' but who did not possess 'noble qualities' could not win honour and glory. 'And therefore', he continued, 'true is that sentence of Cicero, Noble men, except they be vigilant, honest, valiant, and mercifull (notwithstanding their byrth) must needes geve place unto them, which are adorned with those goodly vertues.' A man is happy when 'he is honored of men', and 'this honor is called the reward of vertue'. Rogers illustrated his argument by providing a traditional humanist example of how the temple of honour in Rome had been reached in no other way than by going through the temple of virtue.[80] Although John Foord followed Aristotle and defined nobility as 'ancient riches and virtue', he nevertheless freely admitted that common people could attain nobility by excelling in virtue rather than in fortune.[81] Even the herald John Ferne, who argued that 'Noblenes mixt', combining birth and virtues, was the best one, confessed that 'the inmeasurable highte, of eternall glorye and immortalitie' acquired by virtues 'excelleth the other noblenesse of bloode', and cited Cicero against Aristotle's 'childish' doctrine 'that noblenes (the honor due to vertues) might proceede from riches'. Instead, 'true nobilitye, hath no other fountaine, from whence to fetch her source, then onely vertue'.[82] For William Blandy, 'every man in this lyfe (as on a Theatre or stage) playes one parte or other, which meriteth shame and obloquie, or deserveth (as his owne right) due commendation'.[83]

In his educational handbook Richard Mulcaster explained that 'to become a gentleman is to beare the cognisance of vertue, wherto honour is companion'. He did not feel inclined to give a further account of the issue partly 'bycause the argument is so large ... and so brave a subject cannot chuse but minister passing brave discourses' and partly because there were already so many treatises on the issue. But he nonetheless reminded the reader that 'true nobilitie have vertue for her ground'.[84] In the *Cyuile and vncyuile life* Vincent and Vallentine could easily agree that it was not the external things such as riches, 'apparell and jesture' which made a gentleman but rather 'the inwarde vertues

[80] Rogers, *A philosophicall discourse*, fos. 67^r–69^r. Cf. e.g. Geffrey Fenton, *A forme of christian pollicie gathered out of French* (London, 1574), p. 222.
[81] Foord, *Synopsis politica*, fos. 13^r, 12^v.
[82] Ferne, *The blazon of gentrie*, sig. A3^r, 1, pp. 4, 13–30, and especially p. 76. For Ferne, see James 1986, pp. 379–80, 382. See also Leonard Wright, *A display of dvty, deckt with sage sayings, pithy sentences, and proper similies* (1589), (London, 1616), fo. 4^r.
[83] Blandy *The castle*, fo. 1^v.
[84] Mulcaster, *Positions*, pp. 194–201.

and perfections be in troth of most waight, and cheefly required'; 'true honor consisteth not in the admiration of the common people, but in the vertue of him that therwith is indued'. It followed that they who 'liveth most vertuously ... are fittest for the state'.[85] Haly Heron presented numerous possible answers to the question of the origins of nobility. Ancient poets had suggested that gentry was 'the verye offspring of the Goddes', while ancient philosophers had claimed that nobility derived its pedigree from the sun, the moon and 'manye other celestiall creatures'. The common people held the erroneous view that 'riches' had been 'the beginning of noble birth'. In the same way as Patrizi, Heron commenced his own answer by explaining in Ciceronian terms how civil society had been founded by degrees and how from the foundation of 'civil government' followed not merely 'the crown of princely dignities', but also 'the banner of true nobilitie'. There was no natural nobility and it was consequently 'the worthy fame of vertues alone' that raised man 'to the toppe and type of Honour'.[86]

John Lyly declared that you are not necessarily 'a gentleman' although 'thy ancestours were of nobilitie'; 'a right Gentleman is sooner seene by the tryall of his vertue then blasing of his armes'.[87] Philip Sidney agreed, esteeming, according to Fulke Greville, 'noble actions far above nobility itself'. Although John Rainolds confessed that 'it is a desirable beginning for the course of a happy life to be born of good parents', he was confirmed that 'noble birth ... weakens us in the course of virtue more than it furthers us'. 'It is', Rainolds told his students, 'absolutely stupid and absurd to set the dignity of men in the rotten antiquity of time.' As Cicero and Juvenal had amply demonstrated, 'true nobility does not depend upon ancestral statues, but upon one's own virtues; not upon the titles of one's ancestors, but upon one's own deeds'. The conclusion was inescapable: 'virtue is the one and only nobility'.[88] According to Philip Stubbes, he was 'no Gentleman' who claimed his title by virtue of his 'byrth', because it was 'onely by vertue' that one attained nobility.[89] Edmund Spenser insisted that 'the gentle minde' and 'gentle deeds' demonstrated 'Of what degree and

---

[85] Anon., *Cyuile and vncyuile life*, sigs. M4ʳ, N3ᵛ; see also F4ᵛ.

[86] Heron, *A newe discourse*, pp. 37–8, see also p. 46. Cf. in general e.g. Thomas Crewe, *The nosegay of morall philosophie* (London, 1580), sigs. C1ʳ, G1ʳ; John Bosswell, *Workes of armorie, deuyded into three bookes* (n.p., 1572), fos. 16ʳ⁻ᵛ; George Whetstone, *The honourable reputation of a souldier* (Leyden, 1586), pp. 26–8, 32, 60.

[87] Lyly, *Euphues*, pp. 190–1, 135.

[88] Greville, *A dedication*, in *The prose works*, p. 23; Rainolds, *Oxford lectures*, pp. 301–5.

[89] Stubbes, *The anatomie of abuses*, sigs. C8ʳ–D1ʳ, B6ᵛ–7ʳ.

what race he is growne'.[90] But he asserted even more strongly that it was pompous and vain to 'onely boast of Armes and Auncestrie' without striving for 'vertuous deedes'.[91] In a well-known passage he versed:

> And certes it hath oftentimes bene seene,
> That of the like, whose linage was unknowne,
> More brave and noble knights have raysed beene,
> As their victorious deedes have often showen,
> Being with fame through many Nations blowen,
> Then those, which have bene dandled in the lap.[92]

There is little doubt that the vocabulary of classical humanism was developed with a vengeance in the 1570s and 1580s. The main aim of human life was said to be the advancement of the common good which could only be attained by a relentless pursuit of a virtuous *vita activa*. In articulating the key concepts of humanist tradition, the theorists under discussion were further engaged in developing the consciousness of Englishmen as active citizens. The underlying argument was that the common good could not materialize unless everyone was fully committed to promote this aim by exercising the full range of civic virtues. It is from this point of view that we can perhaps best understand why Englishmen could find republican treatises, such as Patrizi's, so relevant to their own circumstances. Patrizi defined a 'civil man' and 'a good Cittizen' as a person who turned out to be 'profitable to his common weale'; it was the duty of 'all citizens to worke and traveile' in order 'to helpe the common weal, that not onely it be kept in good estate, but that it maye every day encrease better and better'.[93] The vocabulary used by Thomas Rogers, for instance, was strikingly similar. He presented a man who was in so 'harde contemplation' that he was 'unwylling to bestowe his paines in keeping' his country 'from servitude' as a counterpart of 'a civile man' who was 'adorned with all vertues' and who promoted the common good by his 'civile actions'.[94] The public good was, therefore, not totally dependent on the qualities and abilities of the prince, but also, and perhaps in particular, on the virtuous civic participation of the people as a whole. What was needed in order to accomplish this end was not so much any specific skill as a

---

[90] *Faerie Queene*, VI.iii.1, in *Poetical works*.
[91] 'The teares of the muses', lines 79–96, in *Poetical works*, p. 481.
[92] *Faerie Queene*, VI.iv.36.
[93] Patrizi, *A moral methode*, fos. 48ᵛ–49ᵛ; cf. fo. 51ᵛ.
[94] Rogers, *A philosophicall treatise*, fos. 69ʳ⁻ᵛ, 81ᵛ–82ʳ, 84ʳ–85ᵛ; cf. Foord, *Synopsis politica*, fos. 7ʳ⁻ᵛ, where Foord discussed the issue of 'the best citizens'.

more general inclination to serve the commonwealth and a readiness to commit oneself to the advancement of its well-being.

Although it was widely agreed that everyone should actively seek to promote the common good by exercising his virtuous qualities and that this was the best and perhaps the only way to reach the honourable aim, the question can still be raised how these virtues should be put into practice, and what kind of activities should specifically be singled out. In other words, what were the spheres of the citizen's active life? One significant way of displaying one's virtuous character and advancing the common good was to be a soldier. The willingness to defend the fatherland was often directly linked with the cardinal virtue of courage, and since the former was taken to be the duty of every person, courage was frequently interpreted as a chief virtue of the people. According to Valerius, fortitude consisted in a double duty 'to adventure, and to sustaine daungers & adversities'. A major instance of the virtue in practice was 'Citizens fighting for their countrie'.[95] Osorio agreed and presented the greatness of Rome as his example. In Rome men, who had been 'by race and birth no gentlemen', had attained 'the hyghest degree of honour and dignity' by a lavish display of 'their rare and singular fortitude'.[96] Although Patrizi maintained that it was best 'to bee quiet, and to lyve in peace', he nevertheless admitted that one should always be ready to defend one's country. In accomplishing this, it was of the utmost importance to avoid the use of mercenaries and to employ citizens in the defence of the commonwealth.[97] This republican idea of the militia received its fullest treatment in Machiavelli's *The arte of warre* first published in English as early as 1560 and reprinted in 1588.

The same range of beliefs emerges again in the treatises written by the English. Thomas Pritchard wrote that one of the virtuous actions 'towardes our native Countrey' was 'to defend the same' and 'to dye for the honour of thy Countrey as there are many of the Romanes and others Chronicled in Livie'.[98] Rogers believed that one aspect of a 'civile' man was his readiness to defend the fatherland.[99] But the idea of the militia, so central to Italian republicanism, was more fully discussed and endorsed in a number of military tracts. The common

[95]   Valerius, *The casket of iewels*, sig. H7ʳ–8ʳ; cf. sig. E7ʳ.
[96]   Osorio, *The five bookes of nobilitie*, fos. 25ʳ–27ʳ.
[97]   Patrizi, *A morall methode*, fos. 76ʳ–77ʳ, 82ᵛ–83ʳ, 7ʳ, cf. 72ᵛ.
[98]   Pritchard, *The schoole of vertuous lyfe*, p. 30. Cf. e.g. Anon., *Cyuile and vncyuile life*, sig. C1ᵛ.
[99]   Rogers, *A philosophicall discourse*, fo. 198ʳ, cf. Foord, *Synopsis politica*, fos. 13ʳ, 17ʳ⁻ᵛ.

point of departure of these military treatises was the Machiavellian idea
that there was a close connection betwen good arms and good laws.
'Never was theare', Thomas Procter declared, 'a great & famous estate,
whearein armes and lawes, civill governement, and martiall prowesse
florished not together.' Thomas Digges reminded the reader that 'the
whole course of Histories of all times and Countreys' had shown that
'Kingdomes have flourished' when they took care that military skills
were duly maintained and practised, 'and contrarywyse, how most
happie Empires after warlike Discipline have bin corrupted, have fallen
to ruine, and miserable servitude'.[100]

Although there were authors who defended warfare as a professional
vocation,[101] the most common argument was to emphasize that
untrustworthy mercenaries should be avoided and to put the main
emphasis on the employment of a citizen-militia – as suggested by the
'interventionists' of the Privy Council in 1585.[102] 'Not every mercio-
narie' and 'common hirelyng ... is a Soldiour fitte to bee regestered',
Thomas Churchyard wrote, and stressed that as soon as service was
over soldiers must return to their former occupations.[103] According to
Thomas Procter, the employment of mercenaries was the only serious
shortcoming of the 'otherwise moste excellent governement, and
plentyfull provisyon of all thinges, both for peace and warre' of
Venice.[104] One ought to follow the ancient Greeks and Romans who
had fought their wars chiefly 'to purchase fame' for themselves and to
acquire 'honour, and advauncement unto their countreys, and
common wealthes'; they had not availed themselves 'of the spoiles &
prises of their conquests'. Procter could thus summarize his whole
argument in a marginal note: according to Aristotle, 'he loseth the

---

100 T[homas] P[rocter], *Of the knowledge and conducts of warres, two bookes* (n.p., 1578), fo. 48ᵛ, see also
sig. ¶3ᵛ-4ʳ; Leonard and Thomas Digges, *An arithmeticall militare treatise, named Stratioticos*
(London, 1579), sig. A2ʳ, a1ᵛ. See also Thomas Styward, *The pathwaie to martiall discipline, deuided
into two bookes* (London, 1581), sig. A4ʳ; Barnaby Rich, *Allarme to England foreshewing what perilles
are procured, where the people liue without regarde of martiall lawe* (London, 1578), sig. F2ʳ.
101 Geoffrey Gates, *The defence of militarie profession* (London, 1579), especially p. 12. See in general
Jorgensen 1956, pp. 224–30.
102 Guy 1988, p. 287. For the renaissance background, see e.g. Bayley 1961; Hale 1960.
103 Thomas Churchyard, *A generall rehearsall of warres, wherein is fiue hundred seuerall seruices of land and
sea* (London, 1579), sig. M2ᵛ. Cf. Styward, *The pathwaie to martiall discipline*, p. 149.
104 P[rocter], *Of the knowledge of warres*, fos. 35ʳ⁻ᵛ. See in general Thomas Blundeville, *The true order
and methode of wryting and reading hystories* (London, 1574), sig. A3ᵛ-4ʳ. George Whetstone, *The
English myrror: a regard wherein al estates may behold the conquests of enuy* (London, 1586), p. 83. Cf.
also Charles Merbury, *A briefe discovrse of royall monarchie, as of the best common weale* (London,
1581), p. 14.

name of a good Citizen, which preferreth privat profit, before the common weale'.[105]

The strongest analysis of the republican idea of a citizen-militia is to be found in Leonard and Thomas Digges's *Stratioticos*. It was of crucial importance to discard the contemporary corrupt methods – the methods of 'the Barbarous Gothes'[106] – and to adopt the ancient discipline most conspicuously revealed in Roman history. Leonard and Thomas Digges could speak of 'the profession of a Souldior', but they also maintained that scrupulous care should be exercised that soldiers had 'some occupation'. If they were mere professional soldiers they sought 'the warres onely in hope of spoile'. As soon as the war came to an end, the soldier must 'retourne to his Occupation or former calling'. The ultimate lesson of this became evident in the story of Lucius Quintius Cincinnatus who had been called from the plough to dictatorship, had 'guided mightie Armies, over-ruled Kings, and yet [had] thought it no disgrace to returne againe to his private estate, vendicating nothing but the Fame and honour to himselfe'.[107] The most disastrous consequences of a professional army could be gathered from 'the dissolute disorder of [Roman] Emperours', who had disarmed the Roman people and had established 'a Pretorian Garde' instead. This most unfortunate state of affairs, exemplified by the fact that the Pretorian guard had been ready to sell 'the Empire for money to whom they list', had had two fateful consequences. First, after their disarmament, the Roman people, instead of giving laws to the whole world, as they had used to do, had been 'invaded, spoyled, sacked and conquered' by their enemies. Secondly, they had had 'most servilely to abide ... all kinde of injurie and villanie among themselves'.[108] The moral of Digges's reasoning was obvious. The only way to have a good army, which looked to its own glory and to the good of the commonwealth instead of its own private pecuniary gain, was to arm the people. More importantly, the disarmament of the people prompted corruption both from within as well as without the community. The replacement of a militia by a professional army left the people defenceless against alien invaders, and internally against the yoke of tyranny. The citizen-militia was, therefore, not merely a useful weapon

---

[105] P[rocter], *Of the knowledge of warres*, fos. 14ᵛ–15ᵛ. Cf. Ferne, *The blazon of gentrie*, 1, p. 38; Rich, *Allarme to England*, sig. F3ʳ.
[106] Digges, *Stratioticos*, sig. a1ᵛ.
[107] Ibid., pp. 81, 83.
[108] Ibid., sig. A3ᵛ.

against an alien conqueror; it was also an efficacious device against internal tyranny.

The authors of military manuals acknowledged the dual aspect of the active life. According to Thomas Styward, 'Tullie in his first booke of Offices speaketh of a double commoditie these men doe yeeld to their countreie who making warres goe armed, and roabed doe governe the Common-wealth.'[109] 'An other thing also there is', wrote Thomas Procter, 'which maketh a captaine most honourable, & to be as a father unto his countrey, that is, after warres ended, if he can frame him selfe to peace, good government, & to be as profitable unto the cyvill estate by his industrie & policye, as he was by his valure in the warres.'[110] In 1586 Oxford students were asked to dispute whether 'arms should be preferred to *toga*'.[111] It is of course true that in his account of 'the brave Courtier' Edmund Spenser gave a prominent place to martial exercises. But when he described the ways in which the courtier could serve his prince, he spoke not merely about 'Armes and warlike amenaunce' but also about 'wise and civill governaunce'.

> For he is practiz'd well in policie,
> And thereto doth his Courting most applie:
> To learne the enterdeale of Princes strange,
> To marke th'intent of Counsells, and the change
> Of states, and eke of private men somewhile.[112]

But a more unqualified endorsement of the Ciceronian preference for the civil aspects of the *vita activa* was given by the writers of moral treatises. Although it was admitted that warfare was necessary and a true citizen ought to be ready to defend his fatherland, it was argued, often with a direct reference to Cicero, that to take part in the political life of the commonwealth and to act as its governor was the way in which men could acquire the greatest amount of worldly glory. Patrizi emphasized that it was crucial to guarantee that every citizen was able to take part in government in order to maintain the rules of equality and justice and to safeguard the opportunities of all to win honour and glory.[113] For Gabriel Harvey it was only a balanced combination of a Spartan soldier and an Athenian rhetorician which made a perfect life.

---

[109] Styward, *The pathwaie to martiall discipline*, p. 163. Cf. e.g. George Whetstone, *An heptameron of ciuill discourses* (London, 1582), sig. s1ʳ; idem, *The honourable reputation*, p. 69; idem, *A mirovr for magestrates of cyties* (London, 1584), fo. 5ᵛ.

[110] P[rocter], *Of the knowledge of warres*, fo. 18ʳ.

[111] *Register*, vol. II, pt I, p. 171.

[112] 'Mother Hvbberds tale', lines 781–7, in *Poetical works*, pp. 502–3.

[113] Patrizi, *A moral methode*, fos. 5ᵛ–6ʳ; cf. fos. 19ᵛ, 21ʳ⁻ᵛ.

According to Thomas Rogers, those were 'good citizens' and 'civile' men 'who in war, who in peace deserve well of their contrie', those who always 'beare in remembrance the benefits of their contrie'.[114]

The chief task of true nobility consisted in the governance of the commonwealth.[115] According to Valerius, 'a good Citizen' was one who employed his 'civill vertues' in public offices.[116] Similarly, for Haly Heron it was best in all actions to prefer 'the steadfast counsaile of advised policie' to 'the rash enterprise of malaperte boldnesse'. It had long been 'a great question' whether 'the valiant or wise' were 'more profitable' 'in the administration of the common wealth'. Heron himself, however, had no hesitation in answering the question. He wanted to close the whole controversy 'with the opinion of Cicero' that the force of the arms was small without counsel at home. It followed that a man won 'everlasting fame' as a governor rather than as a soldier.[117] The same preference for 'the great foresight' of governors underlay Baynes's dialogue. According to him, it was pertinent to ask whether Scipios and Horatius Cocles had 'deserved theyr immortall fame and estimation in the world, for the greatnesse of their strength, or for the singularitie of their vertue'. The answer, however, was clear. Baynes urged in a truly Ciceronian fashion that they had won honour and praise because of their singularly virtuous characters; pure physical force was the quality of brutish beasts.[118] When Thomas Pritchard discussed what kind of behaviour could be called virtuous, he pointed out that 'a man must of necessitie be able to governe himselfe, before hee be admitted and thought worthy to have submission of others'. Since men attained the highest degree of prudence when they were old, the governance of the commonwealth, as Cicero had explained, was chiefly guided by old men.[119] According to William Blandy, prudence 'resteth in the knowledge of civile governement'; it taught men not merely to govern themselves and their families, but above all 'to rule poletikely great Cittyes and Commonwealthes'.[120]

Traditionally, an area where this active participation in political life

---

[114] Harvey, *Marginalia*, pp. 145, 147; Rogers, *A philosophicall discourse*, fo. 198ʳ.

[115] Osorio, *The five bookes of nobilitie*, fos. 5ᵛ–6ʳ; Sturmius, *A ritch storehouse*, fo. 19ᵛ; cf. also fo. 5ᵛ. Furió [Ceriol], *A very briefe treatise*, sigs. A2ʳ, F1ʳ, N4ʳ; Ferne, *The blazon of gentrie*, I, p. 30; Mulcaster, *Positions*, pp. 184, 192–3, 132.

[116] Valerius, *The casket of iewels*, sig. E6ʳ–8ʳ. Cf. in general Guazzo, *The ciuile conuersation*, fos. 15ʳ⁻ᵛ.

[117] Heron, *A newe discourse*, pp. 51–2, 44–5, 47.

[118] Baynes, *The praise of solitarinesse*, pp. 13–14, 4–6, 11–12. Cf. *A discourse of the commonweal*, pp. 24–5; Rogers, *A philosophicall discourse*, fos. 137ʳ–138ᵛ; Blandy, *The castle*, fos. 10ᵛ–12ᵛ.

[119] Pritchard, *The schoole of vertuous lyfe*, pp. 17–18, 27; in general pp. 17–27.

[120] Blandy, *The castle*, fo. 13ᵛ.

had materialized was in the role of counsellors. Thus it comes as no surprise that this idea was equally vigorously embraced in the 1570s and 1580s. The idea of counsel was often topically linked with parliament. When Thomas Blundeville rendered Furió Ceriol's treatise into English, he claimed that in England parliament was the counterpart both of Furió Ceriol's 'counsell of revenewes' and council of the 'matters of lawe'.[121] Inside Westminster parliament was often regarded as a centre of political activity, with its chief task being counselling. 'The heathen man Tully', as one MP justified his treatment of the issue of succession in 1566, 'said that man is not borne for himself only, but partlie for his parents, partlie for his children, and partlie for his cuntrie. And surely, Mr Speaker, I doe condemne him as very unnaturall that regardeth neither parentes nor children, and him most unnaturall and unworthie to live in any common wealth that regardeth not his cuntrie.'[122] When Peter Wentworth was examined by the committee of the commons for his famous speech of 8 February 1576, which cost him his liberty for a month, he defended his speech declaring that as an MP he was 'no private person'; on the contrary he claimed to be 'publique and a councellor to the whole'.[123]

In his short tract John Foord dwelt long on the issue of the duties of 'the public citizen', i.e. magistrates and their particular tasks, deriving some of his concepts from Aristotle's *Politics* and most of them from Cicero's *De officiis*, as well as *De legibus*.[124] In addition to the office of magistrates, citizens could display the *vita activa* in public assemblies of three different kinds. The first was the senate, which consisted of the king, senators and all the magistrates. A senator was 'raised by merits', and when Foord briefly explained the senator's qualities, he took them directly from Cicero's *De legibus*.[125] The two other assemblies were drawn from the whole community and they were distinguished from each other not so much by composition as by function. When the community was assembled to discuss and decide judicial issues it was called 'the juridical assembly' (*comitia judiciaria*). But when the same community convened to grant liberties, honours and citizenship as well as to choose magistrates, it was known as 'the voting assembly' (*comitia suffragatoria*).[126]

[121] Furió [Ceriol], *A very brief treatise*, sigs. B3ʳ, C3ʳ.
[122] *PPEI*, I, p. 129; see also p. 227.
[123] Ibid., I, p. 435, see also pp. 431, 428.
[124] Foord, *Synopsis politica*, fos. 13ᵛ–14ʳ, fos. 13ᵛ–24ʳ passim, sigs. ¶7ʳ–A1ʳ.
[125] Ibid., fos. 27ʳ, 11ᵛ–12ʳ, 7ʳ.
[126] Ibid., fos. 25ʳ–26ᵛ.

As we have seen, an important aspect of early-sixteenth-century English humanism had been the emphasis on education in achieving the virtuous commonwealth. In the 1570s and 1580s it occupied an equally central place in treatises specifically devoted to issues of education,[127] but it was also vigorously endorsed in moral treatises whether translated or composed by Englishmen themselves. According to Patrizi, learning was a prerequisite for citizenship and it was consequently necessary 'to trayne young children' in learning 'if in tyme to come wee desire to have them ... to be reputed and take in the nomber of Cytyzens'.[128] Thomas Pritchard insisted that the English should imitate the 'care the auncient Romans' had taken 'to traine up their children in Vertue'.[129] Haly Heron claimed that the only way to guarantee that the young would attain 'the perfection of vertue' was carefully to train them 'by good governmente & wholesome instructions'. The 'practise of good education' was amongst the 'most profitable commodities of the common wealth'. Presenting the standard contrast between proper education in learning and that in horses and hunting, Heron could conclude that the former was 'too lightly regarded'.[130] According to Thomas North, history in general and Plutarch in particular outclassed 'all other learning'. The main reason for the preeminence of history was its closeness to action. Other fields of learning were 'private' and thus 'fitter for Universities then cities'; they were 'fuller of contemplacion than experience' and 'more commendable in the students them selves, than profitable unto others'. Histories, on the other hand, were 'fit for every place, reache to all persons, serve for all tymes'.[131] Edmund Spenser's ideal courtier was able to take part in his country's 'civill governaunce', because he had conferred

> with wise discourse
> Of Natures workes, of heavens continuall course,
> Of forreine lands, of people different,
> Of kingdomes change, of divers government,
> Of dreadfull battailes or renowmed Knights.[132]

[127] Ascham, *Scholemaster* (1570), in *English works*, ed. W. A. Wright (Cambridge University Press, 1904), pp. 171–302; Mulcaster, *Positions*; W[illiam] K[empe], *The education of children in learning: declared by the dignitie, vtilitie, and method thereof* (London, 1588); Sturmius, *A ritch storehouse*, Valerius, *Casket of iewels*.

[128] Patrizi, *A morall methode*, fo. 12ᵛ, in general fos. 11ʳ–19ʳ.

[129] Pritchard, *The schoole of vertuous lyfe*, p. 24, in general pp. 21–8.

[130] Heron, *A newe discourse*, pp. 8–9; cf. Harvey, *Marginalia*, p. 145.

[131] Plutarch, *The lives*, sig. *3ʳ.

[132] 'Mother Hvbberds tale', lines 763–7.

John Lyly and John Foord not only claimed that education was of crucial importance for the attainment of virtue, but also gave a short description of the contents of an ideal schooling. These included religion, languages, rhetoric, dialectic and philosophy, and this broad programme was crowned by travelling, preferably by taking part in a diplomatic journey. Foord was fully convinced that if young men carefully followed his plan of tuition, they would become good men and 'best citizens'.[133] It was, however, Lodovick Bryskett who offered the most detailed analysis of the importance of education. 'The foundation of honest and vertuous living', as he put it, was established already during one's childhood. Without a proper training in his youth, a man could not become virtuous later; the only 'way to have cities and commonwealths furnished with vertuous and civil men, consisted in the bringing up of children commendably'.[134]

If education was the means to inculcate virtues into people's minds and to prepare them for civic life, a principal way in which their actual participation in politics and the well-being of their community had been guaranteed in the republican tradition was to hold on to the mixed constitution. This arrangement had also been suggested in England by Thomas Starkey in his reform programme and it had received further treatment in writings of men such as John Ponet and John Aylmer. In the latter part of the sixteenth century we still sometimes catch an echo of the principles of mixed government, as in Thomas Smith's account of England as a mixed state. According to John Vowell alias Hooker, parliament 'is the hiest, cheefest, and greatest Court' of the realm consisting of the three estates of the king, the nobles and the commons. Hooker did not employ the term 'mixed', but he argued that laws were only made with the approbation of these three estates.[135]

According to Fulke Greville, Philip Sidney regarded Poland as a 'well-mixed and balanced aristocracy' and thought that Italy was bereft of the 'excellent temper of spirits' because of the 'tyrannies of Spain and Rome'.[136] In a letter to his brother Robert, he asserted that the English government was similar to that of Venice; in all the other

[133] Lyly, *Euphues*, pp. 123, 136; Foord, *Synopsis politica*, fos. 5ᵛ–7ᵛ.
[134] Bryskett, *A discovrse of civill life*, pp. 42–3, 9, 50–61, 97–119.
[135] Thomas Smith, *De republica Anglorum* (1583), ed. Mary Dewar (Cambridge University Press, 1982), pp. 49–52; John Vowell alias Hooker, *The order and usage of the keeping of a parlement in England* (1572) in Vernon F. Snow, *Parliament in Elizabethan England: John Hooker's Order and usage* (New Haven: Yale University Press, 1977), p. 181. See e.g. Mendle 1985, pp. 56–9.
[136] Greville, *A dedication*, in *The prose works*, pp. 50, 61.

Italian communities there was nothing 'but tyranous oppression, & servile yeilding'.[137] Young Francis Bacon went so far as to assert that 'it may be, in civil states, a republic is a better policy than a kingdom', though he added that 'yet God forbid that lawful kingdoms should be tied to innovate and make alteration'.[138] In 1579 Arthur Hall drew some public reproof when he wrote that the Commons was a young partner in the trinity of the parliament. But he also maintained that the principles of the mixed constitution had only been put into practice in England. With his insular patriotism he expressed some surprise that Plato had been able to develop these principles, although he had known nothing of 'England, and much lesse [of] the English Parliament'. Hall claimed that the three bodies gathered to a parliament had authority not merely to make laws but even to take away 'the Crowne of this Realme'.[139]

More importantly, as Patrick Collinson has convincingly demonstrated, the major members of the English political nation were able to envisage the English monarchy as possessing crucial republican elements, in particular, when the problem of the queen's safety was most pressing. In the 1572 parliament, the future of Mary Stuart was hotly debated and a form of resistance theory was deployed to show that Elizabeth ought to dispense with Mary. The most telling implication was that 'monarchy is taken to be not an indelible and sacred anointing but a public and localised office, like any other form of magistracy'.[140] Twelve years later there was an attempt to solve the problem by the Bond of Association. This was soon to be followed by a parliamentary 'Act for the Surety of the Queen's Most Royal Person'. By swearing to pursue anybody attempting to harm the queen, the signatories of the Bond were advancing a form of republicanism. There was no explicit reference to the succession which implied that authority was to reside in the commonwealth as a whole. But Burghley and his *epigoni* were not content to stop here; in case the queen should die they wanted to make it, in Collinson's apt phrase, 'a regularised Interregnum' – that is to say, they wanted to answer the most pressing question of 'who should succeed'. The solution was sought in the institutions of the Privy

[137] Philip Sidney to Robert Sidney, n.d. (1578/9), in *Works*, III, p. 127.

[138] Bacon, *Advertisement touching the controversies of the Church of England* (1589), in *Letters*, I, p. 85.

[139] [Arthur Hall], 'An admonition to the father of F.A.', an appendix to *A letter sent by F. A. touchyng the proceedings in a priuate quarell ... betweene Arthur Hall, and Melchisedech Mallerie gentlemen, to his very friende L. B. being in Italie* (n.p., n.d. [1579]), sigs. D4ᵛ-E1ʳ. See Mendle 1985, pp. 61–2; Elton 1981, especially pp. 91–8; Neale 1953 I, pp. 407–9.

[140] Collinson 1987, pp. 411–13. See also Bowler 1981; Bowler 1984.

Council and parliament. The former, strengthened by the available members of the Lords and senior judges of the realm, would recall the last parliament which would then settle the urgent question.[141] A dominant section of the political nation from Lord Burghley onwards could conceive of England – under highly exceptional circumstances at least – as a 'Polish style' republic or as 'a mixed polity'.[142]

It is against this background that John Foord's brief account of the prince becomes understandable as well as highly significant. He could extol the prince as a god amongst men, but he also classified him as one amongst the many magistrates. The main difference between the prince and the other magistrates was not so much the inherent and mysterious nature of his authority as simply the fact that his period in office was perpetual, unlike that of other magistrates. This apart, however, the king was almost just like any other magistrate. First, he was elected. Referring to Aristotle's *Politics*, Foord provocatively claimed that the king was elected and that when the senators and nobles held the election, they should appoint the prince amongst themselves.[143] Secondly, and even more to the point of English politics in the early 1580s, Foord listed amongst the extraordinary magistrates, who were elected for an interval time, 'regent' (*interrex*). The regent was, he succinctly defined, 'a magistrate who was legally put in the place of the deceased king by the voting assembly'.[144] Thus, two years before Burghley's secretive plans John Foord had published the idea that it was to parliament that the commonwealth should turn should its prince suddenly and unexpectedly pass away.

In view of this it is perhaps even more astonishing to find that the English displayed a particular reticence about the mixed constitution. Such eminent councillors as Lord Burghley and Sir Francis Walsingham devised a scheme in which England would have strong republican elements, and these plans received publicity in John Foord's

---

[141] Collinson 1987, pp. 413–21. See also Cressy 1982; Guy 1988, pp. 331–3.

[142] Collinson 1987, pp. 419, 421; Lake 1987, p. 336.

[143] Foord, *Synopsis politica*, fo. 15ʳ: 'In electione Regis cavendum, ne quis nisi Senator, aut Eques, isque reqendae reipub. scientissimus ad regiam dignitatem admittatur: quod prudenter Aristoteles quinto lib. polit. admonet.' Aristotle, *Politics*, 1310ᵇ8–10.

[144] Foord, *Synopsis politica*, fo. 22ʳ: 'Est autem Interrex, magistratus in demortui regis locum legitime suffectus, comitiis scilicet suffragatoriis.' See also the chart at the end of the tract. In John Lyly's *Euphues and his England*, Fidus' bees summoned 'a Parliament, wherin they consult, for lawes, statutes, penalties, chusing officers, and creating their king, not by affection but reason, not by the greater part, but the better'. Euphues found this description so convincing that he thought it highly apposite for men to imitate Fidus' bees, *Euphues and his England* (1580), ed. Edward Arber (London, 1868), pp. 263–5.

treatise, but neither he nor any other English author examined in this chapter subscribed to the idea of the mixed constitution, or even had anything relevant to say about the issue. Anticipating subsequent chapters, it is arguable, perhaps surprisingly, that the English were more taciturn about the issues of the mixed constitution during the late sixteenth century than they were during James I's reign.

This is not to say, however, that the idea of the mixed constitution was totally absent from public discussion in the 1570s and 1580s. Michael Mendle has shown how the first wave of presbyterianism in England (Thomas Cartwright and Walter Travers) explored the possibility of mixed government in the service of their cause.[145] Moreover, even if the English writers examined in this chapter felt disinclined to discuss these issues, they were treated in a comprehensive manner in translated treatises. Discussing the different forms of government, Conrad Valerius claimed that 'that Common weale whiche consisteth of them three whiche are esteemed good, Cicero in his bookes *De Repub*: supposeth to be best, by reason it is more excelent, more profitable, and of longer perpetuitie than the rest'.[146] Furió Ceriol embraced the same idea, offering amongst his instances Poland as well as England.[147]

Patrizi opened his whole treatise by posing 'a very olde' question 'disputed upon amongest excellenteste writers in Philosophie: whether it were better to live wel, and safelye to bee governed by a good Prince, and to obey him rulinge in Justice and equitie, or elles to live in a free cittie and Communaltye established by good lawes & traditions'.[148] Although in principle a monarchy seemed to be an ideal form of government, since it enabled the people 'to leade a private lyfe', in practice it proved to lapse easily into corruption. 'Therefore', Robinson rendered Patrizi's argument, 'I judge, that the lyfe of a Civil and well instituted common weale is to be thought far more safer, then of everye Prince, for that is a continuall and almoste an immortall state of lyfe.'[149] The main weakness of monarchy was the fact that it turned out to be impossible to find 'one prince whiche embraceth all vertues' and

---

[145] Mendle 1985, pp. 64–8.
[146] Valerius, *The casket of iewels*, sig. E5ʳ–6ʳ.
[147] Furió [Ceriol], *A very brief treatise*, sig. F1ᵛ–2ʳ. The other translated treatises which argued for the mixed state included [Pierre de La Place], *Politique discourses, treating of the differences and inequalities of vocations, as well publique, as priuate*, translated by Aegremont Ratcliffe (London, 1578), fos. 18ʳ–21ʳ; Bartolome Felippe, *The counseller: a treatise of counsels and counsellers of princes*, translated by J[ohn] T[horius] (London, 1589), pp. 34–5.
[148] Patrizi, *A morall methode*, fo. 1ʳ.
[149] Ibid., fos. 1ᵛ–2ʳ.

even if such a prince were to be found, he would, nevertheless, most easily degenerate.[150] Neither of these disadvantages could arise in a republic where both the nobility as well as the people were involved in government. The chief benefit of such a system was that it could avoid the corruption of the magistrates by virtue of their continuous rotation. It was of crucial importance not merely to maintain the hope of every law-abiding citizen 'to beare rule in tyme to come'; it was of equal importance to assure him who 'hath Jurisdiction or governaunce' to keep constantly in mind 'that not long after, it may come to passe that he must obay others'. Furthermore, power had the inescapable tendency to corrupt its exerciser, as was manifest in 'Julius Caesar, who being continual Dictator, invaded the Publique weale'. It followed, as Robinson translated Patrizi's argument, that 'a magistrate ought to have a determinate & prefixed tyme apointed for ye government & exercise of his office. For, to beare aucthoritie continuallye in a free cittie is hatefull.'[151]

Although it is difficult to judge the exact intentions of Robinson and other translators, there is little doubt that they regarded these republican tracts as relevant to the English context. Evidence that this was indeed the case comes from Richard Robinson. Whilst he was clearly aware of the ultimately republican nature of Patrizi's treatise, he had certain misgivings about it. When Patrizi argued that princes were prone to degenerate, Robinson explained in the margin: 'Hee meaneth of such as are careles for the common weale.' And when Patrizi declared that it was impossible to find a prince who could grasp all virtues, Robinson commented misleadingly: 'The prayse of a Prynce.'[152] Robinson wanted to soften or even to camouflage altogether the sharpness of Patrizi's point. But at the same time he regarded Patrizi's account as relevant and applicable to England. In the epistle dedicatory Robinson explained that whilst 'the greater part' of Christendom did 'so nuzzle themselves in wickednesse', England, in striking contrast to this appalling state of affairs, lived in peace and prosperity. The avoidance of 'civile dissention' in England was mainly due to God's 'unspeakeable love'. But Robinson believed that it also depended on the fact that the queen was 'assisted with so many christal starres of stately light under her, garnishing and savegarding the good government of this her majesties Realme'. The chief benefit brought

---

[150] Ibid., fos. 1ʳ–2ʳ.
[151] Ibid., fos. 4ᵛ–5ʳ, 5ᵛ–6ᵛ, 19ᵛ–20ʳ, 21ʳ, 24ᵛ.
[152] Ibid., fos. 1ᵛ, 2ʳ.

about by her counsellors was the 'most holsome, godly, & politique lawes, and constitutions, for the continual conservation of the publique weale therof universally, free from all private prejudice and publique perturbation'.[153]

The promotion of the common good and the safeguarding of the commonwealth were an outcome of the active participation of governours and counsellors, rather than emanating from the prince alone. In translating Patrizi's treatise, Robinson also endeavoured to guarantee the continuity of this happy state of affairs. Although the book consisted, as Robinson explained, mainly of 'prophane principles of olde time ... for the direction of Mundane matters, in Civyll governemente', it was still highly applicable to a Christian commonwealth. He boldly maintained that 'therein is Copie of matter worthye Memorye and Imitation for every estate and member of a good Christian common weale at this daye'; the book touched 'good order in mayntenaunce of a Monarchye, and the government thereof'.[154] This suggests, then, that when Robinson presented his translation of Patrizi's republican *De institutione reipublicae* to his English audience, he intended its meaning to be taken seriously. Just as the organizers of the Bond of Association took their own semi-republican devices to be the best means of preparing for a possible interregnum, so Robinson claimed that Patrizi taught England how it could avoid the grasp of the continental 'civil dissention'.

In this chapter we have discussed the continuity and revival of the humanist political vocabulary in mid Elizabethan England. There seems to be little doubt that far from fizzling out in the mid sixteenth century, the humanist tradition continued to flourish. However, the question arises of why the English continued to use it. What were they in effect doing by writing or translating these humanist treatises? On the most general level this question can be answered by saying that they did not do this for any one particular reason. In translating Patrizi's *De institutione reipublicae*, Robinson could be said to have endeavoured to stave off the corruption of the English commonwealth and many of the tracts examined in this chapter should perhaps be read against the backcloth of the increasing ideological tension of the 1570s and 1580s. But Haly Heron composed *A newe discourse of morall philosophie* for a certain John Kay and for all those who were in need of some guidance about how to 'be well armed against those daungerous

[153] Ibid., sig. 2.[v].
[154] Ibid., sig. 3.[r].

delights' which ever loomed large at the entrance of the court. The only way, he said, to sail the 'boysterous Sea' of the court or to climb without falling its 'steepe hyll' and 'huge mountayne' was to strenuously embrace the cardinal virtues.[155] In the following chapters we shall see more specifically how the humanist political vocabulary and sometimes even outright republicanism were used in a variety of different contexts and with a variety of different intentions in English political debate before the Civil War.

---

[155] Heron, *A newe discourse*, sig. A2^v–4^r.

CHAPTER 2

Classical republicanism in the margins of Elizabethan politics

It is clear that classical humanist and even republican arguments were prevalent in the mid Elizabethan period. But in order to gauge the most thorough as well as the radical uses of these arguments in particular contexts, we have to move from the centre of Elizabethan politics to its margins. It is significant that the most pervasive and extreme employment of humanist and republican arguments occurred at the margins rather than at the centre of the political community and that they have been little known, at all. This is first an indication of the applicability of republican notions. Classical *polis* and Italian renaissance communities were, of course, urban communities, and it should therefore come as no surprise that political notions derived from these sources could be adapted to an English urban community as well. Similarly, it is hardly original to indicate the instability of an unsettled frontier, such as Ireland. But what is not often appreciated is that both sets of circumstances could offer an apposite context for republican arguments to emerge.

Secondly, the occurrence of humanist and republican arguments at social margins rather than at the centre reveals something of their controversial nature. It was less dangerous to employ them in such obscure places as Tewkesbury or Ireland; as soon as they were brought to the centre, they were marginalized by the use of translations of foreign treatises to convey the message. Finally, the fact that applications of humanist and republican arguments took place only on the fringes of the Elizabethan political world is an indication of the restricted influence which the authors examined in this chapter exerted. Like Thomas Starkey earlier in the century, some of these authors seem to have been almost ignored by their contemporaries and historians alike. This fact tells us about the limits of the applicability of republican parlance in pre-Civil War England. As already emphasized, it never became a major, let alone a dominant, way of speaking in politics, but it was not completely absent. The aim of this chapter is to show that even the most radical Machiavellian form of republicanism could be both understood and used in Elizabethan England.

I

In his helpful summary, Patrick Collinson has reminded us that there were at least three levels at which the sixteenth-century Englishman could become a participant in political life: 'local community, county community and commonwealth or community of the realm'. These were partially 'overlapping' communities, but they were also, in Collinson's apt phrase, 'semi-autonomous, self-governing political cultures'.[1] In the first part of the present chapter, we are concerned with the lowest level, local community.[2] Broadly speaking, the political activities of a town were twofold. If enfranchised, it (or the varied composition of its electorate) was – at least at the time of parliamentary elections – a part of the political nation.[3] At other times a town looked after its own affairs and took care of its own government.

The complexity of the political structure of a town and the extent of its political autonomy depended on whether it had a royal charter. Boroughs were already marked by 'a bewildering degree of institutional variation'; most of them had a number of courts and councils. The prevailing trend, assisted in most cases by the outside influence of central government or local magnates, was towards a more oligarchic form of government at the expense of the common council, although this development did not lead to a complete exclusion of broader participation.[4] Small, unchartered towns were, in many respects, more like the village communities below them than the large corporate towns above them. This meant that their political structure was relatively simple, but that they, nevertheless, experienced some political life of their own.[5]

Of course, contemporaries appreciated the political nature of their local community. For Thomas Wilson, all cities, 'by reason of the great

1 Collinson 1990, pp. 20–1.
2 On the politics of the county community, see e.g. McCulloch 1986.
3 Cf. Hirst 1975, pp. 90–105 for the varied compositions of urban electorates and for their political importance, see Sacks 1992, pp. 101–8. For a different view, see Kishlansky 1986; Tittler 1989.
4 Clark and Slack 1976, pp. 126–40, 29–30; Clark 1977, pp. 12–4, 139–42, 251–5; Barry 1990, pp. 24–30 and references there. For the medieval background, see e.g. Reynolds 1977, pp. 91–130, 171–81.
5 Clark and Slack 1976, pp. 22, 29, 127.

privilledges they enjoy', were 'a Common Wealth among themselves'.[6] According to William Blandy, prudence taught men how to govern themselves and their families, as well as how 'to rule poletikely great Cittyes and Commonwealthes'.[7] In his guide to the writing and composition of letters, William Fullwood emphasized the importance of 'vertue' because 'in this Citie there is great neede of wise men, for to governe the publike affayres'.[8]

Historians have been fully aware of the politics of locality, but they have only more recently begun to see this phenomenon in the context of the development of a civic consciousness. Patrick Collinson has argued perhaps most forcefully for the semi-republican nature of the local community. In his critique of Pocock's thesis of the absence of civic consciousness in pre-Civil War England, he has reminded us of these strictly local but thoroughly political arrangements.[9] The self-government of local communities and their semi-republican measures are clear signs of political awareness, but they were not necessarily inspired by an articulation of an ideological vocabulary – republican or otherwise. To be sure, there have been attempts to uncover an ideology underlying the autonomous political activities of the local community. According to Peter Clark, an 'urban ideology' can be found in puritanism. 'To civic leaders [of Gloucester]', Clark writes, 'trying to govern a community beset by rising population, economic instability, widespread poverty, and other social and political difficulties, puritanism, with its emphasis on public control and godly discipline, had a powerful appeal. Puritan ideology served to buttress and justify measures concerning the poor and lower classes. It further served to consolidate oligarchic authority and to unite the ruling elite during a period of sustained communal stress.'[10]

Now all this may very well be. But it would be rash to infer from the instance of Gloucester that puritanism played the only or even the dominant role in the urban context. Although there is some evidence that the juristic vocabulary of the ancient constitution was already

---

6   Thomas Wilson, 'The state of England anno Dom. 1600', ed. F. J. Fisher, Camden Society, 3rd ser., LII, *Camden miscellany* 16 (1936), p. 20.
7   Blandy, *The castle*, fo. 13ᵛ.
8   William Fullwood, *The enemie of idlenesse teaching the manner and stile how to endite, compose, and wryte all sortes of epistles and letters* (1568) (London, 1571), fo. 54ᵛ.
9   Collinson 1987, pp. 395–7; Collinson 1990, pp. 30–2. Cf. Reynolds 1982; Roy 1988.
10   Clark 1979, p. 184, in general pp. 181–4; see also Clark 1988, pp. 84–7, 89; Clark 1978; Clark 1977, pp. 341, 153–4; Roy 1988, pp. 216–18.

being applied in the urban context,[11] there is also substantial evidence for arguing that humanist and republican vocabularies *were* used to express the civic nature of urban politics and to defend the self-government of local communities. It was perhaps not for nothing that as early as the first half of the fourteenth century extracts from Brunetto Latini's republican *Li livres dou tresor* were copied into the *Liber custumarum* of London.[12]

Many Italian humanist treatises, some of which were translated into English, were, of course, composed in an urban context. Richard Robinson, the translator of Patrizi's *A moral methode*, was a freeman of the Leathersellers' Company in London and dedicated his translation to Sir William Allen, a London alderman, praying for 'the welfare and felicitye of this honourable Cittie'.[13] A sixteenth-century Englishman perusing George Pettie's translation of Guazzo's *The civile conuersation* could read of the importance of public debate, for 'Commonweales, Cities, yea, small Townes, do they not assemble together to choose officers, & to establish orders by common consent?'[14]

Giving a short account of the beginning and florescence of human society, John Vowell alias Hooker argued in 1575 that after the fall men had become 'vagabonds, rungates and wanderers uppon the face of the Earth', but had soon started to desire 'some better kinde of stay & assurednesse of life: and therfore began to devise and to consult, how to provide a remedy for this disease, & salve for this sore'. They could not find a better remedy than 'to be reduced to some kind of government' and Vowell proceeded to cite Patrizi's *De institutione reipublicae* in order to show that people had 'made choise of such as were moste wise, discreet and valiant among them selvyes, whome they appointed to be their Rulers'.[15] Three years earlier he had already pointed out how Patrizi had taught that 'the best order of government of the common welth: procedeth alwais from tholde and ancient Senators'.[16]

---

[11] Anon., *A breefe, declaring and approuing the necessarie and inuiolable maintenance of the laudable customes of London* (London, 1584), sig. A1ᵛ, pp. 3–10.

[12] Reynolds 1982, pp. 22–3; For Latini, see e.g. Skinner 1990a.

[13] Patrizi, *A moral methode*, sig. ₄ʳ; cf. Wright 1958, p. 356.

[14] Guazzo, *The civile conuersation*, fos. 15ʳ⁻ᵛ.

[15] John Vowell alias Hooker, *Orders enacted for orphans and their portions within the citie of Excester* (London, [1575]), sig. A2ʳ⁻ᵛ. See also John Vowell alias Hooker, *A pamphlet of the offices and duties of euerie particular sworned officer, of the citie of Excester* (London, 1584). For Vowell's humanist background, see Snow 1977, pp. 38–49.

[16] John Vowell alias Hooker, *The order and usage of the keeping of a parlement in England* (1572), in Vernon F. Snow, *Parliament in Elizabethan England: John Hooker's order and usage* (New Haven: Yale University Press, 1977), p. 117.

Vowell claimed that in establishing a flourishing commonwealth the examples of Rome and Sparta were to be imitated. The success of Rome had mainly been due to the ingenuity of Romulus, who 'instituted lawes first for Religion and then for pollycies'. Their maintenance had resulted in diligence, just rule and impartial counsel, which, as Vowell argued, quoting Sallust as his authority, had ultimately brought Rome to greatness.[17] This state of affairs had lasted as long as 'eche man lived in his estate, and regarded the common welth, before the private profit ... but when clyming mindes and ambicious heds would rule the roste, when the common state was neglected, and private profit preferred', the greatness of Rome had turned to utter ruin.[18]

The purpose of Vowell's account was not so much to explain how the English commonwealth ought to be organized as simply to extol the government of his hometown, Exeter. He dedicated his treatise to the 'grave & prudent' mayor and 'senators' of Exeter and having pointed out the proper way of ordering a commonwealth, he described Exeter as 'so wel governed by prudent Magistrates' that it had survived the most troubled times. This was mainly due to its 'sure foundation' which had been built 'upon good government and common societie'. Its inhabitants were, therefore, 'not onely valiant and strong, beeing able to withstand the enemie: but also wise, politike and welthy, able to maintain the common societie, and the privat family'.[19] It is thus of some interest to note that John Vowell followed Cicero in his description of the inception of human society, cited Sallust to show how Rome had become great and found Francesco Patrizi's *De institutione reipublicae*, rather than his *De regno et regis institutione*, of particular relevance. More significant still is that all this was done with a view to paying tribute to Exeter. In Vowell's analysis Exeter was seen (in classical republican terms) as constituting a commonwealth of its own, taking care of its foreign and domestic relations and finding room for the citizen to display his virtuous talents.

It is unclear, however, whether Vowell had any more polemical point in mind when he described Exeter as a commonwealth of its own. We have to travel from Devon back to Tewkesbury in Gloucestershire, some ten miles north of the centre of the puritan urban ideology of Gloucester, in order to encounter a fully fledged recourse to classical humanism in the development of a civic ideology in an urban context. Although the freedoms of Tewkesbury had been confirmed and

---

[17] Vowell, *Orders*, sig. A4ʳ; Sallust, *Catiline*, 52.19–23.
[18] Vowell, *Orders*, sig. B1ᵛ.
[19] Ibid., sigs. A4ᵛ–B1ʳ.

extended several times from the beginning of the fourteenth century onwards, the town was granted its first incorporation in 1575.[20] The rise in the status of Tewkesbury was accomplished with the help of the earl of Leicester, whom the inhabitants of the town had obviously approached and who was afterwards rewarded for his intercession.[21] The incorporation determined, amongst other things, that the government of the town consist of two bailiffs and twelve 'principal burgesses' who were to form 'the common council'.[22]

It was to commemorate this historic occasion that the first townclerk of Tewkesbury, John Barston, published a treatise, the *Safegarde of societie*, in 1576. Barston claimed that his treatise had long been in the making and that it was only the earl of Leicester's visit to Tewkesbury and especially his 'late preferments layde to our towne' which had prompted him to publish it.[23] Barston had been at St John's College, Cambridge from 1566 to 1570 and had afterwards gone to London to pursue legal studies. In the charter of 1575, he was nominated as the first townclerk to 'exercise the same so long as he should behave himself well'. In 1589 he was elected bailiff and was presumably still alive in 1609 when his name appears in a list of people who secured the loan by which the manor of Tewkesbury was purchased by the corporation.[24] As well as commemorating the event and paying tribute to the earl of Leicester, to whom the treatise was dedicated, Barston wanted to explain how an incorporated town formed a commonwealth of its own. In writing the *Safegarde of societie*, he was thus using classical humanist vocabulary to extol the civic values of the urban community.

Barston claimed that he had made himself familiar with 'histories of many people, Lacedemons, Atheniens, Romanes & others' and that he had compared the fruits of this reading with what he had gathered from philosophy, a discipline in which he 'had bin somwhat studied,

---

[20] Elrington 1968, pp. 146–7. For medieval confirmations, see Weinbaum 1943, pp. 43–4. Willcox 1940, pp. 4, 211–14 erroneously states that Tewkesbury was incorporated only in 1609 when in fact it received a confirmation and enfranchisement from James I.

[21] Bennett 1830, pp. 42–3, 207.

[22] An abstract of the charter is in ibid., pp. 378–81; see also Weinbaum 1943, p. 44; Elrington 1968, pp. 146–7. The number of principal burgesses was raised to 24 in 1605, and in 1610 a body of 24 assistant burgesses was added to them; Elrington 1968, pp. 147–8.

[23] John Barston, *Safegarde of societie: describing the institution of lawes and policies, to preserue euery felowship of people by degrees of ciuil gouernment; gathered of the moralls and policies of philosophie* (London, 1576), sig. A4ᵛ, A5ᵛ–6ʳ. He claimed that he had begun his writing after finishing his university studies.

[24] Venn and Venn 1927, pt I, vol. I, p. 99, where his name is spelled 'Barstowe'; Bennett 1830, pp. 380–1, 417, 208 n. John Barston 'chandler' appears in a list of freemen of Tewkesbury in 1574, [Day] 1991, p. 181. Cf. Elrington 1968, p. 149.

and greate deale more delighted'. But he had also compared 'the growth of our english lawes' with the laws of other nations.[25] Despite these elaborate comparisons, Barston did not claim any originality for his conclusions or precepts: they were scarcely more than 'borowed speeches, of the store of other authors' and his 'argumente ... often handled of many learned heretofore'. Nonetheless, he expressed a sincere hope that his readers would be delighted 'with the varietie of examples and speeches of learned writers' to be found in his book.[26] Apart from 'the Bookes of holy Scripture', these 'learned writers' were the staple authors of classical learning: the Greek philosophers Plato and Aristotle; the Roman historians Livy, Sallust and Tacitus; the Roman moralists Seneca, Martial and Cicero. Of all these authors it was Aristotle and especially Cicero whom Barston cited and whose authority he invoked most often. In particular, his long discussions on marriage, family and household were mainly derived from Aristotle.[27]

Barston could devote a considerable space to the issues of family and household, but the main purpose of the work was to lay down the principles concerning the organization of the government of towns and cities. The numerous books on 'regiment and common weale' dealt with issues of communities at large, but they also focused attention on 'that special kind of societie and felowship of one people gathered togither in one towne'. Following these books, Barston intended to show how to build a 'societie of people' into a 'commonweale' in general and how to establish 'civill behaviour in towns and cities' in particular: 'how cities are incorporate & maintained', why they were 'put in use', how they were governed and how, unlike 'the rusticke and unmanored sorte sequestred and devided', they could become 'a body politicke and civill in themselves'.[28]

If towns and cities were proper commonwealths in their own right, for what reason were they established as civic communities? Barston answered this in two different ways. On the one hand, he emphasized the importance of peace and tranquillity as a true end of a commonwealth.[29] But he also boldly proclaimed that another central goal of the commonwealth was to uphold liberty. The manner in which laws were

25   Barston, *Safegarde of societie*, sig. A3ᵛ–4ʳ.
26   Ibid., sigs. A7ᵛ–8ᵛ, B1ʳ, B2ʳ.
27   Ibid., sig. B1ʳ⁻ᵛ, fos. 26ʳ⁻ᵛ, 45ᵛ–60ᵛ.
28   Ibid., sigs. A8ᵛ–B1ᵛ, fos. 1ʳ, 4ʳ, 25ʳ⁻ᵛ, 23ʳ.
29   Ibid., fos. 107ʳ, 24ᵛ.

made in the commonwealth ought to be such that it could in no way impair or 'abridge any one his liberty & freedome'.[30] Magistrates should always keep in mind that their first charge was 'to mainteyne liberties'; they must guarantee that 'the common libertie of all bee not made servitude'.[31]

On the most general level these goals could be achieved by establishing what Barston called 'civilitie' or 'civill life'. A chief reason for writing the treatise was to secure 'civilitie', to bring forth 'civill behaviour' – 'a civill and happye life'.[32] In his definition of a 'commonwealth', Barston followed Cicero closely in writing that it consists of 'the riches, the goodes and universall wealth of one people: the institution that is common to all them whyche are governed by one course of love' and can be found wherever people lead 'a civil, mannerly and honest life'.[33] This idea of civic life and the commonwealth took root in municipal communities. It was again Cicero who provided Barston with the best arguments. In 'his Offices' Cicero had put aside 'that infinite comparison of nature, which toucheth all men alike to be of one societie & felowship' and had, instead, focused his attention on the more circumscribed, yet more manageable bonds. Paraphrasing Cicero, Barston argued that there were 'foure principall societies' – country, town, family and friends – which could 'helpe much to civill government'.[34] A town was 'that which one custome, privilege or freedome, hathe by policies united to be one body'. A particularly close connection existed, therefore, between towns and civic life. These 'franchised places' had always been places of 'civill governement and lawdable living'.[35] Men could only embrace liberty proper after founding towns and cities. Nimrod had been the first ruler and the people had at first been 'content every where to subject themselves to kings & princes'. But soon they had 'waxed civil at last' and they had begun 'to know civilitie & embrace freedome'.[36] According to Barston, the highly peculiar character of towns was most apparent in Roman and Venetian examples. Both the Romans and Venetians had honoured 'their freedomes' to such an extent that they had protected themselves against the inflow of new citizens 'for feare of

30 Ibid., fo. 8ᵛ.
31 Ibid., fos. 86ᵛ, 87ᵛ.
32 Ibid., sigs. A4ʳ, A8ᵛ, B1ʳ, fos. 1ᵛ, 23ʳ.
33 Ibid., fos. 25ᵛ–26ʳ.
34 Ibid., fos. 60ᵛ–61ʳ, 66ʳ; cf. *De officiis*, 1.17.53–4.
35 Barston, *Safegarde of societie*, fos. 61ʳ⁻ᵛ.
36 Ibid., fos. 13ᵛ–15ʳ.

hurting theyr freedomes by the singularitie that sometimes creepeth in with new friendes'.[37]

If there was that intimate a connection between liberty, on the one hand, and the commonwealth and the civic life, on the other, then the crucial question of what it meant to live in a commonwealth and to lead a civic life needed to be addressed. There is little doubt that the term 'civic life' was sometimes used to distinguish civic life from barbarian life. But civic life also consisted in promoting the good of the whole commonwealth: 'every societie of people, is established for common weale'; 'the publike societie' should be 'duely honored' by all in their 'private causes' and the ultimate aim should be that 'the common preferment of all may be more easily perfited'.[38] It was of the utmost importance, therefore, that everyone possessed 'countrey love, care of common weale, a weldisposed mynde to preferre the universall of all as willingly as any private cause or singular intente'. This conviction could most easily have been drawn from the teachings of 'the Stoikes' in general and from those of Cicero in particular. Quoting from the first book of *De officiis*, Barston argued that 'no societie is like unto that which every man hath with the common weale. We are carefull and loving of our parents, our children, our friendes, but our native country is the universall parente of us all, for whiche no good man will refuse to lose his life.'[39] It was necessary, 'as the Stoikes confirme', that everyone be willing 'to joyne himselfe, by his private commodities and travels, to profit all other as well as him selfe'.[40]

Liberty depended chiefly on the willingness of everyone to serve the commonwealth and the public good. According to Barston, everyone of 'priviledged persons of one libertie' ought to 'use his calling, to profit all, & to damnifie none, and that must be by preposing private lucre that may not impugne publike utilitie, since that universal cause of that whole common weale is the perticuler cause of every private person'.[41] The most illustrious men of the Roman commonwealth, who had 'thought it gretest securitie to adventure life & goods for the common weale', stood in complete contrast to many of Barston's contemporaries, who, 'in despight as it were of duetie and contempte of their calling', were 'most odious and hateful to god and man', were

---

[37]   Ibid., fos. 61^v–62^r.
[38]   Ibid., sigs. A8^v, B1^v–2^r.
[39]   Ibid., fo. 30^v; *De officiis*, 1.17.57.
[40]   Barston, *Safegarde of societie*, fos. 30^r–31^v.
[41]   Ibid., fos. 31^v–32^r.

'occupied ... to obscure and deface the universall stat of all' and, most importantly of all, took no care whatsoever 'to enlarge the common weale'.[42]

Barston's argument can thus be said to be essentially classical republican in character. Liberty was closely linked with civility, the civic mode of life; freedom was found not so much in nature as in civic society without which men would be living in 'servitude'.[43] Moreover, liberty could be realized only if everyone led the civic way of life, was willing to disregard his own particular good and to promote wholeheartedly the good of the whole community, without which it was impossible to avoid servitude.

Completely in line with the classical humanist tradition, Barston never tired of repeating that there was an exceptionally close link between civic life and virtue. It was 'behavior tempered by vertue' which led to 'civilitie'. When Plato, Aristotle and Cicero had given their accounts of the commonwealth, they had begun 'first of all to set foorth vertue' since 'it is the only cause efficient of a civill and happye life'.[44] Barston followed suit. He asserted that the first thing to be spelled out was that 'the state of civill life' was best explained by 'a morall description of the actes of vertuous living'.[45]

The possession of virtue was thus the indispensable wherewithal to secure civic life and thereby the commonwealth. Virtue was, as Barston went to great lengths to emphasize, 'the fountaine and roote of all that may be called honest and good, the possession whereof must needes be then the only ornament of mans life'. This overarching concept was, as he defined succinctly, 'the very consente or righteousnes of reason it self'.[46] It consisted of four specific qualities: prudence, justice, courage and temperance. Rather than offering detailed definitions and expositions of the contents of these qualities, Barston simply stressed their importance and concurred with Cicero that 'all that may bee called honest, proceedeth from one of these foure'.[47] Virtue taught 'to know office and dutie to such as defende our tranquility, and minister justice to all that are oppressed'. Following his stoic authorities, Barston also maintained that virtue taught men 'howe to pacifie and rule the disordered passions and perturbations of the minde, and to subject the

[42] Ibid., fos. 33ʳ–34ʳ.
[43] Cf. Skinner 1990b, p. 305.
[44] Barston, *Safegarde of societie*, sigs. A4ʳ, A5ʳ, B1ᵛ, fos. 1ʳ, 1ᵛ.
[45] Ibid., fos. 111ᵛ, 25ᵛ.
[46] Ibid., fos. 1ᵛ–2ʳ, 35ʳ.
[47] Ibid., fos. 35ʳ–36ʳ.

motions of our appetites and unrulie wil, to obey reason'. Virtue urged man 'to use reason for the governoure of all his appetites, and to subdue all manner affections to the rule of reason'.[48]

It is clear that the time-honoured humanist notion of the virtuous civic life underlay Barston's idea of the local community of towns. It comes as no surprise, therefore, that Barston turned to a further theme of classical humanism: the question of what qualities constitute a truly noble citizen. It is arguable that the humanist notion of true nobility furnished Barston with an argument to censure the oligarchy of Tewkesbury. According to him, it was a widely held belief that birth and riches made the true citizen. But in his view, this was an utterly wrong way of settling the issue. He was fully convinced that 'dignitie was not ballanced by birth: estimation rayned not in riches: credite came not of continuance'. Denouncing the holder of the opposite view, he averred that 'to bee a gentleman, to bee a riche man, to be an elder, without vertue, withoute wisedome, without experience or knowledge, were counted bare bragges, supercilious sutes, and a naked nothing, to bring a man to dignitie, estimation, or credite'. Instead of ancient lineage or the possession of riches, the only way to be counted a true citizen of an urban community was to embrace virtue. 'In such civill societies of one towne', Barston firmly held, 'each degree likewise was duely made of suche as by wisedome, good moderation, vertuous endevours and knowledge, deserved of the common weale.' He illustrated his argument with the staple example of Cicero and contended that it was better to stand at the beginning of a noble family than to bring up the rear. Cicero had himself been named '*Pater Patriae*' although, as Barston carefully emphasized, 'of long time hys linage was obscured'. Plato, too, had stated most emphatically that those who 'by their vertue and good gifts' attained 'nobilitie by themselves' were '*vere nobiles*, noble men indeede'.[49]

A true humanist, however, Barston thought that it was one thing to identify such a happy commonwealth and quite another to achieve it in practice. The reason why Barston was not content with a mere account of a virtuous commonwealth is not far to seek. One of the themes which runs through his entire work is man's proneness to

---

[48]　Ibid., fos. 2^{r-v}, 35^r. The only stoic concept which Barston criticized was that of 'severe life'. It was improper to claim that that which 'soundeth not of the very inwardes of vertue, were to be condemned'. This stoic severity was 'to grafte men of stone that have no feeling'. There should be, according to Barston, room for 'bodyly health', 'honest pleasure' and 'lawful lucre', fos. 34^v, 41^r.

[49]　Ibid., fos. 62^r–63^v, cf. fo. 28^{r-v}.

corruption: 'the nature of man is so corrupted, that naturally he hateth vertue, & is most shamefully prone to al manner vice'.[50] 'The golden worlde', when 'the very love & commendation of vertue' had been taken as a 'sufficient price, to invite and stirre men to all maner goodnesse', had degenerated into 'these iron times', as 'vertue was exiled, and the rust and canker of vice freated mens hartes to chuse the deapth of evil'. This general corruption was most apparent in man's tendency to abandon honesty, especially for private monetary gain. The 'covetous wretche' was most vividly 'set foorth by Martial in his Epigrammes'. It was of great importance that 'wealth' would 'not tarrie with them that be vertuouse', that 'every man accept his estate' and that 'a civil & honest life' was taken to be 'the chiefest instrument to felicitie'.[51]

Although the commonwealth was thus liable to be corrupted, one of Barston's main aims in the *Safegarde of societie* was to explain how man's depraved nature could be prevented from gaining the upper hand and to lay out the ways in which his instructions could be put into practice in urban communities. One possible way of accomplishing this would be to observe religious duties. Referring again to Cicero and Aristotle, Barston argued that as soon as 'godly religion once goe to wrecke, all trust, all societie of mankinde, justice and all vertue decyeth'. It followed that scrupulous heed should be taken to maintain and to further 'chiefly, and most of all of Christian profession'. Wherever religion was duly embraced in 'uniforme order' and with 'the extirpations of schismes, and divisions', there 'morall policies, even for religions sake, shall worke in all degrees'. There is thus a strong religious element in Barston's tract. His account of the birth of civil society was essentially scriptural: once men had lost 'original righteousnesse', they had been in great need of 'temporall lawes'.[52] Moreover, he asserted that 'godly religion' was the first and principal safeguard of society. In order to guarantee 'the godly discipline of the church', the magistrates should establish and maintain 'good and reasonable lawes'.[53] Religious issues (such as religious uniformity, the repression of schism, observance of religious feasts and almsgiving) loom large in Barston's list of the citizen's duties.[54]

[50] Ibid., fos. 1^{r-v}, 2^v, $4^{-v}-5^r$, sigs. $B1^r$, $A8^v$.
[51] Ibid., fos. 2^v-3^v, 42^r-45^r.
[52] Ibid., sig. $B1^r$.
[53] Ibid., fos. 29^r-30^r; 102^r-105^r.
[54] Ibid., fos. 102^v-105^r, 109^r-110^r.

Another important way of inducing the people to adopt virtue was to take care of their education, because there was an exceptionally close relationship between 'learning' and 'government'. 'Common scholes & learned tutors' were indispensable for the cultivation of virtue; they offered the young an opportunity to be 'nousled in vertue from tender yeeres' so that 'their life may profit the common weale in times of more maturitie and ripenesse'. Schools were, as Plato had already pointed out, 'the Pilote of policies'.[55]

Although religion and education were of great weight in bringing people round to a virtuous life for the common good, it was laws and government which had by far the most crucial place in the Barstonian analysis. It is possible to discern two ways in which Barston treated the issue of law. On the one hand, he presented a typical eulogy of common law, announcing that 'our english lawes' defied comparison. The excellence of common law was partly due to its age; there was 'no comparison' to its 'most credible antiquitie'. But it also overshadowed all other laws, including even Roman law, in contents. Its 'greate equitie, reason, and reasonable grounds therof doe make the practice firme and inviolable'. Barston admitted that when 'the Normans had conquered the lande all was chaunged and nothyng almost suffered that was auntient'. 'Brytons' had not only been given new laws; these new laws had been introduced in a language unknown to them so that the conquerors could more easily abuse them. But the changes which the Norman conquest had brought did not detract from the preeminence of England's ancient common law: 'no nation or people of the world enjoy the lyke privilege of peace and quietnesse, and all manner saftie by their popular lawes, as this noble Iland'.[56]

This encomium of the common law apart, Barston developed another notion of law more in line with the classical republican tradition, in which the law was seen not so much as preventing other people from offending one's private rights or privileges than as coercing everybody to virtue, thereby promoting the common good.[57] Barston informed his readers that his purpose was, above all, to explain that 'the beginning of lawes [was] to incorporate societies unto vertue'. It ought to be apparent to everybody that a commonwealth was 'by lawes confirmed' and that laws were invented and first put into practice

55   Ibid., fos. 2ᵛ, 45ᵛ, 56ʳ–58ᵛ, 102ᵛ–105ᵛ.
56   Ibid., fos. 20ʳ⁻ᵛ, 21ᵛ–22ᵛ.
57   Skinner 1990b, p. 305.

because people lacked the 'inclination to vertue'. Men were reprobates, they hated virtue and the only way, therefore, to build a lasting virtuous commonwealth was by establishing laws to act as 'spurres to pricke men unto vertue'.[58]

It was not enough, however, to have good and profitable laws; equally crucial was their proper application. Whereas moral inducement was employed by philosophers, laws were the methods of 'all politicke good princes and magistrates'.[59] The role of government in attaining a truly virtuous commonwealth raised the most important question: how was the government of a commonwealth to be organized? Although people had at the beginning been 'content every where to subject themselves to kings & princes', they had slowly discovered 'the mane defaltes in princes and Magistrates', once they had come 'to know civilitie' and to embrace 'freedom'. This had been so because 'ambition, avarice and crueltie' had led many princes 'to practise extortion, oppression and tirannie ouer the common people', so much so that 'many were weary and refused all maner [of] regiment and subjection'. It had thus become a crucial question what kind of 'regiment' was best: 'among the learned were stirred great contentions & quarrelling, dispensations of the best state & condition of the common weale'.[60]

Despite the tyrannous inclination of princes, Barston emphasized that 'it is most reasonablie of all concluded for many politike and godly causes, that no state is to be compared to the royall scepter of a King', as the constitutional history of Rome had convincingly demonstrated. The worst form was 'that most pernicious state of Democratia', whereas aristocracy – the 'rule of the honorable and auncient nobles, without a certayne and undoubted Prince' – was almost equally unsuccessful. 'For what perillous commotions, and uprores', Barston asked rhetorically, '[had] vexed the Citie of Rome, as long as the onely Counsell of Aldermenne governed, as in Venice at thys daye?' It followed that the 'lawfull principalitie of one heade and governour, is most of all agreeing to the safetie of the common weale'.[61]

Although Barston had thus come to the conclusion that pure monarchy was the best form of government, he had not yet

[58] Barston, *Safegarde of societie*, sigs. A5ᵛ, A8ᵛ–B1ʳ, fo. 1ʳ⁻ᵛ, see also fos. 4ʳ–13ʳ, 2ᵛ–3ᵛ, 66ʳ.
[59] Ibid., sig. A8ᵛ, fos. 1ʳ, 2ᵛ–3ʳ.
[60] Ibid., fos. 13ʳ–15ʳ.
[61] Ibid., fos. 15ʳ–19ʳ.

exhausted the subject. In the discussion that followed, he not only delimited the prince's authority; he also proceeded to endorse the idea of the mixed constitution. It was the only effective remedy to curb the tyrannous nature of the prince. First, kings should rule by laws alone. 'For if Princes', Barston wrote, 'rule not by lawes, but at libertie, if they bee not themselves subjecte to lawes, but altogither lawlesse, if wilfull will should stand for unwriten law: then might authoritie be doubted lawfull, all government would bee uncerten, and justice should bee wrested to maintaine wrong in steade of right and equitie.' Princes were not above the law, but the laws set strict limits to their rule. As soon as a prince tried to reverse these priorities, he became a tyrant. 'The lawes of the countrey' defined the prince's 'office and function'. 'A King', Barston concluded in an almost conciliar fashion, 'hath not the rule of lawe, but is the only minister and nothing els.'[62]

It was scarcely surprising, therefore, that when Barston discussed the way in which laws were made in England, he emphasized the communal character of the legislative process. Laws were generally made, he wrote, by 'common consent', which in England happened in 'parliament'. The underlying reason was that laws were 'of force and authoritie, when common consent had subscribed therunto, and not before, whiche else avayled nothing of it selfe, to abridge any one his liberty & freedome'.[63] It followed, as Barston later pointed out, that the English government was a mixed one. The way in which English laws had been made accounted for their just and equal nature. In implementing laws, there was no 'more lawfull or laudable order', Barston patriotically claimed, '... than the triple regiment afore spoken of'. Though Barston had not mentioned 'the triple regiment' before, he left no uncertainty as to what he meant. It referred to the ways in which laws were established by 'the free consent and agreement of all three, the prince of all, the noble and universall commons, in common parliament and councel togyther assembled'.[64]

This triple form of implementing laws constituted the strongest safeguard of liberty and a bulwark against servitude. Barston contrasted 'the golden worlde' and the more recent 'iron times', but he also contrasted 'the servitude and bondage of old time' and the 'libertie, peace and quietnesse' of his own times. The former age was a period

---

[62]   Ibid., fo. 19ʳ.
[63]   Ibid., fos. 6ʳ, 8ʳ⁻ᵛ.
[64]   Ibid., fo. 22ᵛ.

when 'people lived ... more beastly in despaire, than regarding honestie or vertue: so hopelesse of manumission and libertie'. They were 'godlesse, and of brutishe condition: on whose neckes Princes and noble men layde such greevous taxes and intollerable distresses, for the building and maintenance of theyr Castles and strong holdes, on which they did trust and depende, more than on politike lawes and lawfull governmente', so much so that 'the whole wealth of the land was in fewe besydes the Prince'.[65] Barston refrained from specifying how Englishmen threw off the yoke of this servitude and came to embrace civility, but he was most outspoken in contrasting liberty, virtue, the civic life and 'the triple regiment' of parliament with servitude, vice, the lack of civility and tyranny.

The main context in which Barston developed the idea of the mixed constitution was that of municipal government. His intention was to 'declare the corporation of a well governed Citie or towne, as they are to be ruled by private lawes and inferious magistrates, and as they are from the rusticke and unmanored sorte sequestered and devided, to be a body politicke and civill in themselves'.[66] A municipal commonwealth was, he boldly claimed in Ciceronian fashion, '[a] multitude or body politike, enuring a civil, mannerly and honest life ... where magistrates do rule, the senate or elders gyve councell, the people use their freedome of consente'.[67] Barston thus conceived of the government of the urban commonwealth as a mixed constitution.

In organizing the government of an urban community, the municipal government of Massilia (Marseilles) had much to commend itself. As Strabo explained, 'the good order of governemente that was used in regiment and rule of their common weale' was taken care of by '600 chiefe burgesses, senators or Aldermen'. From these, fifteen were 'elected and chosen to be magistrates and governours for the yeere'. Finally, three special magistrates were chosen from these fifteen 'to bee judges of the lawe, to keepe courses, to heare and determine trespasses, and to judge every man right'.[68] Although the ideal form of municipal government would thus involve a significant number of 'chiefe burgesses', Barston regarded the example of Roman consuls and dictators or 'Lorde commaunder, and as we call it Mayor', as teaching

---

[65] Ibid., fos. 24^v–25^r, cf. fo. 15^r.
[66] Ibid., fo. 25^v.
[67] Ibid., fos. 25^v–26^r, cf. sig. B2^r; Cicero, *De re publica*, II.33.57, I.35.55.
[68] Barston, *Safegarde of societie*, fos. 78$^{r–v}$; Strabo, *Geography*, 4.1.5. For Cicero, Massilia was a pure aristocracy, *De re publica*, I.27.43.

the central role of one or two magistrates. In some towns the chief
magistrate's task would have been given to ten or twelve 'jurates or
sworne men', but to determine the exact number was not so important
as to follow the general rule 'that many heads do rather endanger and
prejudice tranquilitie'.[69]

Barston emphasized the fact that these chief magistrates should be
'yeerely' elected, because power had the irresistible tendency to
corrupt: 'continuance' could 'easily change' the rulers' 'conditions', so
much so 'that in stede of justice, tyrannie should be used'. Taking
Caesar as his example, he explained the corrupting effect of power:
'when Julius Caesar would have bin Dictator of Rome by patent, many
good men, forseeing what mighte folowe, they abjured the citie, and
some chose to die, and the greatest part betooke them to a private life'.
Experience thus taught that 'honor and estimation wil make most men
to adventure honestie' and that without limiting their term of office
many 'woulde make maisteries and gaynes of offices'. The only
conceivable way of bridling this 'ambition' was therefore to limit the
duration of a magistrate's office to one year.[70]

An equally important question concerning these 'yeerely offices of
magistrates' was: 'who shuld be elected thereunto?'[71] Barston placed
especial emphasis on the same values that we found in his account of
true nobility, thereby revealing his critique of oligarchy. First, 'simple
and ignorant men of handicrafts' were disqualified, both because they
were 'rash' and because they could not suppress their own 'affection'.
Moreover, to an accomplished magistrate, learning was an indispensable asset.[72] But it was of the greatest importance that he was 'an
honest & civil man', which Barston took to mean that he was 'more
careful for common weale, than greedy after gaines: not so wise in his
owne conceit, as submisse & tractable to beare the wisest: not
impugning good councel, not of manifest evill report, not a mayntayner
of quarells, & last of al, not unexpert in the customes of his country'.
The election of a magistrate should, therefore, be based on the
personal merits and virtues of the candidates, not, as Barston was at
some pains to point out, on ancestry or personal wealth: 'How far

[69]   Barston, *Safegarde of societie*, fos. 78ᵛ–79ʳ. Cf. Robert Greene, *The royal exchange: contayning sundry
       aphorismes of phylosophie, and golden principles of morrall and naturall quadruplicities* (London, 1590),
       sig. ¶2ᵛ, where 'the Lord Mayor of London' is said to possess 'absolute governaunce and
       regiment of the Cittie' in contrast to the limited authority of the Venetian 'Duke'.
[70]   Barston, *Safegarde of societie*, fo. 79ʳ.
[71]   Ibid., fos. 79ʳ⁻ᵛ.
[72]   Ibid., fos. 79ᵛ–80ʳ.

deceyved then are they, that make no more a doe to choose a
magistrate, but to find him ancient & welthy, though he lack al things
else besides?'[73]

In his short description of the chief magistrates' duties, Barston put a
high premium on the good of the whole commonwealth. The magistrate 'must forget his private being, so long as his office lasteth, and
should more esteeme publike utilitie than his owne lucre'. He should,
as Cicero had affirmed, embrace 'humanitie' rather than 'prowes of
manhood'; he should preserve equity and justice like Manlius Tor-
quatus, who had been ready to punish his own son; and he should
uphold the laws and customs remembering that 'chaunge and ex-
chaunge of government' had caused Rome's eventual ruin.[74] Rather
than being 'of an abjecte and servile minde', he should be 'a prudente
and politike governour' and remember that 'the maintenaunce of
liberties ... [was] the whole charge of the Magistrates'.[75] As to the
common people, the magistrate ought to bear in mind that 'it shoulde
be lawfull in all free Cities, for every man to speake his conscience'.[76]
Finally, the magistrate should win the common people's 'favoure' and
'forfeite good governement by their necessarie ayde' thinking that
'nothyng may safely be established without them'.[77]

But urban government required two further arrangements, should
the best state of the commonwealth be achieved. First, in addition to
the magistrates there should be 'the senate or elders' whose chief duty
was to give 'councell'. A consummate counsellor ought to have
'experience in things passed', 'due consideration of the tyme presente'
and 'a good understanding of al that may folowe'. He should also know
'whether it be lawfull that is proposed, by what meane it maye bee,
howe necessarie it is, and for what cause' it was proposed. In a word,
he must thoroughly embrace prudence and he would be able 'to doe
good service in counsell for the common weale, and to make him
merite the good reporte and estimation'.[78]

The common people made the triple form of government of an
urban community complete. In line with his earlier denunciation of
democracy, Barston stressed that the common people were but 'a

---

[73] Ibid., fos. 80ʳ–81ʳ. Cf. e.g. Robert Crowley, *A sermon made in the chappel at the Gylde Halle in London, the xxix. day of September, 1574* (London, 1575), sigs. c3ʳ, D2ᵛ–3ʳ.
[74] Barston, *Safegarde of societie*, fos. 82ᵛ–83ʳ, 84ʳ–88ʳ.
[75] Ibid., fo. 87ᵛ.
[76] Ibid., fo. 83ᵛ.
[77] Ibid., fo. 88ʳ.
[78] Ibid., fo. 91ᵛ–99ʳ; cf. sig. B2ʳ.

monstrous beast with manye heades'. The commonwealth would most
certainly be destroyed by 'civill dissention' and concord was thus of
capital importance. The common people must not acquire 'the aspiring
minde' of ambition, but ought to suppress 'their affectes and perturbations' and to swear obedience to the magistrates.[79] In short, towns
should be governed on the principle that 'the fewest must governe' and
'the most of all shoulde obey'.[80] Nevertheless, the common people had
their role to play in the government of towns. They should use 'their
freedome of consente'. In the case of the community of the realm, the
people's role amounted to consent in the law-making process in
parliament. In the urban context, Barston emphasized that the magistrates should not ignore the common people, arguing that the
commons' consent was a 'necessarie ayde' to good government. In
politics of 'all free Cities', it was important to guarantee people's liberty
of speech. Moreover, care should be taken to follow the excellent
Roman rule that nothing should receive the force of law without
tribunal consent.[81] An even more important occasion when the people
could use its 'freedome of consente' was the election of the magistrates.
We have seen how Barston agreed with Strabo that it was the duty of
'600 chiefe burgesses, or senators' to elect them.[82] The actual government of Tewkesbury, determined by its charter, was more oligarchic
than Barston's proposals. It is, therefore, arguable that in extending the
freedom to elect magistrates to such a large body, Barston was again
launching an attack against a tight oligarchy.

John Barston's treatise offers us a complete use of classical humanist
and republican notions in an urban context. The main aim of the
urban commonwealth was to maintain liberty. To make this possible,
Barston envisaged a community where everyone would be willing to
disregard his private good and to practise his civic virtues in pursuit of
the common good. The government of the community was to be
organized as a mixed state where the dominant role was played by the
aristocracy. But it was not an aristocracy based on lineage and
inherited wealth. On the contrary, Barston's exposition of true nobility,

[79] Ibid., fos. 66ᵛ–68ᵛ, in general fos. 66ᵛ–78ʳ.
[80] Ibid., fo. 28ᵛ.
[81] Ibid., fos. 83ᵛ, 88ᵛ.
[82] Ibid., fos. 78ʳˉᵛ. Cf. Greene, *The royal exchange*, sig. ¶2ᵛ, where the 'absolute governaunce' of
      'the Lord Mayour of London' is, nevertheless, described as being ultimately dependent on the
      fact that 'the honourable Cittizens' of London were 'alwaies carefull for the Common-wealth'
      and willing, therefore, to 'elect such a grave, an auncient Magistrate, as for his vertue,
      religion, wealth & worthinesse, may rightly be called *Pater Patriae*'.

and his concept of the mixed constitution in particular, can be taken as a critique of the oligarchic form of municipal government and as a defence of a virtuous aristocracy. Above all, Barston seems to have regarded a self-governing republic as the ideal type of commonwealth, since, as he was most careful to emphasize, its governors were to be elected.

II

A great deal of scholarly attention has been paid to Machiavelli's impact on sixteenth-century England. Englishmen were familiar with Machiavelli's writings from an early date and although the predominant reaction was one of repugnance, there were authors who were inclined to embrace Machiavellian ideas. William Thomas based his secret advice to Edward VI on Machiavelli, and Stephen Gardiner did likewise in his advice to Philip of Spain. In Gardiner's case Machiavelli not only provided pieces of morally neutral advice; he also led the way to a preference for political effectiveness over the claims of morality and religion.[83] Although this last point has often been regarded as the most distinctive feature of Machiavelli's political thought, his republicanism is its most important element for our present purposes.

The idea of a republican Machiavelli was slow to emerge. Reginald Pole had claimed that Machiavelli had written *Il principe* with a view to overthrowing the prince, but it was Alberico Gentili in the 1580s who pointed out that the Florentine had been 'a eulogist of democracy, and its most spirited champion'.[84] There seemed to be a growing interest in Machiavelli's work in general and his republican writings in particular, as shown by the fact that John Wolfe printed both *Il principe* and the *Discorsi* in London with the fictitious imprint 'Palermo'. According to Wolfe, Machiavelli taught 'what difference there was between a just prince and a tyrant, between government by many good men and government by a few bad ones, and between a well-regulated commonwealth and a confused and licentious multitude'.[85] Peter S. Donaldson is undoubtedly right in saying that neither Gentili's remarks nor Wolfe's preface can be taken 'as evidence of any systematic republican

---

[83] For Thomas, see Raab 1964, pp. 40–8; Donaldson 1988, pp. 41–4, and references given there; for Gardiner, see Donaldon, 1988, pp. 48–85, especially, pp. 68–9.

[84] Alberico Gentili, *De legationibus libri tres* (1594), translated by Gordon J. Laing (New York: Oxford University Press, 1924), II, p. 156. The work appeared for the first time in 1584. Panizza 1969, p. 481; Donaldson 1988, pp. 89–90. For Gentili in general, see Panizza 1981.

[85] Donaldson 1988, p. 93, in general pp. 93–5; Panizza 1969, p. 483.

ideology', as Diego Panizza has claimed. There is indeed a long step from such brief remarks to a thorough usage of Machiavellian republicanism. Although it is commonly assumed that this step was only taken in the 1640s and especially in the 1650s,[86] it had in fact been taken as early as the 1590s.

If urban communities, such as Exeter or Tewkesbury, offered favourable circumstances in which humanist and republican vocabulary could be applied, it was Ireland which provided the context for a thorough usage of Machiavellian republicanism. This was hardly a mere coincidence. The inherent stability of the political universe inhabited by Elizabethans and Jacobeans is often alleged to have impeded the emergence of a full-fledged Machiavellian conception of politics dominated by the incessant flux of fortune, and that this could happen only after the complete collapse of the traditional frame of reference in the Civil War.[87] The unsettled frontier society of Ireland, however, makes, an important exception to this rule.

Until the 1530s English governance of Ireland was conducted by an aristocratic delegation of one of Ireland's feudal lords. The Kildare rebellion of 1534, however, prompted Henry VIII to advance a new system of Englishmen to serve as governors in Ireland. In 1541 Henry assumed the new title 'king' of Ireland, and although this decision followed from the break with Rome, it committed England to a full-scale conquest of Ireland. No permanent success was achieved and essentially the same line of policy was continued in the Elizabethan period. When Sir Henry Sidney arrived in Ireland in 1565 to assume the lord deputyship, a renewed programme of conquest was again taken up. Some success was attained, but no conclusive settlement was reached, and in the 1590s England was involved in suppressing a major rebellion.[88]

The continual attempts to extend the English impact in Ireland and the equally continual failures provoked a number of those involved to compose new plans for the conquest as well as its maintenance.[89] Sir William Herbert wrote a Latin treatise *Croftus, sive de Hibernia liber* in 1588/9, and in 1596 Edmund Spenser composed his famous *A view of the present state of Ireland*. But the most remarkable of these treatises

---

[86]　Raab 1964, pp. 157, 161, 163, 168–75, 179–81, 183, 188.

[87]　For a recent statement to this effect, see Sharpe 1989, pp. 25–8.

[88]　See Canny 1976; Ellis 1985; Guy 1988, pp. 356–69; Edwards 1961.

[89]　See especially Quinn 1945; Quinn 1976; Canny 1973; Canny 1976. Earlier printed tracts include Edward Walshe, 'Conjectures concerning the state of Ireland' (1552), ed. D. B. Quinn, *Irish Historical Studies*, 5 (1947), pp. 315–21; Rowland White, 'Discors touching Ireland' (c. 1569), ed. Nicholas Canny, *Irish Historical Studies*, 20 (1977), pp. 446–63.

appeared in 1594 when Joseph Barnes, printer to Oxford University, issued Richard Beacon's modest quarto entitled *Solon his follie: or a politiqve discovrse, tovching the reformation of common-weales conquered, declined or corrupted.*[90]

Herbert's *Croftus* is perhaps the most neglected of these treatises. Yet Brendan Bradshaw has demonstrated that Herbert, writing in humanist Latin and looking to humanist moral and political tradition for the conceptual tools for analysing the Irish problem, offered a comprehensive political programme for reforming the Irish commonwealth.[91] Although Beacon's treatise has not suffered a similar neglect, it has not been given the attention it deserves. Historians of political thought have completely overlooked it and it has mostly been studied in the narrow context of the English conquest of Ireland in the sixteenth century. But even here no adequate account of its contents and argument has been offered. Mostly *Solon his follie* has served as a background to Edmund Spenser's *A view of the present state in Ireland.*[92] This neglect becomes all the more surprising when we recall that scholars have clearly recognized the general importance of the reform programmes composed by the English in Ireland. Nicholas Canny has pointed out that because of the radically different circumstances the English were 'of necessity forced to advance novel solutions' and they consequently developed 'clearly-defined radical programme[s] of reform which would involve the erection of a completely new commonwealth upon firm foundations'.[93] Recently, Sydney Anglo has painstakingly demonstrated Beacon's sources in general and his wide employment of Machiavelli in particular. Nonetheless, although Anglo duly recognizes that Beacon aimed at 'the reformation of a common-

---

[90] Beacon was sometime queen's attorney of the province of Munster in Ireland. Before embarking for Ireland, Beacon had received the standard education of a gentleman. A native of Suffolk, he entered St John's College, Cambridge in November 1567, receiving his BA in 1571 and MA in 1575. After leaving Cambridge, he began his legal studies in Gray's Inn in 1577 and was called to the bar some seven years later. The patent for his attorneyship in Munster dates from December 1586 but by 1591 the post had been conferred on another person: *DNB*; Judson 1947, pp. 165–8. For Beacon's activities in Ireland, see *CSPI* 1586–8, pp. 427, 440; *CSPI* 1588–92, pp. 126, 292, 221–2, where his closeness to William Herbert is attested.

[91] Bradshaw 1988, pp. 140–52.

[92] Canny 1983 p. 8; Cavanagh 1986; Brady 1986b p. 24; Canny 1988b pp. 207–8; Brady 1988; Cunningham 1984, p. 9; Bradshaw 1988, pp. 152–4. Jardine 1990 does not mention Beacon at all. A partial exception is Quinn 1976, pp. 85–6; cf. Canny 1988b, p. 207, who acknowledges its theoretical nature. Bradshaw's argument (1988, p. 154) that Beacon's treatise exhibits 'radical puritanism' is misleading, to say the least.

[93] Canny 1988b, p. 204; Canny 1983, p. 7; Canny 1987, pp. 166–75; Canny 1978; Canny 1988a, pp. 1–29.

weal', he concludes, somewhat in line with other scholars, that 'for Beacon, Ireland is a case not for curative pills, potions and ointments, but for brutal and extensive amputation'. In focusing almost exclusively on Beacon's sources, Anglo still fails to offer a comprehensive account of Beacon's treatise.[94]

The real importance of Beacon's tract lies beyond the narrow Irish context. The treatise merits attention because Beacon was perhaps the first Englishman to make thorough and positive use of Machiavelli's republicanism of the *Discorsi*. Although the fact that Beacon never mentioned Machiavelli's name is perhaps an index of the Florentine's general reputation in England, the ways in which Beacon was ready to use the *Discorsi* drastically alter the accepted view of the reception of Machiavelli's political ideas in early modern England. Even more importantly, in *Solon his follie* Beacon carried on and developed many central themes of classical republicanism. His analysis of political corruption and the remedies he suggested for it not only bear a close resemblance to Machiavelli; they also embody crucial notions of classical republicanism itself. Richard Beacon in *Solon his follie*, it is argued below, is perhaps the most important as well as the most radical exponent of classical humanist political discourse in England before the 1650s.

The humanist approach of *Solon his follie* becomes obvious when we examine its genre, style and scope. Beacon composed it as a dialogue between three interlocutors from sixth-century BC Athens, Epimenides, Pisistratus and Solon. The topic the three Athenians choose to discuss is the policy of Athens (England) towards its colony Salamina (Ireland).[95] The treatise is based on classical examples provided by Athens and even more conspicuously, by Rome. Examples taken from Machiavelli and Guicciardini concerning near contemporary Italian history are also employed.

According to Beacon, the most important task a ruler could accomplish was the 'action of reformation'. The amount of praise, Beacon claimed, which was conferred on Lucius Junius Brutus, the reformer of Rome, was greater than that attained by her founding father, Romulus. In Ireland, therefore, the task Beacon reserved for Elizabeth was similar to the one Brutus had accomplished in Rome.

---

[94]   Anglo 1990, pp. 156, 161. Cf. Davis 1991, p. 340.

[95]   Cf. William Herbert, *Croftus, sive de Hibernia liber* (1588/9), ed. W. E. Buckley, (London: Roxburghe Club, 1887), p. 14, where a similar analogy was drawn between Rome and Sicily and England and Ireland.

'Goe forwarde', Beacon exhorted the queen, 'Brutus, for thy glory in reforming, is farre greater then the glory of Romulus in building and instituting of the citie of Rome.' Beacon boldly equated Elizabeth with the greatest hero of republican Rome, Brutus, who conducted the reform of the Roman commonwealth by expelling the tyrant, Tarquinius Superbus, from Rome, and instituting the republican form of government.[96]

The whole treatise is thus preoccupied with one issue: the reformation of English government in Ireland – 'the sound & universall reformation of this your Realme of Ireland'.[97] Completely in line with other English writers on Ireland, Beacon's aim was twofold. He wanted, in the first place, to demonstrate how the conquest of Ireland could be carried out. More importantly, since he, like most other writers on Irish affairs, acknowledged that there was something seriously wrong with Ireland, he regarded his main task to be an explanation of how these problems could be remedied and the Irish commonwealth reformed.[98] This twofold aim created a certain tension in the book. Although the two themes overlapped on certain issues, as we shall see, there was an obvious discrepancy: the ruthless completion of a conquest was hardly fully compatible with the reformation of a community.

The causes of decline and corruption are discussed several times in the course of the treatise but they emerge most clearly in the third book, where Epimenides takes up Solon's request to scrutinize the issue of decline, and this theme occupies them for the rest of the book. 'A Declination of a body polliticke,' he defines at the outset of his analysis, 'is nothing els but a fall and departure from his first institution, and perfection.'[99] It can be degeneration 'from a just proportion eyther in obeyinge or governing the subjecte'. That is to say, the decline can occur because of the failures of the subjects or those of the government.[100] Furthermore, the tendency of decay belongs to the nature of commonwealths: they are dominated by a cyclical pattern. As Beacon

---

96 Beacon, *Solon his follie*, sig. ¶3ᵛ–4ʳ. Cf. White, 'Discors', p. 446.

97 Beacon, *Solon his follie*, sig. ¶3ʳ–4ᵛ.

98 For the twofold nature of other treatises, see in general Quinn 1947, pp. 303–7. For specific schemes, see also Edward Walshe, 'Conjectures', p. 316; Edmund Spenser, *A view of the present state of Ireland* (1596), ed. W. L. Renwick (Oxford University Press, 1970), pp. 16–17; Herbert, *Croftus*, pp. 16–17; John Davies, *A discoverie of the true causes why Ireland was neuer entirely subdued, nor brought vnder obedience of the crowne of England, vntill the beginning of his maiesties happie raigne* (n.p. [London], 1612), pp. 4–5; E. C. S., *The government of Ireland vnder the honorable, iust, and wise gouernour sir John Perrot* (London, 1626), sig. d2ʳ.

99 Beacon, *Solon his follie*, p. 65.

100 Ibid., pp. 96–7.

put it, from their very being commonwealths 'receive progression, from progression they receive continuance, from continuance a perfection, from their perfection a declination'.[101]

Some of the causes and occasions of decline were mainly impediments to accomplishing the complete conquest and subjugation of Ireland. Solon maintained that there was not a single occasion which 'holde the subject of Salamina, in their disobedience and savage life' more than 'the difference of lawes, religion, habite, and language'. The disorder and violence of soldiers could also stir up discontent amongst the people, which offered opportunities for corruption.[102] Furthermore, certain mismanagements in local government prompted opportunities for decline. Without the active support of the central government, the magistrates placed in a conquered territory would soon face a rebellion.[103]

When Beacon proceeded to treat the more general causes of corruption, he broadened his perspective and employed the central themes of the classical republican tradition. As we have seen, the first way in which corruption could arise was by the people's failure to act in accordance with the right rules. This amounted to their neglect of the values and qualities which directed their attention to the maintenance of the commonwealth. Three fundamental values kept society safe: 'the feare and reverence of God', 'the honour and obedience due unto Princes governours and Magistrates' and 'the love which wee owe unto our Country'.[104] These values entailed 'a just care and regarde of publike affaires', which was achieved through 'heroicall vertues' in the defence of the fatherland. On the most general level the corruption of manners suggested the loss of these values. People were carried away by the feeling of 'an universall securitie' and they ignored not only their religious rites but also 'all their former discipline of warres'. Corruption 'breedeth in men a base opinion and estimation of vertues', and they were ready to replace them with 'pleasures, wantonnesse, vices, and other such private respectes and regardes'.[105] Corruption was thus interpreted as the exhaustion of virtues and regard for the common good. Instead of honouring and promoting them, 'we banish and put to death men of rare and excellent vertues'.[106]

---

[101]   Ibid., pp. 69–72.
[102]   Ibid., pp. 86–91.
[103]   Ibid., pp. 91–2.
[104]   Ibid., pp. 50, 52, 66.
[105]   Ibid., pp. 50–2, 66, 98–9. Cf. in general Herbert, *Croftus*, pp. 46, 51, 9–10.
[106]   Beacon, *Solon his follie*, p. 51.

The people lost their former virtue and regard for the good of their community most easily by certain domestic developments. Beacon mentioned in passing the danger constituted by 'bitter adversities', the general idleness of the people and factions.[107] The most important cause of the corruption of manners, however, and the one to which Beacon devoted most of his attention, was the growth of private riches. A body of people could be 'bewitched with a glistering shew of profit and gaine', and it would be easy for a tyrant to corrupt the people with money so that 'they became rebels and traitoures to their countrie'.[108] Beacon's most telling example was the Romans' universal feeling of security caused by the growth of wealth. It had engendered in them a neglect of their religious institutions and their military valour just at the time of most urgent need. Even worse, they had 'jested and made themselves merry' with those who had given 'them warning thereof'.[109] Their offices as well as 'the voices of election, yea even Justice it selfe' had been sold 'in open market', a development which had ultimately enabled 'Caesar with the money of the Gaules to purchase not onely favour, and offices, but even the libertie of Rome'.[110]

The second and perhaps the gravest danger for a commonwealth was created not by the people but by the government itself, when it failed to maintain 'a just proportion' in governance, and when it departed 'from all the partes and right rules of government'. According to Beacon, misgovernment develops from the imbalance between the nobility and the people in the share of authority and he insists, moreover, that there are two chief ways in which misgovernment could manifest itself. First, when 'the nobility is not respected', a propitious occasion is offered for decline.[111] Another, and yet even more important, manifestation of misgovernment was the absolute supremacy of the nobility. If 'the nobilitie is in so great measure advanced,' Beacon argued, '... they become thereby dangerous & fearful unto the state'. Underlying this was, as Beacon explained, the inherent ambition of the nobility.[112] The absolute supremacy of the nobility was so menacing because by having an excessively powerful role the nobility could hold 'as it were a soveraigne commandement over the commonalty' and not only claim their pieces of land, but

[107] Ibid., pp. 51, 98.
[108] Ibid., pp. 98-9, 51.
[109] Ibid., p. 66.
[110] Ibid., p. 50.
[111] Ibid., p. 75, cf. p. 67.
[112] Ibid., p. 97.

also give them laws. Epimenides could, therefore, conclude that 'nothing giveth greater occasion of declining then the oppression of the commonalty'.[113]

The most striking example of misgovernment, and the one which appears almost as a leitmotif of the whole treatise, is the government of Tarquinius Superbus. The corruption of his government acted as 'a generall distemperature' of the Roman commonwealth, but the outcome of Tarquinius' tyranny was not the fatal decline and corruption of the Roman commonwealth, because it did not coincide with the degeneration of the manners of the people. On the contrary, the Romans were 'constant defendors of their liberties' as well as 'desirous of reformation', and far from ruining their commonwealth they reformed the same. Beacon took pains to explain that 'the forme which Tarquine gave to his ambition, was easilie' repelled 'by Brutus, and Valerius', since 'the manners of the people were not then corrupted'.[114] To confirm his point, Beacon cited positive as well as negative instances from Machiavelli's *Discorsi*. In the first place, Marcus Manlius Capitolinus and Spurius Cassius attempted to advance their 'owne ambition', but again the populace of Rome was uncorrupted, and their plans failed dismally. But as soon as misgovernment was linked with the general corruption of manners, it followed that 'without great resistance it maie not be quenched'. The ambition of Sulla, Marius as well as Caesar (whom Beacon added to Machiavelli's examples) concurred with 'the corruption of manners in the people', and 'the overthrow of that estate' quickly ensued.[115]

Beacon's insistence that there were two different kinds of corruption of commonwealths manifested his adherence to the Machiavellian tradition. Decline could appear as one *ad interitum*, 'a final declination' without any means of reformation. But it could also be declination *ad sanitatem*. This occurred when a commonwealth was faced with serious difficulties which could nevertheless be overcome. Far from regarding these as a calamitous menace to the well-being of the commonwealth, Beacon insisted that they carried with them a positive task of highest importance. The 'contending for honours' between the senate and the people in Rome had not indicated the decline of civil concord, but on the contrary had given 'occasions of

---

113 Ibid., pp. 75–77. Cf. Herbert, *Croftus*, pp. 42–3.
114 Beacon, *Solon his follie*, p. 97; cf. Machiavelli, *Discorsi*, I.16.
115 Beacon, *Solon his follie*, pp. 97–8; Machiavelli, *Discorsi*, III.8.

most happy lawes, and more happy restitution of the declined state of that polliticke body'.[116] Beacon endorsed, to a degree, one of Machiavelli's most original contributions, that one way to sustain virtue in a citizenry was through the encouragement of conflict between different social groups.

Although decline could have positive consequences, Beacon devoted most of his treatise to explaining how a reformation of corruption could be accomplished: 'Sith then this generall corruption of manners doth draw with it so many publicke miseries and calamities, as are before remembred, we can not, except men be altogither voide of humanity and reason, but abhorre even the remembraunce of these lamentable times, and be forthwith kindled with a desire of reformation.'[117] As in the disentanglement of the causes of decline, so in its reformation a tension is apparent between the completion of the conquest of Ireland and the reformation of the Irish commonwealth. Beacon first alluded to this at the very beginning of his treatise. When Epimenides asked the reason for Pisitratus' arrival in Cyprus (i.e. Ireland), he answered that it was his intention to 'leade heere a strong army by the commaundement of the councell of Athens unto Salamina, for the better repossessing and reforming thereof'.[118] The first general rule Beacon laid down was that in effecting a conquest it was best to adopt extreme courses rather than rely on a mean between two extremes. His discussion at this point is based on several chapters of the *Discorsi* in which Machiavelli had surveyed the ways in which a conquered or subjugated people should be treated. Beacon pointed out that there were three major ways of accomplishing the reform of a conquered community. The first method was to imitate king David and Lysander and make 'a thorough alteration and chaunge of auncient lawes, customes, and governement ... not leaving any shadow or resemblance in place thereof'. The contrary method was to follow those who, like Sulla, 'reserved onely unto themselves a principalitie and commaundement' and left the conquered people to enjoy 'their owne lawes'. The third manner was a mean between these two extremes, which had been used by the Florentines in their suppression of the rebellion in Arezzo. They had removed most of their commanders but they had not resumed 'into their handes the landes', nor had

---

[116] Beacon, *Solon his follie*, p. 72; cf. Anglo 1990, pp. 157–8.
[117] Beacon, *Solon his follie*, p. 51.
[118] Ibid., p. 1; cf. Herbert, *Croftus*, p. 17; Spenser, *A view*, pp. 95–6. For Spenser, see in general Jardine 1990; Norbrook 1984, pp. 139–52.

they destroyed 'the principall citie, but [had] preserved the same'. Beacon utterly condemned this line of policy. 'This meane course', he remarked, 'hath never as yet beene founde happy and prosperous.' It followed that they who wanted 'to be prosperous, and make continuance of their state, and governement' must imitate the Romans and either 'so suppresse and sharpely punish the Latines' that they are not able to rebel or 'with bounty and goodnes so winne' their affections that they are not 'willing to rebell'. According to Beacon, the English policy in Ireland had for a long time been dominated by the mean course. The only way to complete the conquest was, however, to abandon that ruinous policy and to embrace either the severe or lenient means.

The decision between these two extreme courses depended on one's resources. Beacon confessed that those whose purpose was 'to performe great actes, and to winne fame and glorie' did best if they chose 'the counsell of Sylla' and employed the lenient method. This, however, required 'a mighty power', and those who did not possess great forces and power but who yet wanted 'to make continuance of their conquest' ought to 'imitate Lysander' and leave nothing intact.[119] The conclusion Beacon drew from his discussion was that the best way to consolidate the conquest of Ireland was to leave nothing unaltered and to construct everything anew.

The first practical rule of completing the conquest was that the opportunity for rebellion offered by differences in laws, religion, habits and language could most easily be prevented by compelling the natives to adopt the laws, language, habits as well as religion of the conquerors. This was proven by the experience of Salamina for, as Solon put it, those parts of it which had embraced 'an uniformity of lawes, religion, habite, and language, with the Cittie of Athens, are founde by daily experience, much more loyal, civil, and obedient' than other parts of the island. The best way to avoid the occasions of decline arising from the cultural differences was to suppress the native indigenous culture.[120]

To consolidate the conquest, it was also necessary to take hostage those who could be expected to cause disturbance.[121] Furthermore, in line with other English authors, Beacon argued that colonies were of

[119]   Beacon, *Solon his follie*, pp. 46–9; Machiavelli, *Discorsi*, 1.25, 26, 11.23.
[120]   Beacon, *Solon his follie*, pp. 94–5. Cf. Herbert, *Croftus*, pp. 38–9, 53, where the same line of policy was recommended; see also *CSPI* 1586–8, pp. 531.
[121]   Beacon, *Solon his follie*, p. 102.

great significance in subjugating a conquered territory. Some writers had maintained that garrisons were more efficient than colonies, but Beacon did not find their arguments convincing. The maintenance of a garrison required continual expense and it revived the discontent of the conquered people. On the other hand, the benefits of colonies were numerous: they required little or no public charge; 'the matter of sedition is remooved out'; colonies would persuade the conquered people 'to embrace the manners, lawes, and governement of the conquerour'. Beacon was convinced that the only way to pacify Ireland and remain strong against possible invaders was to build colonies.[122]

Beacon also agreed with other English writers that to prevent possible rebellions it was best 'to disarme the people, and not suffer them at all to be trained or exercised in militarie discipline, especially where the people be not free, but obedient and tributaries unto us'. Instead, the conquered people should be employed like 'Heilotes to laboure, and plough the grounde', and learning and sciences should be advanced amongst them so that they 'may be drawen from the study and thoughts of innovation and change'.[123]

Scarcely less important was to have soldiers to consolidate the conquest. This could create, however, an occasion for decay in cases where the soldiers were too oppressive. Since the inherent problems of the suppressive soldiers were 'want of pay' as well as 'want of other discipline', the surest way to prevent this opportunity for decline to arise was to look after these two defects. In the case of sufficient pay, Epimenides first argued that the exaction of money should not be forced but should happen by 'the consentes of the subjectes', but he was soon made to change his mind by Solon's compelling argument that 'Princes may lawfully commande and exact the same at the hands of the subject.' The requirement of the people's consent depended on the nature of the commonwealth. If it had been 'from time to time a free estate and not subject to other' as Rome, then all kinds of tributes were 'grievous', and they should not be exacted but in great necessity. If the commonwealth, however, had 'always lived in servitude', like

---

[122] Ibid., pp. 107–14; Herbert, *Croftus*, pp. 36–8; but see *CSPI* 1586–88, pp. 529–30. Cf. Quinn 1945; Quinn, 1976. Well-fortified towns with garrisons were defended by Spenser, *A view*, pp. 119, 125, in general pp. 119–40; Thomas Blenerhasset, *A direction for the plantation in Vlster* (London, 1610), sig. B1ᵛ.

[123] Beacon, *Solon his follie*, pp. 102–3; cf. Herbert, *Croftus*, p. 53; *CSPI* 1588–92, pp. 221–2; Barnaby Rich, *A new description of Ireland* (London, 1610), p. 111. See e.g. Quinn 1945, p. 548. Although Beacon here briefly mentioned the importance of learning, it is still true to say that religion and education were almost totally absent from his account, in striking contrast, e.g., with Herbert, *Croftus*, pp. 44–5, 47, 48–51. For religion, see Bradshaw 1978.

Salamina, then the people were accustomed to 'all impositions and tributes', even for 'the maintenaunce of idle and evill disposed persons'. The conclusion of Epimenides and Solon's discussion was that since the Irish people had always lived under servitude, they were accustomed to all kind of taxes imposed upon them, and the money required for the sustenance of the soldiers in Ireland could be drawn from the local people without their consent.[124]

The final method of consolidating the English conquest of Ireland was to imitate the policy of the Romans in Macedonia and divide the conquered territory into four administrative units and impose capital punishment upon those who went from one area to another.[125] This did not, however, help in avoiding the problem of whether it was best to exclude natives from the offices of the commonwealth or on the contrary to confer the same on them. This seemed to lead Beacon into a dilemma. On the one hand, Solon was made to stress that decline often arose if the natives were secluded from 'bearing of offices or dignity in the common-weale', since thereby 'they remaine possessed with a desire to be restored unto the former liberty'. But Epimenides, on the other hand, pointed out that if the natives were appointed to the offices and dignities of the commonwealth, 'no lesse occasion is given of declining', as shown by the recent events in Salamina. The way out of this dilemma was to grant the people 'offices of profite' and retain the offices of 'commaundement' in the hands of Athenians. With this arrangement 'the multitude shall rest pleased, and the state acquitted of peril and daunger'.[126]

For many a commentator Beacon's treatise has served as a representative example of the advocacy of a ruthless suppression of Ireland, and it would be pointless to deny that it contains numerous arguments to this effect. However, the most formidable and momentous task Beacon set himself to accomplish in writing *Solon his follie* was to explain how the Irish commonwealth was to be reformed. He did not regard Ireland, that is, solely as a target for English conquest and imperial policy; his main task was to demonstrate how a corrupted commonwealth could be restored to its efflorescence. Solon tells Epimenides that just as Epimenides lent him his 'faithfull councell, and best advise for the reformation of the Citie of Athens', in the same manner he now

---

[124] Beacon, *Solon his follie*, pp. 85–91. Beacon derived some of his arguments from Matthew Sutcliffe, *The practice, proceedings, and lawes of armes* (London, 1593), pp. 16–28.
[125] Beacon, *Solon his follie*, pp. 95–6.
[126] Ibid., pp. 93–4; cf. Anglo 1990, p. 160.

moved 'to entreate your most friendly advise for the better reformation of Salamina'.[127] When Beacon pointed out that the best way to subjugate Ireland was the extreme method of starting everything afresh, what he clearly had in mind was not only the conquest of Ireland but also, as he repeatedly said, 'a thorough and absolute reformation of the whole common-weale'.[128]

If the corruption of a commonwealth could be equated with the loss of willingness to promote the common good, the reformation of the community, in its most elementary form, consisted in reversing this degeneration. The aim was, as Beacon put it, to maintain 'with the noble Romaines' the poverty of the people, to withstand 'with Cicero and Cato' 'the flatterie and ambition of Caesar' and, most importantly, to avoid 'safety' and devote all our energies to 'fighting for our Prince and country'.[129]

In line with Beacon's general theme and chief aim, the methods of attaining the proposed goals had distinctively Machiavellian features. Beacon opened his whole discussion with the particular Machiavellian definition of reformation as a return to the original state of purity. 'A Reformation of a declined common-weale,' he defined, 'is nothing els but a happy restitution unto his first perfection.'[130] As with the decay of a commonwealth, so the reversal of this degeneration was either partial or universal. The former comprised 'a reformation of particular mischiefes and inconveniences onely', which called for prompt measures to be taken. But a much more difficult reformation to complete was 'an absolute and a thorough reformation of the whole bodye of the common-weale'.[131] Despite the difficulty of its enactment, the latter provided Beacon with the most important theme of his treatise.

The first general advice of *Solon his follie* concerning the reformation of corruption is to rely on good laws. To forestall further decay, it was crucial to establish laws which, whilst efficiently preventing the pursuit of the private good, at the same time fostered the promotion of the public one. In altering the laws of a commonwealth, either one followed Solon and Numa and changed them 'by little and little', or one imitated the Spartans Agis and Cleomenes and made a rapid and complete change of laws.[132] The solution of establishing new laws,

127 Beacon, *Solon his follie*, p. 3.
128 Ibid., p. 48; cf. in general Herbert, *Croftus*, pp. 16–17, 26–7.
129 Beacon, *Solon his follie*, pp. 98–100.
130 Ibid., p. 5; cf. Machiavelli, *Discorsi*, III.1.
131 Beacon, *Solon his follie*, p. 5.
132 Ibid., p. 44; cf. Machiavelli, *Discorsi*, I.9.

whether gradually or abruptly, was the method of a partial reformation. But Beacon insisted that it was crucial not merely to establish
good and profitable laws; it was of equal importance to look after their
efficient execution. An entire corruption 'could never have possessed
the mindes' of the Salaminian people if 'the exact discipline of law had
in good time beene applied'. A partly degenerated community was not,
as Solon is made to conclude, in need of the change of 'the whole state'
and it was best rather to frame the laws to 'the subject and matter' than
to frame the whole society to meet the laws.[133]

In defining the general scope of the reformation of partial corruption, Beacon followed closely the first chapter of the third book of the
Discorsi. He treated it as an essential element of the maintenance of a
commonwealth that ancient laws and customs should be renewed from
time to time and that the violators of these laws should be severely
punished. What Beacon primarily had in mind was that if a commonwealth was not constantly given fresh life by enforcing its ancient laws,
it sooner rather than later would become completely corrupted; a
commonwealth, that is, needed constant reforming. But it had, of
course, been Machiavelli's final, and most crucial, point that this
restoration should be brought about by 'either good institutions or
good men' rather than by accidents. Again Beacon fully agreed. 'This
reformation made by profitable lawes and discipline thereof' was made
'after two sorts': it was brought about either 'accidentally ... by
occasions' or it was provoked 'by lawes limiting the times certaine for
this reformation'. And Beacon firmly maintained that the reform
carried out 'at times certaine' and the one made 'by lawes and statutes
certaine ... is founde more profitable then the other which is made
accidentally'. In substantiating his claims, Beacon employed Machiavelli's examples – the reformation of Rome after the attack of the
Gauls and the governors of Florence – and quoted from him that 'after
every five years the form of the commonwealth should be restored,
otherwise the discipline of law may not be wel preserved'.[134]

The establishment and execution of new laws was an important
means of restoring a completely corrupted commonwealth as well.
Machiavelli furnished Beacon with instances of the significance of new

---

[133] Beacon, *Solon his follie*, pp. 9, 5–6; cf. Herbert, *Croftus*, pp. 51–2. Spenser argued directly
against Beacon, when he pointed out that 'since we cannot now apply laws fit to the people,
as in the first institution of commonwealths it ought to be, we will apply the people and fit
them to the laws', *A view*, pp. 141–2.

[134] Beacon, *Solon his follie*, pp. 8–9. The beginning of the Florentine example appears in Latin as:
'Singulis quinquennijs redintegrare formam reip: oportere.'

laws in universal reformation. From the opening chapter of the first book of the *Discorsi* Beacon learned that the efficacy of the due execution of profitable laws could be seen in the example of ancient Egypt, which had for a long time 'prevented this generall corruption of manners, which either peace, wealth, security, or otherwise the fertility of place might breed in the hartes of the subjectes'. Similarly, the laws carefully established by 'Romulus, Numa, and other governoures which succeeded them' had been so good that neither their long peace, nor 'the fruitfulnesse of the soile', neither 'the commodities of the sea', nor 'their daily victories' 'could by the space of a long time and many ages; corrupt the manners of the people'.[135]

In his discussion of laws, Beacon was far less concerned with the individual laws or their contents than with the more general issues of their establishment and implementation. It was important 'to remove all occasion, which may move the people or behoulders, to pittie or favour offendours'. Furthermore, the seriousness of the situation left room for disregarding the boundaries of traditional morality. The leaders of those factions which might oppose the reformation should 'be committed to some safe-gard or prison', and 'in cases of great extremities' it was commendable to proceed 'against offendors, without observing the usuall ceremonies of lawe'.[136]

The key to the successful establishment of the new laws was to be found in the winning of the goodwill of the people. As Epimenides put it, because 'the consente of the people, doth give so great furtheraunce unto this action of reformation, it seemeth a matter verie necessarie, that everie Magistrate shoulde retaine the arte, skill, and knowledge, of perswading and inducing the multitude'.[137] Tarquinus Superbus had lost 'the good-will of the people' as well as that 'of the Senate', because he had changed 'the auncient lawes & customes', so much so that he had drawn unto himself 'the authority, as well of the Senate, as also of the liberty of the people'. He had consequently been easily expelled. Brutus, on the other hand, had won the goodwill of the people, and it had therefore been easy for him to complete the reformation of the

---

[135] Ibid., p. 57, see also pp. 19–22, 53, 57–9, 100. Cf. Machiavelli, *Discorsi*, i.i. The only difference between Machiavelli and Beacon was that while the former listed the greatness of the Roman empire ('la grandezza dello imperio') as one of the corruptive factors, the latter saw 'their long peace and rest which they enjoyned in the governement of Numa' as a menace.

[136] Beacon, *Solon his follie*, pp. 14–17, 22; cf. Herbert, *Croftus*, pp. 35, 40.

[137] Beacon, *Solon his follie*, p. 26. In contrast with Beacon, Spenser advised that the government of Ireland should be left intact. According to him, the prince had the absolute power in Ireland, *A view*, pp. 168, 10; cf. pp. 79, 141. See also White, 'Discors', p. 453; E. C. S., *The government of Ireland*, sig. c2ʳ⁻ᵛ who emphasized the importance of parliament.

Roman commonwealth. The same could also be seen in the *Anno salutis* of Florence (1494), when the Medici family had been expelled from the city. This change of government had been accomplished 'without daunger and difficultie', because it had been 'effected by the good-will and consentes of the people'.[138] But a major obstacle to enacting the new and worthwhile laws arose since there was, as Epimenides explained, 'the contrarietie of humours and opinions, lodged in the brests even of the wisest'. These humours were, in practice, associated with two main categories: 'the poore and the rich'.[139]

There were two main ways to win the goodwill of the people and to appease the animosity between the rich and the poor. The first method consisted in the usage of persuasion and rhetoric. Pythagoras had been 'greatlie honoured' because of 'his singular arte and knowledge in winning the affections of the multitude, and in perswading, and dissawing the people'. The importance attached to rhetoric seemed to have obvious links with the active participation of the people in the political life of their community. It is, however, clear that Beacon's discussion of persuasion points less at the active role of the people and more at the methods of manipulating them. The corrupted people could hardly be expected to act virtuously; they had, Beacon argued in a distinctively republican passage, to be induced 'even against their wils' to become 'profitable to the common-weale'.[140] The main aim of persuasion was to induce the people to accept the new laws imposed on them and it was to a considerable extent accompanied by deceit and fraud. A consummate persuader ought to bear in mind that the multitude was not able to discern the 'true causes' of things, and that he ought to appeal to particulars or even concoct fables in order to induce people to follow his will.[141]

The rhetorician must, moreover, be ready 'to delude either faction [i.e. the rich and the poor] by faire promises and sweete wordes'. Another way in which the people could be induced to act as one wished was to coin new terms for old things and thereby to camouflage 'bitter and unpleasant' things with 'pleasing names'.[142] In a highly revealing passage Beacon made Solon espouse the idea that 'for the better justifiyng of this manner of proceeding herein, you shall under-

---

[138]   Beacon, *Solon his follie*, p. 26. For the '*Anno salutis*' of Florence Beacon mistakenly has MCCCCXLIIII.

[139]   Ibid., pp. 10–1.

[140]   Ibid., pp. 27–31.

[141]   Ibid., pp. 34–7.

[142]   Ibid., pp. 31–2, 11–12. Cf. Skinner 1990c, p. 26.

stande, that in a publike magistrate, the same is rightlie tearmed pollicie, but in private persons, the same is not unjustly condemned by the name of deceite'.[143]

It was crucial, however, not to appear to be a deceiver. An accomplished rhetorician ought to imitate Numa and always first perform himself the things he would suggest to the people. In addition, Numa had had recourse to religious institutions. The cogency of Numa's persuasions had been grounded on the fact that he had laid 'before the peoples eies a terrour and feare of their Gods' and had made them believe that his reformation had divine approval.[144]

The second method of establishing and imposing good and profitable laws on the people was to resort to coercion and force. This method to some extent bridged the gap between the completion of the conquest of Ireland and the reformation of the Irish commonwealth.[145] Beacon emphasized, however, that force could only be used if every other course of imposing the reformation had failed. He provided two chief reasons as to why the accomplishment of reformation could prove so difficult that the need for sheer force might arise. There were always those who received personal benefit from corruption; 'this occasion of reformation', Epimenides says, 'is full of difficulties' because 'manie will still be founde, which shalbe discontented therewith'. Further, the inherent nature of the multitude was such that it was always inclined to be 'against such as have authority and commaundement over them'.[146]

The final, and perhaps the most fundamental issue of reformation of a commonwealth by the new laws was the way in which persuasion, fraud and force were adopted. The problem was, in brief, 'into whose handes the same is to be given'. For Beacon, the only way to ensure the success of the reformation was to have a magistrate with wide discretionary authority, a 'man of rare and excellent vertues, by whose constancy and integrity, the envy and malice of the enemy may be quenched'.[147] What Beacon clearly had in mind, and what even a brief look at Roman history tended to confirm, was that the enforcement of the laws for reforming a community was rarely successful without 'a Dictator', who must 'have sufficient powre to execute his vertues and well disposed minde'.[148]

---

[143] Beacon, *Solon his follie*, pp. 11–12; cf. Anglo 1990, p. 158.
[144] Beacon, *Solon his follie*, pp. 31–2, 37–9.
[145] Ibid., pp. 9–10, 11; cf. Herbert, *Croftus*, pp. 35–6.
[146] Beacon, *Solon his follie*, pp. 39–41; cf. Anglo 1990, pp. 158–9.
[147] Beacon, *Solon his follie*, pp. 42–3; cf. pp. 9–10, 22–3, 100–1.
[148] Ibid., pp. 100–1, 22–3, 39–40; cf. Spenser, *A view*, p. 169.

By now it comes as no surprise that Beacon turned to Machiavelli's *Discorsi* in order to find corroboration for his claims. Antonio Giacomini served as an illustration of the importance of appointing a severe magistrate in times of crisis.[149] From Machiavelli one could also learn that 'Hieronymus Savonarole' had failed dismally in his intended reformation since he had not possessed 'sufficient forces' to enforce it, and he had soon become 'oppressed by the envie of others'. But it was not enough to possess adequate forces; it was of equal importance to be determined to employ them if necessity demanded this kind of action. The most telling example of how ruinous it was not to be prepared to coerce the people into reformation was the career of 'Peter Soderin' (Piero Soderini). He had possessed sufficient forces, by which he could 'well have overcome the envy and malice of such as were founde to oppose themselves against him', but he had committed the cardinal error of showing too much leniency at the moment when the only right course of action had consisted of more severe means. Following Machiavelli closely, Beacon emphasized that Piero Soderini had failed to ruin his opponents because he had 'not in time applie[d]' force 'but rather [had] contended with benefites and with a just and honest course of life, to overcome the envie and malice of such as [had] withstoode his reformation'. Soderini's failure to act according to the times had not merely resulted in his own destruction; it had also prompted the overthrow of 'his country and regiment'.[150]

An affirmative example was provided by Moses, who to establish the laws 'which God unto him had delivered', had thought it 'necessarie, with forces to remove such, as being pricked forwarde with envie, did oppose themselves against his intended reformation'.[151] But the strongest example of the forceful methods of reformation Beacon found from Machiavelli in the character of Lucius Junius Brutus. The chief lesson to be learned from Brutus was to act forcefully, mercilessly and quickly. Beacon was clearly fascinated by Brutus' execution of his own sons and repeated the story several times in the course of the tract. If we are to suppress the intemperance of a commonwealth, we must not merely 'with Valerius deny the embassadoures of Tarquine to speake unto the people, least by flatterie they be deluded'; we must also be

---

[149] Beacon, *Solon his follie*, p. 43; cf. Machiavelli, *Discorsi*, III.16.
[150] Beacon, *Solon his follie*, pp. 41–2, 59–60; Machiavelli, *Discorsi*, III.3, 9, 30.
[151] Beacon, *Solon his follie*, p. 41.

ready 'with Brutus ... to condemne and execute even our owne sonnes, corrupted by Tarquine'.[152]

Although Beacon deemed the establishing and enforcing of good and profitable laws to be highly important in the reformation of a corrupted community, and consequently dwelt at length on this issue, he never thought that such laws alone could reform an entirely degenerate commonwealth. Epimenides reprimands Solon for having attempted to change the decadent course of Athens simply by establishing new laws, when it 'was declined by many and infinite disorders' and was in need of more rigorous and extreme methods as well as a more thorough reformation. In Ireland the utter decline prompted by the general corruption of manners could not be reformed 'by the lawes against Captainship, against Coyney and Lyvery, or against the unlawefull custome of supporting and maintaining of rebels or any other new lawe whatsoever'.[153] The methods of the English in their numerous attempts to reconstitute the Irish commonwealth had so far been like Solon's attempts to reform Athens. Many ancient customs, which had originally been granted for the advancement of the public good, had by now 'turned by a generall corruption in the subject, to the ruine of themselves and the lande of Salamina'. It was clear that Ireland was in urgent need of a thorough reformation of her whole society.[154]

How was this entire reform of a commonwealth to be carried out? As we have seen, Beacon believed that decay could arise either because the people failed to pursue the common good or because the government declined from just rule. When both of these factors occurred at the same time a most serious corruption ensued. It followed that in the reform of a universal corruption efficacious remedies should be prescribed for both of these annoyances. Beacon took a complete and universal reformation to mean 'nothing els, but a thorough and absolute mutation and change, of auncient lawes, customes, and manners of the people, and finally of the common-wealth it selfe, unto a better forme of governement'.[155]

If a universal reformation required a change in the form of government, it followed that the partial reformation by the new laws entailed the right kind of government. It was, in other words, only if a

[152] Ibid., p. 100, see also pp. 2, 7–8, 43, 59; Machiavelli, *Discorsi* III.3, 9, 30.
[153] Beacon, *Solon his follie*, pp. 7, 45.
[154] Ibid., pp. 20–1.
[155] Ibid., p. 19.

commonwealth was constituted from the outset in the correct way that its partial decay could be reversed by the force of new laws. In discussing the proper form of government, Beacon drew heavily on Machiavelli. Because the original institution of Athens had been 'meerly popular, corrupt, and unperfit', it had proved to be insufficient to resist 'the tyrannie of such as did aspire unto the principalitie'. The lawgivers in Athens had indeed established 'many lawes for the reformation of the insolencie of the noble men, as also to restraine the libertie of the people', but to no avail: these laws 'could not maintain the same more than a hundred years'.[156] On the other hand, those commonwealths which 'have their first institution and foundation good, though not altogether perfit and complete' could be 'at any time' restored back to their first perfection if they happened to face any form of degeneration. Even more importantly, this 'happie estate thereof may thereby be long continued and augmented', as the Roman example convincingly demonstrated. The first institution of the Roman commonwealth was 'so wel laid by Romulus & Numa, as that after by new laws made for the reformation thereof, as the necessity of that commonweale did require, the same was rendered long, happy, and prosperous'. Beacon did not mention liberty and was thus silent about one of Machiavelli's chief arguments: in spite of the fact that it was set up as a monarchy, Rome had been fortunate enough to have had as its founding fathers such prudent kings that they had enacted laws which had been compatible with liberty. Nevertheless, Beacon entirely agreed with Machiavelli about the happy result of the Roman commonwealth: she had proved to be prosperous as well as long-lasting by virtue of the balanced mixed constitution which she had eventually acquired. The laws and constitutions which had been founded by the kings had enabled Rome to attain 'an happy temper and forme of governement, compounded of three sortes and kindes of governement, namely the Monarchia, Aristocratia, and Democratia'.[157]

The conclusion Beacon drew was to the effect that only those commonwealths which were organized as mixed states were capable of being reformed simply by establishing new laws and changing the corrupted customs of the people. But he also made it clear that Salamina could not be reformed by new laws alone. Consequently, if one wanted to reform Ireland, one had to organize her government

---

[156] Ibid., p. 6. The end of the sentence appears in Latin: 'non eam tamen conservare supra centessimum annum potuerunt'; see also p. 45. Cf. Machiavelli, *Discorsi*, I.2.

[157] Beacon, *Solon his follie*, pp. 6–7.

afresh. Beacon divided this topic into four separate issues. He started by discussing 'the soveraintie and commaundement'. This, he insisted, was sometimes given 'into the hands of one, sometimes in the handes of fewe, and sometimes into the handes of all in generall'. In a distinctly Bodinian manner, Beacon declared that the location of sovereign power, rather than 'the diversity which sometimes appeareth in the forme and government thereof', determined the peculiar character of a commonwealth – whether it was a democracy, aristocracy or monarchy. Moreover, he insisted that this definition embraced every single commonwealth: all of them were constituted after one of these three forms or their corrupted equivalents. When it came to decide 'which institution is to be preferred above others', Beacon had little doubt that a monarchy was 'the most firm and durable'. It was not merely 'freest from trouble', it was also 'most honourable and glorious'. Although an aristocracy most easily avoided 'corruption', the same would be destroyed by the 'envie' and dissention' prevalent amongst the nobles. But 'least permanent' was 'the popular estate', especially if the whole commonwealth was 'mere popular, as well in regard of the soveraintie and commaundement, as of the forme & manner of governement'.[158]

Having made this preliminary concession, however, Beacon moved to praise the mixed constitution. The second issue of the discussion was 'the forme of governement', and Beacon gave his unequivocal assent to the excellence of the mixed state. He firmly believed that a constitution where a balance existed between the one, the few and the many, was by far the most perfect form of government. Solon was made to confess that 'that popular institution, which is equallie tempered, and compounded of the three sortes and formes of governement, after the maner and institution of Rome' was 'more firme and durable'. It was 'this forme of governement' which gave 'a perfection and continuance' to all estates mentioned before.[159] Romulus had aimed at this ideal 'forme of government in the institution of the common-weale of Rome'. First, he had reserved for himself 'the sole and kingly auctority': the command of the army and the power to summon the senators for consultation. 'The person of the Senators' had constituted the aristocracy of the Roman mixed constitution. They had had authority 'to consulte, and publikely to perswade and disswade the attempts for wars, and to discusse all other civill causes, as the state of that common-weale required'. Finally, to perfect the Roman common-

158 Ibid., pp. 60–1.
159 Ibid., pp. 61–2.

wealth, Romulus had added to it a democratic element. 'In the other partes of his governement', Beacon made Solon expound, 'as in framing of his lawes and such like,' Romulus had preferred rather 'a popular liberty, then a Monarchie'.[160]

Although Epimenides had declared that monarchy was the best form of 'soveraintie', he fully agreed with Solon that the mixed constitution was the best 'forme and manner of the institution it selfe'. The chief benefit of this kind of institution was the 'equall proportion' of power which was granted to the one, the few and the many. The distribution of power was made according to 'the dignitie of the one' and 'the liberty of the other'. In the successful tempering of these elements, Epimenides summarized, 'all the skill, arte, and pollicie of governement is wholy contained', so much so that it came 'nearest to the perfection of nature'. 'This', Solon agreed, 'is the best forme of instituting of common-weales.'[161]

The idea of the well-tempered mixed constitution raised the further question of the nature of the balance between the one, the few and the many. First, although it was sometimes necessary to confer 'authoritie absolute' on the one, it was of equal importance to set strict limits on the same. According to Epimenides, 'this authority absolute, without anie limitation of the power it selfe, or of the time and continuance thereof, hath sometimes turned to the great prejudice and danger of such as formerly have graunted the same'. Following closely Machiavelli, Beacon argued that the disastrous results of granting unrestricted authority for a long time were most obvious in the appointment of the *Decemviri* in Rome. In order to make 'a thorough and absolute reformation of the common-weale of Rome', the *Decemviri* had been granted 'the sole and absolute power of Rome'. No magistrate had remained who could have watched over the *Decemviri*; they had become ambitious and Appius Claudius especially had fallen 'into the thoughtes of the principality of Rome'. To achieve his aims, Appius Claudius had strengthened himself 'with friends, & clyents' and had continuously

[160] Ibid., p. 62. Cf. Herbert, *Croftus*, pp. 34–5, 43, where England provided the model for the Irish government.
[161] Beacon, *Solon his follie*, pp. 62–3. Epimenides relied on the example of France. Both interlocutors discounted the fact that the French king's powers in Epimenides' account were much wider than Romulus' authority in Solon's. Anglo 1990, p. 155, n.40 rightly points out that, unlike Bodin, Beacon treated France as a mixed state. It should be noted, however, that at this point Beacon's sharp distinction between 'soveraingty' and the form of government arguably derives from Bodin himself. See Jean Bodin, *The six bookes of a commonweale*, translated by Richard Knolles (London, 1606), pp. 199–200, 755, 785. Cf. e.g. Salmon 1959, p. 22; Keohane 1980, p. 76.

increased his personal wealth. In this way 'a Citizen' had become 'a fearefull enemy to the state of Rome' and the Romans had found themselves in a dilemma. On the one hand, they could not have endured Appius Claudius' 'pride and insolencie' yet, on the other hand, they had been unable to find a safe way to 'suppresse the same without their common peril and daunger'.[162]

To avoid the peril of the *Decemviri*, it was safest, Beacon believed, to pursue the Spartan or Venetian policy. In both commonwealths the chief magistrates had been watched in two crucial areas. First, they had appointed 'certaine watchmen, as daily beholders and observers of all their actions and doings'. Beacon thus endorsed the Machiavellian idea that those who were given great authority must always be watched, lest the unlimited power would corrupt them and they would become tyrants. Secondly, the Spartans and Venetians had set up 'certaine limits and bondes, not lawfull for them [i.e. kings and doges] to exceede'. The most important limit, and the only one which Beacon discussed in detail, was the limit of time. In Rome Caesar's absolute power to reform Gallia had later been 'so long proroged and continued' that in the end Caesar had become 'terrible, as well to the Gaules, as to the Romaines'. By 'making a Dictator perpetuall', the Romans had ultimately lost 'the libertye of their Citie'. In other words, 'authority' could 'easily corrupt the maners of good subjectes'. The only efficient remedy for the situation was that 'every good and faithfull councellour unto the state' followed Cato and resisted 'the proroging of Caesar his governement, least too late with Pompey they acknowledge their errour'.[163]

The final question concerning the princely aspect of the mixed constitution Solon and Epimenides addressed themselves to was 'unto what person may this authority be safely graunted'. The suitable person had to be 'good and honest'; on the other hand, he must not be 'of great might, power and wealth', because this combination would facilitate the degeneration of the magistrate. What Beacon mainly had in mind was that since 'honours change habiyts', it often happened that even the best fell 'by reason of honours and dignities into a generall corruption of manners'.[164]

How was all this connected with Ireland? Beacon's native examples of persons with unlimited power were the ninth and tenth earls of

---

[162] Beacon, *Solon his follie*, p. 23; Machiavelli, *Discorsi*, 1.35, 40.
[163] Beacon, *Solon his follie*, pp. 23–4.
[164] Ibid., p. 24.

Kildare. Because of the combination of his personal standing and official position Gerald FitzGerald had been able effectively to resist the English policies. Similarly, his son Thomas had been able to foment a serious rebellion because of his doubly powerful role.[165] In order to avoid the repetition of a similar situation, Beacon suggested that absolute authority should be conferred on a person who was not already of great might, power and wealth, and that his period of authority was to be strictly limited to one year. In addition, certain institutions should be established to guard against the actions of the magistrate. Although Beacon did not specify the nature of these institutions, the employment of the Spartan and Venetian instances pointed towards a powerful council.

The second issue of the mixed constitution concerned the balance between the nobility and the people, the lack of which was, as we have seen, a chief cause of misgovernment. Beacon believed that, unless the multitude was protected 'from the oppression of the mighty', the temper of the commonwealth would be utterly destroyed. The aim was, in the words of Epimenides, to establish rules 'wherby as well the dignity of the Nobles, as the liberty of the people, may be preserved and defended, according to the example of all common-weales well governed'. The first method for attaining this end was to enact laws. In Ireland, as Solon pointed out, the laws against 'Coiney and Livery' and against 'Captainship' were rules devised to prevent oppression of the people. It was clear, however, that 'good lawes are not sufficient to render a common-weale, happie and prosperous'.[166] What was needed were 'governoures provinciall' to enforce these laws. The chief aim of these local governors was to see that justice was done, since nothing induced the common people to embrace authority and government as efficiently as due enforcement of good laws. This secured to the common people the possession of 'that which is their owne', and by enjoying their property 'they have attained the ende of their desires, and rest for the moste parte contented with the governement'.[167]

It remains to ask whether the local governors should rely more on the people than on the nobles. Exploiting Machiavelli's discussion of how a tyrant should retain his power, Beacon insisted that the governors should always rely on the people. Epimenides pointed out that 'a Monarchie governed popularlie is then secure and voide of

---

[165]   Ibid., pp. 24–5. See Brady 1986a, pp. 41–9, for the problems of the Irish viceroy.
[166]   Beacon, *Solon his follie*, p. 78.
[167]   Ibid., pp. 79–80; cf. Machiavelli, *Discorsi*, 1.45.

perill: for in the multitude or people consisteth the strength and force of every kingdome'. A local governor succeeded if he emulated Nabis, a tyrant of Sparta, and 'endevoured wholie the love and favoure of the people'. If, on the other hand, he imitated Appius Claudius and neglected 'the favoure of the people', he secured nothing except his own ruin. Solon completely agreed with Epimenides. 'It must be confessed', he maintains, 'that in common-weales gained by conquest, you shall advance your governement more assuredly by the favoure of the people, then by the might of the nobilitie.'[168]

Beacon's discussion of the safeguarding of the people was, as is shown by the employment of the examples of Nabis and Appius Claudius, closely linked with the completion of the conquest of Ireland. He wanted to show how the English conquerors could establish their rule over the Irish. But an implication of his argument was to the effect that the government should be organized in a way which prevented the nobles from suppressing the people. If this was accomplished by due execution of good and worthwhile laws, the difficulty was to decide what kind of government could best ensure this: 'what number of judges may suffice herein'.[169] It was safest to avoid one judge, since the nobility corrupts one person most easily. To establish his point, Beacon draws his argument directly from the chapter of the *Discorsi* where Machiavelli showed how difficult it was to formulate laws and institutions to maintain the liberty of the city. But even in the case 'where a fewe are placed for the rule and government' they could be relatively easily persuaded to become 'pleasers of the nobility, and contemners of the people'. Since neither the one nor the few could be trusted, the only solution left was to imitate 'the Venetians'. The Venetians had had the council of ten, 'their *Decemviri*', as well as the college of forty. But the institution of the greatest importance in Venice, and the one which made it so imitable, was the great council, which had possessed the highest authority. Epimenides fully agreed with Solon and concurred that 'this must needes be the best forme of governement', not only since 'many judges are not so easily corrupted as one', but also because 'many are founde to be of greater strength and integritie to resist the displeasure of the nobilitie then fewe'. Finally, Epimenides put forward a familiar argument for the republican form of government when he contended that 'many eies discerne more perfectly then one, and that which escapeth or deceiveth one eie, maie be perceived

---

[168] Beacon, *Solon his follie*, p. 81, and pp. 81–4; Machiavelli, *Discorsi*, 1.40.
[169] Beacon, *Solon his follie*, pp. 78–80.

and that without errour by many; so many wits judge more soundly and sincerely then one'.[170]

Beacon thus maintained that a chief aim of the government of a commonwealth was to preserve the liberty of the people. In order to ensure this, the people must be given a share in government. If they were not given the opportunity to check the few, they would become totally oppressed by them. The people, in other words, must be granted guardianship of their own liberty.

What was Beacon doing with the classical republican tradition whose vocabulary he was using? To answer this, we must recall that, according to Beacon, there were two ways in which corruption could arise within a commonwealth: the decay of the people, or the decay of the government. In reforming the former, it was essential to impose strict new laws upon the people. But with a view to enacting this kind of reform it was necessary that the commonwealth be organized at the outset as a mixed state. Unless this requirement was fulfilled, the reformation of the corrupted manners of the people by establishing good laws could not succeed. Moreover, if the decay of the manners of the people coincided with the corruption of the government, the reformation of this universal corruption could not be accomplished simply by establishing new laws. The government itself also needed to be reformed. The only way in which the universal reformation of an entirely corrupted community could be carried out was to reconstitute its government in accordance with the principles of the mixed constitution. Beacon asserted, therefore, that if the aim was to accomplish 'the sound & universall reformation' of Ireland and to organize the Irish community on a firm foundation, everything had to be constructed afresh and Ireland established as a mixed state. Furthermore, painstaking care had to be exercised to avoid the danger of an overmighty governor. This was achieved by placing a limit of one year on his period of authority and by establishing a powerful council to watch over his actions. Hardly less meticulous care was to be exhibited to safeguard the people against the ambitious nature of the nobility. What was needed to curb the excessive ambitions of the nobility was not merely good laws but above all good institutions capable of enforcing them. The most efficacious way of keeping the nobility in check was to maintain a widely based court of appeal.

Although Epimenides and Solon had come to complete agreement

---

[170] Ibid., pp. 80–1; Machiavelli, *Discorsi*, 1.49.

that the mixed constitution was the best form of instituting a common-wealth, their task was only half-completed. They had heretofore discussed only two of the four proposed issues. The two remaining topics concerned 'the forme and manner of the institution it selfe' and 'the severall endes and scopes of this institution'.[171] The underlying assumption was that corruption could come from both within and without the commonwealth: it could arise from 'the malice and practises of forreine enemies'.[172] In order to check the development of degeneration, scrupulous care should be taken to organize the foreign affairs of the community. Moreover, the way of instituting a common-wealth and the decisions regarding its proper aims were so entangled with each other that Epimenides and Solon treated them together. The manner of setting up a commonwealth, in other words, depended on its chosen end. Again, Beacon's account was essentially Machiavellian in its character.

Solon defined the range of their discussion when he maintained in a distinctively Machiavellian vocabulary that there were both common-wealths which aimed 'at peace' and commonwealths which aimed 'at honour, as the butte and scope of all their actions'. The importance of the decision of the goal of the commonwealth was increased by the fact that the form of institutions of the commonwealth depended on the decision of its aims. A community should be organized, Beacon believed, in a wholly different manner when its aims were peace and longevity than when it strived for glory and empire. Beacon singled out three institutions which a community must build if it was going to attain longevity. First, it should imitate Sparta and 'seclude strangers'. Secondly, again following the Spartan example, it must avoid training its people in 'militarie discipline'. Furthermore, it was scarcely less essential to imitate Venice and 'to possesse a place or fort' which was made invincible by nature as well as by man. Beacon departed from the traditional account by claiming that Sparta did not arm its citizens.[173] Despite this dissimilarity, it is scarcely less important to stress the basically Machiavellian features of Beacon's argument. If a community aimed at peace and permanency, it was safest neither to enlarge the population by admitting strangers nor to train the people in warlike discipline, but on the contrary, to seclude oneself from the rest of the world by constructing the community as a stronghold.

[171] Beacon, *Solon his follie*, p. 60.
[172] Ibid., p. 52.
[173] Ibid., p. 63; Machiavelli, *Discorsi*, 1.6.

On the other hand, if a commonwealth aimed at 'honour and glory, as the butte & scope of their institution', it must act in the completely contrary manner. The first general rule of foreign policy was that 'we are to make preparation for the wars'. The world was a scene of incessant hostile competition: just as the nobility wanted to suppress the people, so entire commonwealths were disposed to dominate each other. The best course of foreign policy therefore required readiness to fight for the commonwealth. It was the chief task of the people to act as soldiers, and those who organized a commonwealth must ensure that the people were 'daily' trained and exercised in 'military discipline'. Furthermore, it was of equal importance 'to render the commonwealth populous'. The commonwealth must be ready not only to admit strangers, but also to have 'many associates & friends'. Following Machiavelli again, Beacon held that if a state aims at greatness, it is necessary to form leagues with 'free Citties and estates'. Both Rome and Switzerland made 'an association with other free Cities and states' and consequently 'they did every where conquere and commaunde'. But neither Sparta nor Athens formed any league and they 'did not long continue their greatnes'. Finally, it was of great significance to be ready to 'deliver the feble, and weake, from the hands of the oppressour'. To pursue this kind of policy was to imitate 'the example of the Romanes'.[174]

The crucial question was 'what manner of institution is most permanent and to be preferred', as Solon put it. Epimenides began his answer by emphasizing the corruptibility common to all commonwealths. It was impossible to find a community which was so constituted that it could ultimately avoid degeneration. The commonwealth which was constituted to aim at empire fell in the end because 'the continual use and trayning in military discipline' rendered the 'citizens' bold and caused fatal discord. But since every commonwealth was sooner or later bound to face corruption and ruin, the attempt to aim at peace and permanence was equally doomed to fail. A long period of peace would engender 'effeminacie, ease, rest, and security', which caused strife and mutinies and these brought about the ultimate destruction of the commonwealth. Nevertheless, although both kinds of community proved to fall prey to corruption, they differed in one crucial aspect. Whereas the commonwealth which in its first institution aimed at peace and permanency left nothing

---

[174] Beacon, *Solon his follie*, pp. 63, 101; Machiavelli, *Discorsi*, II.4.

whatsoever of its memory, the community which pursued empire vanished away in 'the pride of youth' and consequently left 'the image of true glory, as a lively picture, to invest a perpetuall memory of a worthy and excellent Institution'.[175] Solon fully concurred: 'it seemeth then by that which you have said that the institution of that common-weale, which aymeth at vertue, honour, and glorie, is to be preferred before the other, & of princes much more to be desired'.[176] It was best to avoid the example of Sparta and Venice and instead devote all our energies to emulating the Roman manner of organizing the commonwealth.[177]

But Solon enquired whether 'one selfesame common-weale' could 'ayme at the one and the other'. Epimenides rejected this proposal outright. First, when necessity compelled those commonwealths which held peace and longevity as their proper end, and which therefore excluded strangers, to adopt the pursuit of greatness, they were totally incapable of adapting themselves to the changed circumstances and they were in time overcome: 'common-weales which ayme at peace, having but a slender roote, and foundation, laide for the supporting thereof ... may not long be victorious, and hold themselves upright in actions of great importance'. Secondly, even if the commonwealth which strove for peace but which was forced to adopt the opposite line of policy was fortunate enough to attain an empire, 'for want of proper forces to defende' the same, it would immediately lose it. Epimenides arrived at the inescapable conclusion that it was best for common-wealths to pursue the policy of honour and glory. To adopt the peaceful policy of longevity suited only 'servile common-weales', which had always been 'subject to others', as Pisa had at times been to Florence and Salamina to Athens.[178]

What was the point of Beacon's argument? The answer must begin with Beacon's clear distinction between those commonwealths which were servile and those which were not. He made it clear that Ireland should be classified as the former. Ireland had always been a servile commonwealth since it had been subject to England. It was, therefore, safest to organize it like a community which aimed at peace. The best course of policy in Ireland was neither to admit strangers nor to arm the people. We have seen how Beacon emphasized the idea that to prevent

[175] Beacon, *Solon his follie*, pp. 63–4.
[176] Ibid., p. 64.
[177] Ibid., p. 101.
[178] Ibid., p. 64; Machiavelli, *Discorsi*, II.3.

possible revolts in Ireland it was safest to disarm the people and deny them military discipline. England, on the other hand, was not a servile commonwealth. The Englishman was not a servile subject, on the contrary, he was a 'free Citizen'. It was best, therefore, to adopt the policy of aggression, admit strangers, entertain friends and associates and arm the Englishman as well as train him in military discipline.[179] This was the only way to guarantee not merely that he could perform his public duty and safeguard his liberty, but also that his commonwealth could attain glory and greatness. To organize England internally along the Roman lines and to see that its external affairs were conducted along concomitant principles was to ensure, in the first place, that the English conquest of Ireland was carried out and consolidated. In the second place, Beacon was convinced that by adopting the policy he was proposing in *Solon his follie* England could emulate Rome as far as the scope of the commonwealth was concerned. To render England populous and to exercise the people in warlike discipline was to promote the greatness of England. The completion of the conquest of Ireland was but a means towards this loftier goal.

III

In the earlier parts of this chapter we travelled to the geographical margins of Elizabethan England. In this third part we return to the centre of the political nation, not directly but via the marginalized way of translations of foreign political tracts.

Towards the end of the 1590s two remarkable continental republican treatises were translated and published in England. As is well known, Lewes Lewkenor's translation of Gasparo Contarini's *De magistratibus et republica Venetorum* (written in the 1520s and first printed in 1543) was published in 1599. The appearance in 1598 of *The covnsellor*, a translation of the *De optimo senatore libri dvo* (first printed in 1568) by the Pole Laurentius Grimalius Goslicius (Wawrzyniec Grzymala Goslicki 1530–1607), has attracted less attention. Contarini and Goslicius were concerned with explaining and praising the merits of Venice and Poland respectively, and the English translations of their treatises can be partly understood as satisfying the intellectual curiosity about these countries.[180] More to the point, Goslicius' and Contarini's tracts taught

---

[179] Ibid., pp. 102–3.
[180] On Poland, see also [George Carew], 'Relation of the state of Polonia' (1598), ed. Carolus H. Talbot, Elementa ad fontium editiones 13 (Rome, 1965).

the English an important lesson in aristocratic republican theory. As we have seen, classical republican themes had emerged in England before the end of the 1590s in both translations and treatises composed by Englishmen alike. A further example is Robert Hitchcock's translation of Francesco Sansovino's collection of maxims, *Concetti politici* (originally published in 1578), printed in 1590 with the title *The quintesence of wit*. Several of its maxims were not only highly critical of monarchy but openly advocated republicanism. As Hitchcock rendered Sansovino's quotation from Machiavelli, 'all those Contries and Provinces that live in libertie: make great increase, and proceed much more forward then those that live in bondage. For that in a free state is found greater state of people, because mariage amongst them are more free and more desired of men.'[181]

But the appearance of Goslicius and Contarini's important republican treatises, with a strong aristocratic bias, can be said to have thoroughly familiarized the English with this strand of the humanist tradition. Nevertheless, although Lewkenor's translation in particular is well known, it is arguable that its political significance has not been sufficiently recognized.[182] For to see it, and for that matter Goslicius' treatise, merely as a scholarly enterprise is to gravely misunderstand them. In order to grasp what the translators might have been doing in translating these tracts, we should see them, I argue, in their contemporary political context. That is to say, we should interpret them not merely as teaching a lesson about foreign countries but also as carrying a polemical political point.

Despite Beacon's reform proposals, a major rebellion broke out in Ireland in 1595. Ireland was not, however, the only major source of political problems during the 1590s. From 1585 England had been fighting Spain in a war with which the Irish problem had become inextricably entangled. It was fought on the open sea, in the Netherlands and in northern France and could, at any moment, have reached England as well. The war led Elizabeth's government to impose heavy military and economic burdens upon the country and these hardships caused by large-scale war coincided with general economic distress prompted by a sequence of poor harvests and severe outbreaks of plague.[183]

---

[181] Francesco Sansovino, *The quintesence of wit*, translated by Robert Hitchcock (London, 1590), fo. 58ᵛ; see also fos. 89ᵛ, 96ʳ. Machiavelli, *Discorsi*, II.2.

[182] Fink 1945, pp. 41–5; Pocock 1975b, pp. 321–2, 324–5.

[183] See e.g. Power 1985; Outhwaite 1985; Clark 1977, pp. 221–68.

Because of these internal and external factors, England faced a number of grave political problems; so much so in fact that the label 'the crisis of the 1590s' has sometimes been applied. The long war created a shortage of patronage which was exacerbated by the increasing number of educated gentlemen in search of preferment. As competition became fiercer, signs of corruption and venality emerged more obviously.[184] Simultaneously, the Elizabethan court faced its first real factional struggles. The court had long maintained an internal cohesion but the demise of figures such as the earl of Leicester in 1588, Francis Walsingham in 1590 and Christopher Hatton in 1591 altered the situation somewhat, while the rise of the earl of Essex meant that his rivalry with the Cecils escalated into a factional struggle.[185]

Although these developments aroused dissent, the strongest criticism was directed at the issues of purveyance and monopolies. Some of the monopolies were genuine copyrights, but a number of them were exclusive rights to produce and sell certain commodities or even simply to regulate these processes. Whilst lucrative for courtiers who received them, they were burdensome to the public, as they pushed up prices dramatically. Because they rested on a royal prerogative, monopolies were beyond the jurisdiction of the common law courts. Although monopolies were not a completely new phenomenon in the 1590s, their sharp increase provoked widespread and scathing criticism in the parliaments of 1597 and 1601.[186] In 1601 students taking MA degrees debated 'whether the disorders of nations should be traced back to the corruption of discipline rather than to heaven and their sites'.[187]

On top of these economic, political and factional issues came perhaps the acutest of all the problems of the 1590s – the unsolved question of succession. Despite the queen's vigorous attempts to suppress any discussion of the issue, it had from the very beginning of the reign sporadically surfaced in parliament as well as on the stage, and several manuscript treatises had been composed to offer solutions.[188] For obvious reasons, the question became ever more

---

[184] Guy 1988, pp. 391–7; Levy 1986, pp. 102–7.
[185] Adams 1984, pp. 68–70; MacCaffery 1961; Hurstfield 1961; Neale 1963, pp. 145–70. For an interesting discussion of Essex, see James 1986, pp. 416–65.
[186] See in general Neale 1953–7, II, pp. 352–6, 376–93; Russell 1971, pp. 242–51; Guy 1988, pp. 397–403; from the local point of view, see e.g. Williams 1984.
[187] *Register*, vol. II, pt I, p. 172.
[188] See e.g. Neale 1953–7 I, pp. 86–90, 101–13, 129–64; Axton 1977, pp. 11–47.

burning during the 1590s. Early in the decade Peter Wentworth made some vain attempts to kindle discussion but they were quickly suppressed.[189] In 1591 Oxford students presented to the degree of MA debated the manner of electing the magistrate, but in the following year they were told to argue that the well-being of a commonwealth depended on hereditary kingship.[190] The issue of succession was clandestinely treated on the stage which has been called, in this context, 'the freest open forum for political speculation'.[191] Under the pseudonym R. Doleman, Robert Parsons published *A conference abovt the next svccession to the crowne of Ingland.* Published on the continent in 1594, it argued for a catholic succession. Basing his arguments on the tradition of natural law, Parsons claimed that there was no natural form of government but that every commonwealth decided on its own form, which it could therefore change as well. Furthermore, he maintained that the prince could be deposed 'by publique authority of the whole body', thus suggesting an amalgamation of succession and election.[192] Parsons was almost immediately taken to task in several treatises.[193] Although Peter Wentworth died in 1597, his tract on succession was posthumously printed in 1598. Using historical examples and the idea of the original transfer of power from 'the whole Realme' to a prince, he pointed out that although it was up to parliament to assess the validity of the different claims to the throne, it was not in a position to alter the succession.[194] The urgency of the succession question is graphically illustrated by the fact that Thomas Wilson began his description of the state of England in 1600 with this issue, offering a detailed account of every candidate's claim.[195]

It is against this background that we should interpret the translations of Goslicius and Contarini's treatises. It is often pointed out that

[189] Neale 1924; Axton 1977, pp. 89–91.

[190] *Register*, vol. II, pt, I, p. 172.

[191] Axton 1977, pp. 97–130, citation from p. 89.

[192] [Robert Parsons], *A conference abovt the next svccession to the crowne of Ingland* (n.p., 1594), I, pp. 3–13, 33, 130. Cf. Collins 1989, pp. 103–8.

[193] Axton 1977, pp. 95–7; Thomas Craig, *The right of succession to the kingdom of England* (London, 1703); John Harington, *A tract on the succession to the crown* (1602), ed. C. R. Markham (London: Roxburghe Club, 1880); John Hayward, *An answer to the first part of a certaine conference, concerning succession* (London, 1603), see e.g. sig. A3ᵛ.

[194] Peter Wentworth, *A pithie exhortation to her maiestie for establishing her svccessor to the crowne* (n.p., 1598), I, sig. A2ʳ, pp. 5, 50–1, 79–81, 117, II, pp. 6, 46–50.

[195] Wilson, 'The state of England', pp. 2–9.

histories and plays could carry an ideological point, forming a platform where delicate issues could be treated in a veiled manner.[196] In a similar fashion, David Norbrook has recently called attention to the ideological message that Lewkenor's translation may have carried.[197] It is accordingly my argument in what follows that a more accurate reading of these translations is achieved if we regard them, in addition to satisfying an intellectual curiosity, as serving a significant political point.

Contarini and Goslicius pointed out that, far from discussing imaginary commonwealths, they both aimed at explaining the success of their respective commonwealths.[198] More importantly, they both insisted that this success was mainly due to the peculiar manner in which their commonwealths had been established. Other writers had commended the Venetian 'marchandise' and 'the greatnesse' of her empire, but Contarini recapitulated the myth of Venice and argued that it was the 'manner & forme of commonwealthes' which enabled the Venetians to 'enjoy a happie and quiet life'. There had never been a commonwealth, he went on, 'that may bee paragond with this of ours, for institutions & lawes prudently degreed'.[199]

The preeminence of Venice manifested itself first in the fact that her 'soveraity of government' rested on laws rather than on men. It was clear, however, that to be effective laws needed 'a certaine Gardians as Leiftenant', and the question of prime importance was to whom this guardianship of laws should be given.[200] Contarini pointed out that it had long been a matter of dispute 'whether it bee better that one or few have the government of the whole citie, or rather the whole multitude'.[201] In answering this crucial question, Contarini emphasized that the overarching quality should be 'unity'. This was

---

[196] The most conspicuous examples are John Hayward's, *The first part of the life and raigne of king Henrie the IIII* (London, 1599), sig. A3ʳ–4ʳ; William Fulbecke's, *An historicall collection of the continvall factions, tvmvlts, and massacres of the Romans and Italians* (London, 1601), sig. A1ʳ–2ᵛ; Levy 1987, pp. 1–3, 15–21. Cf. the vehemence with which Thomas Bedingfield disapproved of aristocracy and democracy in his preface to his translation of Niccolò Machiavelli, *The Florentine historie* (London, 1595), sig. A4ʳ–5ʳ.

[197] Norbrook 1984, p. 130.

[198] Gasparo Contarini, *The commonwealth and government of Venice*, translated by Lewes Lewkenor (London, 1599), p. 7; Laurentius Grimalius [Goslicius], *The covnsellor: exactly pourtraited in two bookes*, translated by anon. (London, 1598), p. 2. For Goslicius' translation, see Gollancz 1914; Chwalewik 1968, p. 22; and especially Baluk-Ulewiczowa 1988, who points out that there is a manuscript translation of Goslicius' first book, dated before 1585.

[199] Contarini, *The commonwealth of Venice*, pp. 1–6.

[200] Ibid., pp. 10–12.

[201] Ibid., pp. 9, 13.

attained only if, as he was never tired of repeating, there was 'such a mixture of all estates' as could embrace at the same time 'a princely soveraigntie, a government of the nobilitie & a popular authority' 'so that the formes of them all seeme to be equally ballanced'.[202] The democratic element, or 'the forme of a popular state', of the Venetian commonwealth was represented by the great council from whose 'decrees and lawes aswell the senate as all other magistrates derive their power and authority'.[203] The aristocratic element, which consisted in the senate, was the strongest: 'The whole manner of the commonwealths government belongeth to the senate.'[204] Contarini devoted the second book of his treatise to the third element of the mixed constitution – the duke. His authority was strictly limited and he was thus deprived of 'all meanes, whereby he might abuse his authoritie, or become a tyrant'. The chief issue here and the one to which Contarini devoted most space was the election of a new prince. This happened in a most intricate way to ensure that, on the one hand, the people had a part in it, whilst, on the other hand, the ultimate decision was taken by the senators. The decision was made by 'certain several parliaments', as Lewkenor put it.[205]

Although Goslicius' avowed aim was to discuss 'the duetie, vertue and dignitie of a perfect Councellor',[206] he was also concerned with his own country and thus gave an account of an aristocratic mixed state. He first pointed out that of the three pure forms of government, 'the Principalitie and *Optimatie*', had much to commend themselves. But he immediately added that 'some men have thought the moste perfect commonweale, should be tempered and framed of all of the three estates'.[207] This mixture had already been clearly discernible in 'the Lacedemonian government', which had been 'compounded of the nobilitie, (which was the Senators) of the authoritie of one, (which was the King) and the people (which were the Ephori)'. But the most remarkable instance of the mixed consitution was, as Polybius had pointed out, 'the Romane state, because it consisted of the King, the Nobilitie, and the people; supposing that the king for feare of the people coulde not become insolente, and the people durste not disobeye him, in respecte of the Senate'. Cicero had also explained that

---

202 Ibid., pp. 15, 33–4, 67, 83, 146.
203 Ibid., pp. 15–16, 18, 21–2.
204 Ibid., pp. 64–9; cf. in general pp. 64–98, 99.
205 Ibid. pp. 42, 51–62.
206 [Goslicius], *The counsellor*, p. 1.
207 Ibid., p. 18.

the best commonwealth was a mixture 'of the best, the meane, and the base people' and that a commonwealth 'attained perfection when it was governed by a king, a Senate, and consent of the people'.[208] The same preference for a mixed state emerged in the second book, where Goslicius argued more specifically that 'the bodie of our commonweale consisteth in the conjunction of three estates'.[209]

Goslicius' discussion of the prince's role was brief, and the translator had made it even shorter.[210] The king must pursue 'the common commoditie of his subjectes' and 'preserve the rights and liberty of the people'. Although the translator omitted Goslicius' most crucial passage in favour of the elective monarchy, the translation still made it clear that Goslicius took the election of the prince for granted. Confronting an elected prince and a tyrant, he wrote that 'the election of kinges was in time paste proper to the moste vertuous people, unto whome the government of Tyrantes was odious'.[211] With regard to the popular element of the mixed state, 'those people are accounted the beste, which within a good commonweale doe live with justice and libertye'. The 'consente of the people' was a necessary requirement of good laws. But if liberty completely dominated, the commonwealth would be governed 'without vertue and reason'.[212] It was, therefore, best to aim at liberty as well as peace and tranquillity. To ensure this, it was safest, Goslicius held, to rely on the authority of the *optimates*. An aristocracy and the senate, the mean between a monarchy and democracy, was thus like 'a watch-tower'; it provided all the necessary things 'for the state, preventing all seditions, tumultes, and perils that can be attempted' being able to 'finde the perfection of all things'. It was only 'thorough Counsell and authoritie of the Senate' that 'the state would be exceedingly encreased and inforced'.[213] The success of an aristocratic mixed state was most readily seen in the Venetian commonwealth which had 'constantly lived in one forme of government, by the space of a thousand years, or more', as Goslicius restated the myth of Venice.[214]

---

[208] Ibid., pp. 1, 8–19, cf. p. 29.

[209] Ibid., p. 76.

[210] Baluk-Ulewiczowa 1988, pp. 268–71. The omissions concerning religion were much longer, eadem pp. 271–2.

[211] [Goslicius], *The counsellor*, pp. 29, 73–5, 15–16. For the omissions of the translator, see Baluk-Ulewiczowa 1988, p. 268. Although George Carew vehemently criticized an elected monarchy, he, nevertheless, provided a detailed account of the Polish princely elections, 'Relation', pp. 40–53, 107, 130–2, 145–6.

[212] [Goslicius], *The counsellor*, p. 16–18, 79–80.

[213] Ibid., pp. 29–31.

[214] Ibid., p. 18.

Contarini and Goslicius insisted that the mixed constitution should be firmly supported by a virtuous civic life. Contarini was fully convinced that it was before everything else the high degree of wisdom, virtue and patriotism which had made Venice better than Athens, Sparta and even Rome.[215] The case for the active life emerged even more clearly in Goslicius' treatise. Pure contemplation was neither sufficient nor good in itself; it should always be complemented by action. Citizens should be drawn 'to action of governmente', to fulfil their 'civill duetie'. Goslicius insisted that 'such kinde of contemplation and Philosophie which concerneth not the profit, not civill affayres of men, is in trueth improfitable for the state'. For albeit those philosophers were learned and wise, they 'are utterly unfit for government'. But the man who takes part in 'the affaires of government ... becommeth thereby divine, noble, wise, and provident'. 'We therefore doe exhorte all wise men to action, and recommend unto them the commonweale.'[216] The only way to attain the *vita activa* was to embrace knowledge and learning, which led to the cardinal virtues of 'Justice, Temperance, and Fortitude', and consequently made man 'perfect'.[217] Underlying Goslicius' concept of civic life was a particular interpretation of the nature of liberty. For him the citizen's liberty consisted 'chiefly in being capable of offices, to have power to make & correct lawes, to speake freely in matters that concerne liberty, law or injury, not to be arrested or imprisoned without order of lawe or authoritie, nor be unjustly judged, robbed or forced to pay tribute'.[218]

As well as propagating the familiar humanist idea that a virtuous civic life was tantamount to the efflorescence of the mixed constitution and thereby the whole commonwealth, Contarini and Goslicius particularly endorsed an equally traditional assumption about the characteristics of the true citizen. Due to his strongly aristocratic bias, Contarini explained that 'it was ordayned by our auncestors, that the common people should not bee admitted into this company of citizens'. It followed that 'the publike rule' of the Venetian commonwealth was reserved for 'the nobility of lineage'. This argument was not so much directed against obscure but virtuous men, as against those whose only worth consisted in wealth. For Contarini, all who 'were noble by birth,

---

[215] Contarini, *The commonwealth of Venice*, pp. 6–8.
[216] [Goslicius], *The counsellor*, pp. 1, 5–8, 42–3, 59.
[217] Ibid., pp. 12–14. Goslicius also argued that a good citizen did not have to be a good man since he only needed to be 'politique, diligent, and stout' 'in service of the state', although he could otherwise be 'injust, intemperate, and cowardly', p. 37.
[218] Ibid., pp. 79–80.

or ennobled by vertue, or well deserving of the commonwealth, did in the beginning obtain this right of government'. And he was most careful to stress that 'the chiefest honors' should be conferred on those who 'do excell the rest in vertue'.[219]

Despite his equally strong aristocratic bias, Goslicius endorsed even more vigorously the humanist notion that virtue alone was the mainstay of nobility. Although he stipulated that counsellors ought to descend 'from stocke or house of nobilitie or gentrie', he immediately added that he did 'not dislike of those that take the badges of honor from themselves, and make the foundation of their nobilitie upon their owne vertue'. The simple reason for this was that 'vertue entreateth both new and ancient men after one fashion'. This had an immediate bearing upon Goslicius' notion of citizenship. Referring to Cicero, Goslicius maintained that 'those are named Citizens that live according to vertue'. Whereas Aristotle had required that a citizen had 'good parentage, riches, and vertue', Goslicius argued that 'because it seldome happeneth that one man can be owner of them all', it followed that 'vertue alone doth chalenge ... power to make men noble'. Although the membership of 'civill nobility' was given even to those who were 'valiant in the warre of their country', Goslicius followed Cicero in insisting that 'those men whose counsell in time of peace, governed the commonweale wisely, peaceablie and happilie, were preferred before them, that eyther defended or enlarged the same by armes'.[220]

One of the chief benefits of the mixed constitution and a virtuous nobility, which both writers singled out, was the particular way in which these qualities could help the commonwealth to avoid corruption. Corruption took place as soon as men lost sight of the common good and began to pursue their private profit. This could be eschewed, as both Contarini and Goslicius held, first by choosing many magistrates and second by choosing those who indeed possessed virtue. Contarini wrote that 'the offices' should be distributed so that 'the preheminence of publike authoritie might pertaine to many, and not bee engrossed up among a few' since these would be particularly propitious circumstances for the growth of corruption. The underlying argument was that 'nothing is more proper to a commonwealth, then that the common authority and power should belong to many'.[221] Goslicius assured his

---

[219] Contarini, *The commonwealth of Venice*, pp. 16–18, 35.
[220] [Goslicius], *The covnsellor*, pp. 146–8, 33–37.
[221] Contarini, *The commonwealth of Venice*, pp. 32–3.

readers that 'among other things 'which do preserve the commonweale & happines therof, there is nothing better then to elect such men for magistrates, as be induced with greatest wisedome, judgement & vertue'. Magistracy was above all 'an ornament of vertue' and it should be 'bestowed on the best sorte of men, for their vertue and well deserving of the state'. Men were ambitious by nature, and if this characteristic was not bridled, riches and private gain would replace virtue and the public good with the consequence that the commonwealth would face an inevitable disaster. It followed, first, that education had to play a pivotal role in making the citizen virtuous.[222] Secondly, and more urgently, offices should only be distributed on the basis of virtue. As Goslicius maintained, 'great care therfore must be taken in every commonweale, that the offices should not be given rather to the rich then the vertuous men, and that those may be punished, that seeke with money to oppresse vertue'.[223]

The suggestion that these translations were carrying a political message can be criticized from two different angles. First, it is possible to maintain that the English, whose way of thinking was dominated by the concept of a hierarchical body politic, were unable to comprehend a republican universe of active beings. One could also object that the issues which the English found in Contarini and Goslicius were not so much incomprehensible as largely irrelevant to their own context and that they were sources of general 'political wisdom' rather than of 'controversial argument'.[224]

There are a number of ways of answering this criticism. We have already seen that Englishmen were fully capable of translating republican works, and of employing republican notions in order to put forward polemical arguments. The relevance of Contarini' and Goslicius' treatises is further attested by the fact that a number of similar issues was treated and endorsed at the same time in numerous other tracts.

First, the idea of a virtuous true nobility was widely embraced. Admittedly, the earl of Essex may have seen himself as a 'man of arms' bound by the rules of chivalry and may have emphasized his lineage, values which gained currency in such writings as *The booke of*

---

[222] [Goslicius], *The covnsellor*, pp. 43–59.
[223] Ibid., pp. 59–61, 66, 102; in general pp. 59–68.
[224] Cf. Pocock 1975b, p. 350; Sharpe 1989, p. 18. See Salmon 1959, p. 22, for the ways in which Bodin was perhaps seen as 'an encyclopaedia of political wisdom' rather than 'a source of controversial argument'.

S. Albans republished in 1595.[225] But it would be highly misleading to conclude that these conceptions dominated. There is little doubt that the old Roman and humanist idea of virtue as the sole constituent of true nobility acquired great popularity. As one author put it, 'true Nobility consisteth not of great patrimonies and rich possessions, but of godlie & vertuous actions'.[226] This was of course the question to which Giovanni Nenna had devoted his tract *Nennio*, published in English in 1595, reprinted in 1600, and dedicated to the earl of Essex. Nenna pointed out in no uncertain terms that 'this nobility of bloud is not onelie cause of pride, and ignorance, but of unsufferable evil, and inevitable losse'. The only way to become noble was 'to follow vertue and to flie vice'. In his preface to the reader, the translator, William Jones, agreed with Nenna, and not only argued against Aristotle but castigated, in a most forthright manner, those who were 'caried away with fabulous pedigrees'.[227]

Moreover, the mixed constitution and the republican form of government were commended in other treatises of the 1590s. In his encyclopaedia *Of the interchangeable course, or variety of things in the whole world* published in English in 1594, Louis Le Roy wrote that 'there are more excellent personages found in common weales, then in kingdoms; in the which vertue is honoured, and in kingdomes suppressed'. The best form of government was the mixed constitution found most conspicuously in ancient Rome. The only contemporary common-wealths which came near to ancient Rome in this respect were aristocratic Venice and democratic Switzerland. Although Venice was not the greatest empire to be found in history, it was the most durable and most conducive to 'good, and happy life'.[228]

The Venetian government was also eulogized by John Smythe in his

---

[225] Anon., *The gentlemans academie: or, the booke of S. Albans ... reduced into a better method, by G. M[arkham]* (London, 1595), especially fos. 43^{r-v}; for Essex, see James 1986, pp. 416–65.

[226] Bartholomew Chappell, *The garden of prudence* (London, 1595), sig. E1^v. Cf. also e.g. Richard Crompton, *The mansion of magnanimitie* (London, 1599), sig. A4^v, who quoted Sallust; Charles Gibbon, *The praise of a good name* (London, 1594), pp. 20–1, 23; James Perrott, *The first part of the consideration of hvmane condition* (Oxford, 1600), pp. 29–32; Thomas Floyd, *The picture of a perfit common wealth* (London, 1600), p. 113; Robert Ashley, *Of honour*, ed. Virgil B. Heltzel (San Marino: Huntington Library, 1947), pp. 69–70, 34, 37.

[227] Giovanni Nenna, *Nennio: or a treatise of nobility*, translated by William Jones (n.p. [London], 1595), fos. 80^r, 87^r. sig. A3^v–4^r.

[228] Louis Le Roy, *Of the interchangeable course: or variety of things in the whole world*, translated by Robert Ashley (London, 1594), fos. 14^{r-v}, 79^r–81^v, 16^v, 121^v. It is worthwhile to note that Aristotle's *Politics* was for the first time translated into English from Le Roy's French version in 1598. The translation also included Le Roy's humanistic commentary, Aristotle, *Politiqves, or discourse of government*, translated by I. D. (London, 1598). For some suggestive remarks, see Tuck 1979, p. 44.

tract on warfare. According to him, many 'politike States-men' claimed that it was dangerous to arm the people, since this would give them a possibility of rebelling. Smythe argued that it was not the arming of the people but the nature of the government of the community that could give rise to revolts and rebellions. The advice not to arm the people was thus offered so that 'princes and governors should the more safely without any danger of mutiny tyrannize, and exact at their own pleasures upon their subjects'. A corollary of Smythe's argument was that a 'puissant Militia' was the only safeguard against a foreign conqueror, a possible rebellion and a tyrant alike.[229] But since it was mainly the 'lack of justice dulie and equallie ministred' which led to uprisings, it was of utmost importance that justice was duly administered. A case in point was 'the notable Cittie and state of Venice' as well as 'the Cantonnes and confederate people of Suitzerland', after they had established 'a civill and popular State'. Not a single rebellion had occurred in either Venice or Switzerland since their governments had maintained justice and equality so meticulously.[230]

In his own tract, *Of honour*, written towards the end of the reign, Robert Ashley, the translator of Le Roy's work, put forward an even stronger argument for the intimate link between the beneficial nature of a virtuous true nobility and a republican government. Focusing his attention on the question of who was capable of achieving honour, Ashley noted that there were three distinct groups of people. The first group contained those who were 'so heavie and dull spirited that they little differ from brute beastes', while those who were 'so pregnant and high minded that they despise all humane matters, and count them too base for them to deale with' formed the second group. The third group consisted of those who were also 'very desirous of great thinges' but who were at the same time 'moderate in their desires'. The men of the second group were so desirous of fame and honour that rather than needing any incentives for honour, they, in fact, 'had more need of a brydle to restraine them from their over hote pursuit'. But by and large, the consequences of an energetic pursuit of and a bitter contest for honour were favourable. They advanced rather than hindered the common good: honour was 'a great spurr unto vertue'.[231] In some countries the intensity of the quest for honour was further enhanced by 'their institucion and custome'. This was most obvious 'amongst the

[229] John Smythe, *Instructions, obseruations, and orders mylitarie* (London, 1595), sigs. ¶3ᵛ–4ʳ, ¶¶2ᵛ–3ʳ.
[230] Smythe, *Instructions*, pp. 214–15.
[231] Ashley, *Of honour*, p. 40.

Romanes and the Grecians' where 'the founders' of the commonwealths had looked to it that 'their Citizens' could channel their 'great
spirite' to 'great accions'.[232]

The difference between 'dull spirited' and 'high minded' people had
momentous consequences for the organization of the commonwealth's
government. The 'dull spirited' were most easily 'brought under the
yoke of Tyrantes' since they inherently admired tyrants. Even those
who were 'desirous of great thinges' but were 'moderate in their
desires' were eventually 'brought into bondage' as soon as their
'feirsenes' was suppressed. Only the most 'high minded' people were
capable of avoiding the bridle of tyranny. They were 'of more witt and
accomplishment' and they were 'obedient to none but such a one as
ruleth by lawes and institucions and governeth justly, and moderately'.
To illustrate his point, Ashley argued that whereas amongst the
Persians not a single conspiracy against their most tyrannical and cruel
princes had occurred, many of the Greek and Roman princes had been
'banished and slaine bicause they [had] ruled somewhat too severely'.
But it was peculiar to all 'polished nations' that they 'co[u]ld not
indure a proud and arrogant dominion'.[233] Thus the commonwealth
of a 'high minded' and 'polished' people had two definite advantages.
First, the high-mindedness of the people maximized the advancement
of the common good. Since utmost care was taken to confer the highest
honours upon the most virtuous citizens, the high-minded people were
always most careful to embrace virtues and to put them into action. In
Ashley's words, they watched 'night and day that they may seeke to
give better Councell to the state then others'.[234] Secondly, their
commonwealth had a government which ruled according to the laws
since the high-minded people always kept a watch on their superiors
and would not hesitate to rebel should the government degenerate.

Finally, in order to appreciate the claim that Contarini's and
Goslicius' translations had a political point, we have to turn to the
translations themselves. The anonymity of Goslicius' translator and his
several omissions bear witness to the controversial nature of the view
put forward in the treatise. But the tract defies a more accurate

[232] Ibid., pp. 48–9.
[233] Ibid., pp. 49–50. Cf. e.g. Leonard Wright, *A display of dvty deckt with sage sayings, pithy sentences,
       and proper similes* (1589) (London, 1616), fos. 4ʳ⁻ᵛ. According to Wright, although Englishmen
       were 'bound by law', they were 'free by nature'. This meant, first, that they were 'more apt to
       yeeld obedience and dutie, for love of vertue then feare of punishment' and secondly, that
       they were 'more easily governed by friendlie curtesie, then forcible cruelty'.
[234] Ashley, *Of honour*, p. 50.

interpretation of the translator's intentions since there is no preface, dedication or any other comment by the translator. Nevertheless, Goslicius' discussion of the constitutional arrangements prevalent in his own day is of considerable interest. He found traces of the mixed constitution in every commonwealth including France and Spain, although in France the king 'ruleth at his owne discretion' and in Spain the prince had 'authority soveraigne'.[235]

As we have seen, a more genuine representative of the mixed constitution was Poland, where the 'liberty' of the people was 'so great, as the king, without advise of his councel & their authority doth not any thing, neither can the councel determine without the allowance of the King, and consent of the people'. It was mainly by virtue of these principles of the mixed consitution that in Poland laws were exceptionally forceful and people lived 'in great liberty, beeing perswaded that to live according to lawe, is indeed perfect freedome'. According to Goslicius, the same perfect form of the mixed constitution was at work in two other commonwealths. 'The Venetian state', he argued, 'seemeth framed after the same fashion' as Poland. It comes as no surprise, therefore, that there was not a single commonwealth comparable to Venice in quietness and antiquity. Furthermore, an essentially similar set of principles could be detected in England, where, in Goslicius' words, the embodiment of the mixed constitution was seen in 'one common Councell: which in their language is called Parliament', where the king was joined with 'the Nobility and popular order'. England was thus ranked amongst the mixed states of Poland and Venice rather than amongst the monarchies of France and Spain.[236]

Lewkenor's translation is a different matter. It contains a dedication to the countess of Warwick, prefatory verses and a lengthy preface to the reader. A commendation of Venice was central both to some of the verses and to Lewkenor's preface. Edmund Spenser described Venice as the successor of the eastern and western empires, whilst another poet wrote: 'Venice invincible, the Adriatique wonder'.[237] According to Lewkenor, travellers 'would inforce their speech to the highest of all admiration' as soon as they began to talk about Venice. They asserted that it was by far the 'most infinitely remarkable, that they had seen in the whole course of their travels'. And Lewkenor himself fully concurred: 'whithersoever you

235 [Goslicius], *The counsellor*, p. 26.
236 Ibid., pp. 26–8. Cf. [Carew], 'Relation', p. 62.
237 Contarini, *The commonwealth of Venice*, sig. *3ᵛ, *4ʳ. Cf. Fink 1945, p. 43.

turne your eyes, they shall not encounter any thing but obiectes of admiration'.[238] He was ready to admit his own gullibility regarding 'the report of rare and unusuall accidentes', but he considered it far less serious than the outright contempt for new and strange things so typical amongst his contemporaries. Lewkenor wanted, in other words, to dispel suspicions about the use of instances which at first glance seemed to be foreign and irrelevant to the English context, but which on second thoughts turned out to be highly apposite. He criticized, as he put it, those 'who presentlie doe condemne for false fryvolous & impossible whatsoever is not within the narrow lymits of their own capacitie included'.[239]

The admirable nature of Venice consisted partly in its longevity and partly in its empire. It seemed as if it was in league 'with the heavenly powers' since for '13 hundred yeares', it had been 'an estate so perpetually flourishing & unblemished'. It was admired 'for power and glorie', for its 'infinit affluence of glorie, and unmeasurable mightinesse of power'.[240] But the chief reason why Venice should be honoured was the peculiar way in which it was organized, and which ultimately accounted for its greatness and longevity. Spenser firmly believed that Venice 'farre' exceeded all the other commonwealths 'in policie of right'.[241]

There were three features in particular which Lewkenor found highly commendable in the Venetian commonwealth. The first was its ability to hold corruption at bay. If 'no ambitious force' could destroy Venice from without, neither could internal division jeopardize its well-being since 'all corrupt means to aspire are curbd' in Venice.[242] There were more than 3,000 citizens who took part in its political life – not as soldiers, as Lewkenor took some pains to point out, but as 'unweaponed men in gownes' – giving 'direction & law to many mightie and warlike armies'. Nonetheless, Venice had not encountered the perennial problem of factions and overambitious citizens which was traditionally claimed to be inseparable from as well as fatal to aristocratic commonwealths. None of her citizens had been induced to 'aspire to any greater appellation of honour, or higher tytle of dignitie then to be called a Gentleman of Venice'.

---

[238] Contarini, *The commonwealth of Venice*, sig. A1^v–2^r, A2^v.
[239] Ibid., sig. *4^v.
[240] Ibid., sigs. A3^r, *4^r.
[241] Ibid., sig. *3^v.
[242] Ibid., sig. *4^r.

The Venetians' love of their country was so profound and deep that they were content to serve it with all their energy.[243]

The preeminence of the Venetian commonwealth also emerged in the election of its magistrates. Venice had avoided internal discord since, in the words of one poet, her magistrates were 'elected' on the basis of 'vertues'.[244] Lewkenor completely concurred. Not only did the Venetians diligently maintain justice 'pure and uncorrupted'; 'their encouragements to vertue' were hardly less 'infinite'. This encouragement was a consequence of the peculiar way in which 'offices & dignities' were distributed, a way which 'utterly overreacheth the subtilitie of all ambitious practises'. Lewkenor was careful to emphasize that the principles of a truly virtuous nobility had been realized in Venice. All the 'offices and dignitie' were conferred on people whom 'the whole assembly' regarded as 'men of greatest wisedome, vertue and integritie of life'.[245]

The final feature of which Lewkenor strongly approved was the Venetian form of government. Lewkenor insisted that 'the Venetian prince' represented 'a most excellent Monarchie'. He possessed 'all exterior ornamentas of royall dignitie' but his authority was 'wholy subjected to the lawes'. The Venetian 'Councell of Pregati or Senators' embodied 'Aristocraticall government'. This senate, Lewkenor faithfully acknowledged, possessed 'all supreame power' but was totally unable to 'tyrannize, or to pervert their Country lawes'. The final feature of the Venetian form of government was 'their great Councell, consisting at the least of 3000. Gentlemen, whereupon the highest strength and mightinesse of the estate absolutely relyeth'. This 'great Councell', which had not caused any 'tumult' or 'confusion', was 'a most rare and matchlesse president of a Democrasie or popular estate'. For Lewkenor, accordingly, Venice was the embodiment of the mixed constitution.[246]

Lewkenor thus revealed the excellence of the Venetian commonwealth and its government, but perhaps the most astonishing characteristic of his preface is the forthrightness with which he suggested that Venice was a touchstone for the governments of other commonwealths. As a result, to give a picture of the Venetian government was to 'deliver unto other a cleare and exact knowledge' of the different forms

[243] Ibid., sig. A3^r.
[244] Ibid., sig. *4^r.
[245] Ibid., sig. A2^v.
[246] Ibid., sig. A2^{r-v}.

of government so that all could comprehend 'the fruite of all whatsoever other governments throughout the world that are of any fame or
excellency'.[247] Surely it would not be too much to say that one of the
points Lewkenor had in mind when he translated Contarini's treatise,
and criticized those who refused to see the relevance of a foreign
example, was that the English might have something to learn from the
Venetian experience.

[247] Ibid., sig. A2ʳ.

CHAPTER 3

Civic life and the mixed constitution in Jacobean political thought

I

Jacobean political thought has often been studied from the viewpoint of a polarity of opinions between the king and his parliaments. James, together with his Anglican clerics and his lawyers, invoked royal absolutism, whilst the House of Commons attempted to oppose royalist claims by arguments based on their view of the nature and contents of the ancient constitution or, more generally, on theories of contract. This is the focal point of the older – or 'Whig' interpretation.[1] But it is also that of recent studies whether written against, or in defence of, the older account.[2] It is not the aim of this chapter to deny the obvious truth that perhaps the majority of early-seventeenth-century English political discourse centred upon the disagreements between the king and his parliaments and upon the debates on the nature of the ancient constitution. But what I do wish to argue is that the narrow concentration upon these issues, displayed by most scholars, tends to yield an over-restricted picture of the range of Jacobean political thought. It is, in other words, worth our while to take a fresh look at the political writings of the first two decades of the seventeenth century. Although the bulk of political discourse was conducted in juristic parlance – variously absolutist, contractarian or legal in character – it is argued below that the opposing tradition, which emphasized the virtuous citizen's active life, was also present during this period.

The advocates of royal absolutism often directed their arguments against contractarians – both Calvinist and catholic alike, as exemplified by Bartholomew Parsons, the incumbent of Ludgershall, Wiltshire,

---

[1]   E.g. Allen 1938; Judson 1949.
[2]   Smith 1973; Eccleshall 1978; Weston and Greenberg 1982; Sommerville 1986; Christiansson 1991.

in his assize sermon at Sarum in Wiltshire in March 1615. Excoriating Robert Bellarmine, David Pareus as well as the author of the *Vindicae contra tyrannos*, Parsons argued that 'all Magistracie & civil power on earth hath his originall & authority immediatly from the most high, whose dominion is an everlasting dominion, and whose kingdome is from generation to generation: there is no power but of God'.[3] From assumptions like this it followed that the king, in participating in divine grace, was the chief actor in the commonwealth. According to John Buckeridge, man received 'the good of Peace, Protection, Justice, Religion and the like' from the temporal government. Since God had placed government solely in the sovereign's hands, the temporal goods of peace and justice were completely dependent on the monarch.[4] Preaching in Reading in 1619, William Dickinson proclaimed that 'onely the King is the Foundation; and as it were the Selfe-praexistence and axis of the common-wealth, upon whose wel-being and good Lawes the whole state of things, and the good and ill of his Subjects and Cittizens relie'.[5]

From the strong royalist claims it also followed that the subject's active role was severely circumscribed. It was argued not only that the divinely ordained authority must not under any circumstances be actively resisted, but also that it was best for the subject to concentrate on his own private life. The only way in which he could attempt to participate in the public sphere was through acting in the contemplative domain. He should, that is, pray for a good prince.[6] According to George Meriton, the contemplative life of 'Priesthood' far outclassed the active life of 'a Mayor of a Towne or Citty, or a Justice of Peace in

---

3 Bartholomew Parsons, *The magistrates charter examined: or his duty and dignity opened: in a sermon preached at an assises, held at Sarum in the county of Wiltes, on the ninth day of March, last past, 1614* (London, 1616), p. 4. See also e.g. William Wilkes, *Obedience or ecclesiasticall vnion* (London, 1606), pp. 49, 56–60, 63–4; John Dunster, *Caesars penny: or a sermon of obedience ... preached at St Maries in Oxford at the assies the 24 of Iuly 1610* (Oxford, 1610), sig. A2ᵛ–3ʳ, pp. 17–18; Christopher White, *A sermon preached in Christ-church in Oxford, the 12. day of May 1622* (London, 1622), pp. 4, 17–21.

4 Buckeridge, *A sermon preached at Hampton Court before the kings maiestie, on Tuesday the 23 of September, anno 1606* (London, 1606) sig. A3ʳ; Robert Anton, *The philosophers satyrs* (London, 1616), sig. D2ʳ⁻ᵛ.

5 William Dickinson, *The kings right, briefely set downe in a sermon preached before the reuerend iudges at the assizes held in Reading for the county of Berks. Iune 28. 1619* (London, 1619), sig. C4ᵛ; cf. Judson 1949, pp. 192–3, 213–14.

6 E.g. Robert Horne, *The christian gouernour, in the common-wealth, and priuate families* (London, 1614), sig. C4ᵛ–5ᵛ; cf. E. N[esbit], *Caesars dialogve: or a familiar communication containing the first institution of a subiect, in allegiance to his soueraigne* (London, 1601), sig. A5ᵛ, pp. 4, 90–118; George Webbe, *The practice of qvietnes: or a direction how to liue quietly* (London, 1608), pp. 155–6.

the Countrey'.[7] Likewise, Samuel Garey maintained that since it should be the people's desire 'to live a quiet and peaceable life', they ought to confine themselves to *otium* and 'like dutifull members pray for the prosperity of the supreame head'.[8] Isaac Bargrave preached early in Charles's reign that 'obedience' was 'the chiefest of the morall vertues'.[9]

This belief recurred throughout the royalist sermons and pamphlets although rarely with as much conviction and clarity as in William Willymat's treatise, *A loyal svbiects looking-glasse*. In 1603 Willymat had published an adaptation of James I's *Basilikon doron*, entitled *A princes looking glasse*, and, encouraged by the favourable reception, published the companion volume in 1604. Discussing how subjects must abstain 'from taking in hand or intermeddling with any part of the Magistrates office', Willymat emphasized that it did not belong to them to engage themselves in the public life of their community. 'Private subiects' were 'to be ruled and governed'; they had 'no publicke charge nor office to attend upon'. They had nothing but 'only each of them his owne private busines according as his owne place, function, and calling requireth'. It followed, in the first place, that the subject was not entitled to resort to self-help; 'all taking up of revenge for a mans owne proper injurie is here forbidden'. But his passive obedience further entailed abstaining from any public action whatsoever. Following closely Pierre de La Primaudaye's description of the obedience of the subject, Willymat declared that 'all private persons' should exhibit 'moderation' 'in publique affaires, namely that they may not of their owne motion without any calling busie themselves in publike affaires, nor intermeddle in the government'. It was simply prohibited for them to attempt 'any publike thing'. Since the subject was totally devoid of the necessary qualities for taking part in the public life of the community, he ought to refrain from seeking 'to doe any good in the common-weale'.[10]

7   George Meriton, *A sermon of nobilitie: preached at White-hall, before the king in February 1606* (London, 1607), sig. E2ʳ⁻ᵛ, E3ʳ; cf. Todd 1987, p. 222. See also Edward Forset, *A comparative discovrse of the bodies natvral and politiqve* (London, 1606), pp. 45–6.
8   Samuel Garey, *Great Brittans little calendar: or, triple diarie* (London, 1618), p. 6.
9   Isaac Bargrave, *A sermon preached before king Charles, March 27. 1627: being the anniuersary of his maiesties inauguration* (London, 1627), pp. 5–6.
10   William Willymat, *A loyal svbiects looking-glasse, or a good subiects direction* (London, 1604), pp. 47–9, 58–9; La Primaudaye, *The French academie*, translated by T. B[owes?] (London, 1586), p. 609; cf. e.g. Robert Pricke, *The doctrine of svperioritie, and of subiection* (London, 1609), sig. D1ᵛ. When the subject's active role was used to substantiate absolutists' claims, it was argued, as by Henry Howard, earl of Northampton, in 1610, that the subject's active role consisted in giving pecuniary help, *PP1610*, I, pp. 257–85, see especially pp. 263–70; cf. e.g. *PP1610*, II, p. 17. See also Charles Gibbon, *The order of eqvalitie: contrived and divulged as a generall directorie for common sessements* (Cambridge, 1604), pp. 13, 31. For a similar argument in Italy, see Nederman 1993, pp. 512–13.

Contractarian and legal accounts were invoked in the House of Commons to oppose the ascendancy of absolutist interpretation, but both of these traditions defined the subject's role in essentially negative terms. In the natural law tradition, the chief way of speaking about the subject was to define him as possessing liberty, or right in property. A similar assumption underlay arguments based on the ancient constitution. The common law secured both the king's prerogative and the subject's liberty. In Jacobean England these two arguments often appeared together as in George More's traditional advice-book for Prince Henry in 1611. In the time-honoured manner, More entreated the young heir to embrace all the princely virtues like justice, constancy, liberality, learning, religious feeling and clemency and to avoid the opposite vices. The prince should also win and maintain his subjects' love by averting from 'Matchevils principle', according to which, 'the subjects must be made poore by continuall subsidies, exactions, and impositions, [so] that the people may be alwaies kept under as slaves, & feare the Prince'.[11]

More's case of resisting the exaction of subsidies and impositions rested not only on principles of prudence but also on more theoretical underpinning. Enquiring into the inception of political society, he pointed out that a kingdom was established 'by the people'. He embraced the contractarian view that sovereignty had originally resided in the people, and by their consent and choice authority had been conferred on the king. This original contract imposed strict limits upon the royal authority, for the king could neither change the laws of the commonwealth nor take his subjects' property without their expressed consent. 'And as the head of the Physicall body', More taught the would-be king, 'cannot change the reynes and sinewes thereof, nor deny the members of their proper strength & necessary nurriture: no more can a king (who is head of the politicke body) alter or change the laws of that body, or take from the people their goods or substance against their wils.' More coupled this analysis with a more insular interpretation of the ancient constitution. When 'Brute' had arrived 'in this Iland with his Trojans', he had erected 'regall and politicke government' which had been kept inviolate ever since. Although More confessed that 'wee have had many changes', most recently the coming of the Normans, 'yet in the time of all these Nations, & during their

[11] George More, *Principles for yong princes: collected out of sundry authors* (London, 1611), fo. 69ʳ.

raignes, the kingdome was for the most part governed in this same manner that it is now'.[12]

In More's vision, the authority of the king was thus clearly limited. It was confined by the original contract as well as the immemorial custom which defined England as having 'regall and politicke government'. But in so far as the subject was concerned, his role was not one of an active citizen; the original contract and the ancient custom simply secured his absolute property in his goods and land. When the issue of impositions surfaced in Jacobean parliaments, it was essentially these arguments to which the king's opponents resorted. The liberty of the subject tended to be equated with his right in property which was safeguarded by the ancient constitution. This line of reasoning emerges clearly in Nicholas Fuller's speech in opposition to the king's right of impositions in parliament in June 1610. He constructed his account as an argument 'for the freedom of the subject'. The pivotal point was that 'the laws of England are the most high inheritance of the land' and they defined as well as directed both the king and his subjects. The law preserved subjects' 'right and liberty' 'in their lands and goods' and in 'lawful and free trades'.[13]

To conceal the fundamental disagreements between absolutists and their opponents, these arguments were often presented in the 'rhetoric of reconciliation': there was an intimate link between the king's authority and the people's liberty defined by a balanced constitution.[14] This vocabulary was used by the defenders of the king's claims. 'The King's Sovereignty and the Liberty of Parliament', Francis Bacon told a committee of the House of Commons in 1610 in a highly revealing passage, 'are as the two elements and principles of this estate; which though the one be more active the other more passive, yet they do not cross or destroy the one the other, but they strengthen and maintain the one the other ... And herein it is our happiness that we may make the same judgement of the King which Tacitus made of Nerva. *Divus Nerva res olim dissociabiles miscuit, Imperiam et Libertatem*. Nerva did temper things that before were thought incompatible or insociable, Sovereignty

---

[12] More, *Principles for yong princes*, fos. 1ʳ–2ᵛ. Cf. e.g. Richard Middleton, *The carde and compasse of life: containing many passages, fit for these times* (London, 1613), pp. 62, 231, 235–6. Middleton wrote that the prince ought 'to governe and defend the Common-wealth, according to the prescript of the Lawes: therefore is infinite power not to be ascribed to him'.

[13] *PP1610*, II, p. 152. Cf. the interesting discussion of the concept of liberty in Thomas Palmer, *An essay of the meanes how to make our trauailes, into forraine countries, the more profitable and honourable* (London, 1606), pp. 69–70, 117–18.

[14] Sommerville 1986, pp. 134–7; cf. e.g. Hirst 1981; Hirst 1985, p. 124.

and Liberty.'[15] The same vocabulary played hardly less important a role in the arguments of anti-absolutists. Exactly the same quotation from Tacitus was employed a few weeks later by Thomas Hedley in his argument against the king's authority of impositions.[16]

II

Although these modes of thought have customarily been seen as having eclipsed all other patterns of political discourse, some aspects of the Machiavellian vocabulary are generally acknowledged to be found in the court. The court, as Pocock has aptly reminded us, was a world of particularity to which every courtier reacted by employing his particular talents – his virtues.[17] These accounts of the courtier's life have often been seen as a new development in the humanist tradition, where Cicero was replaced by Tacitus as the chief Roman author. This Tacitean interpretation accepted to a certain extent the king's authority as natural, but depicted at the same time the courtly universe as a restless and dangerous world. Although Tacitus' scathing criticism of Roman emperors could yield support to the cause of republicanism, he was most often interpreted as a Machiavellian exponent of reason of state. This interpretation linked Tacitus with scepticism and specifically with a particular kind of stoicism – often, though not entirely accurately, labelled as neostoicism. Tacitus, moreover, came to be linked with Seneca, the outcome of which was an ethic of fortitude and endurance.[18]

There is little doubt that this mode of thought also gained a strong foothold in England. Tacitus' *Histories* (translated by Henry Savile) were first printed in English in 1591 and reprinted in 1598,[19] when the first edition of his *Annals* (translated by Richard Greneway) was also issued (reprinted 1604, 1612, 1622, 1640). Tacitus' terse prose style became, as is well known, a model for those who were critical of the

---

[15] Bacon in parliament 19 May 1610, in *Letters*, IV, p. 177. Cf. *PP1610*, II, p. 98. The Tacitus quotation appeared already in Bacon's *Advancement of learning* (1605), in *Works*, III, p. 303; see also Bacon in parliament 7 July 1610, in *Letters*, IV, p. 202. Tacitus, *Agricola*, 3.

[16] *PP1610*, II, p. 191; cf. e.g. John Davies, *Le primer report des cases & matters en ley resolues & adiudges en les courts del roy en Ireland* (Dublin, 1615) sig. *2ᵛ.

[17] Pocock 1975b, pp. 350–1.

[18] See e.g. Burke 1969; Tuck 1989, p. 65. There is a vast literature devoted to the rise of Tacitean themes in the European context. For particularly lucid analyses, see Salmon 1980; Tuck 1993. For an interesting discussion of 'pragmatic humanism', see Grafton and Jardine 1986, pp. 161–200.

[19] See Womersley 1991; Smuts 1994, especially pp. 30, 40.

Ciceronian style.[20] More important was his currency in his own field; the growing popularity of 'politic history' with its concern with causes and motives has often been ascribed to the impact of Tacitus' historical writings.[21] Perhaps the most important aspects of 'Tacitism' were, however, those of politics and ethics.[22] The popularity of Tacitus gave rise to a distinct genre of political writing – commentaries or essays written around one sentence or passage from Tacitus.[23] Isaac Bargrave claimed in 1624 that 'Tacitus' has become politicians' 'Bible' and that there were 'more Commenters upon him than upon Saint Paul'.[24]

Alongside Tacitus, a number of the continental moral and political treatises of this tradition were translated into English. Justus Lipsius' *Two bookes of constancie* and *Sixe bookes of politickes* appeared in 1594; Guillaume Du Vair's stoic *The moral philosophie of the stoicks* and *A bvckler against adversitie* were issued in 1598 and 1622 respectively; Michel de Montaigne's *Essayes* were printed in 1603; Pierre Charron's *Of wisdome* appeared some time before 1612. Perhaps the most important of these translations, Thomas Lodge's English version of Seneca's prose works was published in 1614 (reprinted 1620), and has recently been described as 'a monument to the Jacobean Neostoic cult'.[25]

Tacitus was employed, in the first place, to point out that the Ciceronian ideal was lofty yet forlorn and that although the consolidation of Octavian's authority had been grounded on the exploitation of deceit, dissimulation and trickery, it had, nevertheless, been the only real choice in the corrupt world. Philip Sidney had already noted that Tacitus excelled 'in the pithy opening the venome of wickednes', and Gabriel Harvey thought it to be Tiberius' 'brave quality and most suttle property' that he 'altogither fayned to do that, which he meant not to do: and not to do that which in deade he meant to do'.[26] Joseph Wybarne explained in *The new age of old names* (published in 1609) the means which Augustus had used to keep 'the Senate in a perpetuall honourable bondage'. He had 'appointed triumphall ornaments for victorious Senators, still reserving the triumph it selfe, for himselfe, and

[20] E.g. Burke 1966; Burke 1969, pp. 151–3.
[21] Levy 1967, pp. 237–85; Levy 1987; Goldberg 1955; Burke 1966; Burke 1969, pp. 153–5. See e.g. Tacitus, *The annales*, translated by Richard Greneway (London, 1598), sig. ¶2ʳ.
[22] See Salmon 1989; Tenney 1941; Bradford 1983; Schellhase 1976, pp. 157–68.
[23] Burke 1969, p. 162; Burke 1991, pp. 484–90.
[24] Isaac Bargrave, *A sermon against selfe policy* (London, 1624), p. 32.
[25] Salmon 1989, p. 199.
[26] Philip Sidney to Robert Sidney, 18 October 1580, in Philip Sidney, *Complete Works*, 4 vols., ed. Albert Feuillerat (Cambridge University Press, 1922–6), III, p. 132. Gabriel Harvey, *Marginalia*, ed. G. C. Moore Smith (Stratford: Shakespeare Head Press, 1913), p. 143.

his successors; and so [had] played with the Romanes, as vermine doe with poultry, sucking the best blood, and leaving the refuse for all commers'. Wybarne believed that Tiberius had learned 'his plot-forme from Augustus'. Their common method had been that 'the name be as little changed as may bee, though the thing bee altered'.[27]

This theme was developed in an anonymous treatise, *Horae subseciuae*, published in 1620 and now thought to have been written partly by William Cavendish and partly by his tutor, Thomas Hobbes.[28] The discussion occurs in a lengthy 'Discourse upon the beginnning of Tacitus', attributed to Hobbes. After a brief introduction, where the 'accidentall' nature of 'the first forme of government in any State' was emphasized and the earlier constitutional history of Rome briefly rehearsed, the author explained how the constitutional development of Rome after the expulsion of the kings had been totally unsteady. The people 'grew perplexed at every inconvenience, and shifted from one forme of government to another, and so to another, and then to the first againe; like a man in a fewer'. The chief reason for this wavering situation had been the rivalry between the commons and the nobles: 'For on whomsoever the commons conferred the supreme authority, the Senate and Nobility still gained in all suites and offices to be preferred before them, which was the cause of most of the seditions and alterations of the State.' The Roman people had soon realized that although it had been necessary to trust the defence of their liberty to someone, at the same time the power had corrupted those in authority, and they had quickly turned against the people and their liberty. 'But indeed the thing they most feared, was, that they saw those who possessed the power for the present, would not give it over, but sought to make it personall, and perpetuate it to themselves.' The Romans were faced with a dilemma for they 'were jealous of their liberty, and knewe not in whose hands to trust it, and were often at the point to lose it'.[29]

Instead of explicating the means whereby corruption might be staved off by limiting the power of those in authority, the author simply

27 Joseph Wybarne, *The new age of old names* (London, 1609), pp. 15–17, 78. Wybarne was also disposed to endorse scepticism, pp. 10–11.
28 Reynolds and Hilton 1993; see also Malcolm 1981. For an account of the arguments of the *Horae subseciuae*, see Saxonhouse 1981. Other English examples of the commentary-style include Robert Dallington, *Aphorismes civill and militarie: amplified with authorities, and exemplified with historie, out of the first quarterne of Fr Guicciardine* (London, 1613). Thomas Gainsford wrote a similar treatise, which remained in manuscript, see Salmon 1989, p. 217.
29 Anon., *Horae subseciuae: observations and discovrses* (London, 1620), pp. 229–34. Cf. Henry Wright, *The first part of the disquisition of truth concerning political affaires* (London, 1616), pp. 45–6.

explained how the constitutional situation in Rome had ultimately led to the consolidation of Octavian's authority. Although Octavian had taken 'upon him the Monarchy by force', he had so settled it that he had afterwards possessed it quietly and 'the State could never recover liberty'.[30] The occasion for Octavian had been offered by civil wars, for they commonly exposed 'a State to the prey of ambitious men'. Finally, the author gave considerable space to a detailed explanation of the ways in which Octavian had safeguarded his acquisition by carefully employing various methods of dissimulation.[31]

This kind of analysis could serve to explain the ultimate necessity for monarchical rule. But Tacitus' writing was a double-edged sword, as attested by James's aversion to 'Tacitism'.[32] A chief way in which Tacitus was used in English political and moral discourse was, however, to link him with Seneca and to lay a particular emphasis on the values of scepticism, private prudence and withdrawal.[33] An apposite example is provided by Fulke Greville who asserted in his *Treatise of monarchy* that monarchy was the best form of government: the king's authority guaranteed the public good, and even if a king would degenerate into a tyrant, the people must not resist him. But scholars have detected more equivocal aspects from the work: a nostalgia for a golden age before monarchy had been established; a belief that the king was no longer enforcing eternal laws but, like a tyrant, practising a statecraft.[34] And yet, as David Norbrook has also emphasized, 'all of Greville's writings come down on the side of obedience and resignation'. Greville contrasted 'those active times and the narrow salves of this effeminate age'. Since the decline of every state was inevitable,

> Soe may grave and great men of estate,
> In such despaired tymes, retire away,
> And yeild the sterne of government to fate.[35]

---

[30] Anon., *Horae subseciuae*, pp. 234–5.
[31] Ibid., pp. 237–42, 249–83. See also e.g. William Cornwallis, *Discovrses vpon Seneca the tragedian* (London, 1601), sig. A1ᵛ, A4ʳ, A5ᵛ, A6ʳ⁻ᵛ.
[32] Bradford 1983; see in general Pocock 1985a, p. 292.
[33] Salmon 1989, especially p. 224. In what follows, I am particularly indebted to this account. See Smuts 1994; Monsarrat 1984, pp. 81–125; Norbrook 1984, pp. 171–4, 182–3; Tuck 1989, p. 65.
[34] Pocock 1975b, pp. 352–3; Norbrook 1984, pp. 160–70.
[35] Greville, *A dedication*, in *The prose works*, p. 7; *Treatise of monarchy*, stanza 108, lines 1–3, in *The remains*, p. 62.

England managed to avoid a civil war,[36] but the political world of the early seventeenth century offered ample opportunities to describe it in terms of flattery and servility, hypocrisy and dissimulation. The court in particular was denounced as a place of vices and corruption. According to Francis Bacon, the court abounded with men whose 'Art' made 'a flourishing estate ruinous & distressed' but who could at the same time 'fiddell very cunningly' and gain 'both satisfaction with their Masters, and admiration with the vulgar'.[37] The court was regarded as completely devoid of virtues. 'The Courtier', Thomas Gainsford defined, 'that is all for shew and complement, is the onely professor of humanitie, master of curtesie, vaine promiser, idle protester, servant of folly, and scholler of deceit.' Nobody should be so foolish as to trust a courtier, for, in a word, 'he neither performeth, what hee commonly sweares, nor remembers in absence, what hee hath formerly protested: so that his oaths and words are like smoake and aire: and his deeds and actions meerly shadowes, and farre from substance'.[38] According to Henry Wright, the court was a place where 'all credit, countenance, honors, and authority' were 'for the most part slippery, and not to be trusted unto'.[39]

The analysis of corruption was often based on the history of imperial Rome. Tacitus' excellence, Richard Brathwait wrote, derived from the fact that he offered 'a dilated compendiary of many declined States, disunited Provinces' and he showed 'the vices of the time, where it was dangerous to be Vertuous, and where Innocence tasted the sharpest censure'. He taught 'men in high estates how to moderate their Greatnesse', but 'others of inferior ranke' could gather from him that it was worthwhile 'rather to live retired, then to purchase eminence in place by servile meanes'.[40] Describing the flattery, dissimulation and corruption of his age, Anthony Stafford made extensive use of Seneca

---

36   John Hitchcock discussed rebellion and civil war in *A sanctvary for honest men: or an abstract of human wisdome* (London, 1617), pp. 120–3, arguing that there were two options open for private persons: 'if they bee men of publike charge and credit they ought to joyn themselves to the better part', but 'if they be private men of a lower degree the best way is to retire themselves to some peaceable and secure place'.

37   Bacon, *Essaies* (1612), in *Works*, VI, p. 587. See also William Covell, *Polimanteia: or, the meanes lawfull and vnlawfull, to ivdge of the fall of a common-wealth* (Cambridge, 1595), sigs. ()3ʳ, D4ᵛ, S1ᵛ; Cornwallis, *Discovrses*, sig. B4ʳ–5ᵛ.

38   [Thomas Gainsford], *The rich cabinet furnished with varietie of excellent discriptions* (London, 1616), fos. 18ᵛ–19ʳ, in general fos. 18ᵛ–21ʳ. Cf. e.g. Robert Dallington, *Aphorismes*, pp. 104–5, 224; Thomas Churchyard, *A pleasant discourse of court and wars* (London, 1596), sig. A3ᵛ–4ᵛ.

39   Wright, *The first part*, pp. 19–20.

40   Richard Brathwait, *The schollers medley: or an intermixt discovrse vpon historicall and poeticall relations* (London, 1614), pp. 10, 13–14; idem, *A survey of history: or, a nursery for gentry* (London, 1638), pp. 38, 50–1; cf. in general idem, *Essaies vpon five senses* (London, 1620); idem, *The golden fleece*

and Tacitus. In England 'more is acted' than 'Machiavell' ever invented, for 'hee was the Theorick: these men for the Practique'. According to Stafford, Tacitus' saying that 'vertues ... are rewarded with certaine destruction' was particularly true in his own age.[41]

One course of reaction to this analysis was to attempt to accommodate behaviour to meet the circumstances. This idea was adopted in a treatise, *Ars avlica or the courtiers arte*, written by Lorenzo Ducci and rendered into English by Edmund Blount in 1607. The courtier served 'his Lord', but this was but a means to the ulterior and 'more principall' goal of 'his owne profit'. When he proceeded to offer a detailed account of *Ars avlica*, Ducci drew much of his material from Tacitus, 'an excellent Master of Courtiers'.[42] A similar attempt was made by Francis Bacon in the *Advancement of learning* where he developed a discipline, the 'architecture of fortune', which formed a part of civil knowledge. Its chief doctrine was 'to teach men how to raise and make their fortune'.[43] According to Isaac Bargrave, all the 'Maximes of State' in Tacitus' commentaries were 'squared by the master-rule of Selfe-Interest'.[44]

Another typical Tacitean reaction to the issues of corruption was the one of retirement. Both Lipsius and Du Vair taught that too strong an affection for the patria was dangerous; one must simply endure the times of troubles, remain steadfast in the face of abrupt changes of fortune and keep aloof from public life.[45] Gabriel Harvey placed a

---

(London, 1611). Cf. Robert Johnson, *Essaies: or rather imperfect offers* (London, 1607), sigs. c8ᵛ–D4ᵛ. It is, however, worth pointing out that despite his admiration for Tacitus, Brathwait held Livy and Sallust in scarcely less high esteem; for Livy, see *A survey of history*, pp. 347–51, for Sallust, see *The schollers medley*, pp. 15–16, and especially p. 94.

[41] Anthony Stafford, *Staffords Niobe: or his age of teares* (London, 1611), especially pp. 5–19, 21–3, 106, 184–5, 191.

[42] Leonardo Ducci, *Ars avlica or the courtiers arte*, translated by [Edmund Blount] (London, 1607), pp. 1–2, 9–10, 15–17, 33; cf. sig. A8ʳ⁻ᵛ; Wright, *The first part*, pp. 19–21, 51–2, 32–3; cf. Remigio Nannini, *Civill considerations vpon many and sundrie histories*, translated from French by W. T[raheron] (London, 1601); Francesco Sansovino, *The quintesence of wit*, translated by Robert Hitchcock (London, 1590); Eustache Du Refuge, *A treatise of the court: or instructions for courtiers*, translated by John Reynolds (London, 1622).

[43] Bacon, *Advancement of learning*, in *Works*, III, pp. 447–73, *Essaies* (1612), in *Works*, VI, pp. 574–5, 550, 549; idem, *Essayes*, pp. 33, 36, 42, and especially pp. 122–4. Cf. Cochrane 1958. See Burke 1969, pp. 156–62, for the Tacitean leanings of this kind of enterprise. For Bacon's admiration for Tacitus, see *Temporis partus masculus*, in *Works*, III, p. 538. Cf. Benjamin 1965; Dean 1941, pp. 172–3; Croll 1971; Berry 1971. See also D[aniel] T[uvill], *The dove and the serpent* (London, 1614), especially pp. 16, 22. For a different interpretation, see Warhaft 1971, pp. 52–3.

[44] Bargrave, *A sermon against selfe policy*, pp. 32–3.

[45] Justus Lipsius, *Two bookes of constancie* (1594), translated by John Stradling, ed. Rudolf Kirk (New Brunswick: Rutgers University Press, 1939), pp. 89–98; Guillaume Du Vair, *A buckler against adversitie: or a treatise of constancie*, translated by Andrew Court (London, 1622), pp. 19–20, 25, 32; idem, *The moral philosophie of the stoicks*, translated by T[homas] J[ames] (London, 1598), pp. 127–9. See also e.g. van Gelderen 1990, p. 208; Oestreich 1982, p. 29; Burke 1991, pp. 491–7.

strong emphasis on the active life, but he also called patience 'an excellent quality' and named 'Constancy' as 'the honorablist Vertue of all Vertues'. Robert Dallington explained that everyone ought to be carefully prepared for sudden change. 'But the resolved man,' he wrote, 'is ever the same, in the period of both fortunes'.[46] In his translation of Seneca, Thomas Lodge advised his reader that he could find in the volume, 'how much thou hast lost in life in begetting vanities and nourishing them, in applauding follies, and intending them'. From this the reader was supposed to infer that 'no time is better spent' than that spent in studying 'how to live, and how to die wel'. Seneca taught that 'to be truely vertuous is to be happy, to subdue passion is to be truely a man ... to live well is to be vertuous, and to die well is the way to eternitie'.[47] Having condemned 'the Jesuites positions', as well as the doctrine held by 'Buchanan and the fayned Junius Brutus' that a tyrant could be resisted, Christopher White emphasized: 'There is no defensive resistance allowed, unlesse thy defence be such, (as Livie only allots to subiects) ... the buckler of patience.'[48]

A similar conclusion was drawn from Tacitus' *Annals* in 'A discourse upon the beginning of Tacitus' of the *Horae subseciuae*, attributed to Hobbes. Whilst virtues of 'deepe wisedome and great, and extraordinary valour' had flourished in republican Rome and generally 'in a free State', the virtue which had acquired prominence in imperial Rome and which had always been 'the greatest vertue' of 'the subject of a Monarch' was 'obedience'. Showing the point of contact of royal absolutism and the Tacitean tradition, the author argued that a prince's subject did not need to possess those virtues which were vital for 'the Art of commanding'. He ought to either lead the life of retirement or apply himself to 'the Art of service', where 'obsequiousnesse' was the chief virtue.[49]

Since the contemporary world was conceived as a place full of decay, deceit and flattery, it was empty of active virtue and the best one could do was to express serene admiration for the great achievements of former ages whilst concentrating oneself on more passive qualities. 'Rise, Sidney, rise:' wrote Anthony Stafford a quarter of a century after

[46] Harvey, *Marginalia*, p. 157; Dallington *Aphorismes*, pp. 115, 64–5, 137–8, 172; Johnson, *Essaies*, sigs. BI^r–4^v, G4^r, G6^v.

[47] *The workes of Lucius Annaeus Seneca, both morrall and naturall*, translated by Thomas Lodge (London, 1614), sig. [xxi^{r-v}]. Cf. William Cornwallis, *Essayes* (1606–10), ed. Don Cameron Allen (Baltimore: John Hopkins University Press, 1946), pp. 167–73.

[48] White, *A sermon*, p. 29.

[49] Anon., *Horae subseciuae*, pp. 305–17.

Philip Sidney's death, 'thou Englands eternall honour, revive, and leade the revolting spirits of thy countrey-men, against the soules basest foe, Ignorance.'[50] But as to his own times, Stafford advocated the contemplative life: the qualities of fortitude, steadfastness and resolution – the extreme suppression of emotions – were the chief characteristics of virtue. In his treatise, *Staffords heauenly dogge* – a biography of Diogenes – he promised to treat 'a strange, inimitable man, who had nothing, yet never knew adversity'. 'The cruell effects of Fortunes malice' had not made Diogenes 'change his minde, nor his countenance.'[51] Stafford combined this stoicism with academic scepticism. Because of his 'wandring ambitious spirit', man had sought to know more with the contrary result that he had come 'to know lesse'. 'All that miserable man now knowes,' Stafford declared, 'is, that hee knowes nothing.'[52] Diogenes' qualities made him the epitome of Stafford's ideal man. 'Vertue', Stafford explained, 'never tooke a deeper root in any mind, then in that of Diogenes.' But this was not the virtue of the active life; rather it was that of a private life, providing proof 'to abide the battery of Fortune'. Stafford was careful to point out that Diogenes was 'no Statist', nor even a citizen of any town 'but of the world', and he therefore excluded prudence and justice from his discussion, focusing his attention on such virtues as temperance, modesty and patience.[53] When Sir John Holles feared that his patron's (Robert Carr, earl of Somerset) fall could jeopardise his own safety, he complained that 'too late I find ... Tacitus his opinion confirmed, that safety dwelleth not in doing well or ill, but in doing nothing'.[54]

The case for the life of retirement was also explored by Thomas Gainsford, Owen Felltham and Joseph Hall. 'The safest way to live under tyrants', Gainsford argued, 'is to do nothing, because of nothing no man is to yield an account.'[55] Felltham, likewise, pointed out that 'retirednesse is more safe then businesse'.[56] Perhaps the fullest account of the *vita contemplativa* was offered by 'the English

50 Stafford, *Staffords Niobe*, pp. 112–7.
51 Anthony Stafford, *Staffords heauenly dogge: or the life, and death of that great cynicke Diogenes* (London, 1615), sig. A5^{r-v}.
52 Ibid., pp. 2–4, 22.
53 Ibid., pp. 20, 26–31, 55. See in general Anon., *The treasure of tranquillity: or a manvall of morall discourses, tending to the tranquillity of minde*, translated by James Maxwell (London, 1611).
54 Cited in Smuts 1994, p. 35.
55 Cited in Salmon 1989, pp. 218–19, see in general pp. 217–19.
56 Owen Felltham, *Resolues diuine, morall, politicall* (London, [1623]), pp. 218–19. See also Anon., *A twofold treatise, the one decyphering the worth of speculation, and of a retired life. The other containing a discouerie of youth and old age* (Oxford, 1612), sig. A2^{v}–3^{r}, A4^{v}–5^{r}, A6^{r}, A10^{v}.

Seneca' – Joseph Hall. In his numerous writings he placed strong
emphasis on the stoic values of forbearance and constancy; every
passion ought to be suppressed, death should not be feared.[57] The
chief moral to be learned from these values was that the only way to
avoid the excess of perturbations was to live 'as a looker on'. It
belonged to the accomplishments of the wise man to seek 'his
quietnesse in secrecy' and 'to hide himselfe in retirednesse'. He
ought to confine himself 'in the circle of his owne affaires'. A man
could be called happy, when he 'knows the world, and cares not for
it', when he 'lives quietly at home, out of the noise of the world'. It
was an obvious sign of 'the inconstancy and lazinesse of the minde'
to be employed 'in some publike affaires'.[58] The private life had two
obvious advantages. First, it enabled man to devote himself to 'the
gaine of knowledge in the deepe mysteries of Nature'. But more
importantly, it gave him freedom 'from the common cares, from the
infection of common evils'. Whether it was a question of international politics – 'whether the Spaniard gaine or save by his peace [in
the Netherlands] ... whether Venice have won or lost by her late
jarres' – or one of the court intrigues – 'who is envied, and who
pitied at Court' – none of these purposeless problems dared to enter
'into the philosophicall Cell'.[59]

These issues form a central theme in Ben Jonson's first Roman play,
Sejanus (1603). Jonson depicted imperial Rome as a place of total
corruption. Sejanus and his clients 'corrupt the times' with their 'filthier
flatteries', argued Sabinus, whilst Arruntius pointed out that the decay
was prompted by the corrosion of the morality of the Romans: rather
than pursuing the good of their commonwealth, men attempted to
advance their own careers. When Silius was accused in the senate, he
declared that his only crime was his moral character; he found himself
'Too honest for the times'.[60]

Corruption manifested itself most clearly at the imperial court.
Those who wanted to make rapid advancement at court had to give
short shrift to issues of morality and instead be ready to do whatever
was necessary for achieving their goal. They should

---

[57] E.g. Joseph Hall, *Characters of vertues and vices* (1608), in *The works of Joseph Hall* (London, 1647),
      pp. 155, 158. For Hall's cognomen, see Monsarrat 1984, pp. 98–100.
[58] Hall, *Characters of vertues and vices*, pp. 155, 157–8. 163; *Heaven upon earth* (1606), in *Works*,
      pp. 66–7.
[59] Hall, *Epistles in six decads*, in *Works*, pp. 270–1.
[60] *Sejanus*, III.168.

Laugh, when their patron laughs; sweat when he sweats;
Be hot, and cold with him; change every mood,
Habit and garb, as often as he varies.

The effectiveness of these methods was most convincingly demonstrated by Macro who declared that 'The way to rise, is to obey, and
please' and who therefore ultimately displaced Sejanus as Tiberius'
chief favourite.[61]

Silius, Sabinus and Arruntius, three Roman nobles who expressed
their disgust for the Tiberian world of corruption, servility and tyranny,
contrasted this period with the healthy commonwealth of previous
ages. Silius argued that although he and his contemporaries had been
born 'Free, equal lords of the triumphed world', they had since become
'the slaves to one man's lusts'.[62] Whereas heretofore every dignity,
including consulship, had been conferred by 'Rome's general suffrage',
in Tiberius' reign they were all for sale.[63] According to Arruntius, all
the republican heroes such as Cato, Brutus and Cassius ('the last of all
that race') had simply 'fled the light'.[64] Arruntius could do nothing but
concur with Lepidius' claim that

the times are sore,
When virtue cannot safely be advanced;
Nor vice reproved.[65]

Unsurprisingly, Sejanus wanted to destroy the historian Cordus since
by praising 'the old liberty', he 'doth tax the present state'.[66]

Despite the contrast between Tiberian corruption and the healthy
republican past, *Sejanus* is pessimistic because those who despised
Tiberius' reign found the reformation of the commonwealth impossible. If a man was not ready for the unscrupulous advancement of his
career, the only option left for him was the life of retirement. When
Latiaris argued that old liberty could be revived by 'active valour',
Sabinus retorted that 'A good man should, and must / Sit rather down
with loss, than rise unjust.'[67] The virtuous senators, lamented Arruntius, had become 'the good-dull-noble lookers-on'.[68] The active values

[61] Ibid., 1.33–5, III.735.
[62] Ibid., 1.60, 63.
[63] Ibid., 1.223.
[64] Ibid., 1.97, 104.
[65] Ibid., III.481–3.
[66] Ibid., II.312, 308.
[67] Ibid., IV.157, 165–6.
[68] Ibid., III.16.

of a 'good patriot' had been replaced by the passive values of preservation and survival:

> Arts, Arruntius?
> None, but the plain and passive fortitude,
> To suffer, and be silent; never stretch
> These arms against the torrent; live at home,
> With my own thoughts, and innocence about me,
> Not tempting the wolves' jaws: and these are my arts.[69]

It is hardly surprising that *Sejanus* got Jonson into trouble with the authorities.[70]

Partly the challenge of absolutist vocabulary but mainly the ascendancy of these Tacitean aspects has led some scholars to see the turn of the century as a decisive point in humanist political discourse. 'By the end of the [sixteenth] century', we are told, 'the dominance of Cicero was over', and the older humanism had comprehensively been replaced by 'a wholly new kind of humanism', with Tacitus playing the central role. The chief ingredients of this new moral outlook were ethical scepticism, the stoic attempt to enter into a state of apathy, as well as the principles of self-interest and self-preservation.[71] As far as England is concerned, there is little doubt that after surfacing in the 1590s this kind of vocabulary acquired popularity in Jacobean court circles and that many an author, as we have briefly indicated above, was preoccupied with these themes. It is clear, however, that neither the growth of royal absolutism, nor the legal accounts of the freedoms of the Englishman, invoked to meet the challenge of absolutists, nor even Tacitean pessimism and its related insistence on the merits of the contemplative and private life, could completely outweigh traditional Ciceronian humanism and its urging of the merits of the active life. But rather than seeing these new emphases, somewhat misleadingly, as the antithesis of classical Ciceronian humanism, such emphases should be interpreted as a part of the humanist political vocabulary. New genres as well as new features – reason of state, dissimulation, scepticism and the neostoic idea of self-preservation – were introduced into humanist political parlance, but these novelties could hardly be said to have

---

[69] Ibid., iv.293–8. Cf. Maus 1984, p. 36.
[70] Maus 1984, pp. 36–7. For an admirable analysis of these themes in *Sejanus*, see now Worden 1994.
[71] Tuck 1993, chapters 2 and 3; Tuck 1990, pp. 63–5, Tuck 1989, pp. 6–11; cf. Tuck 1987, pp. 108–19; Tuck 1983; Levy 1986; Baldwin 1944 ii, pp. 589–90.

completely undermined the older values of the active life, true nobility and cardinal virtues.[72]

Tacitus was not the only Roman historian whose works were published in English at the turn of the century. Philemon Holland's translation of Livy appeared in 1600 and of Plutarch's *Morals* in 1603. Sallust's *The conspiracy of Catiline* and *The Jugurthine war* were issued in 1608. Many of the Tacitean treatises contained numerous traditional elements of Ciceronian humanism. It was 'civil life' attained by virtues which formed Lipsius' chief aim in the *Sixe bookes of politickes*.[73] The same values of the virtuous active life permeated Du Vair's *A bvckler against adversitie*, so much so that, according to the translator, Andrew Court, 'vertue' was 'the maine pillars of civill life and humane societie'.[74] On the other hand, Gabriel Harvey, who is often regarded as a prime example of new pragmatic humanism and who admired Tacitus, also admired Livy and especially Cicero, endorsing, as we have seen, some of the central values of Ciceronian humanism. But he also extolled Cicero's letters to Atticus for their value in politics as well as in 'everyday life'.[75] Moreover, as we shall see, many of the English authors who developed Tacitean themes were ready to endorse the central convictions of classical Ciceronian humanism. To the extent that some scholars have demonstrated the appeal of Tacitean tendencies among court circles, their works have made a valuable contribution to our knowledge about the depth and width of the neostoic moral outlook in early-seventeenth-century England and an important reconstruction of a proper intellectual context for some of the great seventeenth-century contributions to political theory. But to the extent that they have regarded this neostoic and Tacitean movement as entirely superseding the old Ciceronian humanism, hence failing to detect the continuity of Ciceronian values, they have oversimplified the issue. As a matter of fact, it can be argued that some of the early-

---

[72] It should be pointed out that Peter Miller has recently shown that the role of Cicero's moral and political writings in shaping the new vocabulary of reason of state was more prominent than the dominant account allows. Cicero was used alongside Tacitus as an authority for the extreme measures that the preservation of the community demanded. It was above all Cicero's ambiguous discussion of the *honestum* and *utile* which provided respectable support for an argument that the pursuit of the public good justified overstepping the bounds of law. Miller 1994, chapter 1, especially pp. 21–8, 50–1, 57–9.

[73] Justus Lipsius, *Sixe bookes of politickes or civil doctrine*, translated by William Jones (London, 1594), e.g. p. 1; see also van Gelderen 1990, pp. 206–10; Grafton and Jardine 1986, pp. 197–9.

[74] Du Vair, *A bvckler against adversitie*, p. 115.

[75] Gabriel Harvey, *Marginalia*, pp. 122, 133–4. For Harvey's admiration for Tacitus and Livy, see Stern 1979, p. 151.

seventeenth-century moral and political treatises in England are best
interpreted as classical humanist responses to the absolutists' claims as
well as to the challenge of the sceptics and pessimists. In order to fully
appreciate not only the extent of the challenge issued by the advocates
of the private life and the sceptics, but also the nature of the attempts
to meet this challenge, we can do worse than to begin with those
authors who were quite outspoken in their criticism.

III

In 1619, an anonymous tract entitled *The covrt of the most illvstrious and
most magnificent James, the first* was published. The author, 'A. D. B.', was
a foreigner residing at the English court[76] and was preoccupied with
presenting rules for the conduct of a courtier. He had, he told his
readers, resolved 'to divulge and set forth unto publike view, somewhat
concerning the life of a Courtier'. This involved explaining how a
determined courtier could 'wisely and warily' sail 'the deepe of this
difficult and turbulent Sea', how he could escape 'Scylla and Charibdis'
and how he could avoid being 'dasht against the wrath and indignation
of [his] Prince'.[77]

A successful advancement of one's career in the court demanded
several indispensable qualities, and the author offered detailed rules for
a courtier about his apparel, conduct, behaviour and various activities
useful to him.[78] Even more careful attention was paid to the courtier's
behaviour towards his master. The basic rule was that the king's word
was the courtier's law. He should know how to 'carry himselfe in the
change and alteration of a King or Kingdome', and if he 'hath
inconsiderately displeased his Prince'. Above all, he must never
commence anything which is against the king's taste and always know
how to please the king.[79] Furthermore, the courtier should always bear
in mind the true nature of the court – that 'Courts are never empty of
fained friendship'. The courtier's basic course must be to look for 'his
owne well-fare in due time' since, as the author put it, 'every man is the
cause of his owne misery'.[80]

To illustrate his point, the author called attention to the 'most sage

[76]   A. D. B., *The covrt of the most illvstrious and most magnificent James, the first; king of Great Britaine,
       France, and Ireland: &c* (London, 1619), sig. ♠3ʳ.
[77]   Ibid., pp. 1, 4.
[78]   Ibid., pp. 55–6, 110–16.
[79]   Ibid., pp. 60–1, 65–6, 68–9, 97–99.
[80]   Ibid., pp. 67, 146, 153–4, 99–100, 103–4, 105.

Philosopher, and sweet Oratour' who had laid down that 'vertue consists not in words, but in workes'. Although the author could use a Ciceronian maxim to define the courtier's art, he was more prone to appeal to the authority of another Roman author – Tacitus. Life at court was not merely or even chiefly 'a soft, delicate, easie, or calme' life, but was full of dissimulations, infirmities and calamities; everywhere 'full many thornes and thistles doe privily grow up.'[81] In order to describe this darker side of the courtier's pursuits, the author resorted to the Roman historian and claimed that 'wicked and ungodly Courtiers' purchase for themselves 'great power and authority' 'by pretending and counterfeiting the contrary of what they intend'. These courtiers use 'Sejanus as their best tutor and Schoole-maister'. In addition to the rules of dissimulation, Tacitus provided the courtier with the most useful advice of 'Obsequious pliantnesse'. 'By how much the more readie a man is in obsequiousnesse, by so much the sooner shall he be raised to Dignitie and Noblenesse.'[82]

The author dwelt at length on the issues of the architecture of fortune, but it is arguable that his chief polemic lay elsewhere. He pointed out that he had not undertaken the project on his own initiative but had 'urgently [been] solicited thereunto, by the vehement perswasions of some worthy personages, who themselves have observed divers Pamphlets' which had severely castigated the court. The purpose of the tract was mainly to counter those who had offered wholesale criticism of the court. The author scorned 'the perverse petulancie of many Poets, which laid so many odious aspersions upon Courts, as if no vertue had in them any residence'. Because of this belief, these critics retired 'themselves to a certaine unprofitable contemplation, wherein they studie to barke and snarle at the honourable labours and indevours of others, being in themselves absolutely immeritorious'; they held nothing 'more happie, or more blessed then a priuate kind of life, moderated and decorated with the Golden meane and mediocritie'. It was chiefly Seneca, the author believed, who taught 'the tranquillitie and sweete securitie of a Countrey-mans private life'.

The author, in other words, directed his arguments against the exponents of the *vita contemplativa*. The opinions of those who espoused this mode of life had no effect on those who were inclined 'to square their lives and actions, by the rule of true vertue and piety'. Rather than convincing their adversaries, the representatives of the *vita*

---

81 Ibid., p. 10, see also pp. 10–11.
82 Ibid., pp. 91–3, 83; see also pp. 100–1.

contemplativa merely revealed their own insufficiency and incapability of taking 'high action and employment'.[83] It was not the author's purpose 'to discourse of the infelicities or ... the Gay-greivances of a Courtiers life'. Neither did he propose 'to write of the immunities and commodities of the contrarie to this, a private life'. These ends had been accomplished by several other authors. On the contrary, his aim was to offer a defence of the *vita activa*.

He confessed that 'some Courtiers are too immoderately and ambitiously prone, to hunt after honour, preferment, rule and riches, and ... to pleasure and voluptuousnesse'. The inherent malignancy of courtly circles rendered it possible to argue that in fact the retirement of the private life was the most unhazardous way of living. If an aspiring courtier was not prepared 'to endure many evils, inconveniences, and mis-fortunes', it was safest for him to 'forsake the Court, and betake himselfe to a retired and private life'.[84] But it was a foolish mistake to conclude that the whole court and the whole mode of the active life should be condemned. Every way of living – public as well as private – was subject to corruption, and the course of every single life was determined by 'vice or vertue'. The author proposed, therefore, to describe 'certaine rules and precepts of a Courtly and Politicall life'.[85]

The chief aim of a courtier was to be ranked 'amongst the most eminent and illustrious', to be 'esteemed truly noble'.[86] The only way to attain this goal was to remain active; the courtier should always be 'in continuall action'. He should, that is, avoid living 'without employment', since 'this is the meanes to acquire and get a noble name, renowne, and reputation'.[87] Far from yielding to the temptations of the *vita contemplativa*, a courtier ought to strive for the public good through the *vita activa*. Although 'many men, of no meane rancke and qualitie, doe learnedly magnifie, and with much wit dignifie a solitary and private life', the author contended that 'they erre exceedingly, and are in my judgement marveilously mis-taken, which are of opinion, that a private life is in it selfe happie and blessed'. When he turned to the substance of his own argument, he appealed to the authority of Cicero. Following the example of 'divine Plato', 'the most eloquent Orator and excellent Philosopher hath left in writing, in the first Booke of his

83   Ibid., p. 3, sig. ♠3ᵛ–4ʳ, pp. 13–16.
84   Ibid., sig. A1ᵛ–2ʳ, p. 13; see also pp. 13–16.
85   Ibid., sig. A1ʳ–2ᵛ, A4ʳ.
86   Ibid., p. 144.
87   Ibid., pp. 40–1.

Offices that "We are not borne onely to our selves, but our Parents, Countrye, and Friends, doe challenge unto them a part in our being"'. It followed that everyone must avoid 'a private, obscure, and solitary life', because this mode of life was utterly unprofitable, consisting of 'nothing at all beneficiall to the Common-wealth, whereinto, and whereunto they were borne and brought up'. To summarize his whole argument, the anonymous author evoked the authority of Sallust according to whom 'it is a very noble and worthy thing, to doe good to the Common-weale'.[88]

A somewhat more theoretical attempt of a similar nature was made by Francis Bacon. While the anonymous author of *The covrt of James* tried to repudiate those who called the court in question, Bacon had a more philosophical target in mind. He could admire Tacitus and devote a considerable part of his presentation of civil knowledge to the 'architecture of fortune', but he never thought that this was the only, let alone the worthiest, pursuit. Embarking on his doctrine of the architecture of fortune in the *Advancement of learning*, Bacon felt it necessary to justify his undertaking. He admitted that the architecture of fortune was but 'an inferior work' since 'no man's fortune can be an end worthy of his being'. It often happens that 'the worthiest men do abandon their fortune willingly for better respects'. The pursuit of one's own fortune should be but 'an organ of virtue and merit'.[89] Bacon presented an essentially similar argument in the second edition of his *Essayes*, published in 1612. He wrote of the possible discrepancy between the common good and the architecture of fortune since 'extreme lovers of their Countrey, or Masters, were never fortunate'. But personal fortune should never become the chief end of a man's pursuits. Men who were 'great lovers of themselves,' Bacon argued, 'waste the publike'. 'The referring of all to a mans selfe' was 'a desperate evill'.[90] 'The affecting of the Weale of men' Bacon took to be 'the greatest' of all virtues. The only way to justify the architecture of fortune was to take it as an efficacious means of enhancing the public good. 'But power to doe good,' he explained in his essay 'Of great place', 'is the true & lawfull end of aspiring. For good thoughts, (though God accept them) yet towards men are little better then good dreams: except they be put in Act; and that cannot be without power and place; as the vantage & commanding ground.'[91] Bacon turned Ducci's

[88] Ibid., pp. 18–19.
[89] Bacon, *Advancement of learning*, in *Works*, III, p. 456.
[90] Bacon, *Essaies* (1612), in *Works*, VI, pp. 574, 561–2.
[91] Ibid., pp. 545, 550.

argument upside down: the pursuit of the architecture of fortune was but a means to the more valuable aim of the good of the commonwealth.

In assessing the role of moral and civil philosophy, Bacon put forward a fully fledged Ciceronian account of the birth of civil society. Using 'persuasion and eloquence', philosophy had induced men to embrace 'the love of virtue and equity and peace', taught them 'to assemble and unite and take upon them the yoke of laws and submit to authority', and provided them, in short, with the wherewithal to build homes, till the soil and found cities.[92] When he discussed the questions of ethics in the *Advancement of learning*, his analysis was grounded on the same tradition. He began by taking pains to demonstrate what kinds of standpoint he wanted to refute. Following the general scheme of the treatise, he first examined the deficiencies of contemporary moral philosophy. On the one hand, he expressed his criticism towards 'the subtilty of disputations' in scholastic moral philosophy and, on the other, towards 'the eloquence of discourses' of humanists concerned only with the elegant language.[93] The basic weakness of the prevailing moral philosophy was that it had offered 'good and fair exemplars and copies, carrying the draughts and portraitures of good, virtue, duty, felicity'. Since the purpose was, however, 'not to write at leisure that which men may read at leisure' but quite on the contrary 'to instruct and suborn action and active life', it was crucial, instead of simply describing virtue and duty in subtle disputations or in elegant style, to explain 'how to attain these excellent marks'.[94] Bacon thus aligned himself with the general Ciceronian humanist assumption that the main aim of ethics was to teach how virtue might be acquired. A firm commitment to the values of the *vita activa* underlay his exposition of moral philosophy, the central part of which was directed precisely against the advocates of the contemplative life.

Following this scheme, Bacon divided ethics into two halves. The first part dealt with 'the exemplar or platform of good', explaining the meanings of the terms involved, whilst the other dealt with 'the regiment or culture of the mind' explaining how to train men in attaining the marks of ethics. Bacon devoted much space to the issues surrounding this second question, both because of its importance and

[92] Bacon, *De sapientia veterum*, in *Works*, VI, p. 648, translation p. 722; cf. *Advancement of learning*, in *Works*, III, p. 302.
[93] Cf. Bacon's assessment of humanism and scholasticism, *Advancement of learning*, in *Works*, III, pp. 282–7.
[94] Ibid., pp. 418–19.

because it had not been treated properly,[95] but he never thought that even the problems of the nature of moral good had been totally settled. Previous writers, he wrote, had excellently handled 'the forms of Virtue and Duty'. They had no less skilfully described 'the Degrees and Comparative Nature of Good' in their 'comparisons between a contemplative and an active life, in the distinction between virtue with reluctation and virtue secured, in their encounters between honesty and profit, in their balancing of virtue with virtue, and the like'. Nevertheless, they had not provided an exhaustive account of the nature of the good, and it was Bacon's aim, therefore, to offer some particular rules for completing this part of ethics.

There was in everything, he began, 'a double nature of good: the one, as every thing is a total or substantive in itself; the other, as it is a part or member of a greater body'. It was beyond doubt that the latter was to be preferred, since 'the public ought to be much more precious than the conservation of life and being'. Once this issue was settled, Bacon firmly believed, 'most of the controversies wherein Moral Philosophy is conversant' could be easily determined. Once we admitted that virtue consisted of 'the actions and exercises whereof do chiefly embrace and concern society' and that 'in this theatre of man's life it is reserved only for God and Angels to be lookers on', we could readily see which school of moral philosophy was to preferred. 'The question touching the preferment of the contemplative or active life' could be decided.[96]

Bacon first directed his argument – perhaps typically for a Ciceronian humanist – 'against Aristotle' who had erroneously maintained that the contemplative way of living was the most valuable and who had substantiated his claims with arguments which were all 'private, and respecting the pleasure and dignity of a man's self'. Having dismissed the Aristotelian standpoint, Bacon turned his attention to other schools of moral philosophy, which opposed the idea of the active life. He identified his own point of view with the one represented by 'Zeno and Socrates and their schools and successions ... who placed felicity in virtue simply or attended' and, according to whom, 'the actions and exercises' of virtues 'do chiefly embrace and concern society'. Bacon employed this as an index by which he measured various ethical schools. He dismissed, to begin with, 'the Cyrenaics and Epicureans' who placed felicity 'in pleasure, and made virtue, (as it is

95   Ibid., pp. 432–44.
96   Ibid., pp. 419–21.

used in some comedies of errors, wherein the mistress and the maid change habits) to be but as a servant'. Next, he dismissed 'the reformed school of the Epicureans' who, according to Bacon, regarded 'serenity of mind and freedom from perturbation' as true felicity. He further refuted the viewpoint ascribed to Herillus (in 1623 he added, significantly, Pyrrho) and to contemporary Anabaptists according to which happy life consisted of 'extinguishment of the disputes of the mind, making no fixed nature of good and evil, esteeming things according to the clearness of the desires, or the reluctation'. This subjective ethics, calling the validity of objective ethical commitments into question, led 'to private repose and contentment' rather than to the good of the community.[97]

The position Bacon adopted also enabled him to censure 'the philosophy of Epictetus' which taught that 'felicity must be placed in those things which are in our power, lest we be liable to fortune and disturbance'. For Bacon, it was foolish to claim that obtaining 'all that we can wish to ourselves in our proper fortune' rendered us happier than even failing 'in good and virtuous ends for the public' – let alone succeeding in promoting the common good. True felicity consisted rather of 'the conscience of good intentions, howsoever succeeding' than of 'all the provision which can be made for security and repose'. It was much more valuable to fail in lofty attempts to enhance the good of one's commonwealth than to succeed in pursuit of one's own private good. Moreover, Bacon regarded his general argument to be convincing enough to refute the doctrine that man's chief preoccupation must be the pursuit of the kind of life where even the causes of perturbations could be avoided. This ethical standpoint, which had grown 'general about the time of Epictetus', received nothing short of ridicule from Bacon. Neither 'health of mind' nor bodily health were proper goals in themselves for man's life. They were but means to an end. They were external qualities which enabled men to 'refer themselves to duties of society'. Finally, Bacon employed his argument to condemn in general 'the tenderness and want of application in some of the most ancient and reverend philosophers and philosophical men, that did retire too easily from civil business, for avoiding of indignities and perturbations'.[98]

We are not, of course, concerned in the present context with the accuracy of Bacon's descriptions of various schools of philosophy or with his identifications of particular philosophers. But in order to grasp what Bacon was doing in his argument, it is of great importance

[97] Ibid., pp. 420–3; *De augmentis*, in *Works*, I, p. 719, translation v, p. 9.
[98] Bacon, *Advancement of learning*, in *Works*, III, pp. 423–4.

to ask what points of view he criticized and repudiated in the course of his argument. It is clear, in the first place, that it was his aim to refute the Aristotelian concept of the importance of the intellectual virtues and the contemplative mode of life which was linked to them. But he had other and more specific targets in mind. He wanted vehemently to condemn the idea that in order to avoid toil and perturbations one ought to retire from 'civil business'. He wanted, that is, to challenge the contention that the contemplative life was preferable because it enabled a man to avoid perturbation and to reach a state of apathy. One should instead, Bacon announced, endure perturbations in order to become a profitable member of one's community. It was an obvious index of self-love, Bacon argued in the *De sapientia veterum* (1609) that a man wanted to avoid appearing 'in public' or engaging 'in civil business' (*in rebus civilibus*) and to live a 'solitary and private' life.[99] The only means to stave off corruption was to 'row against the stream and inclination of time' by 'industry, virtue, and policy'.[100] 'The care of the commonwealth' was 'a kind of common property which like the air and the water belongs to everybody.' Partly because his 'birth and education had seasoned' him 'in business of state' and partly because he thought 'that a man's own country has some special claims upon him', Bacon had applied himself 'to acquire the arts of civil life'.[101]

Another ethical stand which came under fierce attack was the sceptical view (which Bacon attributed to Herillus and to Anabaptists) that one should refrain from making any ethical commitments. For Bacon, the exponents of this view measured things 'according to the motions of the spirit and the constancy or wavering of belief'. Finally, and most importantly, Bacon repudiated the idea closely connected with the previous two notions that one's own self-preservation was the most crucial ethical value. Although bodily and mental health were important values, they were but means towards the higher end of serving the public good. One of the most often repeated ethical maxims in Bacon's whole corpus is that a man must always be ready to sacrifice himself for the good of the commonwealth.[102] Persuading his

---

[99] Bacon, *De sapientia veterum*, in *Works*, VI, p. 633, translation, p. 705; *Essayes*, p. 317.
[100] Bacon, *Certain considerations touching the better pacification and edification of the Church of England* (1603), in *Letters*, III, p. 105.
[101] Bacon, 'Of the interpretation of nature' (1603?), in *Letters*, III, pp. 84–5.
[102] Bacon, *Advancement of learning*, in *Works*, III, pp. 420–1; *Maxims of the law* (1596), in *Works*, VII, pp. 343, 345; 'A view of the differences in question betwixt the King's bench and the Council in the Marches' (1607), in *Letters*, III, p. 379.

listeners in parliament, Bacon once identified himself with Demosthenes and requested MPs, when giving their votes, to 'raise their
thoughts, and lay aside those considerations which their private
vocations and degrees mought minister and present unto them, and ...
take upon them cogitations and minds agreeable to the dignity and
honour of the estate'. 'For certainly,' he developed the argument, 'Mr
Speaker, if a man shall be only or chiefly sensible of those respects
which his particular vocation and degree shall suggest and infuse into
him, and not enter into true and worthy considerations of estate, he
shall never be able aright to give counsel or take counsel in this
matter.'[103]

In his account of ethics, Bacon grouped together all the distinct
ethical outlooks which he wanted to condemn under the generative
idea of the *vita contemplativa*. This tactical move, which carried with it a
certain degree of plausibility, enabled Bacon to use one single argument against all of these diverse outlooks. It was the *vita activa* tradition
which furnished him with an efficacious argument as a means of
repudiating all of these views. Identifying his own point of view with
Zeno's stoic school and using as his axiom the maxim that good is
preferable when the thing which is good is rather 'a part or member of
a greater body' than 'a total or substantive in itself', Bacon could refute
those who upheld self-preservation, scepticism and apathy as the most
desirable ethical values. Although the fact that Bacon was called 'our
English Tully' is accounted for mainly by his eloquence and his elegant
prose style, the cognomen could also have been attributed to him for
his preference for the *vita activa*.[104]

Bacon's keen awareness of the problems of corruption and his
interest in Tacitus and Lipsius did not prompt him to abandon the
traditional Ciceronian notion of the *vita activa*.[105] On the contrary, he
employed this Ciceronian ideal to repudiate not only the traditional
Aristotelian argument in favour of the *vita contemplativa*, but also and in
particular those who maintained that rather than being an active
participant in the public life of his community a man, and especially a
philosopher, ought to retire himself from civil business, seek 'serenity of

[103] Bacon in parliament 17 February 1607, in *Letters*, III, p. 308.
[104] Stephen Jerome, *Englands iubilee: or Irelands ioyes io-paean, for king Charles his welcome* (Dublin, 1625), p. 32. See in general Penrose 1934, pp. 2–3.
[105] Another example is Daniel Tuvill's *Essaies politicke, and morall* (London, 1608), which is heavily indebted to Bacon as well as to Tacitus. See also the popular Anon., 'The genealogie of vertue', in *The anathomie of sinne, briefely discovering the braunches thereof* (London, 1603), sigs. C7ᵛ–D1ᵛ, E2ʳ⁻ᵛ.

mind and freedom from perturbation' and refrain from any moral commitments. Bacon countered the sceptic and neostoic challenge with a strong restatement of the virtuous *vita activa*. The considerable prominence given to the architecture of fortune in Bacon's presentation of civil knowledge was not indexical of its equal importance. The reason, rather, is to be ascertained in the nature and purpose of the *Advancement of learning*. Bacon intended to offer rules as to how to proceed and develop those branches of learning which previously had been deficiently presented or even overlooked altogether. Whereas the architecture of fortune had been much practised, 'it hath not been reduced to writing'. But the citizen's duty or, as Bacon put it, 'the common Duty of every man, as a man or member of a state', was 'extant and well laboured' and he could refrain from repeating these instructions.[106]

If Bacon could discuss the architecture of fortune whilst embracing the conventional Ciceronian ethics of the *vita activa*, the same was equally true of Fulke Greville and Ben Jonson. Having suggested that 'great men of estate' should seek comfort from retirement, Greville quickly changed his priorities and stressed the crucial importance of the active life: 'Yet whoe are free, must labour and desire.' He claimed that the king's 'best help indeed is happy choice / Of underministers in every kinde', as the example of Alexander Severus demonstrated.[107] Later in the *Treatise of monarchy* Greville went still further, arguing that 'All arts preferred by odds of practicke use, / The meere contemplative scorn'd as abuse.' It was only by educating the people in those arts 'wherof both warr and peace finde use' that 'greate estates' could be maintained 'in reputation'.[108] It should occasion little surprise that, despite his decided preference for monarchy, Greville contrasted between the slaves of tyrants and 'free Citizens' of well-governed commonwealths.[109]

In Ben Jonson's *Catiline* (1611) corruption occurred when people placed their private good before the common good. As Curius revealed the aims of the conspiracy to Fulvia: 'By public ruin, private spirits must rise.'[110] The virtue of frugality was replaced by the prevalence of excessive wealth, and

[106] Bacon, *Advancement of learning*, in *Works*, III, pp. 455–6, 428.
[107] Greville, *Treatise of monarchy*, stanzas 110, 125, 126, in *Remains*, pp. 62, 66.
[108] Ibid., stanzas 484–90, citations from 484, 489, in *Remains*, pp. 156–8.
[109] Ibid., stanza 511, in *Remains*, p. 163.
[110] *Catiline*, II.362.

> Decrees are bought, and laws are sold,
> Honours and offices for gold;
> The people's voices, and the free
> Tongues in the Senate, bribed be.[111]

Unlike in *Sejanus*, however, the solution to corruption was sought neither from the architecture of fortune nor from a life of retirement but from a relentless pursuit of the common good. Cicero praised Fulvia for 'doing office to the public weal' rather than promoting 'private friendship'. And he exhorted Curius to imitate her since our country 'is our common mother, and doth challenge / The prime part of us'.[112]

Although in those parts of the *Horae subseciuae* which have recently been ascribed to Thomas Hobbes, the merits of obedience and obsequiousness loomed large, the main emphasis in those parts which are thought to have been composed by William Cavendish was firmly placed on the time-honoured values of the active life. Like Bacon, Cavendish wrote that contemporary moral philosophy failed to teach a man how to make himself 'either wise or vertuous'. On the contrary, it presented nothing but disputes of 'wisedome and vertue' and definitions as well as distinctions of their nature. The writers of these futile treatises 'onely Syllogize of them, as if they thought it were, Summum Bonum, to define Summum Bonum; or Wisedome, Valour, and Vertue, to know what those notions meant' whereas man desired 'to learne the Art how to governe himselfe in the passages of this life'.[113]

The topic was further pursued in a long essay 'Of a country life', which was strikingly similar to the anonymous *Cyuile and vncyuile life* (1579). Country life was defined as 'such an habitation as implies a retirednes from the presse, busines, and imployment either of city or court'. Although this kind of life contained numerous advantages, it also had its drawbacks. One of the most serious was that 'a totall sequestration in the Country, doth not onely hinder' the country gentleman 'of that preferment, and honor which in all likelihood he may arrive too, but robs the State and Common-wealth where he lives, of an able, and fit minister to doe it service'. It comes as no surprise, therefore, that the country gentleman's 'life must not be wholly

---

[111] Ibid., 1.579–82.
[112] Ibid., III.302–3, 366–7. See Maus 1984, pp. 128–30.
[113] Anon., *Horae subseciuae*, pp. 196–8. The fact that the treatise contains two somewhat contradictory lines of argument fits the recent view that it was written by two different authors. See also John Ford, *A line of life: pointing at the immortalitie of a vertuous name* ([London], 1620), pp. 19–20.

reserved to his owne quiet and particular pleasures; but in that place whereunto he is called, and destined to live, to apply himselfe, and service, for the common and publik good'. The underlying assumption was that man's highest duty was to serve his community. It was utterly condemnable that a man, who knew his abilities, 'voluntarily' concealed and hid them. 'No man is, or ought to be so absolutely master of himselfe', the author declared, 'as to take the liberty of electing that course of life, which onely his owne will, and inclination, governes.' Instead, he ought to 'direct himselfe in that way' which enabled him to put his abilities at the disposal of his country, since 'wee are not borne for our selves ... but to serve the publike'. It was 'one principall end of a mans being in this world, to be serviceable in one kinde or other, to that Kingdome, or Commonwealth where he lives'.[114] Even in that part of the book which has been attributed to Hobbes a sharp contrast was presented between the 'easefull life' and that of 'an active spirit', who continuously laboured 'in production of good effects'. But the point was not elaborated simply because the whole argument 'is so well knowne'.[115]

The humanist ideal of the virtuous public life, so lengthily set out in these treatises, occurred also in educational manuals. James Cleland highlighted in his *Propaideia* the idea that the chief aim of the extensive education of a young nobleman was to prepare him for an active life.[116] William Martyn composed a treatise of instructions for his son studying at Oxford with a view to teaching him the idea that the only way for a man 'to bee compleat' was to embrace virtues and thereby to become 'a profitable member in the Common-weale'. The underlying assumption was that 'virtue consisteth in action, and ... the meditation thereof without practise, is as an unstringed instrument, whereon no man plaieth'. 'It is not enough', Martyn added, 'to boast of the name of vertue, without vertuous deeds and actions, for without them, the name of vertue is fitly compared to a shadow without substance.'[117] The same view was endorsed by Richard Brathwait in *The schollers medley*. He could extol Tacitus, but once again this did not persuade him to abandon the conventional idea that the main area, where history provided useful lessons, was the public life. The chief measure

[114] Anon., *Horae subseciuae*, pp. 138, 141, 165–6, 169–70; cf. pp. 3–4.
[115] Ibid., pp. 335–6.
[116] James Cleland, *Propaideia: or the institution of a young noble man* (Oxford, 1607), pp. 5–6, 50, 69, 119–23, 135–7.
[117] William Martyn, *Youths instruction* (London, 1612), sig. A3ᵛ, pp. 18, 19.

for the excellence of a piece of historical writing was the amount of benefit it could yield to one's country. Brathwait strongly asserted that 'no man [could] be an experienc't Statist, that was not initiated in the reading of Histories' which would yield 'the aptest and exquisitest directions that can attend man, either in publique or private affaires, at home or abroad'. The contents of the lessons of history were not merely the corruption which could be gathered from Tacitus; a 'Senatour' could also learn from historical accounts 'the very natures' of laws and justice. Moreover, history told 'the actions of good men with an Emphasis, to sollicite the Reader to the affection'.[118] History revealed 'such Lawes, Orders, and Precepts, as well Morall as Divine' which could profit and benefit 'their present estate'.[119]

Essentially this same line of thought was developed in numerous moral treatises. John Brinsley, who defended Ciceronian style in his *Lvdvs literarivs* in 1612, came to the fore in 1616 with a translation of the first book of Cicero's *De officiis*. The translation was made 'for the good of Schools' and it was intended to be used with the *Lvdvs literarivs*. It was a volume in three columns, one of which contained Cicero's text in Latin, another Brinsley's translation and the third his comments. Brinsley admonished the reader first to read his comments for understanding 'the matter contained in each Chapter' and only then to proceed to Cicero's text. Resorting to the authority of Erasmus, Brinsley pointed out that Cicero chiefly followed 'the Stoiks ... because these have determined the very best of the end of goodnes, whereunto al Duties are referred'.[120]

In his comments Brinsley did not significantly elaborate on Cicero's arguments; by and large, they were faithful abbreviations of Cicero's conceptions. But Brinsley had no difficulties in ascertaining Cicero's main stance. Beside Cicero's decided preference for the active life (1.21.70) Brinsley commented that 'the life of those who apply themselves to government, for the good of the commonwealth, or to achive great maters: for the same, is more profitable to mankinde, and also more fit for attayining fame and honour'.[121] And when Cicero put forward his celebrated statement that learning should not draw men

---

[118] Brathwait, *The schollers medley*, p. 6.
[119] Ibid., pp. 35, 6–7, 89–116, 1–2, 80, 32, 74. See Fussner 1962, pp. 166–8. In similar vein, Brathwait argued that learning and knowledge of nature was not valuable since it did not conduce 'to the profite of the Repub:', p. 47.
[120] Cicero, *The first book of Tullies Offices*, translated by John Brinsley (London, 1616), p. 2, cf. p. 14. The translation was reprinted in 1631.
[121] Ibid., pp. 145–6.

away from the active life (1.16.19), Brinsley explained the content of this passage to his readers by insisting that by 'studies wee suffer not our selves to bee drawne away from more necessarie imployments'. This was so, because 'all the praise of vertue consisteth in action or performing Duties, from which yet there may be intermissions and returning to studie'.[122]

Anthony Nixon defined duty as 'the end whereunto Vertue tendeth'. Since everything had been created for man, it followed that man himself was created 'for the benefite of man'. It was, therefore, contrary to man's happiness to live 'to him selfe'. Nixon admonished his readers to ponder over this carefully in order to draw the proper conclusion that everybody should dispose 'his actions to the end and purpose of every good worke'.[123] According to Henry Crosse, 'every day offereth a new occasion to doo good, and therefore no one houre ought to slip away without some profitable thing done'. When Crosse explained his reasoning at this point, he repeated the familiar conviction that man was not 'borne onely for himselfe; but as Plato saith, for our friends, parents, countrey, and such common duties, which are the finall endes of every mans labour'.[124]

One of the principal forms of human weaknesses was, according to John Hitchcock, 'the nice kind of life that some men addict themselues unto'. He characterized this manner of living as one where people 'mue up themselves at home, and never see the face of a publike assembly, but live as it were in a well or a bottle'. To lead this kind of life made people utterly 'unfit to be employed for the common wealth, because they see nothing clerely, but a far off and through a hole and vnderstand onely by tradition and report'.[125] Having established this in the first chapter of his treatise – dealing with the 'Theoretike part of Wisdome' – Hitchcock devoted the second chapter to the 'Practicke part of Wisdome'. The justification for such a rationale was not hard to find. As he explained, 'a man is not therefore honest or virtuous, because he knowes what is virtuous or honest, but because he doth the things that are so; *Virtutis omnis in hoc laus est*, the praise of virtue consists

---

122 Ibid., p. 44.
123 Anthony Nixon, *The dignitie of man, both in the perfections of his soule and bodie* (London, 1612), p. 4.
124 Henry Crosse, *Vertues common-wealth: or the high-way to honour* (London, 1603), sig. R3ʳ; see in general sig. G4ᵛ–H1ʳ, R2ᵛ–3ʳ, R4ʳ, S3ʳ. In Walzer's account Crosse's ideas could 'safely be labelled puritanical', Walzer 1965, pp. 207–10. See also D[aniel] T[uvill], *Essayes, morall and theologicall* (London, 1609), pp. 4–6, 23–4; T[uvill], *The dove*, pp. 39–40, which drew chiefly on Bacon's *Advancement of learning*.
125 John Hitchcock, *A sanctuary for honest men*, pp. 34–5, cf. pp. 45–7.

in the action'.[126] But Hitchcock coupled this analysis with the stoic notion that man should 'exempt & free' himself 'both outwardly from popular & multitudinary errors & opinions, and inwardly from passions'. This was accomplished by 'praecaution or praemeditation whereby a man flyeth or extinguisheth whatsoever might kindle or enflame his passions'. This armoured him 'to beare without passion or distemper whatsoever happeneth'.[127]

Similarly, John Ford linked his strong stoicism with the principles of the *vita activa*.[128] On the one hand, he was inclined to confess that 'the toyle in common affaires, is but trash and bondage, compared to the sweete repose of the minde, and the goodly Contemplation of a mans peace with Himselfe'. But, on the other, this belief did not amount to an endorsement of the life of total withdrawal. Rather, it prompted Ford to combine the virtuous public service with inward, stoic resolution.[129] A man must attempt to be 'a good Man', one who voluntarily promoted the common good. He must always have 'an eie, to the North Starre of Vertue: without which, men cannot but suffer shipwrack'.[130] Those people, he argued, whose aim was simply to live were mostly preoccupied with the fear of death, since 'such men that so live, when they dye, both dye finally & dye all'. But those people who endeavoured to 'live well', live with the expectation of death, since 'when they dye, [they] dye to live, and live for ever'. The underlying assumption here was, of course, that by living well a man won honour and glory and when he died his death acted as 'a passage to glorie'.[131] There was yet another reason why the public life was preferable to the contemplative one: virtue materialized in action alone; 'action is the Crowne of Vertue'. 'To be vertuous', Ford invoked, 'without the testimonie of imployment, is as a rich Minerall in the heart of the Earth, un-useful because unknowne.'[132]

If these theorists portrayed an essentially traditional picture of the public life, they adopted a similar perspective towards the means to accomplish the same. It was assumed that men could engage them-

---

[126] Ibid., pp. 50–1.
[127] Ibid., pp. 52–3. See also Anon., *Of affectation: a morall discourse, of some delight, and of much vse for these times* (London, 1607), p. 145. Cf. however, *A sanctuary for honest men*, pp. 58–9, and especially p. 4, where Hitchcock condemned 'Stoicall austerity'.
[128] For Ford's stoicism, see Monsarrat 1984, pp. 236–52.
[129] Ford, *A line of life*, pp. 120–1.
[130] Ibid., pp. 117–27.
[131] Ibid., pp. 2–4, 17–19.
[132] Ibid., pp. 4–6, 9; see also Edward Topsell, *The house-holder: or, perfect man: preached in three sermons lately at Hartfield in Svssex* (n.p., 1609), pp. 72–3.

selves in the public life by their moral qualities – virtues. It was only, that is, by exercising his virtues that a man could hope to discharge his duty and promote the common good. This was, as we have already seen, Bacon's view and the one put forward in *The covrt of James*. Those who had had good education and who were, therefore, 'generous, liberall, and free-hearted' readily understood that 'true glory, reputation, and renowne consisteth in Vertue, which also is especially illustrated and made famous by worthie and meritorious actions and imployments in a Common-wealth'.[133]

The same analysis of the connection between the *vita activa* and virtue also permeated the educational and moral treatises; they repeated the Ciceronian slogan that the glory of virtue consisted in action. And since *negotium* constituted the ultimate aim, the discussion centred around moral virtues, as in Henry Crosse's *Vertves commonwealth*. At the beginning of his treatise Crosse reminded his readers of the importance of Christian virtues and explained that one should never be content to rest on moral virtues. They but fashioned 'the outward man to civill obedience, making that the end which are but motives to the end'. Having made this concession, however, he moved to discuss the moral virtues, and devoted the entire treatise to this theme.[134]

There was wide agreement that it was only by possessing the four cardinal virtues that a man could fulfil his civic mode of life and effectively enhance the common good. This was the opinion of Henry Crosse and John Hitchcock, as well as Anthony Nixon. 'But to prosecute my intent', expounded Crosse, thereby revealing his acquaintance with stoic ideals, 'which is to handle the morall Vertues, and lay open the parts of humanitie, it wil not be amisse to touch by the way the foure chiefe and principall Vertues, called cardinall Vertues.' A little later he pointed out that 'where vertue is wanting in a generall government, that Common-wealth is wholly overthrowne'.[135] According to Richard Brathwait, the chief lesson man ought to learn from history was the centrality of virtue. In a good historian, 'vertue never wants her character, nor vice her reproofe'; the best 'Hystoricall Relations' were such that they induced men to virtue and deterred

[133] A. D. B. *The covrt of James*, pp. 18–19.
[134] Crosse, *Vertves common-wealth*, sig. B1ʳ–2ʳ.
[135] Ibid., sigs. B2ʳ⁻ᵛ, E4ʳ, cf. C3ʳ; Nixon, *The dignitie of man*, pp. 4–6; Hitchcock, *A sanctvary for honest men*, pp. 8off.
[136] Brathwait, *The schollers medley*, p. 7.

them from vice.[136] 'Vertue', Brathwait announced, 'hath in her selfe a soveraigne end, to which all liberall Arts and Sciences (in themselves truly noble and meriting honour) have their aime and recourse.'[137] He claimed that history had such a power that 'where a naturall defect and want of courage was seated', a recourse to history would remedy the situation.[138] The best example of the usage of history in 'imitation in vertue' was to be found in ancient Rome. All of their 'worthy Patritians' had been most careful in their emulation of their predecessors, so much so that their own deeds had become most worthy examples to later generations.[139]

In the fifth book of *Propaideia*, Cleland discussed the young nobleman's 'Dutie' in his 'Civil conversation', beginning his account with the cardinal virtues and stressing above all prudence and justice.[140] William Martyn was thoroughly convinced that a man's outward parts were of no use 'if the inward parts and mind bee not adorned, with such splendent virtues, and with such Gentleman-like qualities'. The possession of four cardinal virtues could make a man 'a profitable member in the Common-weale'. But with a view to becoming a profitable member, it did not suffice 'that a man doth know much, and can doe well, by meanes of that knowledge'. He only became a profitable member of the commonwealth by turning 'into action such effects as his virtues and his knowledge have enabled him to performe'. Unless a man put his virtues into practice by virtuous actions, he could be compared 'to a rare and perfect Diamond, which beeing unpollished, serveth for no use'. He was like a ship 'loaden with Silkes, with Spices, and with Gold' which sank and was, therefore, 'of no value or esteeme'. It was the central claim of Martyn's instructions to his son that a man must first attempt to possess virtues, and then exercise them in his actions with a view to enhancing the public good of his commonwealth. 'I wish and doe advise you', Martyn admonished his son, 'to imploy some times, not onely to reade this discourse often, but also with diligence to meditate, and publikelie to exercise those virtues, and those qualities, which heerein are deservedlie praised, and commended.' The virtuous man should never be content with himself until he had done 'the best, and the most good that he is able'. He must not

---

[137] Ibid., pp. 81–2.
[138] Ibid., p. 5.
[139] Ibid., pp. 9–10, see also, pp. 15–16, 75.
[140] Cleland, *Propaideia*, pp. 163–247, especially pp. 163, 167–8, 198.

cease 'from any toile, if thereby he may profit others, either particularly to themselves, or generally for the good of many, and of the common weale'. Martyn was never tired of repeating that 'it is not enough to boast of the name of vertue, without vertuous deeds and actions, for without them, the name of vertue is fitly compared to a shadow without substance'. Philosophers had offered various definitions of virtue but they all agreed 'that virtue consisteth in action, and that the meditation thereof without practise, is as an unstringed instrument, whereon no man plaieth'.[141]

Although the issues of the virtuous active life already had a conspicuous place in these moral and educational treatises, the extent to which the Jacobean theorists were prepared to go towards the assumptions of republican 'civic' humanists is most perceptible in two more openly political treatises. Rather than taking so much issue with the advocates of the *vita contemplativa*, the authors of these treatises simply assumed the context of the active life. In 1606 Barnabe Barnes published a long treatise entitled, interestingly enough, *Fovre bookes of offices*. In writing the treatise, Barnes was engaged in an attempt to set out the necessary qualities for the active members of the commonwealth. In his preface to the reader, Barnes pointed out that the book was intended to explicate 'certaine speciall qualities and principles ... for generall governement, and the choise both of civill and martiall ministers in every Commonwealth'.[142] He was, that is, writing an advice-book for nobles, counsellors and magistrates. But Barnes intended his treatise for a broader readership. He explained on the title-page that the book was directed to help 'privat persons for the speciall service of all good Princes and Policies'. It was thus Barnes's ultimate aim to treat the issues of the people's participation in the active life of the commonwealth.

Barnes divided his treatise into four books each of which explained in detail one indispensable quality and the area of activity closest to that quality. The division was based on the four cardinal virtues and each one of them governed a particular appointment (temperance – treasurer, prudence – counsellor, justice – judge, courage – soldier). Perhaps the most important was 'civile prudence' which 'doth (as it were) prescribe unto citizens their actions'. By and large, however, a consummate member of the commonwealth was expected to master

---

[141] Martyn, *Youths instructions*, sig. A3ᵛ-4ʳ, pp. 18–19.
[142] Barnabe Barnes, *Fovre bookes of offices: enabling private persons for the speciall service of all good princes and policies* (London, 1606), sig. A3ʳ, p. 1. For Barnes, see Eccles 1933.

all of them, as becomes clear in Barnes's definition of 'citizen'. 'I deeme him worthie to bee reputed a good Commonwealths man,' he stated, 'that being garnished with civile vertues (as with justice and fortitude, which are in themselves moderated with prudence and temperance) can as well in forraine places, and in the warres, as in domesticall and civile affaires, performe the parts of a noble citizen and countreyman.'[143] An accomplished member of his commonwealth, 'a good Commonwealths man' or a 'countreyman' was thus regarded as 'a noble citizen'. He possessed 'civile vertues' by means of which he participated actively in the political life of his community. It was the citizen's prime duty to advance the common good of the whole community; but he was also expected to risk 'his life and substance in difficult seasons for the preservation and safegard of his country'.[144]

This scale of values was even more vigorously embraced by the anonymous author of the curious, Ramist-style tract, *Organon reipvblicae*. It was first printed in Latin in 1605, and although the author's name does not appear on the title-page, the dedication to the king is signed by I. R. The tract was translated almost immediately into English by Edmund Sadler and was published within the year. Sadler wrote that he translated the tract because he regarded its content as important not only for men's private but also, and especially, for their public life. Its material was such that he thought it a pity if it were 'lockt from those which want the perfection of that Language, and yet would be glad from such a methodicall Picture of words, both to forme their dutie to the State, as also to manage their private interests'.[145] The tract was not so much a 'proper' book as a plan for one. Only very occasionally did it form more continuous prose; mostly it was a conglomeration of short notes arranged under several headings. It is perfectly true as the author stated towards the end of the tract: 'this my Epitome'.[146]

As the subtitle of the English translation implied, the main purpose of the tract was to offer a set of rules for conducting 'the course of a Common-wealth'. In pursuing this topic, the author saw the people as active members of their community, as members contributing their

---

[143] Barnes, *Fovre bookes of offices*, p. 87.
[144] Ibid., pp. 87–8.
[145] [I. R.], *Organon reipvblicae* (London, 1605); [I. R.], *Organon reipvblicae: or the north starre of pollicie, by which the course of a common-wealth may be directed* (London, 1605), sig. A3ᵛ. See sig. E4ʳ for Ramus. The translation is hereafter referred to as *The north starre*. In the translation the dedication to James is removed and is replaced by one to Sir Julius Caesar.
[146] [I. R.], *Organon reipvblicae*, sig. D3ᵛ: 'haec mea Epitome'; *The north starre*, sig. E4ʳ.

own special abilities towards the common good. The commonwealth was interpreted, that is, as a community of active beings and attention was focused on their role rather than on that of the prince. Although the original edition was dedicated to James, a central theme of the tract was to explain the citizen's public role in the commonwealth. 'Wee ought to contend at all times, not with privie grudges and hatreds, but whether of all can best deserve of' the 'Prince and Countrey, and doe most good for it.'[147]

The author's point of departure was the fact that far from being guided by divine eternal laws, the world of politics was rather an uncertain business. A commonwealth resembled closely 'the fraile nature and unconstant minde of men'. Therefore, they were 'variably tosled hither and thither' and sometimes 'advanced from small to great' and yet sometimes 'throwen downe from their greatnesse into divers perils of things'. In addition to these fluctuating courses of commonwealths, even their normal course was full of 'innumerable perills'. In order to avert these perils, it was vital, in the first place, to claim God's protection and help. But equally indispensable was the ability to use one's own talents. With a view to facing the challenge of the perils caused by the fluctuations of time, a commonwealth had to employ the abilities of its own members. It was of decisive importance to invent 'the best pollicies' (*optima consilia*) for avoiding all these fatal dangers. What was required above all was 'an excellent sharpnesse of the wit, and an admirable quicknesse, and wisedome'.[148] The author's purpose was to explain what means needed to be designed so that this aim could be achieved.

The first general conclusion the author drew was that 'the best pollicies' could only be produced through a constant display of virtues. 'There is no treasure more commodious to a Prince and Commonwealth,' he announced, than 'vertues, wisedome, fidelitie, and valour.'[149] He was in complete agreement with the widespread belief that it was only by embracing the four cardinal virtues that the dangers could be averted; the people could advance the public good

---

[147] [I. R.], *Organon reipvblicae*, sig. DI[r]: 'Certare oportet, omni tempore, non privatis simultatibus & odijs; sed vter omnium melius de principe & patria mereri, & plura in eam beneficia conferre possit.' Cf. sig. B2[r]: 'Cavendum, ne rerum privatarum respectus, publicis rebus noceant, & officiant.' *The north starre*, sig. EI[v], cf. CI[v].

[148] [I. R.], *Organon reipvblicae*, sig. BI[r], 'Excellens etiam ingenij solertia, & in consilijs optimis inveniendis celeritas & sapientia admiranda requiruntur.' *The north starre*, sig. B3[v].

[149] [I. R.], *Organon reipvblicae*, sig. BI[r]: 'Nullus Thesaurus principi & Reip. vtilior, quam Consiliarij, virtute, prudentia, fide, & fortitudine, praestantes.' *The north starre*, sig. B3[v].

only by adopting these virtues. A substantive part of the tract was consequently devoted to presenting them.[150] The reason for calling them 'cardinal' virtues was that 'as the doore is turned upon the hinge [*cardo*], so on these, mans life is turned and ruled'. But these virtues, the author insisted, had two other names. They were sometimes called 'Humane' by virtue of the fact that they 'are gotten by mans study', and sometimes 'Consuetudinall', since they were acquired through custom. Most importantly, however, they were called 'Politike' (*Politicae*) virtues, since 'by these a civill life [*vita civilis*] is ordered'.[151] The author of the *Organon reipvblicae* was employing the humanist concept of the civic life to describe the proper organization of the commonwealth.

Anthony Nixon opened *The dignitie of man* by discussing the four cardinal virtues and quoted *Organon reipvblicae* in order to demonstrate that they were called 'Politique' virtues, because 'by these a civill life is ordered'.[152] Later, when he treated the issues dealing with 'Policie', Nixon admitted that 'Civill policies are not the workes of man onely, but proceed from the Providence of God.' This did not, however, restrain him from quoting the *Organon reipvblicae*: 'an excellent sharpnes of the wit, and an admirable quicknes, and Wisdome, are requisite in inventing the best Policies'. The maintenance of the commonwealth and its possible success were dependent on the ingenuity and the virtues of its members. In answer to the question, 'what signifies Policie?', the author referred to 'the manner of life used by some politicall person'. A commonwealth, moreover, was said to be corrupted, when 'the increase of private commoditie' was sought. On the other hand, the commonwealth was healthy, when 'the publique profit of the Citizens' was duly respected.[153]

Although the Ciceronian ideal of a virtuous civic life was so strongly and widely reiterated, there is little doubt that several English writers were also disposed to come to terms with the new arguments of reason of state: when the preservation of the common good was at stake, one

---

150 [I. R.], *Organon reipvblicae*, sigs. B3ʳ–C1ʳ; *The north starre*, sigs. C2ʳ–D1ʳ.

151 [I. R.], *Organon reipvblicae*, sig. B3ʳ; *The north starre*, sig. C2ᵛ.

152 Nixon, *The dignitie of man*, pp. 4–6. As Ennis 1940, pp. 398–400 has pointed out, Nixon's whole account was heavily indebted to La Primaudaye's *The French academie*. But he also quoted the *Organon reipvblicae*. The opening words of his dedication were taken more or less directly from the dedication of Edmund Sadler; in his discussion of virtues and laws, Nixon directly quoted several passages from the *Organon reipvblicae*; perhaps most importantly he took, as we shall see, his assessment of the form of government from the same source, *The dignitie of man*, sig. [A3ʳ], pp. 87, 116–20, 122–3; *The north starre*, sigs. A3ʳ, C3ᵛ, B2ᵛ–4ʳ, C1ʳ, C2ᵛ–3ʳ.

153 Nixon, *The dignitie of man*, pp. 115–19.

should be ready to discard conventional morality. Perhaps the best-known author to endorse this argument is Francis Bacon. In his discussion of the architecture of fortune, Bacon could claim that his precepts were those of 'good arts' as against those of 'evil arts', which he ascribed to Machiavelli.[154] Nevertheless, he agreed with Justus Lipsius that, while an excessive use of dissimulation was imprudent, it was prudent to have 'Dissimulation in seasonable use; And a Power to faigne, if there be no Remedy'.[155] The reason was not far to seek. In places where flattery and baseness loomed large, there was no need for traditional virtues.[156] Princes' courts answered this description, for those who were 'brought up from their infancy in the courts of kings and affairs of state scarce ever attain to a deep and sincere honesty of manners'.[157] But it was not merely princes' courts where honesty was lacking; it was a more general rule in 'state-prudence [*prudentia civilis*] ... to distrust, and to take the less favourable view of human affairs'.[158] In 1614 Bacon told the House of Commons that 'we live not in Plato his Commonwealth, but in times wherein abuses have got the upper hand'.[159] It was futile to rely on 'the solemnity and sanctity of the oath in treaties and compacts of princes', because 'all are too weak for ambition and interest and the licence of power'. 'There is adopted therefore', Bacon concluded, 'but one true and proper pledge of faith; and it is not any celestial divinity. This is Necessity (the great god of the powerful), and peril of state, and communion of interest.'[160]

Similar arguments were often based on the distinction between a private person's morality and that of a political community. According to Robert Dallington, 'necessitie gives a larger latitude, and freer scope to the manage of great affaires'.[161] Using Tacitus, Cicero and Bacon as his authorities, Daniel Tuvill fully concurred. 'The law of mens actions', he began, 'is one, when we respect them only as men; and an other when wee consider them, as partes of a politike body.' It followed that 'publike actions, done for the preserving and well-ordering of a State or common-weale, may seeme sometimes, seeme (I say) to have in them ...

---

[154] Bacon, *Advancement of learning*, in *Works*, III, p. 471.
[155] Bacon, *Essayes*, p. 22.
[156] Bacon, *De sapientia veterum*, in *Works*, VI, p. 728.
[157] Bacon, *De augmentis*, in *Works*, V, p. 27.
[158] Bacon, *Novum organum*, in *Works*, IV, p. 91.
[159] Bacon in parliament, *Letters*, V, p. 52.
[160] Bacon, *De sapientia veterum*, in *Works*, VI, pp. 706–7. See also, John Melton, *A sixe-folde politician: together with a sixe-folde precept of policy* (London, 1609), sigs. Q1ʳ, P7ᵛ–8ʳ; John Stephens, *Essayes and characters ironicall, and instructive*, 2nd impression (London, 1615), pp. 158–9.
[161] Dallington, *Aphorismes*, p. 101.

some ruder lineaments and traces of unjustice'. A public person must 'so fashion and conforme his carriage, that the benefit of the publike weale maybe the onely marke and scope of his endeavours'.[162]

It is this same line of thought which seems to guide John Hitchcock's discussion of prudence. Hitchcock, we recall, argued for a virtuous active life and offered an account of the four cardinal virtues. In addition, he wanted to distance himself from those who 'may be without essential honesty and piety'.[163] But when he explored the cardinal virtue of prudence he gave his unqualified endorsement of the principles of reason of state. According to Hitchcock, 'in the Justice of a Prince we must not bee too strict; for (in as much as it is a matter of no small moment well to governe a State) it is expedient for a Prince enterchangeably to assume the skinne of the Foxe and the Lion'. It followed that the prince should 'doe that for the good and safetie of himselfe and the weale publike which in private persons were vicious and unlawfull'.[164] Hitchcock gave a list of 'eight things expedient in a Prince, although some question the lawfulnesse'. The list included not only distrust, dissimulation and secrecy, but also items of more straightforward advice. A prince must 'clip the wings of anyone that is like to soare too high in the State'; he should be ready 'in a time of necessitie and povertie of the State' to 'take by authoritie the wealth of the richest'; and he ought 'to cancell the lawes or priviledges that are any way prejudiciall to the authoritie of the Prince'.[165]

IV

The meticulous attention paid to the issues of the *vita activa* and the closely connected theme of civic virtues was often accompanied by an equally thorough discussion of another classical republican theme. This was the question of what constituted true nobility. The persistent occurrence of this topic is an important index for the continuity of Ciceronian humanist values. Although its emergence could be seen as an integral part of humanist political discourse, it is of some importance to bear in mind that to maintain the humanist idea of true nobility was not merely to repeat a time-honoured truism; it was also to argue against those contemporaries who endorsed the contrary view. In

162 T[uvill], *The doue*, pp. 36–40.
163 Hitchcock, *A sanctuary for honest men*, pp. 4, 54–5.
164 Ibid., pp. 85–6.
165 Ibid., pp. 86–8.

preaching before the king in February 1607, George Meriton employed all his rhetorical skills to deny the humanist contention with its levelling claim that true nobility should be based on merits. He was thoroughly convinced of his opponents. They were stoics, he claimed, 'the old brokers of parity' as well as their successors, 'the English Switzers of these our dayes' who put forward the incredible claim that inherited nobility was 'a meere fiction'. According to their preposterous arguments, Meriton declared, nature 'is an equal parent unto all' and 'God made but one Adam, not one of silver to be the father of Nobles, and another of earth to beget the common sort.' They further made the unfounded assertion that 'none are barred of their way to vertue, or hindered of their course to true felicity'. Drawing a close analogy between men and metals as well as plants, where there was 'great difference of seeds and branches', Meriton announced that 'it avayleth much from what stock one descendeth'. It was chiefly lineage which determined that 'some are noble, some ignoble, some ingenuous, some base, some quick of apprehension, some dull: some fit to rule, some to serve'. Since children often carried 'the markes of their fathers, grandfathers' and so on, it was reasonable to judge that 'they retaine in their minds, the propensions, inclinations, and as it were the sparkes of their auncestors'.[166] The same conclusion was endorsed by the civil lawyer John Cowell who held that those were 'gentlemen' whose 'bloud and race doth make [them] noble'. And at the beginning of *The compleat gentleman* Henry Peacham defined nobility as not only 'a certaine eminency, or notice taken of some one above the rest', but also and in particular 'the Honour of blood in a Race or Linage'.[167]

Against these arguments many authors asserted that true nobility consisted in the possession of virtues. Nobility by virtue was affirmed already by Henry Peacham who added to his definition of inherited nobility the observation that a man could lose it 'by his vice and basenesse'. The chief ingredient of nobility was thus not ancestry or riches but virtue alone. 'Since all Vertue', Peacham argued in a familiar manner, 'consisteth in Action, and no man is borne for himselfe,' but on the contrary, to become 'beneficiall and usefull to his Country', it followed, in the first place, that there was no nobility 'in contemplation'. True nobility consisted thus of virtuous actions for the public good, as had occurred in Rome where, since honour had been

[166] George Meriton, *A sermon of nobilitie*, sigs. B2^v, B3^r–4^r, C1^r–2^v; cf. however, sigs. C4v–D1r, D4v.
[167] John Cowell, *The interpreter: or booke containing the signification of words* (Cambridge, 1607), s.v. 'gentleman'. Henry Peacham, *The compleat gentleman* (London, 1622), p. 2.

'highly prized, every one [had] aymed at Nobilitie, and none [had] refused the most desperate attempts for the good of his Countrey'. But it also followed that one's lineage and wealth were totally irrelevant in so far as true nobility was concerned. 'Neither', Peacham wrote, 'are the truly valorous, or any way vertuous, ashamed of their so meane Parentage, but rather glorie in themselves that their merit hath advanced them above so many thousands farre better descended.'[168]

The same preference for a virtuous true nobility was expressed in Ben Jonson's *Catiline*. When Sempronia claimed that 'virtue, where there is no blood: 'tis vice', Fulvia retorted that 'Twas virtue only, at first, made all men noble'.[169] Cicero emphasized the same point even more strongly:

> I have no urns; no dusty monuments;
> No broken images of ancestors,
> Wanting an ear or nose; no forged tables
> Of long descents, to boast false honours from.

By calling himself 'a new man', Cicero underscored the fact that he owed his advancement entirely to his own 'virtue'.[170] Catiline, as depicted by Cicero, was the complete opposite: despite his illustrious background, Catiline failed to live up to his 'excellent gifts of fortune and of nature'.[171]

An important discussion of nobility is to be found in Thomas Scott of Canterbury's treatise on civil nobility. Thomas Scott, an important local politician and MP in Canterbury, is famous for his puritan diary, and his ideas are mostly accounted for by his godly religion.[172] Scott's *A discourse of polletique and civill honour*, written in 1619, is a vehement critique of the contemporary manner of granting honour and nobility; 'that plague of sellinge and prostituting of honour'. The importance of the matter was intensified, since 'the confusion of order and honor' would ultimately lead to 'the confusion and ruine of state'.[173] There were two chief ways in which Scott sought to justify his position. On the one hand, he emphasized the inherited nature of nobility. It was important, as he succinctly put it, 'not to make any knights ... but of

---

168 Henry Peacham, *The compleat gentleman*, pp. 1–5, 9–10; cf. idem, *Minerva Britanna: or a garden of heroical deuises* (London, 1612), p. 54.
169 *Catiline*, ii, 122, 127.
170 Ibid., iii, 14–17, 19, 21.
171 Ibid., iv, 120.
172 Clark 1978; Clark 1977, p. 341; Cust 1987, pp. 175–85.
173 Thomas Scott, *A discourse of polletique and civill honour* in G. D. Scull, *Dorothea Scott* (Oxford: Parker & Co, 1883), pp. 156, 152. For the suggested dating, see Clark 1978, p. 11n.

eminent desert'. In other words, knighthood and nobility was rooted in one's pedigree, and Scott measured his own importance in the local community with the help of genealogy.[174] 'Vertue', he quoted King James, 'followeth oftest noble bloud, or noble rases.' And it was of course Aristotle who had taught that there were slaves by nature and that 'as a man begetts a man, and a beast a beast, soe good Parents do begett good children, Noble parents, noble children'.[175]

On the other hand, Scott also criticized current fashions of conferring nobility by appealing to the humanist idea of virtuous true nobility. As a result, Scott turned at this point to Cicero and Seneca. Since everyone was descended from Adam, it was wise 'not to trust too much to our birth'.[176] Nobility derived thus from one's own virtues. 'Nobilitie of birth' was completely insufficient without 'vertue, desert and abilitie'. Paraphrasing Francis Bacon, Scott argued that 'Conditores, the founders of states and soe of houses, are ever worthie the first and cheife degree of honor.' The same lesson could be learned from Cicero who had rather been 'the builder of a newe house' than 'the uphoulder' of an old one.[177]

There are two conclusions to be drawn from Scott's account of civil honour. It is, in the first place, somewhat misleading to attribute all his ideas to godly religion. Clearly, as far as his idea of true nobility is concerned, Scott owed an obvious debt to the staple sources of the humanist tradition. Furthermore, although he emphasized the importance of birth, his final point was that irrespective of one's descent, true nobility depended on one's virtues and learning and that it was only this virtuous nobility which was capable of taking care of the government of the local community as well as the commonwealth.[178]

Yet a more unqualified endorsement of the humanist slogan *virtus vera nobilitas* emerges in those educational, moral and political treatises we have examined in this chapter. In teaching Prince Charles, Patrick Scot quoted the prince's father that 'oftimes vertue followes nobilitie of blood', but only in order to contrast this with the idea of true nobility derived from Erasmus, Petrarch, Juvenal and Sallust. 'It is', Scot told the prince, 'a ridiculous and ostentive humour, to glory in the merit of others vertue; for certainly the splendour of ancestours, is the greatest

---

[174] Scott, *A discourse*, p. 160; Clark 1978, p. 7.
[175] Scott, *A discourse*, pp. 185–7. For Fulke Greville's similar position, see James 1986, pp. 404–5.
[176] Scott, *A discourse*, pp. 188–9, 188–194 passim.
[177] Ibid., p. 192; Bacon, *Essayes* (1597), in *Works*, VI, p. 532.
[178] See Scott, *A discourse*, p. 195.

staine, that can faint degenerating posterity.' Everyone should be able
to say: 'I am the beginner of my nobilitie.'[179] James Cleland began his
treatise with a preface 'describing who are Nobles, and the nature of
Nobilitie'. According to him, men are equal in their birth as well as
death. But 'in the middle course' between birth and death there are
some who 'excell & are more noble then others'. From the very
beginning of mankind those who were called nobles did not inherit
their status but were always chosen and elected. Nobility was thus
completely based on personal virtues. Nobody should ascend higher
'then their owne vertuous actions merited'. It was not 'the great
revenues, faire possessions, pleasant Palaces, manie Lordships and
infinite riches' which made a man noble, but 'the glorious Character of
Vertue'. Cleland felt able to declare that 'Vertue onlie is able to make
thee Noble.'[180] William Martyn argued that he who 'soweth virtue,
shall reape honor'. 'A wise man', he added a little later, 'placeth his
contentment in nothing more, then by the active distribution of his
vertues, to make himselfe the more famous.' Like Patrick Scot, Martyn
extended this idea of meritocracy even to the domain of princes. He
reminded his readers that 'the power of Monarchs, and of Kings, must
be supported by the goodnes of their vertues'. This was so, since he was
'much more generous whom his vertues, then he whom his ancestors
have made noble'. It followed, therefore, as Martyn was willing to
point out, that 'much more is he to be admired, that swayeth a
kingdome by his vertues, then he that ruleth it by the only priviledge of
his enobled and heroicall discent'.[181]

It was also one of the most commonly held convictions in moral
treatises that nobility was achieved by virtue alone. To prove that
'many moe are made honourable by diligence, then by Birth', one
author pointed to the fact that in raising 'their Common-wealth' the
Romans had 'stoode not upon termes of blood'. In comparison with his
own times the author could lament: 'then Vertues gave Titles, nowe
Titles sell Vertues.'[182] According to Anthony Nixon, 'the signes of an
honorable minde' were to avoid 'Honour, Riches, or Dignitie' and
instead to aspire to 'vertue'. In answering the question – 'how must we
ascend to true Honour?' – he resorted to the Roman example of the

[179] Patrick Scot, *A table-book for princes: containing short remembrances for the gouernment of themselues and their empire* (London, 1621), pp. 57–62.
[180] Cleland, *Propaideia*, pp. 1–10; Morrice, *An apology*, sig. B3^{r-v}.
[181] Martyn, *Youths instruction*, pp. 18, 19–20. Cf. Richard Brathwait, *Times curtaine drawne: or the anatomie of vanitie* (London, 1621) sig. G3^{v}–4^{r}.
[182] Topsell, *The house-holder*, pp. 90–2.

temples of virtue and honour and concluded that 'it appears that
Vertue is the way to Honour'.[183] Glory, another author explained, was
nothing but 'a shadow of vertue, which doth accompanie even the
unwilling'.[184] Henry Crosse claimed not only that virtue was 'the
spurre of Honour' but also that it was not 'the aboundance of wealth
and great dignitie, that maketh a man truly noble: but the possession of
Vertue'. Although 'that nobilitie is most to be honoured' where virtue
'hath long continued in the house of a Gentleman, without corruption
of bloud', those were '*veré nobiles*, truly noble', who 'for Vertues sake
onely are seated in the place of honour'. He who relied on 'his riches,
parentage, office, place, dignitie' in his pursuit of honour was climbing
'a rotten ladder'.[185] The author of *The covrt of James* argued strongly
against inherited nobility. Although the glorious deeds of forefathers
should not be buried in oblivion, the author exhorted the would-be
courtier to eschew extolling his 'Pedegree' as well as 'the smoakie
images of' his 'Progenitours'. The underlying reason was that 'since all
men had nothing but Dirt and Slime for their first and great Grand-
father', the idea of inherited nobility was utterly pointless. 'Doe not
therefore proudly, and disdainefully', the author advised, 'glory in thy
Grand-fathers, or great Grand-fathers Eminence.' If one wanted to
excel and exceed others in achievement, the only way to accomplish
this was to rely on one's own qualities. 'Let thy nobilities originall and
foundation', the reader was instructed, 'be founded and grounded on
Vertue, whereof assuredly tis farre better to have beene the first Author
and Occasioner, then ... being well begun by others.'[186]

   Similarly, Joseph Hall characterized the object of his chapter named
'Of the truly-noble' as one who 'stands not upon what he borrowed of
his Ancestours; but thinks he must worke out his owne honor'.[187]
Richard Brathwait emphasized the regular occurrence of those who
were born 'of nothing' but yet who 'by some private indowments' for
the good of their country ascended to the pitch of 'highest honours'.
Cicero had been reprimanded for this kind of snobbery, but, as

---

[183] Nixon, *The dignitie of man*, p. 85. Cf. Brathwait, *The schollers medley*, pp. 76–7, 82; Ford, *A line of life*, pp. 57–9; Felltham, *Resolues*, pp. 302–4.

[184] Anon., *Of affectation*, pp. 19–22.

[185] Crosse, *Vertves common-wealth*, sigs. c4ʳ–D2ᵛ, D3ᵛ–4ʳ. Cf. e.g. George Webbe, *The path-way to honor* (London, 1612), pp. 12–13, 17–18; [Richard West], *Wits ABC: or a centurie of epigrams* (London, n.d. [1608]), sig. B2v.

[186] A. D. B., *The covrt of James*, pp. 53–4.

[187] Joseph Hall, *Characters of vertves and vices: in two bookes* (London 1608), pp. 51–6. Cf. e.g. [Michael Scott], *The philosophers banqvet: newly furnished and decked forth*, 2nd edn (London, 1614), pp.107–9; Anton, *The philosophers satyrs*, pp. 25, 29.

Brathwait pointed out, 'Dependance of Auncestors conferre small or no glory to us, if our succeding worth shew not a correspondency to our Prodecessours glory.' The morality of this was, as Brathwait sought to prove by his examples, that the qualities 'of proper Nobility [were] not derived from their fathers greatnesse, but from their owne eminence'. Explaining why he put so much emphasis on virtue, he pointed out that 'Vertue alone is crowned, Vertue in her selfe is of all possessed: She it is alone by which man is eternized.'[188] Walter Ralegh wrote in *The historie of the world*: 'if honour (according to L. Vives) be a witnesse of vertue and well-doing: and Nobilitie (after Plutarch) the continuance of vertue in a race or linage: then are those in whom vertue is extinguished, but like unto painted and printed papers.'[189]

Most importantly the same belief appeared in Barnabe Barnes's *Foure bookes of offices* as well as in the *Organon reipvblicae*. In his discussion of who were the aptest choices for counsellors, Barnes remarked that they should be elected 'out of the true nobilitie', which under the prince 'should governe and amplifie the Commonwealth'. Pursuing the topic further, Barnes defined what he meant by 'true nobilitie'. This term referred to those who were 'notable amd approved for their vertues and honour' while at the same time encountered 'neerely with the dignities of their blood and families'.[190] Having made this concession, Barnes went on to embrace the most typical humanist concept of true nobility. He declared: '*Sola namque virtus vera Nobilitas est.* For very Nobilitie is composed of vertue onely.' The adoption of this humanist slogan enabled Barnes to argue that 'a king may make apt Counsellors of very meane men (*Qui maioribus suis virtute praelucent*): Which give more light of vertue than their ancestors'. If the king followed this rule, his court would soon become 'a Schoolehouse or Colledge of sapience and vertue'.[191] According to the author of *Organon reipvblicae*, a commonwealth did not flourish if good men were obscured and their deeds 'adorned with no praise of due honor', whilst their corrupted compatriots were munificently rewarded.[192] The well-being of a commonwealth required, on the contrary, that 'due testimony' was given 'to

188 Brathwait, *The schollers medley*, p. 82. See also John Davies, *Microcosmos: the discovery of the little world, with the government thereof* (Oxford, 1603), pp. 124–8, who also cited Cicero.
189 *The historie of the world*, I.ix.iv, p. 184.
190 Barnes, *Foure bookes of offices*, p. 28.
191 Ibid., p. 32–3, cf. pp. 65, 72, and p. 115, where Barnes resorted to the central third book of Francesco Patrizi's *De institutione reipublicae*. See also Thomas Sutton, *Iethroes covnsell to Moses: or a direction for magistrates: a sermon preached at St Saviours in Southwarke. March 5. 1621* (London, 1631), pp. 17–18.
192 [I. R.], *The north starre*, sig. E1r; *Organon reipvblicae*, sig. C4v.

vertue'. Everyone, that is, should be rewarded in accordance with their merits. 'Let vertue', the author declared, 'be the chiefest merit for promotions' and added a little later: 'Let not the more noble, but the better judgement obtaine the victorie.'[193]

It should be emphasized that such central notions of classical humanism as *negotium* and *vera nobilitas* were not necessarily by themselves incompatible with support for a strong monarchy. Robert Cotton is an apposite example of those who coupled humanist ideas with a notion of sovereignty.[194] As we have seen, John Hitchcock argued for the *vita activa* at the same time as he insisted that a prince could overstep the boundaries of law. Many of those who were employed by the king's government saw themselves as leading an active life. The anonymous treatise, *The covrt of James*, employed humanist arguments to defend the courtier's life. Francis Bacon's espousal of *negotium* was scarcely directed against James's government, whose loyal servant he of course was, but rather against the rise of the new moral outlook of scepticism and self-preservation, which was, on the other hand, closely linked with the court.

Nevertheless, there is little doubt that the ideas of *negotium* and true nobility were used not merely to portray the self-image of the king's servants or to emphasize the general importance of the people's active role in the public sphere, but also to launch a more particular ideological attack on the contemporary political system. The future republican poet George Wither published his highly controversial collection of moral poems *Abvses stript, and whipt* in 1613. This long work was exceptionally popular (there were four printings in 1613 and one each in 1614, 1615 and 1617), and it got Wither into troubles with the authorities who imprisoned him for a while in 1614.[195] In *Abvses stript, and whipt* Wither impugned the morality of the contemporary political life with exceptional outspokenness. Dedicating the work to himself, he noted: 'Some no doubt will mistaste my plainnes, in that I have so bluntly spoken what I have observed, without any Poeticall additions or faigned Allegories.' Rather than using the examples of 'old ages past' or 'wise-mens Sayings' to express his withering criticism, he was, he said, 'resolv'd to tie my rimes / As much as may be to the present times'.[196] In one of the epigrams

---

[193] [I. R.], *The north starre*, sig. ci^{r-v}. 'Sit virtus, ad dignitates, meritum summum.' 'Vincat sententia non nobilior, sed melior.' *Organon reipvblicae*, sig. b2^{r-v}.

[194] Sharpe 1979, pp. 235–47.

[195] Pritchard 1963.

[196] George Wither, *Abvses stript, and whipt: or satirical essaies, diuided into two bookes* (London, 1613), sigs. b1^{r-v}, k2^{r}.

written by a friend (Th. C.), Wither was contrasted with 'time-pleasers', for unlike them he 'freely speak'st the truth'. He was thus 'Another Cato' save 'more daring'.[197]

Wither's forthrightness was evident both in his description of the decay and corrosion of the English commonwealth and in his pre-scribed remedies. He claimed that he had perceived 'The confus'd actions of this present age'; everything he saw around him 'was ill'. The 'present age' was a scene 'Of Villany, of Lust, and all uncleane / And loath'd corruption'. The purpose of his book, Wither declared in an epigram to the earl of Pembroke, at the end of the volume, was to reveal 'th'abuses of these wicked Times'.[198] Although there were several particular areas where corruption arose, Wither was convinced that it emerged most clearly in two highly crucial ways with disastrous results. First, it had caused a general tendency to place the private good before the public one and thus to lead a solitary rather than active life. According to Wither, some people held 'them wise and vertuous' who lived in 'A heremitall solitariness', which opinion proceeded from 'imbecillity' and which resulted in 'Non-ability'. It comes as no surprise that it was Cicero whose authority Wither found compelling.

> For man (saith Tully) borne to other ends
> The for to please himselfe; a part to have,
> The common-weale doth look, and parents crave
> A part; so doth his friend.[199]

The other and even more important way in which the decay affected the whole commonwealth was by corrupting the idea of nobility. There was already a widespread but repulsive habit of identifying nobility with wealth and riches.

> Yea there be idle theeving Rogues a many,
> That have no Vertue, nor will ne're have any;
> Yet for their wealth shall highly, be respected,
> When honest men their betters, are neglected.[200]

Equally dangerous was to regard birth and lineage as true qualities of nobility. 'Noblenesse of Birth' was nothing but 'vaine', unless the family had retained 'Some noble qualitie'.[201]

[197] Ibid., sig. B5^r, cf. sigs. K2^r, L2^v.
[198] Ibid., sigs. C6^r, X3^r.
[199] Ibid., sig. Q4^v–5^r.
[200] Ibid., sig. G2^r.
[201] Ibid., sig. G2^r.

Riches and wealth, birth and pedigree, even a title had nothing to do with true nobility, which consisted in nothing but virtue. The vulgar could think that a rich man with a long pedigree and a pompous title was noble, but 'in a wise-man's eyes' this appeared nothing but obtuse. Only those who were 'rais'd by Vertue' not merely had 'most worthinesse' but were also 'most ancient', because their nobility was obtained by the same means as 'all Great men [had] first obtained their Fame'.[202]

v

If the arguments presented in Jacobean England about the importance and desirability of the virtuous public life were essentially classical humanist in character, this was equally true when we turn to analyse the ways in which they thought this mode of life could be acquired in practice. It was widely agreed that this could only happen through an extensive education in the *studia humanitatis*. John Ford believed that a man could hope to attain virtue and thereby act virtuously if he began the training for this as early as possible,[203] whilst Thomas Scott of Canterbury maintained that education was the safest way for men 'to make good, or improve' their birth.[204] The same idea was extensively discussed by Henry Crosse, according to whom the means to virtue was 'diligent education & training up youth in discipline'. Education was nothing less than 'the maine pillar that holdeth up & underprops the government, without which no Common-wealth could stand & peaceably continue'.[205]

But the idea that education was necessary for the inculcation of virtue in people's minds was most extensively explored, of course, in the educational treatises which can in this respect be seen as a direct continuity of the earlier, singularly English, tradition of educational manuals. Cleland pointed out that the institution of youth was a crucial element in 'a wel governed Common-weale' and included logic and mathematics in his curriculum, but gave the most prominent place to 'the Grammar, and Humanities'.[206] Henry Peacham lamented how

---

[202] Ibid., sig. P5ᵛ. Cf. idem, *A satyre, written to the kings most excellent maiestie* (1614), in idem, *Iuuenalia a collection of those poems* (London, 1622), sig. EE3ʳ⁻ᵛ.

[203] Ford, *A line of life*, pp. 7–8.

[204] Scott, *A discourse*, pp. 193, 188, 195.

[205] Crosse, *Vertues common-wealth*, sig. G4ʳ; cf. in general Hitchcock, *A sanctuary for honest men*, pp. 5, 142–52; Nixon, *The dignitie of man*, p. 77; Leonard Wright, *A display of dvty*, fos. 1ʳ⁻ᵛ.

[206] Cleland, *Propaideia*, pp. 21, 79–85; cf. e.g. [I. R.], *Organon reipvblicae*, sig. D4ᵛ.

parents were ready to invest more money in 'a fellow who can but teach a Dogge, or reclaime and Hawke' than in 'an honest, learned, and well qualified man to bring up their children'. He provided an even more detailed and staggering list of subjects which a young gentleman should master. The basis of his education rested, however, on the pillars of rhetoric, history and moral philosophy.[207] Thomas Morrice reiterated that 'good education' advanced and preserved 'true Nobilitie'. But many parents paid more careful attention to receiving into their service 'a Cooke, a Falconer, or an Horse-rider' than to getting a proper 'Schoolmaster' for their children. 'They doe not much care', he lamented, 'whether hee bee well learned, or hath taken any degree of Schoole, or is lawfully allowed to teach, or hath any good methode in teaching, or hath had experience and approbation in the trayning up of children, and doth understand and speake perfectly pure English, Latine and Greeke, with the right accent and true pronunciation thereof.'[208]

The humanist education also furnished Barnes and the author of the *Organon reipvblicae* with the chief way of attaining virtues and thereby the commonwealth. According to the latter, the four cardinal virtues were not natural qualities, but were acquired by perseverance alone. A matter of crucial importance in the maintenance of the commonwealth was, therefore, to pay sufficient attention to the issues of 'the education of youth'. 'Good education is called the foundation of wisedome.'[209] Questions concerning morality and politics were to be learned from both holy scriptures and 'Prophane Authors' including Aristotle, Cicero, Seneca and Tacitus. In learning it was important to perceive 'what wee learne' and to keep 'that which wee learne', but most vital was to see to it that something was brought forth and framed from our learning, and this was 'a worke of continuall exercise'.[210] History was a key subject since, 'as Cicero saith', it was 'the mistresse of life, and the witnesse of times'. The reason why history was most useful training for the future active members of the commonwealth was ascribed to the fact that 'the nature of man continueth the same'. 'Onely the persons and Actors of the Historie,' the author wrote, 'doe succeede new every age; and the names being changed, the stories are now told as it were

[207] Peacham, *The compleat gentleman*, pp. 30–7, 42–55.
[208] Morrice, *An apology*, sigs. B4ʳ, C7ᵛ–8ᵛ.
[209] [I. R.], *Organon reipvblicae*, sig. C4ʳ; *The north starre*, sig. D4ᵛ; Barnes, *Foure bookes of offices*, pp. 60–2, 67.
[210] [I. R.], *Organon reipvblicae*, sig. A3ʳ⁻ᵛ; *The north starre*, sig. B1ʳ–2ʳ. Cf. [Richard West], *The schoole of vertve, the second part: or, the young schollers paradice* (London, 1619), sig. A5ᵛ.

of our selves.'[211] In addition to moral philosophy and history, rhetoric was an indispensable discipline. The author raised this issue already in his discussion of learning, pointing out that one should 'speake well' as well as 'speake eloquently'. Towards the end of the tract the theme of rhetoric was pursued further, and the reader was offered an epitome of things of weight in persuasion and dissuasion.[212] This ideal model of consummate learning was contrasted sharply with the prevalence of ignorance and idleness in the contemporary ruling class. 'Oh shame!' the author exclaimed, 'men unwise, and of a grosse braine, Despisers of learning ... Do beare the Scepters, rule the people, and governe Cities.' Far from being interested in learning, these rulers continued to uphold the traditional customs of nobility; they 'have onely care of dycing, Or to feede dogges, horses and hawkes, And to leade a childish life in continuall sportes'. This degeneration and despicable mode of life was the chief reason for 'so manie thousand scabbes of errors, so manie sinkes of follies, so manie thousands of mischievous deeds'.[213]

The emphasis on the active life and on education in the *studia humanitatis* as a means to it was closely linked with a sharp critique of futile scholastic learning, with accompanying stress on the utility of learning. Although Cleland was of the opinion that 'the generalities & Quodlibets of Schoolemen' were to some extent good, he emphasized that one must avoid descending 'into their distinctions' instead of 'a fruitful wombe, for the use and benefit of a mans life'.[214] The strongest case to this effect was presented by Francis Bacon. As we have seen, he argued that moral philosophy should aim at teaching how to practise virtue in the active life. In the *Advancement of learning* Bacon employed all his rhetorical skills to condemn 'the Schoolmen' and their degenerate learning which consisted of 'a number of subtile, idle, unwholesome, and (as I may term them) vermiculate questions'.[215]

The conviction that the feature of greatest importance in learning

---

[211] [I. R.], *Organon reipvblicae*, sig. c4^r: 'Historia ... est vitae magistra, testis temporum ... natura hominum eadem manet ... Personae tantum, & Actores Historiae, singulis aetatibus, novi succedunt; &, mutatis nominibus, quasi de nobis fabulae nunc narrantur.' *The north starre*, sig. D4^v.

[212] [I. R.], *Organon reipvblicae*, sig. D2^r–3^r; *The north starre*, sig. E3^r–4^r.

[213] [I. R.], *Organon reipvblicae*, sig. c4^v: 'Proh pudor! ignari Sophiae, crassique cerebri, Doctrinae osores (quibus est sola alea curae, Aut nutrire canes & equos, volueresque rapaces, Continuisque iocis puerilem ducere vitam) Sceptra tenent, populo praesunt, vrbesque gubernant. Hinc mille errorum scabies, tot stultitiarum Colluvies: hinc & tot millia flagitiorum.' *The north starre*, sigs. D4^v–E1^r.

[214] Cleland, *Propaideia*, p. 88.

[215] Bacon, *Advancement of learning*, in *Works*, III, p. 285, cf. pp. 418–19. It should be noted that Bacon commended 'the colleges of the Jesuits', pp. 276–7.

was its practical utility has long been identified with Bacon. Only recently, however, have scholars tended to link this aspect of Bacon's thinking to the humanist tradition.[216] Dedicating the *De sapientia veterum* to his *alma mater*, Bacon announced: 'Certainly I am of opinion that speculative studies [*contemplativæ*] when transplanted into active life [*in vitam activam*] acquire some new grace and vigour, and having more matter to feed them, strike their roots perhaps deeper, or at least grow taller and fuller leaved.'[217] It is important to bear in mind that there was nothing exceptional in Bacon's arguments; they were endorsed equally strenuously by a number of other theorists examined in this chapter.

James Cleland opened his chapter, entitled 'Howe profitable learning is, and how hurtful ignorance is unto a Noble man', with a traditional lamentation over the prevalence of the 'false and fantastical opinion' that 'ignorance is thought an essential marke of a Noble man'. Those who professed learning were ridiculed as 'clerks or pedants', and if a child did not love 'an Hawke and a Dogge', this was taken as a token of his degeneracy. To oppose these prevailing attitudes, Cleland placed chief emphasis on the usefulness of learning in the active life. An ignorant man could perform no public service, he was totally 'unapt for all dignities, offices or Charges' of the commonwealth.[218] William Martyn similarly stressed the importance of virtue, but added that it did not suffice 'that a man be vertuously enclined'. In addition to the embracement of virtue, 'he must likewise be furnished with learning, and with wisedome'. The chief benefit of deep learning was said to be found in its helping to put virtue into action. It was only when a man was able to combine virtues with learning that he was able 'to make a profitable dispensation and distribution of his vertues, for the good of himselfe and of other men'. To summarize his point, Martyn announced that 'concerning the necessity of being learned, (for the better practising of religion, and of vertuous actions) you must know, that without learning, you shall be unprofitable to the common-weale'. A man could achieve nothing 'excellent' without labour and pain and 'learning being so gotten doth not only make men excellent, but she is (indeed) the excellency of man'.[219]

[216] Vickers 1984; cf. Skinner 1978 1, p. 107; Shapiro 1983, p. 18; McNamee 1971. Cf. Cochrane 1976, pp. 1050–2.

[217] Bacon, *De sapientia veterum*, in *Works*, VI, p. 621, translation, p. 691.

[218] Cleland, *Propaideia*, pp. 134–9; cf. Peacham, *The compleat gentleman*, pp. 18–21; A. D. B., *The court of James*, pp. 6–7.

[219] Martyn, *Youths instructions*, pp. 24, 31, in general pp. 24–33.

The successful statesman's indispensable qualities and the crucial importance of learning are central themes of Shakespeare's *Coriolanus*. It was statesmen or senators who took care of the common good. As Menenius told the citizens,

> The senators of Rome are this good belly,
> And you the mutinous members. For examine
> Their counsels and their cares, digest things rightly
> Touching the wel o'th'common, you shall find
> No public benefit which you receive
> But it proceeds or comes from them to you.[220]

Coriolanus' uncompromising disposition and therefore his tragic end can be explained by his incompleteness as a statesman. He was a man of valour and true honour, but he can hardly be said to have been a consummate statesman. The virtue of courage and valour was, in fact, his only virtue, and warfare his only sphere of action; for him, action *meant* warfare. Coriolanus thus completely ignored the civic aspects of the active life.

The predominance of courage made Coriolanus proud and insolent, which amounted to intemperate behaviour. It was the tribunes who most strongly accused Coriolanus of lack of temperance, but even Menenius exhorted him to act 'temperately', which advice Coriolanus of course failed to follow.[221] Moreover, Coriolanus did not embrace justice. Although he did not act like a cunning fox, he was nonetheless prepared to act like a lion. More importantly, his striving for personal glory led him to the most serious form of corruption. He put his private honour before the common good of his country: he was about to invade Rome in order to exact revenge on the Romans.

Eloquence was an invaluable asset for a statesman; it could turn even a woman into a senator. When Volumnia used eloquence in persuading Coriolanus to refrain from attacking Rome, Menenius hailed her as a true statesman:

> This Volumnia
> Is worth of consuls, senators, patricians,
> A city full: of tribunes such as you,
> A sea and land full. You have prayed well today.[222]

[220] *Coriolanus*, i.i, 146–51.
[221] Ibid., iii.iii, 28, 67.
[222] Ibid., v.iv, 51–4.

But not only did Coriolanus fail to master the complexities of rhetoric; for him, idle and empty rhetoric epitomized the useless civic sphere of *negotium*. He pointed out that 'when blows have made me stay, I fled from words'.

> I had rather have one scratch my head i'th'sun
> When the alarum were struck than idly sit
> To hear my nothings monstered.[223]

Eloquence was simply a sign of base behaviour because it consisted in nothing but flattery and dissimulation.

Coriolanus' most serious defect and the one on which all his other shortcomings ultimately hinged was his utter lack of wisdom and learning. Preferring sword to schoolmaster, he failed to embrace learning and thereby the essential virtues of *negotium*. According to Volumnia, Coriolanus' son was his 'father's son' because he 'had rather see the swords and hear a drum / than look upon his schoolmaster'.[224]

VI

Having devoted a considerable amount of attention to the issues of the active life and true nobility, the writers examined in this chapter confronted the question of how men could expect to lead the active life and fulfil their truly noble qualities in practice. One way of answering this question was to project the venerable image of counsellor. This idea emerges in Bacon's writings, who even asserted that because of the exceptionally powerful position of learned counsellors, 'the governments of princes in minority (notwithstanding the infinite disadvantage of that kind of state) have nevertheless excelled the government of princes of mature age'.[225] As we have seen, the idea of the counsellor was also central in Barnes's *Fovre bookes of offices* and in the *Organon reipvblicae*. The purpose of Barnes's book was, as he wrote in the opening pages, to offer 'instructions for noblemen, and sage Counsellors of any Common-wealth'. If the king was 'absolute in his parts onely', 'the state' could not be prosperous. This could only be achieved when 'his Senatours' were furnished with 'dutifull diligence and proportion of vertues'.[226] The author of *Organon reipvblicae* claimed that the most necessary thing for a

---

[223] Ibid., II.ii, 70, 73–5.
[224] Ibid., I.iii, 56–7.
[225] Bacon, *Advancement of learning*, in *Works*, III, p. 270; *Essaies* (1612), in *Works*, VI, pp. 553–6.
[226] Barnes, *Fovre bookes of offices*, pp. 24–5, sig. A3ʳ.

prince or a commonwealth was virtuous counsellors.[227] According to Barnaby Rich, in the time of war 'the common wealth is defended by Souldiers' and 'in the time of peace it is preserved by Counsaylers'. 'Souldiers and Counsaylers therefore,' he concluded, 'have bin ever thought most fitte to governe'. It was important to keep in mind, Rich added, that 'a happy and a blessed common wealth it may bee called that is governed by the wisedome and vertue of noble personages'.[228] Thomas Morrice expressed a similar outlook when he pointed out that education and learning advanced 'true Nobilitie', since it enabled men to become 'wise Councellours' of their commonwealth.[229]

However, not all of these authors confined the sphere of *negotium* exclusively to that of counselling, but some were willing to extend it to the more general governance of the commonwealth. First, it was pointed out that to take care of the running of the local community was the duty of true nobility. Thomas Scott of Canterbury stressed that only those who met these requirements should be appointed as sheriffs, commissioners of the peace or other local governors. The same also applied to the governors of towns. Scott's insistence that true nobility should assume authority brought him close to the idea of an aristocracy. 'It is just and profitable for the Commonwealth', he wrote, 'that Rustiques follow the Plough, and the flockes, and heards, Mechaniques theire Trades, and that the noble beare rule. As it was in the Roman State, and all other flourishing Commonwealths, which noe longer flourished then they were carefull of this rule of well ruling.'[230] Anthony Cade drew on Cicero when he argued that 'good laws are perished for want of good men to preserve them in life ... So the Roman Common wealth expired (with Tully) not for want of good Lawes but of good men to keepe life in them.'[231]

In 'Of a country life' of the *Horae subseciuae* (attributed to William Cavendish), a true noble's local duties were listed even more meticulously. First, he ought to suppress 'the disordered and unruly life of those under his authority & command' and prevent 'all bold & contemptuous behaviour' and 'all seedes of seditions and quarrels'.

---

[227] [I. R.], *Organon reipvblicae*, sig. B1ʳ: 'Nullus Thesaurus principi & Reip. vtilior, quam Consiliarij, virtute, prudentia, fide, & fortitudine, praesantes.' *The north starre*, sigs. B3ᵛ, D4ᵛ.

[228] Barnaby Rich, *Opinion diefied: discouering the ingins, traps, and traynes, that are set in this age, whereby to catch opinion* (London, 1613), p. 12. Cf. e.g. Stephens, *Essayes and characters ironicall, and instrvctive*, p. 90.

[229] Morrice, *An apology*, sig. B4ʳ; cf. Martyn, *Youths instruction*, pp. 24–6.

[230] Scott, *A discourse*, p. 186.

[231] Anthony Cade, *A sermon of the nature of conscience* (London, 1621), sig. A2ᵛ, pp. 9–10, cited in Peck 1993a, p. 171.

Above all, he must bear in mind in his role of local governor that he should stand above competing factions and moderate them by 'the vertue of his authority'. Secondly, it belonged to the duty of a country gentleman 'not only to prevent il, but to do good'. This was accomplished 'in the sollemne and publike meetings, for distribution of Justice'. Conducting himself on these occasions with 'an excellent restraint of partialitie and favour' and 'without private ends', a true gentleman was able to enhance the good of his country and to induce other men to imitate his example.[232]

As well as discussing the idea of counselling and the governance of the local community, some of these theorists felt inclined to accept, at least to some extent, the more genuinely republican idea that the active life was not confined to the exclusive coterie of counsellors, but should instead be extended to a larger body of virtuous men. According to Cleland, learning was vital for a true noble, since it enabled him 'to sit in a Kings Privie Councell, to have a voice in the Parliament house, to undertake an embbasage, or to bee imployed in some other honorable charge for the publike'.[233] John Ford called him 'a publike man' who was employed 'in affaires for his Countrey, Prince and Commonwealth', and later, in the definition of the scope of his actions, Ford emphasized that 'places of Authority in a Commonwealth' should be disposed to virtuous men who could be called '*Bonus Ciuis*', or 'a good Statist'.[234] Similarly, since parliamentary participation was considered as a service for the common good, MPs could be conceived as political actors.[235]

The essay 'Of a country life' in the *Horae subseciuae* asserted that the locality was not an adequate arena of activity for the country gentleman. A retired country life was not sufficient for a gentleman since this made him unable to gather the experience of public life available only in the city and at court. Although learning acquired by extensive reading was important for a gentleman, it was not adequate since the world, especially as it stood presently, was so variable. Knowledge based merely on books could not, therefore, guide a man safely through the ever-changing landscape. Practical experience was indispensable for a gentleman in the managing of his own affairs. But more importantly, practical experience made a

---

232 Anon., *Horae subseciuae*, pp. 141–5, see also pp. 147–8.
233 Cleland, *Propaideia*, pp. 135–7, 144–6, 51; Wright, *A display of dvty*, fos. 4^r–5^r.
234 Ford, *A line of life*, pp. 52–4.
235 Sacks 1992, pp. 91–3.

gentleman capable of performing his duty towards the commonwealth. It enabled him to act as a 'minister' or statesman.[236] In his
apology for schoolmasters, Morrice maintained that the acquisition
of 'vertuous Learning' made men 'worthy Governours of their
Countrey'. He summarized his whole argument by invoking the
authority of Thomas Elyot to the effect that those who were not
learned could not act as 'politique Statesmen, or wise Councellours,
or discreet Governours'.[237]

The idea that the *vita activa* should not be confined to the
exclusive group of counsellors, but must include as wide a body of
virtuous citizens as possible, was most clearly set out in Barnes's
Fovre bookes of offices and in the anonymous *Organon reipvblicae*. We
have already noted how Barnes maintained that 'a good Commonwealths man' displayed his 'civile vertues' and acted as 'a noble
citizen'. The chief way in which this could materialize was when
citizens took care of the government of the community. 'Their
whole care and studie', Barnes wrote, should 'bee bent to maintaine
the reputation of that Common-wealth, where they governe under
their prince.'[238]

A striking feature of the argument presented in the *Organon
reipvblicae* was the serious curtailment of the role of the prince. The
original edition was dedicated to James and the author paid lip
service to the king with a dedicatory remark: 'to whom this kind of
small work could rather be offered than to him who presides over the
highest government of the commonwealth'.[239] Nonetheless, in the
tract the king's power or his indispensable qualities and characteristics
were hardly mentioned at all. As a result, the chief responsibility for
the maintenance of the commonwealth did not lie with the king but
on the contrary with a larger body of citizens. As we have seen, the
tract emphasized *negotium* and discussed the four cardinal virtues
implying that they should be possessed by the whole body of the
people. 'The Law, equitie, execution of Lawes, the dexteritie of the
Magistrates,' the author listed as the true sinews of the commonwealth, 'are the patrimony of a Common-wealth.'[240] It is possible to
catch an echo of the republican priority of liberty. Although the laws

---

[236] Anon., *Horae subseciuae*, pp. 163–71.
[237] Morrice, *An apology*, sigs. B3^r–4^r, B7^r, C6^v.
[238] Barnes, *Fovre bookes of offices*, p. 88, cf. pp. 28, 57.
[239] *Organon reipvblicae*, sig. A2^r: 'Cui enim potius offerentur istiusmodi opuscula, quam ei qui Reipublicae summo gubernaculo praesidet.'
[240] [I. R.], *The north starre*, sig. C1^v.

had to restrict excessive liberty, at the same time they had to secure 'moderate liberty' which was 'profitable for every one, and for the Common-wealth'.[241]

But the republican nature of the arguments of the *Organon reipvblicae* emerged most clearly when the author discussed how to ensure that the people could perform their public duty. He quoted Cicero to the effect that when 'Judges and magistrates doe well and justly execute their offices ... there it must needes be, that the same Common wealth do florish, and flow with all good things'. In this commonwealth the people applauded and praised 'the excellent beautie of vertue shining in their superiours', and so attempted to follow their example.[242] To ensure that this state of affairs continued and that magistrates executed their offices, certain strategies had to be assumed. First, as we have already seen, promotion should be based on virtues and personal merits. Secondly, care should be taken that 'there be successive Magistrates'. If this was not taken seriously and the same magistrates stayed long in power, the continuous exercise of power would corrupt them. The calamitous results of such practice could be seen in the Roman triumvirates. By having a continuous succession of magistrates, it was possible to avoid the situation where they might become 'proud with continuall government'. The rotation of magistrates helped in preventing their own decline, but it also ensured that the 'hope of advancement' would 'comfort' as many as possible.[243]

Finally, the rotation of magistrates served to promote the health of the commonwealth by ensuring that the most virtuous members of the commonwealth became magistrates. 'Where there bee fewe which desire offices,' the author contended, 'there the common wealth is in danger.' Severe competition for office, in other words, ensured that magistrates were men of true virtue. 'Let no estate of men', he added, 'bee deprived of hope to attaine anie preheminence.' The competition for office was itself maintained by the system where everyone had a chance to be promoted. The underlying assumption was that a system

241 Ibid., sig. B4^r–C1^v, B1^v–2^v; cf. Wright, *The first part*, pp. 46–50.
242 [I. R.], *Organon reipvblicae*, sig. B2^v: 'Vbi iudices & magistratus suis officijs, pro sua imperiique dignitate, egregie & iuste perfunguntur, eam Remp. facile florere, omnibusque bonis affluere necesse est; populo applaudente & collaudante excellentem virtutis pulchritudinem, in superioribus.' *The north starre*, sig. C1^v.
243 [I. R.], *Organon reipvblicae*, sig. A4^v; *The north starre*, sig. B3^r. Contrast this with Charles Gibbon's definition of equality – 'one to Rule and the rest to obey is the onely square of equalitie', *The order of eqvalitie*, p. 5.

of magistracy based on meritocracy would provoke contest amongst men, so much so that everyone pursued virtue and the whole commonwealth would in effect benefit from this competition by having the most virtuous magistrates. 'By rewards & honors,' the author remarked, 'excellent wittes are stirred up with a more earnest vehemency of minde, to the study of vertue.'[244]

In Ben Jonson's *Catiline* the republican answer to corruption was developed in some detail. In Act I the chorus lamented the corruption of the commonwealth but in Act II it explained the way in which this decay could be reformed. The good of the commonwealth hinged on the election of new consuls. Those who had voice in the election should

> make a free and worthy choice,
> Excluding such as would invade
> The commonwealth.

They should pay attention to the candidates' 'faith' and 'conscience' rather than to their 'face' and 'fame'. Good consuls had all the central virtues – wisdom, fortitude and justice – and they counted 'life, state, glory, all they gain' as 'the republic's, not their own'. They simply imitated the great heroes of the republic – Brutus, Decii, Scipios – and they proved to be 'truly magistrates' and 'make happy states'.[245]

VII

So far in this chapter we have examined two closely related, central concepts of humanist political thought – the active life and true nobility – and how they could be promoted and how jeopardized. Although English writers of the early seventeenth century mainly drew – the common classical sources apart – on the northern humanist tradition as well as on its forerunner, the Italian literature of advice-books for princes, the contrasting tradition of republican humanism also had a discernible impact at the time. This is clear enough from the occasional exertions of this literature in discussions of the active life and true

---

244 [I. R.], *Organon reipvblicae*, sig. c4ᵛ: 'Vbi pauci candidati, status in periculo.' 'Nulli hominum ordini, praecludatur, ad quamcunq; dignitatem ... spes.' 'Praemijs & titulis, splendida ingenia, ad virtutis studium, accriori animi impetu, concitantur.' *The north starre*, sig. EI^r. The same idea was endorsed e.g. by Nixon, *The dignitie of man*, pp. 81–3; Wright, *The first part*, pp. 61–3; Hitchcock, *A sanctvary for honest men*, p. 16; Crosse, *Vertues common-wealth*, sig 14ᵛ; Joseph Wybarne, *The new age of old names*, pp. 55–6; and most strongly by Anon., *Horae subseciuae*, pp. 11–30: 'To desire precedence above others in respect of ones service, or merit is a good emulation', p. 26.
245 *Catiline*, II.371–406.

nobility. But the continuing impact of 'civic' humanism is most obvious in the treatment and endorsement of the mixed constitution.

There is a surprising degree of unanimity amongst scholars that the idea of the mixed constitution exercised no influence in English political discourse of the early seventeenth century.[246] Nevertheless, I find it difficult to concur with this. There is of course little doubt that the classical theory of the mixed constitution never assumed a central, let alone a dominant, place in the political vocabulary of Jacobean Englishmen. But neither was it completely lost on them. The moral and educational treatises we have been studying in this chapter had little to say about the machinery of government; they did not, in other words, discuss how the government of their commonwealth should be organized. This is not to say, however, that the Jacobeans failed to draw on the literature of classical republicanism in so far as government organization was concerned.

The issues of the mixed constitution surfaced, to begin with, in a number of translations. In 1607, the 1598 translation of Laurentius Grimalius Goslicius' *De optimo senatore* was reprinted with a new title of *A common-wealth of good covnsaile: or, policies chiefe counseller*. In 1615, Edward Grimeston rendered into English Pierre d'Avity's *The estates, empires, & principallities of the world*, where it was claimed not merely that in England 'all absolute power consists in the Parliament', but also that the government of Venice exceeded every other form of government. Venice had long enjoyed 'a golden age, living in tranquilitie and peace, and encreasing dayly in prosperitie and wealth'. Although this proceeded 'chiefely from the will of God', d'Avity found it impossible to deny that it also grew 'by a well ordered government instituted by wise men'. The chief benefit of the Venetian government was that it was neither 'a government of many, nor of few' nor even a 'government of one alone: but it is composed of all the three kindes of governments, out of which they have made one that is perfect'.[247] The whole success story of Venice was told by Thomas de Fougasses in his *The generall historie of the magnificent state of Venice* translated into English in 1612.[248]

---

[246] Weston 1960; Hinton 1960; d'Avack 1975; Eccleshall 1978, pp. 120–1; Weston and Greenberg 1981, pp. 8–34; Pocock 1975b, p. 355; Sommerville 1986, pp. 57–8; Mendle 1973, p. 222; Mendle 1985, pp. 3, 111; Nippel 1980, pp. 218–37; Collinson 1990, p. 23; Smith 1973. But see recently W. Klein 1987.

[247] Pierre d'Avity, *The estates, empires, & principallities of the world*, translated by Edward Grimeston (London, 1615), pp. 10–11, 526–7, see also pp. 529–30. Cf. W. Klein 1987, p. 214.

[248] Thomas de Fougasses, *The generall historie of the magnificent state of Venice*, translated by W. Shute (London, 1612), sig. A3ʳ.

Three years later an anonymous treatise entitled *A description of the vnited Prouinces* described the Netherlands as a country of freedom and liberty and as a country where the prince was elected and where 'the other Rulers and States that were chosen out of the Nobilitie and Commons, had as much power or superintendance over the King, as the King had over them'.[249]

The cement of the English monarchical system did not inhibit a number of Englishmen from perceiving the advantages of a republican mixed government or even detecting its traces in their own commonwealth. Thomas Smith's famous description of the mixed constitution was reprinted three times during James's reign.[250] Francis Bacon had written in 1589 that a republic may be better policy than a monarchy. In 1608 he reminded himself of the 'Bookes in commendac[ion] of Mon[narchy] mix[ed] or Aristoc[racy] and told the king a few years later that 'the senate of Venice' was 'the wisest state of Europe'.[251] Bacon asserted that a prince became a tyrant when he took 'all into his own hands' and did not care 'for the consent of his nobles and senate [*ordinum et senatus*]', but administered 'the government by his own arbitrary and absolute authority'.[252] In the *Advancement of learning* he wrote that 'it was ever holden that honours in free monarchies and commonwealths had a sweetness more than in tyrannies'.[253] He scarcely used the term 'free monarchies' in the same sense as James I. For Bacon, a free monarchy was something akin to a republic.

Similarly, Walter Ralegh argued in *The historie of the world* that whereas kings were 'unwilling to pay great thankes', 'free Estates' were 'bountifull in giving thankes',[254] but in his tract on war he set greatest store by the nobility in the political life of a community. He pointed out that many 'learned writers abroad have declared' that 'the commonwealth was best governed' in England. Although Henry III had 'yielded to the growing greatness and privileges of the commons' in order 'to lessen the power of the nobility', Ralegh completely agreed with those 'politicians' who affirmed that 'nobility preserves liberty

---

[249] Anon., *A description of the prosperitie, strength, and wise government of the vnited Prouinces of the Netherlands* (London, 1615), sig. A3ʳ–4ʳ; cf. sig. B2ʳ, where the government of the Netherlands was described as 'a Democraticke gouernment'.

[250] For Smith's importance, see W. Klein 1987, pp. 214–15.

[251] Bacon, 'Commentarius solutus' 28 July 1608, in *Letters*, IV, p. 73; Bacon to James I, 31 August 1617, in *Letters*, VI, p. 246.

[252] Bacon, *De sapientia veterum*, in *Works*, VI, pp. 630–1, translation pp. 702–3.

[253] *Works*, III, p. 316. See also, Greville, *A dedication*, in *The prose works*, p. 14; but cf. *Treatise of monarchy*, stanza 594, in *Remains*, p. 184.

[254] *The historie of the world*, v.vi.ii, p. 717.

longer than the commons'. In so far as longevity was concerned, 'Solon's popular state came far short of Lycurgus's by mixed government; for the popular state of Athens soon fell, whilst the royal mixed government of Sparta stood a mighty time.' Because of the prominent place of the nobility both 'Sparta and Venice enjoyed their freedom longer than Rome'.[255] Joseph Wybarne argued that since 'the Nobility is interessed in the Commonwealth', it was not possible 'that any State, eyther auncient or moderne, can be preferred to it for politicke and discreete Governement'.[256]

When Barnabe Barnes came to discuss forms of government, he began by declaring that 'according to the generall opinion of all good writers, there are six formes of policie'. Proceeding to the first one – monarchy – Barnes cited Bodin to demonstrate that kings were above the law by virtue of their law-making power.[257] He then briefly introduced all six forms of government and stated that monarchy was by far the best of them. Having established this, however, Barnes quickly moved to treat the constitutional development of ancient Rome. When the kings had been expelled from Rome, the commonwealth had been 'by the Senate managed a long time'. After the aristocratic phase the Roman people had retained 'a Democraticall state', which was tempered 'with the moderation and authorities royall, and with the Patricians, as appeared in the Consulate estate, and in the Senators'. 'So that', Barnes asserted, 'out of the Soveraigne rule of a kingdome, being revived in the Consuls; out of the government Aristocraticall, represented by the Senators; and out of the Democracie, manifested in the Plebeian Tribunes, a firme and absolute Commonwealth was fashioned.' Without using the term 'mixed', Barnes claimed that Rome had acquired its most stable and durable form of government when it was organized as a mixture of all three pure forms. To explain what he had in mind, Barnes pointed out that the 'most perfect and excellent' monarchies in his own time consisted of these three elements. They were 'established by the Senate or Counsell of most prudent persons, advanced for their true nobilitie to that place with a kind of consent and approbation of the commons'.[258]

---

[255] Walter Ralegh, 'A discourse of the original and fundamental cause of natural, arbitrary, necessary, and unnatural war' (1614–16), in *Works*, VIII, pp. 295–6.

[256] Wybarne, *The new age of old names*, pp. 78–9.

[257] Barnes, *Fovre bookes of offices*, p. 63.

[258] Ibid.,, pp. 63–5. Cf. Fulke Greville, *Treatise of monarchy*, stanzas 304–6, in *Remains*, p. 111, where republican Rome is presented in similar terms, in striking contrast with Greville's later discussion of the same theme.

Later in the third book of his treatise, Barnes discarded the Bodinian concept of the king's law-making authority. Enquiring into the nature of laws, he remarked on their constant change and argued that this only happened in parliament. 'When the billes of those houses [of parliament]', Barnes explained, 'are once exhibited, past, and inacted, they cannot be repealed without another Parliament, by generall consent of the Prince and of all persons.' He further named 'our Parliamentall lawes' 'the Civill law' partly because they respected 'this Realme and Commonwealth generally', but mainly by virtue of the method of making them. 'For as these our Statute Lawes of England', Barnes wrote, 'are only made & established by the popular consent and unanimitie; whereupon they take title of commonwealthes Laws.' This way of making laws by popular consent was not the distinctive mark of the English commonwealth alone, but was characteristic of 'all free Cities'. According to Barnes, 'the civill Laws of all free Cities' were 'devised and established for the generall behoofe of those particular States, by consent of all the free Citizens, and thereupon called civill Lawes'. Ancient Athens furnished Barnes's instance: 'such were the lawes of Solon and Draco, unto which the people of Athens (that had during the Greeke monarchie been a free State, and royall Commonwealth) were subjected in particular.'[259]

A Scot, Robert Pont, enquired into the nature of the different forms of governments at the beginning of his dialogue on the Anglo-Scottish union. The dialogue was opened by Irenaeus summarizing the topic of their former discussions. He pointed out how Polyhistor, another interlocutor, had 'breifly described what Aristotle setteth downe at large, and shewed that of the three formes of government, monarchicall, aristocraticall, and democraticall, the cheif and principall' was 'princely power'. But Polyhistor had also argued that monarchy ought to be joined with aristocracy so that 'of this twofold kinde a sweet and pleasant harmony of governing might be composed'. This conclusion had been confirmed by 'Aristotle and Plato' who both 'commend this mixt kinde of rule, and by good proofes shew it to excell all other'. Nevertheless, Polyhistor's final point was that the mixture of monarchy and aristocracy was the form of

---

[259] Barnes, *Foure bookes of offices*, pp. 134, 129–30; cf. also p. 73 where England and Venice are described as 'free Cities'. Cf. R[obert] J[ohnson], *The new life of Virginea: declaring the former successe and present estate of that plantation being the second part of Noua Britannia* (London, 1612), sig. E2ᵛ–3ʳ.

government prevalent in both England and Scotland. 'You', Irenaeus argued, 'did farther prase even for this amongst other the Britons' commonwealth (I meant that of Great Britaine), and proved it to take place with the very first entrance of those nationes that peopled the country, and to be confirmed by the lawes, English and Scottish.' The foundation of the English as well as the Scottish commonwealth was such that 'one kinge by the counsell of his nobility ruled all'. If this balance between the monarchy and the aristocracy was not maintained, it either grew into tyranny or into 'timocraty'. The first case occurred when the prince was not 'guided by the holesome and sage advice of his counsellors'.[260]

William Stoughton defended his argument against prelacy by identifying the commons with the democratic element and the Lords with the aristocratic element of the mixed government. Rather than being a pure monarchy, the English 'people ever since the time they first began to be a people, have had their witts long exercised, with the sence and feeling, of the reasons & principles, aswell of Democracie, as also of Aristocracie'. The way of making laws in parliament was 'a mere Democraticall consultation' while 'the reasons, and principles of Aristocracie' were 'alreadie in the minds of the Peres, the Nobles, the Judges, and other great men of the Realme'.[261]

In 1621, William Loe, a former chaplain of James, presented an essentially similar account of the English form of government. 'The inferiour Courts', Loe insisted, 'are erected for the good of the subject in smaller causes, and the Parliament in supreame causes is conveened, wherein the King himselfe (albeit he hath royall assent in all) yet by Law, Reason, and Religion, he is legally limited and concluded.' This was one of the excellences of the English system, for 'no wicked Nimrod can offend by strong hunting, no cursed machevillian, by damnable Statizing, nor any griping Zacheus by

---

[260] Robert Pont, 'Of the union of Britayne', in *The Jacobean union: six tracts of 1604*, ed. Bruce R. Galloway and Brian P. Levack (Edinburgh: Scottish History Society, 1985), pp. 1–3.

[261] [William Stoughton], *An assertion for true and christian church-policie* (n.p., 1604), pp. 352, 361–4. Cf. Judson 1949, pp. 331–2; Mendle 1985, pp. 98–102. Mendle's discussion is somewhat misleading at this point. First, he repeats the common claim that there was an absence of the mixed government in the early seventeenth century, yet he states that 'Stoughton developed quite the fullest and most penetrating version of the mixed constitution that had yet appeared in England.' Secondly, he explains the alleged disappearance of the mixed constitution during the period by claiming that the king associated it with the presbyterian cause against bishops; yet he has to confess that Stoughton's book, which was indeed directed against bishops, did not meet official displeasure (p. 102).

forged cavillations'. Loe first reminded his readers of the fact that 'wee live in a Common-wealth under a Monarchy which is the most absolute forme of governement'. But he immediately pro-ceeded to describe the English parliament as a mixture of the three different forms of government. 'And seeing in the high Court of the State,' he wrote, 'which wee call a PARLIAMENT, which consists of a three-fold State, and all of God, the King as the Monarchy, the Upper-house the Aristocracy, and the Lower-house as the Democracy, which nathlesse hath freedome and libertie, both of suffrage, voice, and vote.'[262] Englishmen were obviously capable of conceptualizing the government of their commonwealth not merely as a Fortescuan *regimen politicum et regale* but also as a classical mixed government.

Although the author of the *Organon reipvblicae* indicated a complacent view of the powers of virtues in the promotion of the common good, he was clearly aware that this ideal state of affairs could hardly be carried out without certain institutional factors. A commonwealth, the author believed, was utterly destroyed if it was not maintained by 'Religion and pollitique Lawes'. He did not elaborate on the former, but paid attention to the 'pollitique Lawes'.[263] Of greatest importance was to frame the laws relating to the constitution and form of government. The author conventionally listed the three good and the three bad forms, pointing out that monarchy is the form which 'is with us at this time'. He also presented instances of each of the six forms from Roman history. Monarchy was represented by the first kings while Tarquinius Superbus, Sulla and Caesar stood for tyrants. The rule of consuls formed his example of aristocracy, and the triumvirates of Caesar, Crassus and Pompey as well as Octavian, Antonius and Lepidius furnished instances of oligarchy. Roman democracy consisted of 'the pollicy of the civill Magistrate: who expelled the Decemviri', whereas 'the authority of the raging and most audacious Commons, who, when Antonius was mooved and provoked with anger, most wickedly and villanously murdered Cicero, and many states of Rome', stood for anarchy. It is noteworthy that whereas the author's positive examples came from early Roman history, Caesar's authority was classified as tyranny.

The author refrained from drawing any clear-cut preference

---

[262] William Loe, *Vox clamantis: Mark 1.3: a stil voice, to the three thrice-honourable estates of parliament* (n.p., 1621), pp. 28–9, 41.

[263] [I. R.], *Organon reipvblicae*, sig. B1ᵛ–2ᵛ; *The north starre*, sigs. B4ʳ–C1ᵛ.

between either the three good or the three bad forms of government. This is not to say, however, that he failed to reveal his own ideal form of government. He did not specify his preferences from the pure forms mainly because he held that none of them was sufficient in itself. 'It is to be noted,' the author pointed out, 'that a Commonwealth and the most perfect kindes of governments, are very seldome found absolutely simple, but fitly composed amongst themselves.' He expressed, in short, serious doubts that there could exist a pure monarchy, aristocracy or democracy. But he also believed that the best and most durable form of government was a mixed one. It is often seen, he wrote, that 'a certaine mixture is voluntarily admitted amongst them'. They were 'so mixt and tempred, that in a triple forme (as in a mervailous and sweet harmonie) one counsell signifieth as it were one minde'. Finally, the author stated that a commonwealth retained the name of the dominant part.[264]

If Anthony Nixon's discussion of the four cardinal virtues and their political character was derived almost word for word from the *Organon reipvblicae*, this was equally true of his scrutiny of the different forms of government. Nixon opened his chapter 'Of Policie' by defining what he meant by the term. 'It is', he argued, 'the regiment of a Citty or Commonwealth: the bond of all society.' The proper end of government was 'publique benefit'. When he explained the good and bad forms of government, he quoted almost verbatim the definitions put forward in the *Organon reipvblicae*. Having laid down the tripartite divisions of government he posed the question: 'How are these kindes of governments disposed?' Citing the *Organon reipvblicae* in response, Nixon wrote: 'It is to be noted that a common-wealth, and the good, and most perfect kindes of government, are very seldome found absolutely simple, but fitly composed amongst themselves: For a certaine mixture is voluntarily admitted amongst them, yet so mixt and tempered, that in a triple forme (as in sweet harmonie) one counsell signifieth as it were one minde.'[265]

---

[264] [I. R.], *Organon reipvblicae*, sigs. A4ʳ–B1ʳ: 'Notandum est, quod perraro Resp. & perfectissimua gubernandi genera absolute simplicia, sed concinne inter se composita inveniuntur. Mistura enim quaedam inter se voluntarie admittitur; adeo tamen mixta & temperata, vt in triplici forma (veluti Harmonia mira & iucunda) vnum consilium, vnam quasi mentem significet et: Nomen tamen Resp. retinet, a parte digniore, caeteris imperante.' *The north starre*, sig. B2ᵛ–3ᵛ. The discussion bears a close resemblance to that of Thomas Smith, *De republica Anglorum*, pp. 49–52.

[265] Nixon, *The dignitie of man*, pp. 115–18.

Perhaps the most unequivocal and sophisticated exposition of the mixed constitution was put forward by Henry Wright in *The first part of the disqvisition of trvth concerning political affaires*. In the second chapter, entitled 'Of the best forme of a common-wealth', Wright first introduced arguments for every particular pure form of government. 'According to many mens opinions', he introduced rule by one, 'the Monarchy ... ought to be preferred.' Relying mainly on the authority of Cicero, Sallust, Tacitus and Livy, Wright presented a cluster of traditional arguments favouring rule by one man. Monarchy was the oldest form of government; it was the one which 'best agreeth to nature' as well as 'to reason'; it resembled 'the divine Regencie'. It had also been contended that without the authority of one it was quite impossible to retain 'long concord and agreement' in a commonwealth. The superiority of kingship had also been attested by the observation that in times of difficulties democracies and aristocracies 'were glad to abandon the former kinde of government' and instead rely on a kind of monarchy by conferring 'the absolute power, strength and authoritie upon one onely'. Finally, it was possible to justify monarchy by pointing out that the tyranny of one was less unbearable than the tyranny of many. It was easier to persuade one tyrant to respect the common good than 'for many to bee disposed to goodnesse'.[266]

Those who favoured democracy did so because they believed that it maintained equality. Then 'all are subject to the lawes alike', and magistrates are 'placed by common suffrage, who judge according to the lawes' and then all 'counsels and consultations' are referred 'to the good of the Common-wealth'. Moreover, George Buchanan had advocated democracy by contending that if many were 'joyned together', they 'can better judge of all matters then one alone'. The underlying reasoning was that 'it may very well bee thought, that in every one of those many, there are certaine sparkes of Vertue, and excellencies of gifts, which concurring and put all together, must needs make an absolute judgment'.[267] Aristocracy had been preferred, according to Wright, by 'those taken to have beene of the wisest'. They claimed that in an aristocracy 'the counsels and consultations of the best men, excelling others in vertue and wisdome' guaranteed the maintenance of the public good. The success of Sparta and Venice had often been

[266] Wright, *The first part*, pp. 7–8.
[267] Ibid., pp. 8–9.

invoked to suggest that 'the Aristocraticall state was more durable
then any other forme of government'. The rule of the most virtuous
enabled a commonwealth to accommodate itself 'to all times and
occasions'.[268]

Having explicated the arguments put forward in defence of every
particular form of government, Wright did not decide the case for any
of these but provocatively claimed that these arguments were neither
good nor convincing. It was a relatively simple task to show the
weaknesses of these arguments and thereby to substantiate the further
claim that none of these three forms of government was sufficient in
itself. It is important to bear in mind that in presenting the various
arguments for the different forms of government Wright was simply
explaining what sort of arguments were usually put forward in
upholding them. But when he proceeded to advance the weaknesses of
these arguments and the deficiencies of the pure forms, Wright was
making claims of his own.

The major weakness of democracy was that since counsels and
decrees came from the people, they were governed rather 'by meere
chance' than by grave wisdom based on experience and learning.
'This forme of government', Wright judged, 'is worst of all.' Although
the longevity of aristocracy could be adduced from the instances of
Sparta and Venice, Wright declared that 'experience hath made it
manifest to the world' that as a matter of fact this was not the case.
Those who 'for a while have justly and uprightly governed the
Common-wealth, not long after have abused their power and
authority to the gathering of riches'. Power had the tendency to
corrupt its possessors which was a particularly serious problem in
aristocracies, as was easily discernible in the instance of 'the Decemvi-
rate'. A scarcely less serious problem of aristocracy was constituted by
the issue of succession. Because aristocracies were normally derived
from nobility native rather than nobility dative many a time it
happened that the successors of virtuous governors turned out to be
utterly corrupt. Underlying Wright's analysis at this point was the
humanist idea of true nobility. It was often the case that 'the sonnes
of vertuous parents ... became extreame insolent'. So, true nobles
were not those who could claim a long and fine line of ancestors, but
those who proved to be virtuous in their own life. Since these two
qualities, a long line of ancestry and a virtuous mind, rarely

[268] Ibid., pp. 9–10.

concurred, it followed that aristocracies which were based rather on blood than on virtues quickly degenerated. 'I conclude', Wright held firmly, 'That the Aristocraticall government cannot stand long firme, and stable, much lesse to bee permanent and durable.'[269]

The problems of a pure monarchy were similar to those of an aristocracy. Wright began his analysis with a dichotomy that every 'Monarch is either tied to rule, according to the lawes of the kingdome hee possesseth, or he is not'. In the latter case, when the prince is not bound by the laws, 'all men will confesse with me, that Monarchy may easily degenerate, and grow into tyranny'. If the laws, in other words, did not check the king, he would become a tyrant. But even if the king was bound by the laws of his kingdom, 'that forme of Commonwealth may not bee durable'; it was ultimately impossible to evade the ensuing corruption. Although the laws could check a ruler as long as he reigned, they were not able to make his heir virtuous. 'For very seldome', Wright announced, 'falleth it out, that to a wise and godly Father, a Sonne of that stampe, and endowed with like vertues, should succeed.' The confrontation of a corrupt king and good laws always ended up with the subjection of the laws. The reason was not far to seek. A degenerate prince would also corrupt his subjects and the authority of the law would ultimately become subdued. 'Now, whenas by the perverse, carelesse, or bad carriage of the Monarch toward his people, the manners of his subjects are once corrupted, it must of necessitie follow, that either the lawes are of small force, or none at all.' All these arguments enabled Wright boldly to conclude his discussion: 'And so farewell to that forme of governement.'[270]

If democracy was bad in itself and if it was not possible to check the growth of corruption either in an aristocracy or in a monarchy simply by establishing laws which would in principle coerce the ruler(s) to behave virtuously, the question emerged as to how the government of a commonwealth should then be organized. How was a commonwealth to be rendered durable? At the beginning of his answer Wright emphasized that one should conform with tradition. In general, the best form of government in a commonwealth was that which was 'already established'. The underlying assumption was that people were so used to the form of government which had been established in their

---

[269] Ibid., pp. 11–12.
[270] Ibid., pp. 10–11.

community that 'it would be a very hard matter' to accustom those who were used to living under a monarch to 'a free forme of government' and, contrariwise, it would be almost an impossibility to reduce a free people 'to live under the obedience and command of one absolute Ruler'. The moral of Wright's reasoning could be seen not only in 'the Easterne Countries' which 'were ever devoted to live under one sole Monarth', but also in the fact that 'no forme of government would please the Athenians and Helvetians ... but a Democracy: None the Lacedaemonians but an Aristocracy'.

Wright did not explicitly relate his discussion to the circumstances of his own country, but he was careful to point out that to change the established form of government in a community was not recommended. Nevertheless, he was fully convinced that none of the pure forms were good in themselves. 'I utterly', he declared, 'deny all right formes of Common-wealthes, as the Monarchy, Aristocracy, and Democracy, to bee absolute and perfect.' Although 'in them-selves they are good ... yet accidentally, they many times become evill, as well for that they last not long, as that they so easily degenerate'. The argument Wright had been developing seemed, therefore, to lead to the inescapable conclusion that the mixed constitution was the best and most durable. 'To conclude therefore', he argued, 'I hold that forme of Common-wealth to bee best, which is compounded of the temper of all these, or at leastwise is so mixed of a Monarchy and Aristocracy, that one (indeed) for the Majesty of the State should bee the chiefe Commander, but his power should be governed and his Counsels ordered by the decrees and wisedome of the Senate.' This mixed form of government could resist the corruption inherent in the pure forms and every form contributed its characteristic virtues to the whole. The mixed state enabled, in Wright's view, the prince to retain 'his splendor and dignity, the Senate their power and authority, and the people their lawfull liberty'. He did not specify the particular nature of the mixture, but it seemed to be leaning towards aristocracy.[271]

Wright was thus engaged in an attempt to render the commonwealth stable and durable. With a view to doing this it was, he argued, of utmost importance to organize the government in a way which secured this aim. Yet since every pure form of government was inherently prone to corruption, the only way to acquire durability was to mix the

[271] Ibid., pp. 13–15.

three pure forms. In arguing this, Wright embraced the classical belief that the intrinsic and unavoidable decay of political authority could only be stopped by organizing the government as a mixture of the three elements – the one, the few and the many.

CHAPTER 4

Francis Bacon, Thomas Hedley and the true greatness of Britain

One of the most important political issues of the early years of James I's reign was the union of England and Scotland. Although James advanced his schemes for union cautiously and desired to use the parliaments of both kingdoms as much as possible, it was primarily the English House of Commons which would be blamed for its failure.[1] But, whatever the ultimate result of the project, it aroused heated discussions not only on the floor of the House of Commons, but also in writings available outside its walls. The practical issues of the union and its theoretical underpinnings apart, one of the emerging themes was that of civic greatness.

The king himself linked the union with the idea of civic greatness. Speaking at the opening of his first English parliament, 19 March 1604, James posed a rhetorical question, 'hath not the union of Wales to England added a greater strength thereto?' Wales was 'a great principality', but it 'was nothing comparable in greatness and power to the ancient and famous kingdom of Scotland'. The logical conclusion was that the union of England and Scotland would create a truly great monarchy.[2] Many of the treatises of union written in the course of 1604 followed suit, pointing out that civic greatness would be a chief benefit of the union. Political changes, it was argued, were always difficult and dangerous, but the intrinsic value of the union far outweighed any danger: in this case 'the increase of Empire' occurred by peaceful methods rather than by wars or conquest. The nature of the union consisted, William Cornwallis wrote in March 1604, of 'the greatnesse, that from a weakned & almost breathlesse state, is come to be the most

---

[1] Galloway 1986; Levack 1987.

[2] J. R. Tanner, *Constitutional documents of the reign of James I AD 1603–1625* (Cambridge University Press, 1930), p. 26.

opulent, strong and entire Empire of the world'. 'Our encreased dominions', he proclaimed, '... have made us terrible to the world without any terror to ourselves.'[3]

According to the Scot, Robert Pont, 'the first fruit springing out of this roote [of the union] ... is the enlarging of the empire',[4] whilst another Scot, John Russell, argued that the union would lead to 'the bettir knitting, enlarging and preserving thairof in ane heich and soverane monarchie'.[5] John Hayward employed a similar vocabulary. 'All true testimonies', he wrote, 'doe agree, that the greatest perfection of glory, beautie, stabilitie or strength, is either occasioned by union, or therein found.' If the main domestic consequence of the union was peace, the chief foreign benefit resulting from it was 'the enlargement both of dominion and power'.[6] The theme of civic greatness did not fall into oblivion with the encomia of the new king's inaugural year. It remained a staple topic in the treatises dealing with the furtherance of the union, as exemplified by Thomas Craig, David Hume and John Thornborough.[7] In 1610 Thomas Gainsford rhymed:[8]

> So now the English haue a new increase
> Of Northern friends, in vallour like the rest,

3   [William Cornwallis], *The miracvlovs and happie vnion of England and Scotland* (London, 1604), sig. B1ʳ⁻ᵛ, B4ʳ⁻ᵛ. In the datings of the tracts I rely on Galloway 1986, pp. 56–7.

4   Robert Pont, 'Of the union of Britayne', in *The Jacobean union: six tracts of 1604*, ed. Bruce R. Galloway and Brian P. Levack (Edinburgh: Scottish History Society, 1985), pp. 17, 20.

5   John Russell, 'A treatise of the happie and blissed union', in *The Jacobean union*, p. 136, also p. 116. See also Anon., ['A treatise about the union of England and Scotland'], in *The Jacobean union*, pp. 42–3.

6   John Hayward, *A treatise of vnion of the two realmes of England and Scotland* (London, 1604), pp. 2, 3, 4–5, 6. See also e.g. Henry Spelman, 'Of the union', in *The Jacobean union*, p. 163.

7   Thomas Craig, *De unione Britanniae tractatus*, ed. C. Sanford Terry (Edinburgh: T. & A. Constable, 1909), pp. 241, the original 25, see also e.g. p. 357. David Hume, *De vnione insvlae Britannicae tractatus* (London, 1605), pp. 5–6; John Thornborough, *The ioiefvll and blessed revniting the two mighty & famous kingdomes, England & Scotland into their ancient name of great Brittaine* (Oxford, n.d. [1605]), p. 23, see also p. 22; cf. idem, *A discovrse plainely proving the euident vtilitie and vrgent necessitie of the desired happie vnion of the two famous kingdomes of England and Scotland* (London, 1604). The theme of civic greatness did not appear in John Gordon, *The vnion of Great Britain* (London, 1604), idem, *Enotikon: or a sermon of the vnion of Great Britannie, in antiquitie of language, name, religion, and kingdome* (London, 1604).

8   T[homas] G[ainsford], *The vision and discovrse of Henry the seuenth: concerning the vnitie of Great Brittaine* (London, 1610), p. 7. Incidentally, it can be noted that in the early 1620s an author argued that the Anglo-Scottish union could not be strengthened but by 'armes in some fortunate warre, wher honour and danger may be equally devided, and no jealousie or contention rise, but of well doing, one victory obtayned by the joint valour of English and Scots'. This 'will more indelibly Christen your Majesties Empire greate Brittaine, then any acte of Parliament or artifice of State'. Anon., *Tom tell troath: or a free discourse touching the manners of the tyme* (n.p., n.d. [1622?]), p. 28.

So that all broyles of bordering warres must cease,
And now this Ile may more advance her crest:
What power soever dares her Lions wake,
Tis in their power a due revenge to take.

Even more conspicuously, the issue of the greatness of states surfaced when James visited Oxford in August 1605. The university organized academic disputations in different fields of learning to honour the learned king. The last disputation was on moral philosophy, and one of the two topics was 'whether it be more to defend, or enlarge the boundes of an Empire or Kingdome?' James was highly interested in the disputation – especially in the question of civic greatness – and spoke 'with such learning, as Apollo, if his Tripos were up againe' and 'many times urged contrarieties to finde out the certaintie, indeavouring in knowledge to winne a full and compleate perfection'. Being the last disputation of the day, however, there was a shortage of time, and the arguments were 'verie compendious and briefe'. Afraid that 'his Majestie should bee wearied with tediousnesse or proxilities, the Proctors did cut off the Opponents verye suddainelye' and before 'all the Opponents had disputed, they spoke to the Moderator that he should conclude'. The king, however, intervened, having noticed that 'there was one left out, which had not disputed, [and] his Majestie gave commaundement that hee should dispute also, so desirous hee was of hearing'.[9]

Although contextually linked with the union, the issue of civic greatness also emerged in other areas of political debate in the early years of James's reign. In 1606 an English translation of René de Lucinge's *The beginning, continvance, and decay of estates* (originally published in 1588) appeared on the stalls of London booksellers. The tract had been prompted by 'the fortune of the Ottomans, and the increase of their greatnesse'. Although the writer enquired into the ways in which the Ottoman empire could be destroyed, he also took pains to discuss in detail the ways in which civic greatness could be attained and preserved.[10] A similar range of questions was discussed in Giovanni

---

9   [Anthony Nixon], *In the royall entertainement of his moste excellent maiestie, the queene, and the prince: the 27. of August last; 1605* (London, 1605), sigs. C4ᵛ–D2ʳ. Isaac Wake, *Rex Platonicus: sive de potentissimi principis Iacobi Britanniarvm regis, ad illustrissimam Academiam Oxoniensem, adventu, Aug. 27. anno 1605* (Oxford, 1607), pp. 103, 108ff. See also Thomas Bodley's description in Trevor-Roper 1945.

10   René de Lucinge, *The beginning, continvance, and decay of estates: wherein are handled many notable questions concerning the establishment of empires and monarchies*, translated by John Finet (London, 1606), sig. b1ʳ, b2ʳ. Cf. Brathwait, *The schollers medley: or an intermixt discourse vpon historicall and poeticall relations* (London, 1614), p. 77.

Botero's treatises, which were translated into English around this time. It first emerged in 1601, in the second English edition of Botero's *Delle relationi universali* (originally published in 1591–2).[11] In 1606 Botero's *Delle cause della grandezza delle città* (originally published in 1586) was rendered into English.[12]

But the idea of civic greatness had a scarcely less conspicuous place in Barnabe Barnes's *Fovre bookes of offices*. In the fourth book, devoted to the cardinal virtue of courage, Barnes referred to the rules offered 'by the politicke Florentine Secretarie to Petro de Medici' giving advice on how 'to conserve and augment, th'empire' and pointed out that 'the amplification of Empire' was 'most noble and loveable'.[13] As late as 1616 we find Henry Wright asking the ways in which a kingdom might be got and kept as well as 'how a new-got Kingdome may be enlarged'.[14]

The greatness of states was discussed during the first years of James's reign to such an extent that it raised objections. In Aristotelian fashion Edward Forset asserted that the main end of a government was 'to make the state happie', which he carefully distinguished from 'the largenesse, the power, or the well shewing composure' of the same. Studying the differences between 'religion' and 'policy' in 1608, Christoper Lever came to realize that they differed radically in so far as their rules and ends were concerned. Although a commonwealth relying on 'the judgement of sense and politique advice onely' pursued 'greatnes' as its chief end, it ought to 'square out her forme of government by religious rules', and aim at 'goodnes'.[15]

One of the first writers, and certainly the most important, to devote

---

[11]   Giovanni Botero, *Delle relationi vniversali: parte seconda* (Rome, 1592), pp. 1–11. The earliest translation, *The travellers breviat: or an historicall description of the most famous kingdomes in the world*, translated by R[obert] J[ohnson] (London, 1601) did not contain this discussion, but it appeared in *The worlde, or an historicall description of the most famous kingdomes and common-weales therein*, translated by R[obert] J[ohnson] (London, 1601), pp. 1–10. I have used the 1608 (London) edition, entitled *Relations, of the most famovs kingdoms and common-weales thorovgh the world*.

[12]   *A treatise, concerning the causes of the magnificencie and greatnes of citie*, translated by Robert Peterson (London, 1606). A new translation was published in 1635, *The cavse of the greatnesse of cities: with certaine observations concerning the sea*, translated by Sir T. H. (London, 1635).

[13]   Barnabe Barnes, *Fovre bookes of offices: enabling private persons for the speciall service of all good princes and policies* (London, 1606), p. 172. For earlier examples see e.g. John Dee, *General and rare memorials pertayning to the perfect arte of navigation* (London, 1577); Bartolome Felippe, *The counseller: a treatise of counsels and counsellers of princes*, translated by J[ohn] T[horius], (London, 1589), pp. 166–70, which is based on Machiavelli.

[14]   Wright, *The first part: of the disqvisition of trvth concerning political affaires* (London, 1616), pp. 26–7.

[15]   Edward Forset, *A comparative discovrse of the bodies natvral and politiqve* (London, 1606), p. 4; Christopher Lever, *Heaven and earth, religion and policy: or, the maine difference betweene religion and policy* (London, 1608), pp. 49, 53, 95.

a considerable space to these issues was Francis Bacon. In 1603 in *A brief discourse touching the happy union of the kingdoms of England and Scotland*, he connected the Anglo-Scottish union with civic greatness.[16] The theme also appeared in his argument in Calvin's case in 1608 and in his *De sapientia veterum*.[17] Bacon's two most important statements on civic greatness, however, were his long speech in the House of Commons on 17 February 1607, and the unfinished tract 'Of the true greatness of the kingdom of Britain'. 'Fo[r] greatness (Mr Speaker)', Bacon told his colleagues in the House of Commons, 'I think a man may speak it soberly and without bravery, that this kingdom of England, having Scotland united, Ireland reduced, the sea provinces of the Low Countries contracted, and shipping maintained, is one of the greatest monarchies, in forces truly esteemed, that hath been in the world.'[18] Finally, a few years later, in 1612, Bacon published the second edition of his *Essayes*, where the last piece was entitled 'Of the greatnesse of kingdomes'.

It is essential to an understanding of Bacon's political writings to recognize that he was preoccupied with the same range of questions as his contemporaries, since there is a tendency to insist that Bacon's writings are independent of their restricted historical context and that they form an example of classic texts making sense 'on their own' and having a transhistorical audience.[19] Furthermore, it has often been claimed that Bacon's different writings form a consistent unity and that the proper ideological context of his writings on civic greatness is his scientific writings.[20] Finally, this contention has often, though not always, given rise to another claim, according to which Bacon's project was essentially modern.[21] Bacon's idea of civic greatness was modern, we are told, since it was 'mercantile imperialism' as well as 'the imperialism of Baconian science'.[22]

---

16 In *Letters*, iii, pp. 90–9, see especially pp. 92, 95–6.
17 Bacon, 'The case of the post-nati', in *Works*, vii, pp. 664–5; *De sapientia veterum*, in *Works*, vi, p. 642, translation p. 715.
18 Bacon in parliament 17 February 1607, in *Letters*, iii, p. 323. Cf. Epstein 1977, p. 97, n.40 where 'Of the true greatness of the kingdom of Britain' is called a 'tract on union'.
19 Weinberger 1985, p. 19; White 1968, p. 11.
20 White 1958; White 1968; Whitney 1986, pp. 50–4, 197–8; Weinberger 1985, pp. 132–3; Martin 1988, pp. 1, 3–4, 204–5, 164; Rice, 1963, pp. 49–53; Greenleaf 1964, pp. 202–3.
21 The most important studies which do not see anything particularly modern in Bacon's project are Martin 1988; and Webster 1975, pp. 420–65, 341, chapter 1.
22 White 1958; Whitney 1986, pp. 10, 11, 197–8, 99, 105; Weinberger 1985, pp. 19–21, 28, 9, 25–6; Weinberger 1980, pp. vii, xviii; Greenleaf 1964, pp. 201–3; Bock 1937, pp. 42–3; Hill 1965, pp. 96–9. See also in general J. Klein 1987; Wheeler 1956; Kanerva 1985; Kraus 1926; Eiseley 1962.

It is, however, arguable that the attempt to excavate a hidden consistency underlying the seeming contradictions between different works of Bacon is an anachronistic undertaking imposing our values on Bacon's writings. First, in emphasizing the role of commerce in Bacon's concept of civic greatness, scholars have overlooked the fact that Bacon clearly distinguished the pursuit of wealth and riches from the quest for true greatness. Secondly, and more importantly, in treating science as an integral part of the greatness of states, scholars have overestimated the unity of Bacon's thought. He never mentioned science in his writings concerning true greatness. There was rhetorical similarity between the propagation of the augmentation of learning and civic greatness, but they stood in diametrical opposition in so far as the qualities which they necessitated were concerned.[23] Instead of perceiving Bacon's scientific writings, or the birth of modernity, as constituting the intellectual context of his writings, perhaps we should consider him as a classical republican in his moral and economic thought. We have already seen in the previous chapter how Bacon carried on the English tradition of classical humanism by defending the central values of the *vita activa* against the advocates of moral scepticism and relativism and the closely associated idea of the *vita contemplativa*. It now remains to see that Bacon's most important political writings of the first decade of the new reign were not merely composed as answers to the central issue of the contemporary political debate – the Anglo-Scottish union – they also utilized some of the chief themes of the classical republican tradition. The Machiavellian tradition provides us with the ideological context of Bacon's writings on civic greatness.[24] Scholars such as Charles Webster and Christopher Hill have interpreted Bacon from the standpoint of mid-seventeenth-century puritan science. I should like to suggest, however, that James Harrington's analysis of Bacon offers a better point of departure for reading Bacon's writings on the true greatness of states.

[23]   Cf. Box 1982, p. 41; Whitaker 1970; Neustadt 1987.

[24]   Bacon's general debt to and connection with Machiavelli as well as their common preoccupation with the theme of civic greatness has been recognized by many scholars. It is arguable, however, that scholars have tended to concentrate mainly on producing complete lists of Bacon's Machiavelli citations, and by doing this have separated particular passages from their meaningful contexts and failed to produce interpretations which see Bacon as a follower of a tradition rather than as a borrower of a few separate ideas. See Orsini 1936, especially pp. 50–2. This is the source of virtually all of the later studies at this point. See Allen 1938, pp. 32, 58–9; Raab 1964, pp. 73–6; Rossi 1968, pp. 110–15; Jardine 1974, pp. 166–8; Marwil 1976, p. 107; White 1958, pp. 473–6; Luciani 1947; Liljeqvist 1894, pp. 334–5; Kraus 1926, pp. 19–31.

Bacon's profound interest in the greatness of states marks a shift in the development of English humanism. Although civic greatness had emerged before, as had the idea of the armed citizen, neither had assumed a central place, but remained matters of secondary importance. A partial exception is Richard Beacon's *Solon his follie*. But even there civic greatness and the armed citizen were far from main themes, in comparison to the reform of a corrupt commonwealth. Bacon can thus be said to be the first Englishman to ponder on civic greatness as a theme in its own right. Furthermore, Bacon's deep concentration on the issue of civic greatness prompted him, as we shall see, to set aside the issues of happiness and well-being. This is not to say that he found these concepts completely irrelevant, for as we have seen in the previous chapter, he displayed deep interest in them. But when he treated the questions of civic greatness he took no account of happiness and well-being. In addition, Bacon's enthusiasm for the greatness of the state alerted him, as we shall also see, to recent developments in the theories of civic greatness on the continent. But rather than following these new trends in an acquiescent manner, he in fact restated the older and essentially Machiavellian theory, which enabled him to mount a sharp attack against the newer theory. Most importantly, because of the great popularity of Bacon's writings, it was he more than anyone else who familiarized the English with the Machiavellian theory of *grandezza*. Bacon's Machiavellianism, in other words, exercised a profound influence on subsequent English political discourse. He can be seen as the beginner of a new, indigenous vein of classical republicanism, which found several followers in the decades before the Civil War and which culminated in the writings of James Harrington.

Bacon's point of departure in his assessment of civic greatness was the great difficulty of the enterprise. Although it was relatively easy to measure the size of the territory of a state, the measurement of its power and strength was a most intricate undertaking – than 'which there is nothing among civil affairs more subject to error'.[25] This had several important consequences. First, the over-estimation of the intrinsic strength of a state could lead to 'many inconsiderate attempts and insolent provocations'. But from the erroneous measurement of the intrinsic power of a state could also proceed   a   failure   to   seize   every   available   opportunity   to

---

[25]   Bacon, 'Of the true greatness of the kingdom of Britain', in *Works*, VII, p. 47 (hereafter referred to as TGKB); cf. 'Of the greatnesse of kingdomes', in *Works*, VI, 587.

enhance its greatness.[26] Finally, the difficulty of the true appraisal of civic greatness ensured that it was a rare statesman who could properly gauge the power and strength of a state. Bacon took pains to demonstrate at the beginning of the essay 'Of the greatnesse of kingdomes' that while the finding of counsellors who could advance their own career but who proved to be ruinous for their common-wealths was a simple task, the discovery of 'politikes & Statesmen' who could 'make a small estate great' was a more formidable one. Thus, after explaining how civic greatness could be acquired, Bacon con-cluded his essay with a statement of scepticism noting that the rules of greatness were not followed but were 'commonly left to chance'.[27]

If erroneous opinions about civic greatness were so often voiced, it can be asked what was the way in which reliable information about the successful methods of acquiring greatness could be gathered. According to Bacon, there was only one way to political wisdom: one's judgement should be 'grounded upon reason of estate'; it was pointless to speak 'of mathematical principles' when 'the reason of state is evident'.[28] He advised his colleagues in the House of Commons to look 'into the principles of estate' and to 'true reason of estate'.[29] The key to political wisdom, to 'true reason of estate', he insisted in a familiar manner, lay in the systematic use of history.[30] In reading on the Statute of Uses in Gray's Inn during the Lent vacation in 1600, Bacon argued that precedents of former ages could be employed since 'states and commonwealths have common accidents'.[31] When revealing his idea of civic greatness to the Commons, he said that 'a position of estate' was to be 'collected out of the records of time' and contended that 'the time past is a pattern of the time to come'.[32] In case of the true greatness of states, Roman history offered the best example for imitation. It was best, he pointed out in a philosophical paper written at the same time, to dismiss the induction by enumeration in front of the superior single example provided by Rome. 'Aristotle', Bacon argued, 'it is said, wrote a book in which he gathered together the laws and institutions of two hundred and fifty-five cities; yet I have no doubt that the

---

[26] Bacon, TGKB, p. 47; cf. e.g. de Lucinge, *The beginning*, pp. 56–66, 82–90.
[27] Bacon, 'Of the greatnesse of kingdomes', in *Works*, VI, pp. 587, 588.
[28] Bacon, TGKB, pp. 50, 51.
[29] Bacon in parliament 17 February 1607, in *Letters*, III, pp. 312, 314.
[30] For Bacon's method, see in general Clark 1970.
[31] Bacon, 'Reading on the Statute of Uses', in *Works*, VII, p. 407.
[32] Bacon in parliament 17 February 1607, in *Letters*, III, pp. 319, 311.

customs and example of the single state of Rome are worth more than all of them combined, so far as military and political prudence are concerned.'[33]

Bacon's keen awareness of recurrent errors in the appraisal of civic greatness prompted him to correction. He contrasted 'popular errors' to 'the sounder sort of judgements', which were grounded on 'reason and examples',[34] and promised in 'Of the true greatness of the kingdom of Britain' to begin 'by confuting the errors or rather correcting the excesses of certain immoderate opinions'. Having done this, he intended to propound and confirm 'those other points of greatness which are more solid and principal, though in popular discourse less observed'. In proposing this order of procedure Bacon was, first, following his own instructions. He had assured his audience at Gray's Inn in 1600 that 'it is the nature of all human science and knowledge to proceed most safely by negative and exclusion, to what is affirmative and inclusive'.[35] Secondly, and more importantly, by using this order of presentation, he made it clear that he intended to intervene in a contemporary debate. He wanted, in other words, to refute some of the claims put forward about the attainment of civic greatness and to uphold more solid principles.

Although accurate appraisal of power and strength was a difficult task, Bacon's theoretical starting point was similar to that of Machiavelli. According to Machiavelli, a commonwealth could either pursue civic greatness and glory or hold longevity as its chief goal. The organization of the commonwealth depended on its chosen end; in the former case it should adopt the policy of Rome, while in the latter it should imitate Sparta. But, in practice, the pursuit of durability was forlorn, for it was, he argued in a celebrated passage, impossible to be successful in the policy of longevity. The only real option was to consider the possibility of civic greatness.[36] We have already seen that Richard Beacon adopted Machiavelli's line of reasoning, and Bacon fully agreed. Rather than arguing in the context of the juxtaposition of civic greatness and longevity, he took it for granted that whereas Roman policy proved to be immensely

[33] Bacon, *Redargutio philosophiarum*, in *Works*, III, p. 569; I have modified Farrington's translation, see Farrington 1964, p. 115. Cf. *Advancement of learning*, in *Works*, III, p. 335; *Charge touching duels* (1614), in *Letters*, IV, p. 404. See in general Fischer 1857, p. 288.

[34] Bacon, TGKB, pp. 55, 49–50.

[35] Bacon, 'Reading on the Statute of Uses', in *Works*, VII, p. 398.

[36] Machiavelli, *Discorsi*, I.6.

successful as far as the greatness of their state was concerned, that adopted by Sparta was a failure in all respects.[37] Bacon, in other words, embraced the Machiavellian idea that empire and civic greatness was the only real option for states.

An important argument for the modernity of Bacon's 'imperialism' is constituted by the claim that it was commercial 'imperialism'. When we turn to Bacon's writings on civic greatness, however, we can see him emphasizing the corrupting nature of riches. One of the most 'immoderate opinions' put forward, Bacon opined, was that monetary values were of crucial help in attaining civic greatness. A central mistake in contemporary theories of greatness was that too much importance had been ascribed 'to treasure or riches'.[38] The underlying assumption was that, far from enhancing civic greatness, riches and treasure debased the indispensable qualities. As early as the Christmas revels for the court in 1594, Bacon distinguished between virtue and wealth; the fifth counsellor advocating virtue advised the prince to 'advance men of virtue and not of mercenary minds'.[39] Bacon's insistence that riches were but 'the baggage [i.e. hindrance] of Vertue', would be utilized by James Harrington.[40] Although Bacon conceded that in certain circumstances riches increased 'true greatness',[41] his account is organized around the polarity between virtue and riches. 'We', Bacon advised the Commons, 'Shall refer our counsels to greatness and power, and not quench them too much with consideration of utility and wealth,' and added later that it was utterly futile to 'think nothing but reckonings and audits, and *meum* and *tuum*, and I cannot tell what'.[42] Bacon contrasted 'effeminate' and 'merchant-like' states with 'magnanimous' states, arguing in a law-case that, since the laws of England 'looketh to the greatness of the kingdom', England was not a 'merchant-like' state, and did not ponder on 'husbandlike considerations of profit'.[43] Explaining the same idea in 'Of the true greatness of the kingdom of Britain', he contended that 'no man can be ignorant of

---

[37] Bacon, TGKB, pp. 52–3.

[38] Ibid., p. 48; cf. 'Of the greatnesse of kingdomes', in *Works*, VI, p. 587.

[39] Bacon, *Gesta Grayorum*, in *Letters*, I, p. 339.

[40] Bacon, 'Of riches', in *Essaies* (1612), in *Works*, VI, p. 566; James Harrington, *The common-wealth of Oceana* (London, 1656), p. 145.

[41] Bacon, TGKB, pp. 58–61. The most important of these conditions was the Machiavellian idea, according to which, money should be 'so disposed, as it is readiest and easiest to come by for the public service and use', p. 59, see also p. 61; cf. Machiavelli, *Discorsi*, II.19.

[42] Bacon in parliament, 17 February 1607, in *Letters*, III, pp. 323, 325, cf. p. 313; cf. also *Letters*, II, p. 86.

[43] Bacon, 'Lowe's case of tenures', in *Works*, VII, p. 548; 'The case of post-nati', in *Works*, VII, pp. 664–5.

the idolatry that is generally committed in these degenerate times to money, as if it could do all things public and private'.[44]

For Giovanni Botero, the cornerstone of civic greatness was riches and profit. 'This profit', he argued, 'is of such power, to unite and tye men fast unto one place; as the other causes aforesayd, without this accompany them with all, are not sufficient to make any city great.' Botero summarized his account by declaring that 'profite is the verie thing from whence, as from the principall cause the greatnesse of citties groweth'. The only way to achieve civic greatness was to promote 'the industrie of men, and the multitude of Artes'.[45] Closely related to this was Botero's insistence that 'the fruitfulnes of the country' was 'the second cause of the greatnes of a city'.[46] John Hitchcock followed this line of argument pointing out that treasure was 'the sinewes of the State'.[47] Similar argument, with a particular emphasis on the navy, was presented by Walter Ralegh, who may have translated Botero's treatise. According to Ralegh, 'whosoever commands the sea commands the trade; whosoever commands the trade of the world commands the riches of the world, and consequently the world itself'. As long as the Venetians had maintained their navy, they had proved to be 'great and powerful princes', but as soon as they had abandoned this maritime policy, they had lost their greatness.[48]

The prevalence of these arguments that riches and wealth were of crucial importance has led some scholars to assume that Machiavelli's 'out-dated claim that men, not gold, provided the sinews of war was dropped' altogether.[49] Nevertheless, when Bacon was denouncing the importance of riches and wealth in the pursuit of civic greatness, he

---

44 Bacon, TGKB, p. 55. 'A discourse of Rome', in Anon., *Horae subseciuae: observations and discovrses* (London, 1620), pp. 331–4 (ascribed to Hobbes), offers a similarly traditional account.

45 Botero, *A treatise*, pp. 11–13, 14, 48–50, 55–9, 18–29. See also William Fulbecke, *The pandectes of the law of nations* (London, 1602), fos. 68ʳ–75ʳ; John Wheeler, *A treatise of commerce* (London, 1601), p. 7; Justus Lipsius, *Sixe bookes of politickes or civil doctrine*, translated by William Jones (London, 1594), p. 82.

46 Botero, *A treatise*, pp. 15–17, 13. [Giovanni Botero], *Observations vpon the liues of Alexander, Caesar, Scipio*, translated by anon. (London, 1602), sig. E8ʳ⁻ᵛ. Incidentally, this was also Machiavelli's point of view, *Discorsi*, I.1.

47 John Hitchcock, *A sanctvary for honest men: or an abstract of humane wisdome* (London, 1617), pp. 91–5.

48 Walter Ralegh, 'A discourse of the invention of ships, anchors, compas, & c' (1604–16), in *Works*, VIII, pp. 317–34, pp. 324–5; idem, 'A discourse touching a war with Spain', in *Works*, VIII, pp. 299–316, pp. 302–3. Cf. also [John Keymer?], 'Observations touching trade and commerce with the Hollander, and other nations', in Ralegh, *Works*, VIII, pp. 351–76, pp. 353, 365–7, 375–6. Lefranc 1968, p. 666.

49 Miller 1994, p. 32.

aligned himself with Machiavelli. His argument, in other words, stood in stark contrast to that maintained, for instance, by Botero and Ralegh. And he not only condemned treasure and opulence; he also claimed that in the measuring of greatness too much had been 'ascribed to the fruitfulness of the soil, or affluence of commodities'.[50] All these values were direct antitheses of civic greatness and, far from helping its pursuit, they tended to debase the qualities which were necessary to its attainment. Indeed, Bacon wrote that civic greatness always rose from poverty and barren soil.[51] Moreover, in contrast to publicists such as Edward Forset who wanted 'to make the state happie' instead of great, Bacon set out in 'The true greatness of the kingdom of Britain' to speak 'of that which is proper to the amplitude and growth of states, and not of that which is common to their preservation, happiness, and all other points of well-being'.[52] Finally, Bacon's sharp dichotomy, between the size and riches of a state, on the one hand, and its internal qualities, 'the forces and power', on the other, bears a close resemblance to the humanist division between lineage as well as riches and true virtuous nobility. It is arguable that when Bacon composed his tracts on the true greatness of states he was engaged in writing treatises on *vera nobilitas*.

According to Bacon, the most important quality and characteristic of a truly great state was warlike disposition; civic greatness consisted 'in the valour and military disposition of the people it breedeth: and that in this, that they make profession of arms'.[53] This contention was often repeated in the course of the debate of the first decade of the seventeenth century. Barnabe Barnes wrote that 'where militarie science and exercise is frequent, there good laws are in most force and honour: for it maintaineth and magnifieth every Commonwealth and state'.[54] It was perhaps most forcefully argued in de Lucinge's treatise on the greatness of Ottoman empire. The Ottomans' success was

50   Bacon, TGKB, in p. 48; cf. however, Bacon in parliament 17 February 1607, *Letters*, III, p. 310. The same idea was endorsed e.g. in W[illiam] Crashaw, *A sermon preached in London before the right honorable the Lord Lawarre, Lord Gouernour and Captaine Generall of Virginea* (London, 1610), sigs. E4^v–F1^r.

51   Bacon in parliament 17 February 1607, in *Letters*, III, p. 324. TGKB, p. 55–7, 59; cf. *Advancement of learning*, in *Works*, III, p. 275. Cf. [Cornwallis], *The miraculous and happie union*, sig. C1^r; Craig, *De unione*, pp. 357, 413–15; Anon., *Horae subseciuae*, pp. 330, 333–6; Brathwait, *The schollers medley*, p. 9.

52   Bacon, TGKB, p. 49.

53   Ibid., p. 48. For the actual wording, cf. Lipsius, *Sixe bookes*, p. 144.

54   Barnabe Barnes *Foure bookes of offices: enabling private persons for the speciall service of all good princes and policies* (London, 1606), p. 162, see also in general pp. 171–4. Cf. e.g. Hayward, *A treatise of union*, pp. 5–6.

completely based on the fact that they 'fashion their whole dessignes to the war, and bend all their thoughts and studies to the exercise of armes, rejecting all others course, and pleasing themselves onely in what may stand them in stead for that profession'.[55]

The idea that valour and military disposition were necessary for civic glory recurred throughout Bacon's writings on true greatness. He connected civic greatness and warlike ability as early as his long parliamentary speech in 1607 and reiterated the connection in his argument in Calvin's case, and in *De sapientia veterum*.[56] But the theme was most extensively explored in 'Of the true greatness of the kingdom of Britain' and in the essay 'Of the greatnesse of kingdomes'. What was needed above all, he emphasized in the former, was 'martial virtue and discipline'; the import of every other quality was scrutinized in relation to this basic value.[57] 'It is necessary', Bacon announced, 'in a state that shall grow and inlarge, that there be that composition which the poet speaketh of, *Multis utile bellum*.'[58]

There were two distinct aspects to Bacon's conception of valour and warlike disposition. First, the people must have courage and warlike spirit. Like tiny grains of mustard seed there were states which had the appearance of small states, but were apt to grow, by virtue of the warlike and courageous spirit of the people. There were, Bacon pointed out, 'States that are great in Territory, and yet not apt to conquer or inlarge: and others that have but a small dimention or stemme, and yet apt to be the foundation of great Monarchies'.[59] But it was not enough to possess the spirit. Bacon firmly endorsed the idea that a thought without an ensuing act was completely futile. 'For good thoughts,' he wrote, '(though God accept them) yet towards men are little better then good dreams: except they be put in Act.'[60] The military virtue and spirit was completed by the concrete warlike ability and the art of war.[61]

[55] de Lucinge, *The beginning*, p. 4, in general pp. 3–8; cf. e.g. Wright, *The first part*, p. 27.

[56] Bacon in parliament 17 February 1607, in *Letters* III, p. 313; 'The case of the post-nati', in *Works*, VII, pp. 664–5; *De sapientia veterum*, in *Works*, VI, p. 642, translation p. 715; 'Lowe's case of tenures', in *Works*, VII, p. 548.

[57] Bacon, TGKB, pp. 53, 55, 58.

[58] Ibid., p. 59.

[59] Bacon, 'Of the greatnesse of kingdomes', in *Works*, VI, p. 587; Bacon in parliament 17 February 1607, in *Letters*, III, p. 323.

[60] Bacon, 'Of great place', in *Essaies*, (1612), in *Works*, VI, p. 550.

[61] For a short account of the basic rules of the art of war, see Bacon, *De sapientia veterum*, in *Works*, VI, pp. 641–3, translation pp. 715–17.

Since military disposition and the actual art of war were indispensable for every state which pursued civic greatness, warfare lay at the
heart of Bacon's concept of the true greatness of states. To emphasize
the force of his argument, Bacon contrasted military virtues with
qualities such as the territorial size of a state and 'the strength and
fortifications of towns or holds' as he put it in 'Of the true greatness of
the kingdom of Britain'. A few years later he added that 'walled
Townes, stored Arcenals and Armories, goodly Stables, Elephants' as
well as 'Number in Armies, Ordinance, and Artillerie' were of no use
without the military virtue of the people. They were nothing 'but a
Sheep in a Lions skin', Bacon wrote, 'except the breed and disposition
of the people be militarie'. They were, in short, 'mercenary aides' –
one of the epithets Bacon contrasted most strongly with true civic
greatness.[62] But, expressing his opinion on this issue, Bacon was not
merely repeating a self-evident truism; he was also arguing against
those who, like de Lucinge, maintained that fortifications were of great
importance in warfare.[63] It was of utmost importance, according to
Bacon, to appreciate that the quality which was needed above all in the
pursuit of civic greatness was military virtue and valour. Fortresses and
artillery were not so much in themselves inimical to civic greatness, but
the feeling of security to which they gave rise as well as the misleading
scale of priorities which they engendered usually ruined the quest for
civic glory.[64]

The final, and perhaps the most important, polarity in Bacon's
account of the people's bellicose virtues was the one between military
valour and riches. He vigorously opposed those who argued that
money was a crucial element in war. This was central in Lipsius,

[62]   Bacon, TGKB, pp. 48, 49–55; *A brief discourse*, in *Letters*, III, p. 96; cf. 'Of the greatnesse of
kingdomes', in *Works*, VI, p. 587. For a strikingly similar wording for the virtue of courage, see
Anon., 'The genealogie of vertue', in *The anathomie of sinne, briefly discovering the braunches thereof*
(London, 1603), sig. H7ᵛ. Although Giovanni Botero argued in *Relations of the most famous
kingdoms and common-weales* (sig. BIʳ⁻ᵛ) that a prince could obtain rule and dominion over
another amongst other things 'by largnesse of Territory', this principle was refuted in *A
treatise*, p. 1. Botero opened his treatise by asserting that 'the greatnes of a Citty, is sayd to be,
not the largenes of the scite'.

[63]   de Lucinge, *The beginning*, pp. 14–23 where the argument is directed against Machiavelli; cf.
also Giovanni Botero, *The reason of state*, translated by P. J. and D. P. Waley (London:
Routledge, 1956), pp. 117–18.

[64]   Cf. Hale 1975. It is arguable that, when Ralegh argued that Alexander would easily have
conquered Rome had he chosen to make the attempt, he was criticizing or even poking fun at
this aspect of Bacon's argument; see Ralegh, *The historie of the world* (London, 1614), v.i.i, pp.
309–10: 'It were needlesse to speake of Treasure, Horses, Elephants, Engines of batterie, and
the like: of all which, the Macedonian had aboundance; the Romans having nought save men
and armes.'

Botero, Ralegh as well as in de Lucinge's account of the success of
Turkey. De Lucinge opened his discussion by explaining that in
warfare 'the most necessarie and profitable is to have alwaies store of
money in our coffers'. 'This is', de Lucinge insisted, 'the sinew of
warre, and the onely meanes to hasten forward occasion, and attaine
... to a happie end of his enterprises.'[65] According to Botero, 'money is
an advantage of great importance, forasmuch as ther is nothing more
necessary in warres, or of more use in peace'. It followed that 'mony
worketh these two notable effects to the augmentation and continuance
of the greatnes of kingdomes and estates'. It provided and maintained
forces, and it offered opportunities to weaken or at least to withstand
the enemy.[66]

But, according to Bacon, money was helpful in warfare only if the
enemy had the same amount of valour as you, since 'the better
monied state will be the better able to continue the war, and so in
the end to prevail'.[67] In the case of foreign war, however, this rarely
happened; it was only in civil wars that money played a crucial part.
In every other case money yielded to valour. It is in this context that
we have one of Bacon's best-known references to Machiavelli.
'Neither', he told the Commons, 'is the authority of Machiavel to be
despised, who scorneth the proverb of estate taken first from a
speech of Mucianus, that Moneys are the sinews of wars; and saith
there are no true sinews of wars but the very sinews of the arms of
valiant men.'[68] When Bacon set forth the same maxim in 'Of the
true greatness of the kingdom of Britain', he added that Machiavelli
had perceived its truth with 'his eyes in his own times and country'.
The Florentine had witnessed how an ill-provided French army
made 'their passage only by the reputation of their swords by their
sides undrawn, through the whole length of Italy' without encoun-
tering any resistance, in spite, or rather because, of the fact that
Italy was 'at that time abounding in wealth after a long peace'.
'But', Bacon concluded, 'it was not the experience of that time

---

65   de Lucinge, *The beginning*, pp. 69–70; Lipsius, *Sixe bookes*, p. 136; Ralegh, *A discourse touching a war with Spain*, in *Works*, VIII, p. 314; idem, 'Of the art of warre by sea' (1608–9), in Pierre Lefranc, *Sir Walter Ralegh écrivain: l'œuvre et les idées* (Paris, 1968), pp. 597–601, p. 600.

66   Botero, *Relations*, sig. B3ᵛ–4ʳ. Cf. e.g. Robert Dallington, *A survey of the great dukes state of Tuscany. In the yeare of our Lord 1596* (London, 1605), p. 43; Hayward, *A treatise of union*, p. 6; Spelman, 'Of the union', in *The Jacobean union*, pp. 162, 173; Fulbecke, *The pandectes*, fos. 68ʳ–69ʳ.

67   Bacon, TGKB, p. 58.

68   Bacon in parliament 17 February 1607, in *Letters*, III, pp. 323–4.

alone, but the records of all times that do concur to falsify that conceit, that wars are decided not by the sharpest sword but by the greatest purse.'[69] The Roman empire was not destroyed by 'some constellation or fatal revolution of time', but by the effeminacy of its former valour.[70] The same idea clearly emerged in the fourth book of Barnes's *Fovre bookes of offices*, where he wrote that 'all places naturally munited and fortified are nothing without the willing aide of men valiant to defend them by force' and that 'treasure is wonne by the sword, and not the swords vertue by treasure'.[71] The inherent danger of money in warfare was exactly the same as that of strongholds and artillery: the wrong and eventually ruinous scale of values which went with it prevented the ultimate success of the pursuit of civic greatness. Military virtue always found money, but money never found military virtue.

From the centrality of military virtue and warlike disposition, it followed that constant warfare was a crucial element of the quest for civic greatness. Peace was, therefore, inimical to a state pursuing glory. 'No body', Bacon wrote, 'can be healthfull without exercise, neither naturall body, nor politike; & to the politike body of a Kingdome or estate, a civill warre is like the heate of a fever: but an honourable forraine warre is like the heate of exercise.' The underlying assumption was, as Bacon put it, that 'in a slothfull peace, both courages will effeminate, and manners corrupt'.[72]

In 1596 Bacon associated the flourishing of 'civil knowledge' with the continuous exercise of bellicose qualities. Writing on behalf of the earl of Essex to the earl of Rutland, he maintained that civil knowledge was ruined either 'by civil wars', or by 'wealth' and 'too great length of peace'. In times of peace and prosperity, men became interested in 'the study of *artes luxuriae*' instead of pursuing proper learning. 'If it seem strange', Bacon went on, 'that I account no state flourishing but that which hath neither civil wars nor too long peace, I answer, that politic

---

69   Bacon, TGKB, p. 55–6. Cf. in general Barnes, *Fovre bookes of offices*, p. 172.
70   Bacon, TGKB, p. 53.
71   Barnes, *Fovre bookes of offices*, p. 172.
72   Bacon, 'Of the greatnesse of kingdomes', in *Works*, VI, p. 588. The maxim appeared for the first time in 'Observations on a libel' (1592), in *Letters*, I, p. 174. The same idea was endorsed e.g. by Forset, *A comparative discovrse*, p. 44; Barnes, *Fovre bookes of offices*, p. 162; Greville, *Treatise of monarchy*, stanza 539, in *Remains*, p. 170; John Wybarne, *The new age of old names* (London, 1609), pp. 32–3; Robert Johnson, *The new life of Virginea: declaring the former svccesse and present estate of the plantation being the second part of Noua Britannia* (London, 1612), sig. F4^r–v; Dallington, *Aphorismes civill and militarie amplified with authorities, and exemplified with historie, out of the first quarterne of Fr Guicciardine* (London, 1613), pp. 1, 143.

bodies are like our natural bodies, and must as well have some exercise to spend their humours, as to be kept from too violent or continual outrages which spend their best spirits.'[73]

Although the flourishing of civil knowledge required circumstances and qualities similar to those required by civic greatness, the notion that the most crucial quality for a great state was warlike disposition clashed directly with Bacon's idea of the advancement of learning.[74] In the famous letter sent with a part of *Instauratio magna* to Toby Matthew in 1609, Bacon described himself: 'Myself am like the miller of Huntingdon, that was wont to pray for peace amongst the willows; for while the winds blew, the wind-mills wrought, and the water-mill was less customed. So I see that controversies of religion must hinder the advancement of sciences.'[75] While civic greatness demanded warlike disposition and consequently also wars, science made its advancement in peace alone. Towards the end of the *Advancement of learning* Bacon argued that one of the reasons why his own times were so conducive to learning was 'the present disposition of these times at this instant to peace'.[76] Two years later in 1607 he expressed the same firm belief that his own age would witness the advancement of learning, since 'the balance of power' in Europe would maintain peace which 'is fair weather for the sciences to flourish'.[77] The fact that Bacon believed in the advancement of science through universal peace as he was elsewhere arguing that warfare was indispensable for civic greatness, suggests the distance between his search for the progress in science and his idea of civic greatness. Science was an international pursuit progressing only in universal peace. The quest for civic greatness was the opposite; it was a purely national undertaking demanding not only warlike disposition, but continuous wars.

Although valour, courage and military virtue were the essential characteristics of a state which aimed at empire, these qualities were hardly maintained and their ultimate object scarcely accomplished

---

[73] The earl of Essex to the earl of Rutland (1596), in *Letters*, II, pp. 11–12.

[74] Cf. Liljeqvist 1894, p. 335; Box 1982, p. 41.

[75] Bacon to Toby Matthew, 10 October 1609, in *Letters*, IV, pp. 137–8.

[76] Bacon, *Advancement of learning*, in *Works*, III, pp. 476–7; cf. however, 'Of the interpretation of nature', in *Letters*, III, p. 86. In addition to universal peace, amongst the factors which made Bacon's own time so conducive to the augmentation of sciences was 'the leisure wherewith these times abound, not employing men so generally in civil business, as the states of Graecia did in respect of their popularity, and the state of Rome in respect of the greatness of their monarchy', pp. 476–7. This was against the ideal of the *vita activa* which Bacon so vehemently defended in the *Advancement of learning*; see Chapter 3, pp. 139–45.

[77] Bacon, *Thoughts and conclusions*, in Farrington 1964, pp. 94–5; the original, *Works*, III, p. 613.

without the other qualities enunciated in 'Of the true greatness of the
kingdom of Britain'. The first in the list of the six true qualities, and
the only one treated in detail, was 'a fit situation'. This was composed
of three aspects, all of which were perfectly applicable to the kingdom
of Britain (although the unfinished treatise breaks off before Bacon
reached the section of application). The region of a great monarchy
should be 'of hard access', but at the same time 'in the midst of many
regions'. Finally, the region needed to be 'maritime'.[78] This property
brings us to another practical quality of a truly great state. It was
crucial, Bacon maintained, that a state possessed 'the commandment
of the sea'.[79]

The third indispensable practical feature of a great state was a
large population. Although it was above all the military virtue of
the people which brought about civic greatness, it was extremely
difficult to achieve durable success without a large population.[80]
One method of increasing the population was to acquire colonies
as the Romans had done.[81] A second procedure for attaining a
large population, again following the Romans, was to form leagues
with other states.[82] The most important method of increasing the
number of inhabitants, however, was to admit strangers. This line
of thought appeared first in 1603 in Bacon's discourse on the
union. 'So likewise', he wrote, 'the authority of Nicholas Machiavel seemeth not to be contemned; who enquiring the causes of
the growth of the Roman empire, doth give judgement, there was
not one greater than this, that the state did so easily compound
and incorporate with strangers.'[83] A few years later in parliament
he attempted to prove 'a position of estate, collected out of the
records of time' that the union of the kingdoms must be fortified
by a further union of naturalization and presented Rome and

[78]   Bacon, TGKB, pp. 48, 62. Cf. Robert Cotton, *An answer to such motives as were offer'd by certain
military-men to prince Henry* (London, 1675), p. 96.
[79]   Bacon, TGKB, p. 49. Cf. e.g. de Lucinge, *The beginning*, pp. 72–3; Ralegh, 'Of the art of warre
        by sea', in *Works*, VIII, pp. 600–1.
[80]   Bacon, TGKB, p. 49. Cf. e.g. Botero, *A treatise*, pp. 87–8, 33–5, [idem], *Observations*, sig.
G4^v–6^v.
[81]   Bacon, 'The case of the post-nati', in *Works*, VII, p. 661. Cf. e.g. Barnes, *Foure bookes of offices*, p.
172; Anon., ['A treatise about the union'], in *The Jacobean union*, p. 44. It can be noted that the
theme of civic greatness was a common topic in the treatises of colonies, see e.g. R[obert]
J[ohnson], *Nova Britannia: offring most excellent fruites by planting in Virginia* (London, 1609), sigs.
B1^r, C2^r, E2^v.
[82]   Bacon, *A brief discourse*, in *Letters*, III, pp. 93–5. Cf. Barnes, *Foure bookes of offices*, p. 172; Anon.,
        ['A treatise about the union'], in *The Jacobean union*, p. 44.
[83]   Bacon, *A brief discourse*, in *Letters*, III, p. 96, see also p. 95.

Sparta as his instances. Bacon answered those who charged that England could not sustain any increase of population[84] with a rhetorical question: what is the most dangerous consequence of this increase? 'Look into all stories', he argued in his own reply, 'and you shall find it none other than some honourable war for the enlargement of their borders, which find themselves pent, upon foreign parts; which inconvenience, in a valorous and warlike nation; I know not whether I should term an inconvenience or no.'[85] In his argument in Calvin's case, he declared that those states which have been fit for empire, 'have been ever liberal in point of naturalization'.[86] And since England was a 'magnanimous nation', the law of England 'open[ed] her lap to receive in people to be naturalized'. The same argument appeared in 'Of the true greatness of the kingdom of Britain' as well as in the essay 'Of the greatnesse of kingdomes'. Since Sparta had not naturalized foreigners, it had happened that after 'they had embraced a larger empire, they were presently surcharged'. But Rome, by virtue of its policy of naturalization had achieved civic greatness.[87]

If civic greatness is to be achieved by a large population displaying valour and military virtue in martial enterprises, it remains to ask how we can guarantee not merely the occurrence but also the continuation of these values. It is to this issue that Bacon devoted some of the most important parts of his writings on the true greatness of states. In answering this question he concentrated on the social and political factors underlying warlike disposition and consequent civic greatness. Some scholars have argued that, for Bacon, a strong monarchy secured the coming of true greatness.[88] Bacon himself, however, was almost completely silent upon the role of the king. There is no mention, in his writings concerning civic greatness, of either the king's power or his

---

[84] Bacon's speech was a reply to Nicholas Fuller who had claimed that England would become over-populated; see Notestein 1971, p. 222.

[85] Bacon in parliament 17 February 1607, in *Letters*, III, pp. 319, 313.

[86] Bacon, 'The case of the post-nati', in *Works*, VII, p. 664–5, see also p. 661.

[87] Bacon, TGKB, pp. 52–3; 'Of the greatnesse of kingdomes', in *Works*, VI, p. 588. Cf. e.g. Thornborough, *The ioiefull reuniting*, pp. 68–70. It can be noted that Gerard de Malynes argued in *The maintenance of free trade, according to the three essentiall parts of traffique* (London, 1622), p. 67, that whereas demoracies and aristocracies sought 'by all meanes to make their Countries populous by the inhabiting of all nations for the increase of their meanes', monarchies avoided 'the multitude of forraine nations to inhabite within their Government'.

[88] Martin 1988, pp. 1, 3–4, 204–5, 164; Rabb 1969, p. 182.

necessary qualities and characteristics.[89] It was the business of 'politikes & Statesmen' to 'make a small estate great'.[90] Although he did not enquire, as Machiavelli had done, into the question of the constitutional arrangements of a truly great state, the emphasis in Bacon's treatises on civic greatness was on the virtues and qualities of the people. This is particularly apparent in his discussion of the social and political elements underlying civic glory. Here, in particular, he endorsed some of the central notions of classical republicanism. One of the central issues of greatness was 'that every common subject by the poll be fit to make a soldier, and not only certain conditions or degrees of men'.[91] The practical dimension of this principle followed from the idea of a large population: the great number of inhabitants was itself negligible, if its majority failed to act as soldiers. But the idea also had an ideological dimension.

By stressing that every subject should be fit to act as a soldier, Bacon was embracing the classical concept of the armed citizen. This theme surfaced in several early-seventeenth-century treatises of civic greatness. According to a Scot, both the English and Scottish people were 'mightie, free and bellicose nations'.[92] Similarly, Francis Trigge, referring to Botero, pointed out that 'the common Souldier' was 'the glory of England', and concluded that 'in some sort these Commons may seeme to bee the sinewes of the Common-wealth'.[93] That the infantry was the most important part of the army was beyond doubt for Barnabe Barnes, who coupled this assertion with a condemnation of mercenaries. Barnes opened his analysis by stating that 'such ... as propose honor for the meed of their travels are cold, resolute, of a quiet and unbroken spirit, knitting up all their vertues in that action to which the whole force of mind & bodie must be bent'. Mercenaries, however, were unable to offer this kind of lavish display of virtues. They fought 'for a little wages' alone; they 'cannot combat with that true courage and martiall alacritie which native contrimen will'. 'Native souldiers', on the other hand, did not fight for money but of 'necessity' and 'in hope of a glorious conquest'. Since 'the largest

---

[89]   The issue of the king's power occurred towards the end of 'Of the greatnesse of kingdomes' where Bacon remarked that 'it is in the power of Princes or Estates by ordinances and constitutions, and maners which they may introduce, to sowe greatness to their posteritie and succession', *Works*, VI, p. 588.

[90]   Bacon, 'Of the greatnesse of kingdomes', in *Works*, VI, p. 587.

[91]   Bacon, TGKB, pp. 48–9.

[92]   Anon., ['A treatise about the union'], in *The Jacobean union*, p. 47.

[93]   Francis Trigge, *To the kings most excellent maiestie: the humble petition of two sisters; the church and common-wealth* (London, 1604), sig. F1ᵛ–2ʳ, F2ᵛ.

portion of just reputation happeneth to themselves' they were ready to employ all of their virtues in the cause of their nation.[94]

In the preceding chapter we saw how Barnes developed the civic aspect of the *vita activa*; carrying arms and defending one's country was thus just another form of the civic life, and another way to safeguard one's own liberty as well as that of the whole commonwealth. It was perhaps Machiavelli to whom Barnes was referring when he revealed his own pessimism concerning the maintenance of liberty. He argued: 'the reason why so fewe free people and States are in comparison of former times, and such a defect of true lovers and of valiant champions of liberties in comparison of former ages (as a wily Commonwealths man hath noted) is, that people in hope of beatitude, and towards the fruition of a second comfortable life, devise in these dayes how to tollerate and not to revenge injuries.'[95] There was, then, a close link, in Barnes's scheme, between liberty, virtue, and bearing arms; values which stood in complete contrast with security, servility and unwilling-ness to fight for the fatherland. Most of his contemporaries, Barnes continued, kept 'their swordes and armes rustely sheathed and cased, when a vehement necessitie doth importune the contrarie' and by 'sottishly nuzzling themselves in sluggish securitie, [they] utterly con-demne the lawfull meanes and courses of warre, restoring that needfully by force of swords, which no law nor charmes of perswasive words can accomplish'.[96] The danger of employing mercenary troops was emphasized even more strongly by Ralegh, who wrote that the point was 'well observed by Machiavel'. The Dutch revolt had succeeded despite rather than because of the mercenaries fighting for the Dutch. According to Ralegh, mercenary troops were employed by tyrants, because they disarmed all their own subjects for fear of rebellion. The proper way of organizing the defence of a country, however, was to imitate the Roman example and arm the citizens.[97]

It was this idea of the armed citizen that underlay Bacon's concept of civic greatness. Although his emphasis on the commandment of the seas has led some scholars to claim that the navy was the most important element of his military scheme, Bacon himself argued that 'the infantery' was 'the nerve of an Armie'.[98] Thus the principal task of

94 Barnes, *Fovre bookes of offices*, pp. 190–1, 171.
95 Ibid., p. 173.
96 Ibid., p. 173.
97 Ralegh, *The historie of the world*, V,ii,ii, pp. 377, 380, 386.
98 Bacon, 'Of the greatnesse of kingdomes', in *Works*, vi, p. 588; cf. *Letters*, iii, p. 36. For de Lucinge, the cavalry was the most crucial part of the army, *The beginning*, pp. 144–6.

the majority of the people was to carry arms, to be ready to fight for
their commonwealth. A matter of even more decisive importance was
to avoid the usage of a professional army. Bacon's constant advice that
a state pursuing civic greatness ought to concentrate almost exclusively
on warlike disposition, that the people ought to 'make profession of
arms',[99] and his continuous insistence on martial 'discipline' seem to
point to the idea of the standing army. But this is hardly the case. His
idea that *every subject* should be capable of bearing arms and his social
analysis of a truly great state suggest the contrary. Bacon was most
emphatic that mercenaries should be avoided at all costs; if a state
relied on 'waged Companies of forraine Armes, and not' on its 'owne
Natives', it would never achieve long-lasting greatness.[100]

By identifying courage with the people, Bacon endorsed the republican idea that a central part of the active role of the people was their
martial character. Warfare was the area in which the people demonstrated their public spirit – military virtue. The powers of fortune were
exceptionally great in wars. But the effeminate states alone were under
her spell, and those states which had warlike people and strong military
valour could overcome fortune.[101] Bacon approved of Xenophon's
saying that 'we have now but those two things left, our arms and our
virtue; and if we yield up our arms, how shall we make use of our
virtue?'[102] Underlying Bacon's argument was the Machiavellian idea of
the armed citizens of the Roman republic. The inescapable conclusion
was that the only way to successfully pursue civic greatness, or even to
survive in the predatory world, was to attain a large population and to
arm it. Almost as soon as Sparta had been forced to acquire an empire
(i.e. when it had been forced into a martial policy) it had been
destroyed.

Bacon coupled this moral evaluation of the armed citizen with an
argument that society should be organized in a way which enabled the
people to perform their military role. To ensure that the people were
capable of cultivating valour, certain material standards should be met.
Bacon opened his analysis by stressing that sedentary and indoor arts
were not conducive to military character; these 'nice manufactures', by
requiring 'rather the finger than the hand or arme, have in their nature

---

[99]   Bacon, TGKB, p. 48, cf. p. 59.
[100] Bacon, 'Of the greatnesse of kingdomes', in *Works*, VI, p. 587.
[101] Bacon, *Of the colours of good and evil* (1597), in *Works*, VII, p. 79; 'Character of Iulius Caesar', in
       Works, VII, p. 344.
[102] Bacon, *Advancement of learning*, in *Works*, III, p. 313. For Bacon's source, see Wolff 1913 II, pp.
       27–8.

a contrariety to a disposition militar'.[103] His argument was a reiteration of a commonplace derived from Vegetius that certain professions made better soldiers than others simply by increasing their members' strength and capacity to endure pain and hardship.[104]

On the other hand, the argument carried with it two closely related but distinct ideological implications. Instead of being hardworking, warlike people were 'a little idle', for they loved 'danger better than pain'. It followed that if the people were to retain their military virtue and fulfil their duty as active members of their community, they should in the first place maintain their virtue by continuous exercise – 'neither must they be too much broken of it, if they shall be preserved in vigor'.[105] But it was of equal importance to ensure that they abstained from direct involvement in economic life. Bacon did not explain, however, as he would do a decade later, how the economic life of a state pursuing civic greatness was to be organized.

The other element of Bacon's social analysis was his explanation of the material position of the armed citizen. Instead of seeing him as a man engaged in commerce, Bacon conceived him as a cultivator, a sturdy, free Roman farmer; 'it is', he argued, 'the Plough that yeeldeth the best soldier'.[106] He stressed the relative freedom of farmers. To guarantee that the community had a good infantry and that the subjects were able to carry arms, a large body of 'middle people' was required, men who were not dependent on a landlord but instead owned their own pieces of land. There were several means to ensure this. First, it was important that taxes and subsidies were not too high. Bacon was fully convinced that 'a people overcharged with tributes' would never be 'fit for Empire'.[107]

Another means to ensure that the state had a large body of 'middle people' was to inhibit the disproportionate increase of the nobility, because a sharp increase in the numbers of nobles would mean that farmers would become dependent on landlords. And in losing possession of their land, they would lose their willingness and their 'heart' to devote themselves to their commonwealth by fighting

---

[103] Bacon, 'Of the greatnesse of kingdomes', in *Works*, VI, p. 588.

[104] Vegetius, *The foure bookes contayninge a plaine forme and perfect knowledge of martiall policye*, translated by John Sadler (London, 1572), I.7, fos. 3^{r-v}; Lipsius, *Sixe bookes*, p. 150. Cf. de Lucinge, *The beginning*, pp. 23–6; William Leighton, *Vertve triumphant, or a lively description of the foure vertves cardinall* (London, 1603), stanza 132; Matthew Sutcliffe, *The practice, proceedings, and lawes of armes* (London, 1593), p. 67.

[105] Bacon, 'Of the greatnesse of kingdomes', in *Works*, VI, p. 588.

[106] Ibid., p. 588. Bacon endorsed this view as early as 1601, in *Letters*, III, p. 36.

[107] Bacon, 'Of the greatnesse of kingdomes', in *Works*, VI, p. 587.

for it. Finally, it is arguable that Bacon's reasoning pointed towards the Machiavellian idea that dependence on landlords made people lose the moral independence which was indispensable for participating in the public life of their commonwealth. 'Nobilitie & Gentlemen multiplying in too great a proportion,' Bacon observed, 'maketh the common subject grow to bee a pesant and base swaine driven out of heart, and but the Gentlemans laborer.'[108] In his natural analogy, he pointed out that it was in commonwealths just as it was 'in copices, where if you leave your staddels too thick, you shall never have cleane underwood, but shrubbes and bushes'. It was therefore of crucial importance that the plough was maintained 'in the hand of owners, and not of meere laborers'.[109] If a state wanted to become great, it should be organized in a way which enabled its people to perform their main function – the participation in military affairs – and this was made possible, if the people retained their material as well as moral freedom and independence through owning their farming land.

Bacon's final characteristic of true greatness, regarding the qualities of the people, concerned the government of the community. Civic greatness, he maintained, 'consisteth in the temper of the government fit to keep subjects in heart and courage, and not to keep them in the condition of servile vassals'.[110] He thus drew a sharp distinction between 'servile' people and people capable of achieving greatness in the political as well as in the material arenas. The moral independence of the people and their willingness to employ their virtue for the public good required both proper social organization and proper arrangement of the political institutions of the community. Bacon, that is, attributed to the organization of the government the responsibility for preventing the people's servitude. Defending the naturalization of the Scots, he told the House of Commons that the Scots were, like the English, not 'tractable in government'. Indeed this quality was incident to all martial people, as was evident 'by the example of the Romans'. They were like

---

[108] Ibid., pp. 587–8. Cf. Thomas Wilson, 'The state of England anno Dom. 1600', ed. F. J. Fisher, Camden miscellany, 16 (1936), pp. 18–19, 38–9, according to whom, 'the yeomanry of England' had already decayed and become but 'servants to gentlemen'. Cf. however, 'Lowe's case of tenures', in *Works*, VII, p. 548.

[109] Bacon, 'Of the greatnesse of kingdomes', in *Works*, VI, p. 588. It can be noted that Joseph Swetnam regarded war as one of 'arts, trades and sciences' and contended that yeomen were 'idle'; Joseph Swetnam, *The schoole of the noble and worthy science of defence* (London, 1617), pp. 16, 75–6, 79–80.

[110] Bacon, TGKB, p. 49.

'fierce horses', 'of better service than others, yet are they harder to guide and manage'.[111] The attainment of civic greatness required that free people were not governed or directed at will. This was the price a state had to pay if it wanted to achieve civic glory and empire.

How were the political institutions of a community to be organized? Unfortunately in the unfinished 'Of the true greatness of the kingdom of Britain' Bacon never reached detailed analysis of the idea of 'the temper of the government'. Nonetheless, something of what he might have had in mind can be gathered from his other writings on civic greatness. In *A brief discourse*, he noted that laws which formed a principal part of the union fell into three parts: 'Laws', 'Manners' and 'Abilities and Freedoms'. Although in Calvin's case in 1608 Bacon would argue that the liberties of the Romans were 'the devices commonly of popular or free estates' and, therefore, 'unfit for monarchies', which granted unconditional citizenship,[112] five years earlier he resorted to the same Roman liberties in defining the freedoms of the Englishman. According to Bacon, the Romans had had four particular liberties. The first one '*Jus Connubii*' was out of use in Bacon's time, since marriage was open between diverse nations. But the other three had still an accurate equivalent in England. The right of citizenship, '*Jus Civitatis*', answered to naturalization. The last two, however, were the most interesting. While the Romans' liberty – '*Jus Suffragii*' – 'answereth to the voice in Parliament, or voice of election of such as have voice in Parliament', that of, '*Jus Petitionis* answereth to place in counsel and office'.[113] Bacon defined the basic political capacities of the Englishman, sitting in parliament and giving counsel, with the help of Roman liberties.

What was Bacon doing in this argument? The interpretation of the Roman policy of naturalization as the proper pattern for the Anglo-Scottish union, and the definition of the Englishman's fundamental spheres of political activity with the help of the model of the Roman citizenship, furnished Bacon with an argument against those who

---

[111]   Bacon in parliament 17 February 1607, in *Letters*, III, p. 315. See also John Melton, *A sixe-folde politician: together with a six-folde precept of policy* (London, 1609), sig. P8ʳ⁻ᵛ. According to Melton, the heroes of republican Rome 'helde true valour, and Magnanimitie to consist in avoyding of subjection, and that the quiet and patient tolleration of adverse fortunes, drawing under the yoak of obedience, and subscribing to domination, rule and superiority, was basenesse & brutishnes'.

[112]   Bacon, 'The case of the post-nati', in *Works*, VII, p. 649.

[113]   Bacon, *A brief discourse*, in *Letters*, III, p. 97; cf. 'The case of the post-nati', in *Works*, VII, p. 661.

expressed fears of Scottish participation in English offices. This was one of the most heated political issues associated with the union, and many an Englishman was apprehensive that vacant offices would be filled by Scots.[114] By showing that the capacity to hold office and have voice in parliament belonged to liberties which were granted in the act of naturalization, Bacon and the other advocates of the union were able to argue that the bestowal of these freedoms followed naturally from the complete union.

A similar argument was put forward for instance by John Hayward, Alberico Gentili, Thomas Gainsford, John Doddridge, Walter Ralegh and John Thornborough, who noted that the 'free denisons of Rome' had enabled the Romans 'to participate in honour, magistrates, and dignities' and that this was a worthy example to be imitated. Alberico Gentili referred to the crucial passages of Machiavelli's *Discorsi*, Lipsius' *Admiranda, siue, de magnitudine Romana* and to Cicero's *Pro Balbo*.[115] Similarly, Thomas Craig claimed that 'unless all distinctions between the two countries are removed, and equal access to dignities, honours, and immunities be allowed, perfect union is not attainable'. To prove his point, Craig offered a set of arguments based on the history of the Roman republic. First, 'the jealousy between the plebs and patricians' concerning 'the consulate and all other public offices' had compromised the interests of Rome. Secondly and similarly, a bitter war had broken out between the Romans and the Latins over the fact that the latter had been excluded from being eligible for consuls. 'Why', Craig posed the question, 'restrict honours and administration to one and leave the other in an almost servile situation?' The only way to acquire a lasting union was to offer everyone an equal 'hope of attaining the reward and promotion which are wont to stimulate men to excellence'.[116]

[114] Levack 1987, p. 60, and pp. 59–62; see also *State trials*, II, cols. 564, 574. The conference of both houses on naturalization on 25 February 1607 discussed an act to naturalize all ante-nati 'with certain conditions and restrictions for bearing offices judicature, or having voice in parliament', *Somers tracts*, I, p. 133.

[115] Thornborough, *The ioiefull reuniting*, pp. 68–70, Hayward, *A treatise of union*, pp. 19–22; John Doddridge, 'A breif consideracion of the unyon', in *The Jacobean union*, pp. 147–8; T[homas] G[ainsford], *The vision and discourse*, p. 17; Ralegh, *The historie of the world*, v.ii.ii, p. 382; Alberico Gentili, 'De vnione regnorum Britanniae', in *Regales disputationes tres: id est, de potestate regis absoluta: de vnione regnorum Britanniae: de vi ciuium in regem semper iniusta* (London, 1605), pp. 44–5; Machiavelli, *Discorsi*, II.3, 4; Justus Lipsius, *Admiranda, siue, de magnitudine Romana libri quattuor* (Paris, 1598), pp. 47–56, especially pp. 47–8; Cicero, *Pro Balbo*, XIII.31.

[116] Craig, *De unione*, pp. 329–31, 333–4, 344, 351–2, 441–3, 467; cf. Henry Spelman, 'Of the union', in *The Jacobean union*, p. 182; de Lucinge, *The beginning*, pp. 47–8; Botero, *A treatise*, pp. 30–3; [idem], *Observations*, sig. G5^v–6^r.

Although some theorists felt qualms about directly applying the Roman model to the Anglo-Scottish union,[117] Bacon showed no such hesitancy about the usefulness of the Roman model of bestowing citizenships. He constantly employed the example of the Roman policy of naturalization to urge the complete naturalization of Scots in England. And he used the Roman concept of citizenship to define the liberties and freedoms of the English, in order to show that they should be extended to the Scots as part of the union.

The Roman liberties that were of crucial importance for Bacon's particular argument for the union carried with them a contention of a wider ideological importance. It was only through the exhibition of the people's virtue that civic greatness could be attained, and this required a community where the conditions of participation in public life were fulfilled. With a view to preventing the people from losing their 'heart and courage' and becoming 'servile vassals', the government of the state should be organized so that the people retained their ability to take part in its political life. This becomes clear in Bacon's February 1607 parliament speech. According to Bacon, 'the points or parts of Naturalization' could not be better expressed than by 'the ancient distinction of *Jus Civitatis, jus Suffragii vel Tribus*, and *Jus Petitionis sive Honorum*'. To be a citizen entailed the capacity of voting and bearing office. Explaining what he had in mind, Bacon told the Commons that 'all ability and capacity is either of private interest of *meum* and *tuum*, or of public service'. There were two spheres of action, the private and the public, and whilst the first consisted of looking after one's private property, the latter was not constituted simply of safeguarding the private sphere, but also of serving the public. Elucidating further what he meant by public service, Bacon announced that it 'consisteth chiefly either in Voice, or in Office'.[118]

It was, therefore, a central feature of the English political system that the basic conditions for the people's public service were maintained. A state pursuing civic greatness should, in other words, be organized so that it was certain not merely that the people were armed, but also that their ability to participate in political life – through having a voice in parliament and opportunity for office – was secured. The armed citizen took part in the civic life of his commonwealth by assembling for battle and for parliament. Illustrating the nature of a warlike nation, Bacon argued: 'we see that, in the very summons of parliament,

---

[117] Anon., ['A treatise about the union'], in *The Jacobean union*, pp. 42–3, 58–9, cf. 44–5.
[118] Bacon in parliament 17 February 1607, in *Letters*, III, p. 309.

the knights of the shire are required to be chosen *milites gladio cincti*; so as the very call, though it were to council, bears a mark of arms and habiliments of war'.[119] It was only when everyone set aside their narrow private interests and dedicated themselves to the public good that a state could attain civic greatness. Although Walter Ralegh disagreed with Bacon about the role of money in the attainment of civic greatness, he wholeheartedly agreed with him about the importance of civic virtue. Summing up Bacon's idea of civic greatness, he wrote: 'Certaine it is (as Sir Francis Bacon hath judiciously observed) That a State whose dimension or stemme is small, may aptly serve to be foundation of a great Monarchie: which chiefly comes to passe, where all regard of domesticall prosperitie is laid a side; and every mans care addressed to the benefit of his countrie.'[120]

It comes as no surprise, therefore, that Ralegh's account is also strikingly similar to Bacon's in so far as the close connection of the citizen army and a certain type of government is concerned. Whereas mercenary troops were usually employed by tyrants, a citizen army entailed 'the moderate government of the Romans'. Since they had been free, the Romans and the Latins had been particularly willing to fight. Slaves could be 'furious' and 'outragious', but they always wanted virtue. Only those who lived 'under a pleasant yoke' were courageous as well as 'stout fighters'. Ralegh found this argument so compelling that he was astonished how rarely it had been followed up: 'The moderate use of souereigne power being so effectuall, in assuring the people unto their Lords, and consequentlie, in the stablishment or enlargement of Dominion: it may seeme strange, that the practise of tyrannie, whose effects are contrarie, hath beene so common in all ages.'[121]

Bacon's account of the social and political underpinnings of a truly great state formed a startling contrast to that presented in de Lucinge's *The beginning, continuance, and decay of estates*. In the second book of his treatise, de Lucinge enquired into the means of preserving greatness once it was attained. The chief responsibility in the maintenance of an empire lay in organizing of its social and political structure. The first rule was carefully to ensure that the subjects 'have alwaies neede of him that is their Commander'. The sultan was 'Master of the persons, habilities, goods, houses, and possessions of his vassals'. But it was not

---

[119] Bacon, 'Lowe's case of tenures', in *Works*, VII, p. 548.
[120] Ralegh, *The historie of the world*, v.iii.xiii, p. 496.
[121] Ibid., v.ii.ii, pp. 376–7, 382–6. Cf. however v.iv.v, p. 607, where mercenary troops were said to prevail against the militias of 'free States'.

merely their homes, lands and other goods which the subjects had
solely by the favour of the sultan: they owed their very lives to him.
'And in a word', de Lucinge argued, 'their being and life depending
indifferently upon the Prince, their principall care is to winne his
favour.' It was scarcely surprising that the subjects called themselves
'slaves of their Prince'.[122]

The next step in safeguarding an empire was to take care of possible
popular commotions. It was, in the first place, important to disarm the
people, so that they would 'forget both the use and courage to handle'
arms. In order to keep the subjects under 'so barbarous a yoake', it was
of the highest importance for the sultan to maintain 'a general peace
and tranquillity throughout his estate'; to make certain 'that justice be
equally distributed' and that the people had 'plenty of victuals, and all
other usuall commodities'. As de Lucinge put it, it was best 'to lull
asleepe their fury'. Under these circumstances 'every one maketh the
best of his fortune and liveth quietly at home, embracing that naturall
desire of holding his owne', and 'they rest free from the thought of
plotting or understanding sturs and rebellions'.[123] The final step in
organizing the empire was to have a standing army always ready to
suppress possible commotions. The prince, de Lucinge argued, ought
to maintain 'a great number of horse and foot alwaies armed, alwaies
in pay, and distributed in garrisons thorow out his Empire, especially,
in places most proper to resist or assaile'.[124]

The central features of Bacon's concept of the true greatness of
states – that every subject ought to be fit to act as a soldier and that
'the temper of the government' must not keep subjects 'in the
condition of servile vassals' – can perhaps be seen as a sarcastic
repudiation of the values put forward by de Lucinge. On several
occasions Bacon firmly maintained that the English as well as the
Scottish were military in character. In *A brief discourse*, Bacon
remarked that union entailed the unification of 'these two mighty
and warlike nations'[125] and he told the Commons that Britain had
'the best iron in the world, that is the best soldiers of the world'.[126] In
Calvin's case he described England as 'a warlike and a magnanimous

---

[122] de Lucinge, *The beginning*, pp. 95–6.
[123] Ibid., pp. 102.
[124] Ibid., p. 105; see in general pp. 96–8, 105–8 for the details of the professional army. It should
be noted that de Lucinge disassociated himself from the policy conducted in Turkey, p. 96,
cf. however, p. 95.
[125] Bacon, *A brief discourse*, in *Letters*, III, p. 92.
[126] Bacon in parliament, in *Letters*, III, pp. 313, 325, cf. p. 315.

nation fit for empire'.[127] The point he was making was that the new united kingdom of Britain, if not destined, was at least eminently qualified, to attain civic greatness. Britain met the conditions of a fit situation. More importantly, it fulfilled the social and political require-ments of a truly great state. It was a populous and warlike state, and its social structure was based on armed citizen-farmers, ready to die for their country. Finally, its political institutions were such that the people were well equipped to participate in political life by answering the summons for a parliament, and by playing the honourable role of a counsellor.

The lively debate about civic greatness calmed down with the end of the union project in 1608. The theme emerged only sporadically during the next decade, and although Bacon published 'Of the greatnesse of kingdomes' in 1612, he had by then turned his attention to other political issues. It was only during the major crisis of the 1620s that similar issues surfaced with equal vigour. And it was then that Bacon returned to the theme of the true greatness of states, developing his earlier ideas and making his final contribution to English political debate. His tract 'Of the true greatness of the kingdom of Britain' remained, however, unpublished as well as unfinished. This was no doubt partly because the union project for which it had been intended had come to an end. But there is little doubt that the general thrust of Bacon's idea of civic greatness also had something to do with it. Considering James's fame for peaceful policies and in particular the great emphasis he laid on peaceful methods for attaining an empire (through union), the extent to which Bacon's conception of civic greatness implied an aggressive advocacy of martial enterprises might account for the incompleteness of his tract. Furthermore, the utmost importance Bacon attached to warfare in his essay 'Of the greatnesse of kingdomes' put him in surprising and even awkward company.

A central argument in George Wither's *Abuses stript, and whipt* (published in 1613) called for a radical change in James's foreign policy. Wither could expatiate on the *vita activa* and *vera nobilitas*, but he also claimed that meticulous attention should be paid to external relations. The peace which God had brought about had made the English

---

[127] Bacon, 'The case of the post-nati', in *Works*, VII, pp. 664–5; cf. 'Lowe's case of tenures', in *Works*, VII, p. 548.

'feareless, careless and secure', and they had passed 'slightly' their 'former care of Martiall discipline'.[128]

> We have not onely let all care alone,
> But also are so drunken with delights,
> And drown'd in pleasure, that our dulled sprits
> Are so o'reclog'd with Luxury; we droupe,
> More fit for Venus then for Mars his troupe.

Wither urged a drastic change of this development: the English should renounce their 'presumption' and prepare for war. To accomplish this, 'a Parlament' should be called and those 'Martiallists' who had long been 'disgrac't' should 'be lov'd againe'.[129] There is little doubt that Wither's outspoken statements about foreign policy played a central role in his imprisonment in 1614.[130]

More importantly, the vocabulary Bacon employed in favour of the royal project of the union had been borrowed by Thomas Hedley, one of the most vigorous opponents of the king's new impositions, in his famous speech in James's first parliament in June 1610. The importance of this speech has been recognized by scholars; it is often quoted in studies of Jacobean political thought, mainly to highlight Hedley's close allegiance to the common law.[131] Michael Mendle alone has clearly detected the republican traits of Hedley's oration and has recently labelled it as 'the profound, sadly ignored Machiavellian–Baconian speech'.[132]

The weight and significance of Hedley's address was wide and multifaceted. The bulk of the speech relied upon the familiar vocabulary of the common law. But towards the end of the speech Hedley added the classical republican vocabulary to that of common law; an apposite example of the fact that the boundaries of political vocabularies were fluid enough to be combined without apparent contradiction and without sacrifice of persuasive force. There was a touch of irony to Hedley's speech: not only did he speak right after Bacon;[133] his

---

128 George Wither, *Abuses stript, and whipt: or satirical essaies, diuided into two bookes* (London, 1613), sigs. s4^r–5^r, H5^{r-v}.

129 Ibid., sig. s5^{vi}, in general sig. s5^v–7^r.

130 See Pritchard 1963.

131 Sommerville 1986, pp. 90–1, 94–6, 98, 134, 135, 148; Sommerville 1989, pp. 57, 60; Pocock 1987a, pp. 270–4; Sharpe 1989, p. 285; Hirst 1981, pp. 86–7; Christiansson 1991, pp. 70–1; Sacks 1992, pp. 118–19; cf. Notestein 1971, pp. 365–6.

132 Mendle 1985, p. 190, n.24; Mendle 1989a, p. 116.

133 Notestein 1971, p. 365; *PD1610*, p. 72.

arguments were directed, amongst other things, against those of Bacon. Hedley employed Baconian arguments to counter Bacon's arguments.

When Hedley gave his oration, the topic of the debate was whether the king had the right of impositions. Hedley opened his long speech by claiming that the previous speaker (i.e. Bacon) had digressed from the matter under debate but that he had, in his 'slow and imperfect pace', 'a more direct and open way to walk'.[134] After some preliminary remarks, Hedley proceeded to 'examine the question in hand' and was fully convinced that he could 'give a certain judgment' whether the king's right to impose was 'any part of the common law or no'. Since the common law had been defined as 'the best reason or the quintessence of reason', the king's right of impositions had to be proved to be 'tried and allowed by the wisdom of time for many ages together to be good and profitable for the commonwealth'. Bacon had erred, therefore, when he had claimed that 'this question was not a question of *bonum et malum*, but of *vera et falsa*'.[135]

Hedley's definition of the common law suggested that if 'it is ill for the good of the commonwealth, ergo, no law'.[136] Since the good of the commonwealth was the end of the common law, 'whatsoever, then, crosseth this end, the law will not digest it, but reject it as unsavory as soon as time, the trier of truth, hath found it out, and that notwithstanding any former precedents or judgments'. So a former judgment of a law court (such as Bate's case) in no way prevented judges making a contrary decision, since the whole excellence of the common law was based on the fact that it was 'tried reason', which was taken to mean that it was constantly redefined in the light of new circumstances. If this were not the case, Hedley argued, quoting Bacon's *Advancement of learning*, judges would have been devoid of 'versatile *ingenium*' and 'subject to the reproof of *idem manebat neque idem decebat*'.[137]

Hedley's delivery was dominated by common-law vocabulary until the final argument which he opened with a familiar contention: 'My last reason is drawn from the ancient freedom and liberty of the subjects of England, which appeareth and is confirmed by the great

---

[134] *PP1610*, II, pp. 170–1; cf. however, p. 180, where Hedley confessed, after a long discussion of the excellence of the common law, that he was 'necessarily drawn to digress'.

[135] Ibid., II, pp. 172–6. For Bacon, see *Letters*, IV, p. 191; cf. Bacon in parliament 28 February 1607, in *Letters*, III, p. 327.

[136] *PP1610*, II, p. 176.

[137] Ibid., II, pp. 176, 178–9; Bacon, *Advancement of learning*, in *Works*, III, p. 465, cf. p. 454. The first phrase is taken from *Livy*, 39.40, while the other one is a paraphrase from Cicero, *Brutus*, 95.327, where Cicero wrote '*remanebat idem nec decebat idem*'.

Charter of the liberties of England, but more plainly and particularly by reports and judgments printed and published in our law books.' But the liberty of the subjects was only one of the twin pillars of 'the felicity and happiness of all kingdoms'. It was wholly useless without the other – 'the sovereignty of the king'. Making use of Bacon's speech delivered in the committee of grievances on 19 May, Hedley pointed out that the truth of this pair became manifest in Tacitus' description of how Nerva had combined two things which customarily had been thought to be incompatible – liberty and sovereignty.[138] Whilst Bacon's point had been to suggest that the Commons should not intrude in the area of the king's sovereign power, Hedley wanted to show, instead, that the king should not exceed the proper limits of his power. But in accomplishing their respective ends, they both employed exactly the same juristic vocabulary. As Hedley put it, the sovereignty of the king consisted chiefly in 'honor or government' whilst 'the liberty of the subject' embodied 'matter of profit or property'.[139]

But Hedley went on to couple this argument with the republican idea of the armed citizen. The liberty of the subject, he told the Commons, furnished him with 'such ingenuity and freedom as maintains him in spirit and courage'.[140] Hedley thus embraced a central doctrine of the classical republican tradition. Military disposition was the citizen's chief area of action and his liberty was closely connected with his military virtue. Although in his writings on civic greatness Bacon had made the same association, his employment of Nerva's example stopped short of this. This republican argument was linked in Hedley's analysis with the idea of liberty rooted in property. Whereas in other spheres 'the bound and freemen are almost alike', their difference emerged most clearly in the area of property. If 'the liberty of the subject in his profit or property' was taken away 'a promiscuous confusion of a freeman and a bound slave' ensued.[141]

It is important to note that Hedley cited Cicero's *De officiis* in defence of the inviolability of private property. The earl of Northampton argued later in the same session that Cicero had exhorted the citizen to

---

138 *PP1610*, II, pp. 190–1. For Bacon see *Letters*, IV, p. 177, *PP1610*, II, p. 98. It can be noted that Nicholas Fuller commented on Bacon's speech: 'though Mr Solicitor's speech were full of rhetoric and art, yet it had some good substance in it', ibid., II, p. 98. Cf. also Bacon, *Advancement of learning*, in *Works*, III, p. 303; Bacon in parliament 7 July 1610, in *Letters*, IV, p. 202. The same passage from Tacitus was again used by the Speaker in the 1626 parliament, see *PP1626*, I, p. 31.

139 *PP1610*, II, p. 191.

140 Ibid., II, p. 191.

141 Ibid., II, pp. 191–2.

devote his time 'upon moral studies for the service of his country'. But this did not mean that he should be like 'those empirics that trifle out the time idly about questions impertinent either touching the precedent errors or future directions'. The subject should not, in other words, ponder over problems regarding the questions of prudence. Moral studies amounted simply to taking care of 'their sovereign's necessity', to giving pecuniary help.[142] In startling contrast, Hedley quoted Cicero to the effect that the commonwealth could not violate citizen's property rights. 'Tully', he told the Commons, 'though an heathen yet a wise man, makes it a principal point in state administration *ut suum quisque teneat neque de bonis privatorum publice diminutio fiat* [that everyone has his own and that there is no loss of private property in the interest of the public].' To provide security for private property had been a principal reason for founding the commonwealth. 'This then', Hedley concluded, 'may give proof to the state that the prerogative of princes should not dive too deep into the profit or property of their free subjects.'[143]

Property was thus the chief ingredient of the subject's liberty, and its safeguarding lay at the heart of founding a commonwealth. Hedley, of course, wanted to prove that despite his sovereign rule in area of government, the king could not violate the subject's property rights.[144] But his emphasis on property enabled him to argue further that 'a man's lands and goods' increased 'spirit and courage to the professors thereof'.[145] Underlying Hedley's argument was the Aristotelian idea that in order to be able to bear arms and to be a citizen a man ought to have inherited property. He was, in other words, describing the material basis of armed citizens. He completely agreed with the view that 'gentry' was 'nothing else but ancient riches'. It was not, however, the amount of property which created liberty and citizenship, but simply the ability to possess and thereby to exercise power over it. 'But', Hedley maintained, 'it is not so much to lose all a man's wealth as the power of holding it, for that is nothing else but bondage, or the condition of a villein, whose lands and goods are only in the power of his lord, which doth so abase his mind, even the lack of liberty in this point, that he is neither fit to do service to his country in war nor peace, for the law enables him not so much as to serve in a jury, and

---

[142] Ibid., I, pp. 264, 267. Cf. in general Nederman 1993, pp. 512–13.
[143] *PP1610*, II, p. 192; *De officiis*, II.21.73; II.22.78.
[144] See *PP1610*, II, pp. 192–3.
[145] Ibid., II, p. 194.

the wars design him but to the galleys or the gallows.'[146] If a man lost his material independence, he also lost his moral independence, and his ability 'to do service to his country'.

Without liberty in their property, subjects would become 'little better than the king's bondmen' and consequently unfit to bear arms. To be 'the king's bondmen' would 'so discourage them and so abase and deject their minds, that they will use little care or industry to get that which they cannot keep and so will grow both poor and base-minded'.[147] In England, however, this was not yet the case. England met the material conditions of a warlike commonwealth. Because the Englishman had his ancient liberty, he was an able soldier. Hedley contrasted sharply 'the peasants in other countries' who were not free and who were 'no soldiers nor will be ever made any' to free Englishmen. 'Every Englishman', he argued, 'is as fit for a soldier as the gentleman elsewhere.'[148]

If England could enjoy 'the blessings and benefits' of an absolute monarchy – benefits which Hedley refrained from spelling out – it was scarcely less fortunate in enjoying, to an equal degree, the benefits of 'a free estate'. Because of the peculiar nature of the English common-wealth, it could easily defend itself against any threat from without. The military virtue of the Englishman grounded on his freedom in property maintained and safeguarded the whole kingdom.[149] This was the essence of 'the blessings and benefits' of 'a free estate'. Moreover, the armed citizens who enabled England to withstand the corruption coming from without could also help her play a more honourable role. England had, Hedley reminded his colleagues in the House of Commons, 'prevailed with a perpetual happy success to the everlasting honor of the realm and the admiration of all the world'. Although Hedley did not argue that England could pursue civic greatness, as explicitly as Bacon did, his employment of the example of the Romans who had performed 'vast exploits' and had become 'conquerors' pointed in this direction.[150]

It was, however, a cardinal error to suppose that the amassing of wealth could produce great success. Hedley was careful to emphasize the fact that riches never brought civic glory. He first cited Bacon's

[146] Ibid., II, p. 194.
[147] Ibid., II, p. 194.
[148] Ibid., II, pp. 194–5.
[149] Ibid., II, p. 195.
[150] Ibid., II, p. 195.

(and Machiavelli's) favourite example – the story of Solon and Croesus. The moral of this story was that 'gold is not sure to find good soldiers, but good soldiers are sure to find gold'. The same lesson could be learned from Roman history. For had they 'warred with gold', they could hardly have proved successful, but since they had been 'warring with iron', they had become 'conquerors and [had] never wanted gold'. The underlying assumption was obvious. 'It is', Hedley spelled out by paraphrasing Bacon, 'the sinews of men's arms then (namely a valiant, populous and military nation), as hath been well observed and collected by one of the worthies of this House, that there are the true sinews of war and hath made our nation so renowned through the world.'[151]

What was Hedley's point? This Baconian argument enabled him to prove the great harm of impositions and to counter the arguments that since money was crucial in warfare, it was prudent for the subject to contribute. Salisbury had argued at the beginning of the session that it was a prudent line of policy to have money ready, and that people's willingness to contribute was the measure of their love towards their country. James had put it in even plainer terms. 'If I must maintain you', the king had told the both Houses in March, 'in peace and defend you in time of war, it must be by money, which is the sinews there of.'[152] And as we have seen, a similar argument cast in a Ciceronian vocabulary of *negotium* was put forward by the earl of Northampton later in the session. In paraphrasing Bacon, Hedley was thus not merely following a theoretical tradition in a servile way; he was also mounting a more particular attack on the importance of money in warfare and thereby on the king's authority for impositions.

Hedley drew two conclusions from his discussion. In the first place, he maintained that warlike disposition and military virtue were neither natural characteristics nor qualities depending on outward circumstances. It was not 'the nature of the people or climate' which enhanced a people's military virtue. The warlike disposition of a people mainly descended from 'the laws, liberties, and government' of the community. The valour of the people, Hedley claimed, was upheld by the 'maintenance of houses, of husbandry and tillage' as well as by avoiding 'depopulation', and finally by 'restraining great and mighty men from

---

[151] Ibid., II, p. 195; *Letters*, III, pp. 323–3, 313. Since the example of Solon and Croesus appeared almost immediately before the passage Hedley was paraphrasing, it is possible to assume that he also took that example from Bacon.

[152] *PP1610*, II, pp. 15–17, I, p. 50.

wronging or oppressing the common people'. In order to have valorous people, it was important to organize society so that the farmer could retain ownership of his land, and the noble could not oppress him.[153]

The other, and more important, conclusion Hedley drew from his social analysis of the armed citizen was to the effect that to take one brick away would ruin the whole building. If the property of the people were touched, their liberty would be destroyed. And this would not merely corrupt their military virtue, ultimately, it would also entail the demolition of the whole commonwealth with a vengeance. 'But once take this ancient liberty from the commons,' Hedley explained, 'so that they perceive their lands and goods not absolutely their own but in the absolute power and command of another, they will neither have nor care for that wealth and courage that now they have, but a drooping dismayedness will possess and direct them or deliver them up to desperate resolutions; for seeing their liberty and condition no better than the bondmen or the peasants in other places, their courage will be no better than theirs.'[154]

But how was all this connected with impositions? They were, after all, customs imposed upon foreign trade rather than upon the farmer. In order to demonstrate the connection, Hedley pointed out that what applied to the farmer, applied *mutatis mutandis* to the merchant. He claimed that 'the wealth and strength of the realm' rested as much 'in the merchant as in the ploughman'. This was so because the merchant increased, on the one hand, the strength of 'the navy and mariners which are the walls of this island' and, on the other hand, 'the wealth and treasure of the kingdom'. It followed, according to Hedley, that if 'great men' or 'the king's prerogative' oppressed and discouraged either 'the merchant or ploughman', then 'the wealth and strength of the king and kingdom must needs decline'. Because of its peculiar geographical surroundings, England needed valorous mariners as well as soldiers,[155] and it followed that any infringement on the subject's (whether farmer's or merchant's) property would commence corruption. As Hedley put it himself: 'And impositions, if unreasonable, touch all the commons as well as the merchant, and so doth touch and impeach the wealth, strength, and honor of the king, and may so

---

[153] Ibid., II, p. 196. It should be remembered that Bacon developed his similar social analysis only in 'Of the greatnesse of kingdomes' in 1612, although the embryo was already there in TGKB, pp. 48–9; see also *Letters*, III, p. 36.

[154] *PP1610*, II, p. 196.

[155] Cf. Nicholas Fuller, 23 June 1610, in ibid., II, pp. 160–1.

weaken the king and kingdom that he will want both gold and iron, both men and money, and so will be unable to defend himself and kingdom with his own force.'[156] If the king had the power to impose, he was also bound to resort to foreign help; he 'must depend on other princes or states' and employ 'mercenaries'. Some 'great and ample kingdoms and monarchs' had been able to maintain, besides their own forces, 'a sufficient number of mercenaries' to the extent that 'some wise statesmen have held it as good to lose with their own as win with others' arms'. But Hedley repudiated the value of mercenaries. Although they could serve well, it was his firm opinion that England 'must (as it hath done) stand of its own strength, which (as hath been said) resteth principally in the liberty and wealth of the commons'.[157]

The conclusion Hedley drew from his argument was that impositions without the consent of the subject were not merely against the common law, but were also a most imprudent line of policy. 'That prerogative, then,' Hedley concluded, 'that shakes this so long settled freedom of the subject in point of profit or property, hazards ... to unjoint the whole frame of this so ancient, honorable and happy state, so prudently compact of the sovereignty of the king and the liberty of the subject.'[158] By reducing the courage of his subjects, the king would not only jeopardize his own treasure; he would also compromise his whole realm. The decrease in valour of the people meant that the king could not defend his realm by his own forces, but would have to resort to foreign help. And this was the most perilous menace.[159]

Although Hedley had gone a long way towards employing Bacon's notions, there was a striking difference between their social analyses. Bacon concentrated exclusively on the role of farmers. In arguing that sedentary and indoor arts were contrary to military disposition, he was consciously belittling the role of merchants. Hedley, on the other hand, wholeheartedly included merchants among his warlike people. One does not have to go far to find the reason. To demonstrate the imprudence of impositions it was reasonable for Hedley to include

---

[156] Ibid., II, p. 196.
[157] Ibid., II, pp. 196–7.
[158] Ibid., II, p. 197.
[159] It should be noted that Hedley circumscribed the people's active role to the military sphere and left government to the king. The common law allowed 'to the subjects such ingenuity and freedom as maintains him in spirit and courage and yet contains him in all duteous subjection'; ibid., II, pp. 191, 192. Cf. Forset, *A comparative discovrse*, p. 18 (see also p. 21): 'If the people be tractable, and truely serviceable, with all dutious subjection, in the nature of right alleagiance, then as loving subiects, by their forwardnesse in cooperating with him, they give strength and stay unto his government.'

merchants, for the efficacy of his line of reasoning hinged upon the maritime nature of England. This difference contains a touch of irony. Bacon's idea of the true greatness of states has often been seen as an embodiment of commercial imperialism because of his insistence on the control of the seas. But it was in fact Hedley (as well as Ralegh) – not Bacon – who embraced merchants, and thereby commerce, in his conception of a warlike nation and a great state.

CHAPTER 5

Thomas Scott: virtue, liberty and the 'mixed Governement'

If the Anglo-Scottish union formed a major political issue during the first years of James I's reign, the question of how to respond to the European crisis acquired an equally dominant position in English politics towards the end of the reign. England had been entangled in the European crisis from the very beginning, ever since James's son-in-law Frederick had accepted the Bohemian crown offered to him after the Bohemians had renounced their allegiance to the Archduke Ferdinand, heir-apparent to the Holy Roman emperor. Although James had tried to persuade Frederick to turn down the offer and had consequently not acknowledged Frederick as king of Bohemia, the situation changed dramatically when the Catholique League not merely crushed the Bohemian army, but also occupied Frederick's hereditary Palatinate on the Rhine with Spanish troops. Frederick and Elizabeth were popular in England and their popularity grew further with the Spanish intervention. The English parliament, which met in 1621, earnestly pleaded with the king to restore the Palatinate to Frederick by force. James also condemned the Spanish intervention since it upset the status quo, but he preferred a peaceful settlement. He assumed that Spain controlled catholic Europe and placed his hopes on the negotiations about a marriage between Prince Charles and the Spanish Infanta which had been going on since 1614. These negotiations looked like foundering in 1618 over the issue of toleration for English catholics, but the pursuit of a negotiated settlement of the international crisis revived hopes of a Spanish match. Nevertheless, these came to an abrupt end in 1623 when Charles and Buckingham made their hazardous trip to Madrid. In the course of their stay in Madrid it seems to have become clear to Buckingham that the Spaniards were not fully committed to the restoration of the Palatinate to its rightful heir, Frederick. When they returned from Spain in October 1623 Charles and Buckingham met with huge popular acclaim and were determined to persuade James to change his peaceful line on foreign policy to a more martial one.[1]

The outbreak of a major European conflict with strong ideological implications kindled wide public discussion in England. The king endeavoured to restrict public speech about state matters.[2] A critic of royal policy told the king that 'I can come into no meetinges, but I finde the predominant humor to be talking of the wars of Christendome and honour of theire country, and suchlike treasons', whilst a catholic apologist for the Spanish match complained in 1623 that the propaganda campaign against Spain and the match had led 'the people of London ... to snarle and murmur, even at the verie name of Spayne: and everie artificer presumed, as an Aristarchus, to censure the king for that negotiation, as for an error of state'.[3] A few years later George Wither could still claim that 'These times do swarme with Pamphlets, which be far / More dangerous, then mortall poysons are.'[4] This lively debate has been charted in detail by Thomas Cogswell in his recent study of the period between 1621 and 1624. He distinguishes two periods, the dividing line being Charles and Buckingham's return from Madrid in October 1623. Before this the king's policy for solving the Palatinate crisis met with criticism, despite James's attempt to curb it. Whilst the *rapprochement* with Catholic Spain led some to praise peace and to produce Anglo-Spanish grammars and dictionaries, as well as to promote a more ecumenical stance by the Church of England, opponents of the Spanish match watched the developments with growing dismay. The government's control of the press was exceptionally tight, but Cogswell has been able to detect ways in which contrary opinions were publicly aired in sermons and in print as well as in manuscript pamphlets. 'For both James and his subjects,' he concludes, 'the pursuit of a Spanish match had been an ordeal. Never before in James's reign had a single political issue so deeply divided the kingdom.'[5] Yet by 1624 the situation had dramatically altered. A belligerent foreign policy was more openly advocated and the villain of

---

[1]   See Cogswell 1989a, pp. 6–20, 36–54, 57–69. For a succinct, balanced account of English foreign policy during these years, see Lockyer 1989, pp. 17–21; see also Russell 1979; Adams 1983; Adams 1985; Young 1985.

[2]   Cogswell 1989a, pp. 20–1, 32.

[3]   Anon., *Tom tell troath: or a free discourse touching the manners of the tyme* (n.p., n.d., [1622?]), p. 1; M[atthew] P[attenson], *The image of bothe churches, Hierusalem and Babel, vnitie and confusion: obedience and sedition* (Tornay, 1623), p. 1.

[4]   George Wither, *Britains remembrancer containing a narration of the plague lately past* (n.p., 1628), fo. 246ʳ.

[5]   Cogswell 1989a, pp. 20–53, the quotation is from p. 50; Cogswell 1989b.

the first act, the duke of Buckingham, suddenly became the hero of the second.[6]

In his lucid analysis of the period 1621–4, Cogswell primarily aims at showing first how the political nation reacted to the king's peaceful foreign policy and secondly how the 'Patriot' coalition was organized in 1624. But as far as the ideological underpinnings of the pamphlets are concerned, Cogswell has surprisingly little to say. He has traced the changing religious stances of the tracts, but on the whole he focuses on revealing that the literati of 1621–3 were talking about *arcana imperii*, that they proposed in only thinly veiled suggestions that England ought to help foreign protestants and that in 1624 there was a strong and more open campaign for martial intervention. The religious aspect apart, Cogswell does not pause to ask whether those who publicly voiced their opinions employed some theoretical tools in their attempts to grasp the political world they inhabited. Although it is of course true that the majority of pamphleteers were perhaps not concerned with any wider theoretical implications, it does not follow that this is true of all of them.

The best known as well as the most prolific pamphleteer of this brief but remarkable period was Thomas Scott. Scott studied both at St Andrews and at Peterhouse, where he received his BD in 1620. He wrote his first pamphlet *Vox populi* (published in 1620) whilst still in Scotland in 1619. In the course of the next four years he was to publish more than twenty pamphlets, all dealing with the problems of England's role in the European crisis. Although Scott's life and his writings raise formidable biographical and bibliographical problems,[7] a considerable amount of scholarly attention has been paid to them. According to the traditional account, Scott opposed the king's foreign policy, thereby expressing the opinions of 'the intelligent Protestant groups notably the London middle class'.[8] As far as his theoretical outlook is concerned, Scott is placed amongst those puritans who argued that the law should circumscribe the king's authority.[9] More recently, Peter Lake has argued that Scott's radicalism is not to be found in 'his publicly expressed opinions' but rather in 'his actions', that is, in 'his career as a pamphleteer'. A central aspect of Scott's

---

[6]   Cogswell 1989a, pp. 281–307. James Howell, *Dendrologia: Dodona's grove, or the focall forest* (n.p. [London], 1640), pp. 170–3. See also Limon 1986.

[7]   See Adams 1973, pp. 448–62; Adams 1976.

[8]   Wright 1943. Cf. van Eerde 1968.

[9]   Judson 1949, pp. 328, 333–4, 342–3.

argument was the 'activist view of government and citizenship'. According to Lake, the ideological setting for this idea of political activism and for so much else in Scott's writings must be sought in his religious background. The most important political contribution of puritanism, we are told, was the formation of an active citizenship. According to Lake, Scott's 'view of the world' enabled him 'to transfer "puritan" attitudes concerning a proper personal understanding of and zeal for true religion and further reformation directly into that enlarged political arena. This puritan contribution to the formation of an ideal of active citizenship ... may be the most important effect of puritan ideology on the political attitudes of the period.'[10]

Although the thesis presented by Lake has gained wide acceptance,[11] there are two factors which must lead us to question it. First, in stressing the formative nature of active citizenship, he tends to imply that we are here dealing with an entirely novel feature of English political discourse. But this amounts to a failure to recognize that the ideas put forward by Scott and other like-minded puritans can scarcely be said to be new. In fact they had been expressed in England throughout the sixteenth century as well as the first decades of the seventeenth. Secondly, Lake has overrated the puritanical elements in Scott's ideas. Scott can of course be classified as a puritan in his religious outlook and this may be said to have had several implications of great importance for his political ideas. But in so far as his advocacy of active citizenship is concerned, Scott's arguments are almost exclusively classical republican in character.

The main aim of the present chapter is to analyse Thomas Scott's ideas of politics, relating them to the classical humanist tradition we have been exploring and thus to substantiate my reservations about Lake's thesis. It should be emphasized that I do not wish to deny the central role of religion and anti-popery in Scott's writings. Many of his arguments were put in exclusively religious terms. He pointed out that 'this great businesse of Religion' was 'the foundation of all'; as he argued elsewhere, it was that 'which wee alwayes prize and preferre

---

[10]   Lake 1982, pp. 807, 813, 824; Walzer 1965, pp. 206, 210, 282. The rapprochement with Spain could also be opposed by restating the king's supremacy in religion; Thomas Proctor, *The right of kings: conteyning a defence of their supremacy* (n.p. [Amsterdam], 1621), sig. A2ʳ, pp. 3–4, 10; Edward Forset, *A defence of the right of kings* (London, 1624), pp. 50–1. Cf. Thomas Reeve, *Mephibosheths hearts ioy vpon his soveraignes safetie: deliuered in a sermon in the church of Great Yarmouth in Norfolke, the 19. day of October. 1623* (London, 1624), pp. 18–20, who ascribed a dominant role to the king in promoting the common good.

[11]   See Sommerville 1986, p. 45; Lake 1989, p. 89; Cust 1986, pp. 76–7; Cust and Hughes 1989, p. 21; Hughes 1991, pp. 87, 89. See, however, the brief remarks in Butler 1985, pp. 160–1.

before all other respects'.[12] But Scott was also using history to prove his points. On one occasion he wrote that his argument was not only 'a Paradoxe in divinity', but also 'a law universall, both of nature, & nations'. And since, as Scott put it, 'the more noble the nation is, the more frequent the examples', he employed instances drawn from Greek and Roman history.[13] He espoused the principle that 'by precedent examples men commonly judge of future events'. It was best to proceed 'by comparing time past, with that which is like to follow'.[14] It is therefore argued that, in addition to the religious features, it is possible to trace a distinctive humanist analysis of the commonwealth through Scott's writings and that it is only when we also recognize this element in Scott's polemic that we can begin to appreciate the full nature of his enterprise.

An important point which should be borne in mind is the Scottish background of Scott's career. It is a well-known fact that for a number of reasons Scottish politics was particularly prone (in comparison to English) to humanist and republican trends of political thought. The lack of an apocalyptic vision and of legal traditionalism, the constant instability of national politics as well as a strong sense of aristocratic civic virtue as a bulwark against tyranny contributed to the Scottish susceptibility to humanist and civic ideas.[15] The impact of Scottish humanism on English political discourse is obvious at least at two specific moments. The first of these was the Anglo-Scottish union debate. As we have seen in the previous chapter, this debate not merely provoked a number of Englishmen and Scots to study the problems of civic greatness; it also prompted them to enquire into the nature of citizenship. Another and even more specific moment when Scottish humanism can be said to have impinged on English political thought is Thomas Scott's pamphlet campaign. He was, as has been said, a graduate of St Andrews and began his publishing career in Scotland.

---

12 [Thomas Scott], *Vox regis* (n.p., [Utrecht], n.d., [1624]), p. 66; [idem], *Synmachia: or, a trve-loves knot* (n.p., n.d., [1624]), p. 14; see also e.g. [idem], *Vox Dei* (n.p, n.d., [1623?]), p. 49; [idem], *The Belgicke pismire: or stinging the slothfull sleeper* (London, 1622), p. 5. See in general [idem], *Englands ioy, for svppressing the papists, and banishing the priests and iesuites* (n.p., 1624), p. 13; [idem], *Aphorismes of state* (Utrecht, 1624); [idem], *Digitus Dei* (n.p., n.d., [1623]), pp. 20, 39.

13 [Scott], *Vox Dei*, p. 35. Cf. in general e.g. Abraham Gibson, *Christiana-polemica: or a preparatiue to warre ... a sermon* (London, 1619), sig. A6ʳ⁻ᵛ; Thomas Sutton, *The good fight of faith: a sermon preached at Saint Mary-acts in London, vnto the gentlemen of the Artilley Garden, the 19. of Iune, 1623* (London, 1624), pp. 27–8.

14 [Thomas Scott], *A relation of some speciall points concerning the state of Holland* (The Hague, 1621), p. 16; [idem], *An experimentall discoverie of Spanish practises or the covnsell of a well-wishing souldier, for the good of his prince and state* (n.p., 1623), p. 29.

15 Williamson 1979, especially pp. ix, 86–116; Mason [s.a.]; Norbrook 1987.

As we shall see, Scotland played a significant role in some of his arguments. It is arguable, therefore, that Scott's Scottish background can in part account for the striking degree of humanism and republicanism in his pamphlet campaign.

'The generall Torrent of discontent that raigns with such a seditious noyse over your whole Kingedome' had not yet made an 'open breach uppon your peoples obedience', but had certainly 'very much weakned theyr affections'. This is how one author described the political situation in England in early 1622. The reason for this 'generall Torrent of discontent' was twofold. It was caused both by 'Dishonour abroad', and by 'Discord at home'.[16] In 1624 John Randol preached that 'ye have corruptions within, [and] provocations without'.[17] As Lake rightly reminds us, Scott too was not merely preoccupied with English foreign policy; he was equally concerned with the underlying domestic developments. International politics was full of intrigues, frauds and dishonesty. 'In these warres and times of wickedness', Scott wrote, 'so many outrages & cruell bloodsheddings were committed, that Nero's opening of his mothers wombe was not comparable.'[18] But the international events had important reverberations in England. Whilst the alarming news of 1623 was spreading, Scott reminded the king of the fact that everyone who searched 'into the Spaniards proceedings' could see that Spain would corrupt the whole of England.[19] Elsewhere, he was even more pessimistic, pointing out that 'the corruption of manners hath broken downe our Walles, and let in that Trojan Horse laden with trumperies'. 'To conclude all,' he wrote, 'this Nation of ours at this day, outsinnes all the nations of the world, even in their proper sinnes for which they have beene infamous.'[20] It was useless to dwell on particular problems when 'not only this or that member, this or that finger or toe, but the whole body is corrupted'.[21] The good news of October 1623 and the consequent shift of direction

---

16   Anon., *Tom tell troath*, p. 5, see p. 6, for further description of corruption.
17   John Randol, *A sermon preacht at St Maries in Oxford, the 5. of August: 1624: concerning the kingdomes peace* (Oxford, 1624), p. 18.
18   [Thomas Scott], *Boanerges: or the humble supplication of the ministers of Scotland, to the high covrt of parliament in England* (Edinburgh, 1624), sig. c3ᵛ.
19   [Thomas Scott], *An experimentall discoverie*, p. 7; cf. his, *The Spaniards perpetvall designes to an vniversall monarchie* (n.p., 1624), sig. **1ᵛ.
20   Thomas Scott, *The proiector: teaching a direct sure, and ready way to restore the decayes of the Church and state both in honour and revenue: delivered in a sermon before the iudges in Norwich, at summer Assises there holden, anno 1620* (London, 1623), sig. A3ᵛ, p. 34; cf. *Digitvs Dei*, pp. 31–2; *Englands ioy*, p. 5.
21   Thomas Scott, *The high-waies of God and the king: wherein all men ovght to walke in holinesse here, to happinesse hereafter: deliuered in two sermons preached at Thetford in Norfolke, anno 1620* (London, 1623), p. 80.

in English foreign politics did not fully change Scott's mind and in 1624 he still talked of 'the generall grievances of the Church and State'.[22]

What did Scott mean by corruption? To begin with, there is little doubt that he associated it with religious issues. He declared that 'the whole body [of England] is corrupted', and noted that every place 'swarme with schismes, sects, heresies, and private spirits'.[23] But where the exact nature of corruption was concerned, Scott resorted to a familiar stock of images. It is significant that he was engaged in the translation of Trajano Boccalini's *The new-found politicke*, often described as a prime example of the exhaustion of Italian republicanism.[24] In *Vox popvli* he expounded that, whilst enriching themselves, 'tymeservers milk the estate and keep it poore'.[25] Those whom Gondomar had managed to 'Hispaniolize' 'for their private ends (as all temporisers do) neglected the publicke good either of Church or Common-wealth'.[26] In his definition of England's corruption, Scott placed his greatest emphasis on 'an itch of private wealth which ever forerunnes and effects the ruine of the Common-wealth'.[27] The first conclusion Scott drew from his analysis of corruption can be expressed at its simplest by saying that in a corrupted commonwealth people neglected the common good and instead pursued their own private interest. Many critics of the royal policy arrived at the same judgment. John Randol believed that the world was full of 'Oeconomicall hunters ... that hunt for the provision of their owne houses' and neglect 'the publick welfare of the state'. According to the author of *Tom tell troath*, 'the olde compasse of honour is quite forgott'. People knew 'no other route, then that of thair owne fortunes: according to which they tacke and untacke all publicke affaires'.[28]

This familiar idea occurs throughout Scott's writings. In 1621 he

---

[22]   [Scott], *Vox regis*, p. 18, see in general pp. 18–24. Cf. [idem], *A briefe information of the affaires of the Palatinate* (n.p., 1624).

[23]   Scott, *The high-waies of God*, p. 80.

[24]   Trajano Boccalini, *The new-found politicke, disclosing the secret natures and dispositions as well of priuate persons as of statesmen and courtiers*, translated by J. Florio, T. Scott and W. Vaughan (London, 1626); Thomas Scott, *Newes from Pernassus: the politicall touchstone, taken from Mount Pernassus* (Helicon, 1622); Skinner 1978 i, pp. 168, 188–9.

[25]   [Thomas Scott], *Vox popvli: or newes from Spaine* (n.p., 1620), sig. B3ᵛ; cf. sig. B4ʳ.

[26]   [Scott], *Boanerges*, sig. D4ʳ.

[27]   Scott, *The high-waies of God*, p. 80.

[28]   Randol, *A sermon*, pp. 3–4, also pp. 6–7, and especially p. 25; Anon., *Tom tell troath*, p. 6; [Alexander Leighton?] *The interpreter wherin three principall termes of state: much mistaken by the vulgar are clearely unfolded* (n.p., 1624), pp. 12, 14. This tract was previously ascribed to Thomas Scott, but was probably written by Leighton, see Condick 1982.

argued that there were 'two great hinderances' which commonly appeared together: 'Jealousie and respect of our owne benefit'. 'When any man', as Scott explained his idea, 'bendeth his wit and all his actions only to seeke his owne benefit; he thinkes every thing too much that another man hath, when he cannot have a part therein.' Those who had nothing but their own private gain in mind were 'the meanes and causes of the ruyne of all Common-wealths'.[29] Corruption made people lose their sense of judgement and, instead of esteeming the common good, they would begin to value the art of amassing private riches as the most desirable quality. The people's resulting moral character could be described as effeminate and as loving 'Luxurie'. They did nothing but sleep 'in securitie' and enjoyed their 'sensuall pleasures', 'bewitching pastimes' and 'brutish passions'.[30] Complete apathy among the people was therefore an unmistakable sign of corruption.

According to Scott, corruption affected the whole commonwealth, but most conspicuously and dangerously the nobility. Central to Scott's whole pamphlet campaign was the idea of a totally corrupt court. Describing the characters who were to be blamed for the corruption of the commonwealth, he said: 'I will conclude with him that is the cause of all this, and that's the Courtly Thiefe.'[31] These 'Monopolists' were amassing 'all our private Wealth'; in their mischievous lives, they wholly degenerated from the virtues of their progenitors. Scott was convinced, as he put it in his typical flowery style, that 'their breede is from the lazie scumme of counterfeyt Gentilitie, who bearing those Armes idely, which their diligent Predecessours have purchased as badges of some honorable atchievement, doe thereby disgrace their Originals, as if they were priviledged to be vicious by the redundancy of their predecessors vertues'. These men, irrespective of whether they were 'base in their originals' or had degenerated 'from the nobilitie and vertue of their Ancestors', directed their efforts to 'undo the publique for their private and inordinate desires'.[32] Scott later added that it was most typical of his own corrupt times that the more a man was able to 'inrich himselfe by the losse of others, yea by the losse of all ... the more wise he is thought to bee, and the more worthy of

---

29 [Thomas Scott], *A relation of Holland*, p. 18. Cf. also *The Belgicke pismire*, pp. 30–1; [Thomas Scott], *The Belgick souldier: dedicated to the parliament: or, warre was a blessing* (Dort, 1624), p. 39.
30 [Scott], *The Belgicke pismire*, pp. 12, 44, 82–3, 26. Cf. e.g. Thomas Barnes, *The wise-mans forecast against the evill time* (London, 1624), pp. 36, 43, 45.
31 Scott, *The high-waies of God*, p. 79.
32 [Scott], *The Belgicke pismire*, pp. 26–8.

preferment'.[33] The degeneracy of the nobility was primarily due to its education. It was, Scott wrote, 'farre unfit for true Nobilitie to be educated in an idle course of life, and trayned up onely to hunt, to hawke, or daunce, or drinke, or court, or play', which were 'the ordinarie exercises of these degenerate times'.[34]

If corruption held sway long enough, it would not confine itself to the morality of the individuals but would infect the whole common-wealth. A long period of corruption led, in other words, 'to the yoke of slaverie'. Servitude could arise in two important ways; first, when people lost their vigilance and all their energy to serve the community, devoting their attention instead to their private good. With his typical verbosity Scott emphasized that 'to waste and impoverish a plentifull Estate like a Prodigall, to sucke the life bloud out of the Common-wealth, thereby to deject the spirits of men with their fortunes, and so subjugate them under the yoke of slaverie, to draw all the juyce and marrow from the veints and bones of a people, requires no great wit to bring about'. Slavery was brought about by people's idleness – 'the idle and secure people were drowned in the generall Deluge'.[35] This kind of life dejected them and consequently imposed the yoke of slavery upon them. To illustrate his point, Scott took Cato's view that men's feeling of security and their inclination 'to shackle and manacle, to bridle and saddle themselves in silkes and velvets, in gold and silver' 'threatneth and introduceth slaverie'.[36] If a man became subject to the vices of prodigality, idleness and sloth, his heart would become effeminate, which would pave the way for 'a State fit and supple for any other subjection'.[37] There was thus a direct road from the promotion of private riches through idleness to the slavery of the entire commonwealth.

But an even more insidious way in which slavery could victimize a community was through the abuse of government. By becoming a cruel tyrant, the king reduced his realm to slavery, as the examples of

---

[33] Ibid., p. 34. Cf. George Wither, *Wither's motto: nec habeo, nec careo, nec curo* (n.p. [London], 1621), sigs. B1^{r-v}, D5^{r-v}; Edward Sutton, *The serpent anatomized: a morall discourse* (1623) (London, 1626), pp. 9–10, 13–14, 39–40 and especially p. 11; Anon., *Tom tell troath*, p. 4, where the corruption of the court was partly explained by the influence of merchants who were only concerned with 'what toucheth their owne profit'. An indication of this influence was the fact that 'one of their occupation, is made Treasurer'.

[34] [Scott], *The Belgicke pismire*, p. 31.

[35] Ibid., p. 38. Cf. [Leighton?], *The interpreter*, p. 14.

[36] [Thomas Scott], *A tongve-combat, lately happening between two English souldiers in the tilt-boat of Grauesend* (London, 1623), p. 64.

[37] [Scott], *The Belgicke pismire*, pp. 81–2.

Roman emperors amply demonstrated. 'We see', Scott wrote, 'Claudius the dullard, Nero the Mountibanke, Caligula the debosht drunkard, (that had neither wit nor honestie) could doe this as well and as readily, as Tiberius, that had wit without honestie.'[38] Although Scott used Roman emperors to illustrate how a tyrant could bring about the yoke of slavery, it was of course the Spanish monarchy which furnished his main instance. If the United Provinces were to have peace with Spain or to be 'in subjection to Spaine', Scott argued in 1622, they would be nothing but 'slaves'. The reason was not far to seek. Wherever the king of Spain goes, 'he sets himselfe downe like an absolute and tyrannical Lord, silencing all Lawes but his owne, which are as those of the Medes and Persians; yeas as those of Draco written in blood'.[39]

In the context of England this meant that the king would turn tyrant if he disregarded parliament and sought to oust the majority of the political nation from the main sphere of active life. According to Scott, 'publique persons should do publique actions in publique' which he defined as taking place 'in the Gates of the City, in the Kings high-way, in the eye of all'. This was the way to guarantee that the public good was duly respected, for when public actions were done in private, they not merely became 'chamber-workes'; they did nothing but promote 'privacy and parciality'. Scott's most telling example was the seventh king of Rome, Tarquinius Superbus, who, according to Scott, 'made the name of a King odious at Rome, because he ruled all *Domesticis consilijs* by chamber-Councell'.[40] The instance of Tarquinius was highly relevant because a similar danger was threatening English public life. In *Vox popvli*, Scott boldly maintained that there were many counsellors around the king 'who blow this cole fearing their owne stakes, if a Parliament should inquire into their actions, that they use all their art and industrie to withstand such a councell; perswading the King he may rule by his absolute prerogative without a Parliament'.[41] In 1624 he claimed that he had heard 'a generall despaire close up the hearts of all men, that they should never see Parliament againe'.[42] Scott's rhetoric left a strong impression that there were men around the king who advocated the policy of disregarding parliament, and in seeking to

---

[38]   Ibid., p. 39.
[39]   Ibid., p. 56.
[40]   Scott, *The high-waies of God*, pp. 69–70; *Livy* 1.50. Cf. e.g. [Thomas Scott], *Englands ioy*, p. 7.
[41]   [Scott], *Vox popvli*, sig. B3ᵛ. Cf. [Leighton?], *The interpreter*, p. 7.
[42]   [Scott], *Vox regis*, p. 23.

do this they were, in fact, causing James to become a Tarquinius Superbus. In Scott's definition of 1624, 'a Parliament where Prince and People meet and joyne in consultation, is fit only for that weightie and important worke, in whose even ballancing, the weale of a State doth consist. And without this Councel, the greatest Peere or Officer, yea, the greatest profest Engineere in State stratagems, may easily erre upon either hand, many degrees from good government, and so fall into an Anarchy or Tyrannie.'[43]

Scott was not content, however, with a description of a corrupted commonwealth. He also wanted to show how the growth of corruption could be halted or even avoided altogether. It is arguable, in other words, that it was Scott's main aim to explain the ways in which the most serious trouble ravaging the English commonwealth could be cured or eradicated. The first remedy for corruption lay in reversing the dominant values. In one of his most important pamphlets, *The Belgicke pismire*, Scott declared that the two first things to be done were 'to full the veines of a decayed estate' and 'to inrich a Common-wealth'.[44] If Scott was fully convinced that corruption was closely linked with people privileging their own private gain, he was scarcely less persuaded that citizens of a healthy commonwealth placed the good of the community before any consideration of personal gain. When crucial issues of the commonwealth, such as the one of peace and war, were to be decided, 'wee must not consider nor respect any mans particuler interest, but the benefit and commodity of the generality'. There was no real advantage 'in seeking after our owne particuler benefit', since its pursuit meant that 'the generall commodity is lost' and if this happened, 'the particuler cannot continue'. 'It ought to be', as Scott concluded his examination of the state of Holland, 'a Maxime in all good and politicke Governments, to doe Justice, and procure the good of the generality, and particuler profit will of it selfe come unto you.'[45] If one wanted to reform a degenerate community, it was essential to change people's morality; instead of preferring their own personal interest, they ought to place the good of the commonwealth above anything else. Whereas Tarquinius Superbus was Scott's most telling example of a tyrant, Cato epitomized republican virtues. 'We have', Scott proclaimed, 'more neede of a Cato to reforme our corrupt

43 Ibid., p. 68.
44 [Scott], *The Belgicke pismire*, p. 39.
45 [Scott], *A relation of Holland*, pp. 5, 18–19. Cf. [Leighton?], *The interpreter*, p. 7.

manners, then of a Cicero, or Antony, or Salust, to purifie and polish our Language.'[46]

But Scott argued that merely to convert people's private interest into an attachment to the common good was not sufficient; complete reform also required a change in other areas. Instead of luxury and wealth, the people should esteem frugality. More importantly, they ought to denounce slavery and cherish, above anything else, freedom and liberty. Scott quoted Willem Verheyden *in extenso* to demonstrate the crucial importance of liberty.[47] In *The Belgicke pismire*, the third necessary measure to stave off corruption was 'to restore libertie'.[48] In other words, Scott adopted, to some extent, the republican scale of values. If there was a strong link between the growth of private riches and slavery in Scott's account, that between frugality and liberty was as close. A Cato could easily observe that 'ancient and commendable frugality ... maintaines their liberty'.[49]

Scott's contention, that frugality could reform a corrupted commonwealth, promote the common good and ensure liberty, raises a practical problem of the utmost importance: what was the key to these qualities? Again, Scott turned to the humanist vocabulary for an answer. The way to foster the common good and to uphold liberty was to lead the *vita activa*. Using the metaphor of the body, Scott pointed out that 'nature makes use of any parte in any office, for preservation of the whole man from ruine'. Since every member of a body, he went on, 'partak's with the head and whole body, in paine or pleasure, in honor or dishonor, therefore it concerns every member, to looke to the preservation both of themselves in perticuler, and of others in generall'.[50]

As we have seen, this idea of the active life in Scott's writings has commonly been ascribed to his puritan background. There is of course little doubt that the more fervent protestants in general and Scott in particular sometimes expressed religion in distinct terms of action. William Hull told his listeners in a sermon that 'in this spirituall Theater, not idle contemplatives, but active performers of vertuous offices, are honoured with crowns celestiall' and that therefore 'the

[46]   Scott, *The high-waies of God*, p. 84.
[47]   [Thomas Scott], *The second part of Vox populi: or Gondomar appearing in the likenes of Mathiauell in a Spanish parliament* (Goricom [i.e. London], (1624), sig. D2ᵛ–3ʳ.
[48]   [Scott], *The Belgicke pismire*, p. 39.
[49]   [Scott], *A tongve-combat*, p. 64.
[50]   [Scott], *Vox Dei*, pp. 25–6. Cf. e.g. J[oh]n R[eynold]s, *Vox coeli: or, newes from heaven* (Elesium [i.e. London], 1624), pp. 35–6.

active and contemplative life meete both in the true Christian'. According to Thomas Taylor, 'Christian prudence' was not 'a contemplative, but an active knowledge'.[51] In *The arte of happines*, Francis Rous spoke about 'the fellowship & communion of Saints' in a similar manner. They were 'all Brethren and Countrimen, and withal Pilgrims in a strange Countrie'. If they were to survive, they ought amongst other things to 'excel in vertue' and 'confirme and provoke one another to good works'.[52] In another treatise, Rous referred directly to the debate about the respective merits of the contemplative and the active life. It was possible to argue that being closer to heaven 'Contemplation is heerein more excellent then Action.' Nonetheless, contemplation ought to be combined with action. 'For Contemplation', Rous expounded, 'is then most commendable when it is expressed in deeds, and not when it is meerly borne and buried in thoughts.'[53] Similar ideas can be found in Scott's writings. In *The Belgicke pismire* Scott claimed that man 'was not created to idlenesse', but to enjoy labour and 'to preserve by industrie what God himselfe had created'. 'In the action,' he added, 'there is *terminus a quo* implyed, and *terminus ad quem* expressed.'[54]

The idea of the active life, however, was scarcely a puritan invention. On the contrary, the puritan insistence on the *vita activa* was, as Margo Todd has shown, a mixture of Christian and humanist values, which she calls 'Christian humanism'.[55] Rous could exploit the notion of the *vita activa* in a religious context, but the arguments he was employing were scarcely more Calvinist in character than his argument that the church needed continual amendments and a return to its origins. Whereas in 1622 he simply observed that 'it is an observation of secular Policie, That all States, with time gather rust, and therfore by often reviews, they are to bee reduced to the first grounds of Vertue and Justice, which setled their Foundations', five years later he explicitly

---

[51] William Hull, *The mirrovr of maiestie ... set forth in fiue sermons* (London, 1615), pp. 45–6. Thomas Taylor, *Circumspect walking describing the seuerall rules, as so many seuerall steps in the way of wisedome* (1619) (London, 1631), pp. 31–2.

[52] Francis Rous, *The arte of happines* (London, 1619), pp. 399–403; cf. p. 411.

[53] Francis Rous, *Diseases of the time, attended by their remedies* (London, 1622), pp. 208–21. For Rous, the pursuit of private gain comprised 'the privatnesse of contemplation' and this was to 'neglect the profit of the publike', p. 17. Cf. in general his *Meditations of instruction, of exhortation, of reprofe: indeavouring the edification and reparation of the house of God* (London, 1616), pp. 1–3, 330; idem, *Oile of scorpions: the miseries of these times turned into medicines and curing themselues* (London, 1623), sig. A7ᵛ–8ᵛ; William Evans, *A translation of the booke of nature, into the vse of grace* (Oxford, 1633), pp. 24, 40–1.

[54] Scott, *The Belcigke pismire*, pp. 1, 12.

[55] Todd 1987; see also Todd 1983.

referred to Machiavelli at this point.[56] This is equally true for Thomas
Scott. His idea of the active life was not limited to religion, nor was it
only expressed in religious terms. In *Vox regis* Scott defended the
contention that the marriage of a prince concerned the commonwealth
as much as the prince himself. This was so, he argued, since 'everie
mans vocation bindes him to prevent evill, and to doe good. So that,
whensoever I have opportunitie to doe it, I have a calling to doe it.' A
man was not only a Christian, he was also 'a Subject', and hence it was
his duty to work 'for the benefit of the State and Church'.[57]

In his last pamphlet, *Sir Walter Rawleighs ghost*, Scott described the
Elizabethan hero as a man whose mind was 'actively disposed'.
Although Ralegh had possessed excellent qualities for *otium*, he had
never given up *negotium*. For all Ralegh's inclinations which could have
drawn 'thy minde from all other obiects, and to have setled thee upon
this Theorie, that solitarinesse is the most excellentest condition
belonging unto mankinde', but 'yet all this thou didst neglect, and both
contradict and disprove'. The life of contemplation was totally 'unfit
for thy greatnesse'. Scott was convinced that 'thou wert not borne for
thy selfe but thy Countrie'.[58] The same priorities also emerged elsewhere in Scott's writings. 'It is my duty', said Henry Hexham in his
introduction to one of Scott's pamphlets, '... to doe thus; for my
meanes receive of the States obligeth my tongue, hand, heart, and
whole man, to promote their just cause in wordes, writings, actions,
prayers.' He 'that doeth not thus thinke speake, write, and doe, having
the same ingagements, where occasion is presented' was deemed to be
a 'traytor'.[59] In his assize sermon delivered in Norwich in 1620 and
printed in 1623, Scott preached that a man 'must give an accompt for
the imployment of his talents'. He should avoid gathering wealth and
focus on doing 'God service, and other men good'. Cicero helped him
to explain what he had in mind; 'as Heathens could say', the chief rule
of public justice was that '*Non solum nobis nati sumus, sed partim patriae,
partim parentibus, &c.*'[60]

In Scott's analysis the active life was not only the direct antithesis of
sloth and idleness; it was equally at variance with the *vita contemplativa*.
Preaching at Thetford in Norfolk in 1620, Scott told his listeners that

---

56   Rous, *Diseases of the time*, sig. A7ʳ–8ʳ; idem, *The onely remedy, that can cure a people when all other
remedies faile* (London, 1627), pp. 208–10.
57   [Scott], *Vox regis*, pp. 14–15.
58   [Thomas Scott], *Sir Walter Rawleighs ghost: or Englands forewarner* (Utrecht, 1626), pp. 15–16.
59   [Scott], *A tongve-combat*, 'The epistle dedicatorie', sig. A2ʳ⁻ᵛ.
60   [Scott], *The proiector*, p. 6. Cf. Taylor, *Circumspect walking*, sig. A2ᵛ–3ʳ.

men had two ways before them – 'the way of knowledge and under-standing' and 'the way of Practise or Action'. The former consisted of 'Faith or Religion' whilst the way of action was chiefly formed by 'conversation, manners and fashion of living and dealing betwixt man and man, in vice or in vertue'.[61]

The same traditional line of argument also emerges in Scott's account of learning. He insisted that learning was an indispensable quality, but was even more adamant that it was utterly useless as long as it was not combined with action. A man could not be called truly wise although he was 'a great Scholer' and 'a great Philosopher' being 'seene in the hidden secrets of nature', mastering all 'the Arts' as well as all 'the Languages' and superseding even Aristotle in learning. Neither could he be truly wise even though he understood 'the whole bodie of Divinitie' and was able 'to resolve all the knotty controversies that are in the world, or may bee imagined'. Nor could a man even claim to attain true wisdom while being 'a great and perfect Politician, diving into those *arcana Imperij* that are sealed up in silence', whilst acquainted with 'all forraine Countries and Customes' and with 'the natures of all people' and able to 'dissemble more artificially then Machiavell'. A man could not be called a wise man until he could put his learning to active use. 'For he that will be wise,' Scott insisted, 'must not onely labour for wisedome, (that is, to get the *Theory* or bare *Speculation* thereof as it is a *Science*) but when he hath gotten that he must labour with wisedome also, or else hee can effect nothing: that is, he must shew his wisedome in action.'[62] The reason was straightforward. A man was truly wise only when his learning materialized in action, because '*virtus in actione consistit*'. Wisdom was not given to men so that they 'should sit still and sleepe with it, or play or dally with it, as with a pleasant companion'; the purpose of this quality was simply 'to direct us in vertuous undertakings'.[63]

If Scott's idea of the *vita activa* bears a close resemblance to the Ciceronian ideal, this is equally true of his idea of the qualities which enabled a man to lead this kind of life. He argued in Ciceronian fashion that the key to public service and the promotion of the common good lies in virtue. Instead of pure contemplation, everyone should aim at 'vertuous undertakings'. And in his discussion of the nature of virtue, he further evinces his fidelity to the humanist tradition.

[61] Scott, *The high-waies of God*, pp. 6–7.
[62] Scott's italic.
[63] [Scott], *The Belgicke pismire*, pp. 37–8.

It is above all the cardinal virtues of courage and prudence that a man needs in order to enhance the good of his community. Scott vehemently admonished his countrymen: 'cease to be foolish, and become wise; cease to be a Sluggard, and become diligent; cease to be fearefull, and become couragious and active'.[64] It is 'humane and politique providence' which helps us 'foresee that which in our actions and dealings is fit to be foreseene and prevented'.[65] 'Consideration', as he defined it, 'is a serious examination of any businesse, with the causes, effects, beginning, continuance, and issue thereof.' It is simply 'a rumination of the judgement, pondering, and revolving some matter in hand, untill the same be perfectly digested, settled, and disposed by reason'.[66]

Scott's example of 'a good Commonwealths-man' was a pismire (i.e. ant) who, as he took pains to explain, 'forecasts where best to provide herselfe, and then diligently takes the oportunitie of the time for her best advantage'. Furthermore, her wisdom was such that 'shee doth not onely and barely know this by a naked speculation; but considering it aright, shee puts it in practise, and makes use of every occasion, for the full and finall accomplishment of her purposes'.[67] Later in the same treatise, Scott spelled out the relevance of the pismire's example to human life: 'Now, since wisdome is so requisite for the life of man, as that without it a man is worse then a Pismire; and, since wee see to be wise, is not only to know by speculation, nor only to goe and to consider, but also to resolve, to practise, and to execute what wee know, and have considered.'[68] To be devoid of prudence 'keepes men in slouth'; they are unable to ponder upon 'the reward of glorie' which they would only attain by their 'good and vertuous actions'.[69]

It is thus no exaggeration to state that one of Scott's main aims in his pamphlet campaign was not only to lay bare the serious menace to the English commonwealth but also to indicate the way out of this

---

[64] Ibid., p. 16; cf. *A relation of Holland*, pp. 16–19.
[65] [Scott], *A relation of Holland*, p. 1.
[66] [Scott], *The Belgicke pismire*, p. 14.
[67] Ibid., p. 25.
[68] Ibid., p. 43; see also *The high-waies of God*, pp. 6–7. According to Francis Rous, 'the maine Faultinesse of these Times, is a Disproportion, betweene Knowledge and Action; or rather a meere resting in knowledge short of Action', *Meditations of instruction*, p. 1. Cf. John Everard, *The arriereban: a sermon preached to the company of the Military Yarde* (London, 1618), p. 47; J[ohn] R[eynolds], *Votivae Angliae: or the desires and wishes of England* (Utrecht, 1624), sig. B2ʳ, A3ᵛ. For a strikingly similar rhetoric, see Secretary Edward Conway's strategic plans cited in Cogswell 1989a, p. 70. See also [Alexander Leighton], *Speculum belli sacri: or the looking-glasse of the holy war* (n.p., 1624), pp. 32–3.
[69] [Scott], *The Belgicke pismire*, p. 14.

corruption. His confidence in the possibility of the reform of the English commonwealth remained unshaken in the face of the bad news of 1623. In *Vox dei* he offered a cluster of examples, including some of the central heroes of republican Rome – Mucius Scaevola, Scipio Africanus and Horatius Cocles – and wondered whether someone 'desires further satisfaction, and thinkes these examples of antick liberty, & vertue, too farr out of fashion, to be revived in these dayes, degenerating from true nobility, and declining headlong towards security'.[70] The reform of this degeneracy depended, to a great extent, on whether the people could be persuaded to change their heart. To accomplish this Scott used a distinctively classical republican vocabulary. The best means of upholding liberty was to lead a virtuous active life and thereby to serve the common good. If only the people could be persuaded to change tack, the commonwealth could be reformed and the people's liberty maintained. 'Finally,' Scott concluded the second sermon printed in *The high-waies of God*, 'let none amongst you bee seene idlely to sit at home, whilst these things are doing in the full Country, as if it did not concerned you: but ride, runne, and deale seriously herein, as for your lives and liberties which depend heere-upon.'[71]

Although Scott maintained that it was everyone's duty to be actively involved in the promotion of the public good, he reserved a special role for the nobility. Having strongly disparaged the contemporary idea of nobility, Scott felt it was necessary to point out that it was not his intention 'to disparage the Nobilitie' as such but on the contrary 'to preserve it intire from mixture and coagulation'.[72] He levelled unmitigated criticism at the corrupt nobility of his day, and was equally determined that 'antick liberty, & vertue' were closely linked with 'true nobility'.[73] In one of his pamphlets Scott sought to argue that it was of great importance to confer 'honors and rewards' on those who deserved them. Since there was a 'Common Error' 'That Commonweales are incapable of this power to conferre honors', Scott resorted to the history of Rome for corroboration. 'Amongst the Romans', he observed, 'severall rewards and honors of all sorts [had been], distributed freely and constantly to the best deservers.' This had been

---

[70] [Scott], *Vox Dei*, p. 37, cf. pp. 70–1. It was of course a commonplace to offer the Elizabethan period as a model to be emulated, e.g. Anon., *Tom tell troath*, pp. 2, 6; John Taylor, *An Englishmans love to Bohemia* (Dort, 1620), p. 4; Randol, *A sermon*, p. 4; Cogswell 1989a, pp. 95–8.

[71] Scott, *The high-waies of God*, p. 87.

[72] [Scott], *The Belgicke pismire*, p. 28; *Vox Dei*, p. 57.

[73] [Scott], *Vox Dei*, p. 37.

done with a view to encouraging 'all of every ranck, high and low, the witty and valiant, in their severall kindes, to do their best, and to adventure for the publique good'. This kind of system, Scott assured his readers, where honours were conferred on the basis of merits alone, 'would animate and stirre up noble spirits to excellent actions and enterprizes through emulation'.[74] Elsewhere he pointed out that the idea of a meritocracy was exemplified by the governors of the contemporary Netherlands as well as by Roman consuls. In both cases 'the wisest and worthiest persons' were employed, in spite of the fact that they were 'without traine, or pompe, or titular vanities; and many of them [were] raised for their experience, fidelity and wisedome, from meane stations, to treade in those high steps of authority and superioritie'.[75]

In *The Belgicke pismire* Scott opened his discussion of nobility by quoting Aristotle to the effect that nobility proceeded from excellent lineage. Conversely, the wrong kind of nobility was exemplified by those who had either degenerated from 'the nobilitie and vertue of their Ancestors' or were 'base in their Originals'.[76] But in general Scott's treatment of the issue was dominated by a different set of values. The true nature of nobility became clear as soon as attention was focused on 'Antiquitie'. When 'the desire of dominion' had begun 'to disturbe the whole World', people had had 'to elect out some of the strongest' for protection. 'And to these', Scott proceeded, 'they gave both titles and priviledged, to incourage their diligent attention on their offices.' The moral of this ancient instance was obvious. Nobility was based on personal qualities rather than ancestry, or as Scott put it: 'Thus it appeares, that Nobility was first from Office, not from nature.' Although the eldest son could inherit his father's 'titles and lands', his 'most vertuous and active' son was 'the heyre of his fathers honors'.[77]

Even 'Principalitie it selfe', Scott added, 'springs from this low but fruitefull root.' It followed, therefore, that 'virtue' alone determined 'nobility'.[78] He insisted that at birth men were equal and it was only their later lives that determined their worth. According to him, 'all have alike common entrance into the world; the King and the beggar; the foole and the Philosopher; and that only the difference betwixt

74 [Scott], *Synmachia*, pp. 26–8.
75 [Scott], *A tongve-combat*, p. 50.
76 [Scott], *The Belgicke pismire*, pp. 27–8.
77 Ibid., pp. 29–30.
78 Ibid., p. 28.

Man and Man was, in the different use of themselues, and the choyce of their wayes heere, where there was a way of wisedome and vertue, and a way of ignorance and vice propounded to all'.[79] The same point was versed by George Wither in 1621:

> I care not for that Gentry, which doth lye
> In nothing but a Coat of Heraldry.
> One Vertue more I rather wish, I had;
> Then all, the Herald to mine Armes, could add:
> Yea, I had rather, that by my industry
> I could acquire some one, good quality.
> Then through the Families, that noblest be
> From fifty Kings, to drawe my Pedigree.[80]

Scott's strong emphasis on the importance of virtuous actions as the chief quality of true nobility had an immediate bearing upon the role the nobility was expected to play in the public life of the commonwealth. The maintenance of the commonwealth hinged on their active participation. It was the 'vocation' of 'true Nobility' to promote the common good. 'For all the honors & priviledges of the ancient Nobilitie', Scott argued, 'were granted upon this ground, that they had worthily acted something for the generall benefit of many.'[81] Any attempts 'to purchase honour without some worthy action fore-going, or for any man to conferre this without merit concurring' was doomed to fail; it was not 'truely to be Noble, but the idole of Nobility'.[82] Scott never tired of repeating that 'Nobilitie' sprang 'from action'; 'the workes that Nobility is originally tyed unto, are actes of bountie, justice, charity, piety, loyalty, and prudence'. True nobility ought 'to watch and warde, and study, and counsell, for the Common-wealth'. It had been created 'for the generall service of the State in publique imployments'.[83]

For those who pursued the virtuous active life with vigour and success Scott retained his most honorific term 'commonwealth-men'. He defined 'worthy Commonwealths-men' as those who 'with his Majesties good liking, the peoples generall applause, to Gods glorie, the States good, and their owne personall honours, have liberally and freely layd open the Grievances of all good men, and with solid arguments inveighed against the Abuses of the Time, presented to their

---

[79] Scott, *The high-waies of God*, p. 1. Cf. Sutton, *The serpent anatomized*, pp. 11, 17–18.
[80] Wither, *Wither's motto*, sig E1ᵛ–2ʳ.
[81] [Scott], *The Belgicke pismire*, p. 28.
[82] Ibid., p. 30.
[83] Ibid., pp. 30–1; *Vox Dei*, pp. 1–3, 16–17.

censure and correction, in the high Court of Parliament'.[84] His concrete example of a 'commonwealth-man' was Cicero who 'is a member, a servaunt, a childe, of the Common-wealth; yet is he truly what he is, called the father, of the Common-wealth'.[85] In *The Belgicke pismire* Scott sharply contrasted 'the effect of privacie, whilst every man cares onely for himselfe, and neglects the Common-wealth' with what he called 'the practise of the Pismire' who represented 'a good Common wealths man'. Quoting Bacon's three-part division of studies, Scott argued that there were three spheres of life: those of 'a Naturalist', 'a Moralist' and 'a Polititian'. When a man acted as 'a Polititian', he became 'a good Citizen, a good Common-wealths-man'.[86]

The meticulous attention which Scott paid to the issues of the active life raises the further question of the nature and range of actions the people in general and the true nobility in particular were expected to perform. In answering this question, Scott followed a familiar path. In the first place, it was the duty of the people and of the nobility to be willing to defend their country – a characteristic which corresponded to the virtue of courage. Whereas the wrong kind of nobility were perpetuated by an education which trained noblemen for an idle course of life, the creation and maintenance of true nobility were crucially dependent on the right kind of education, which brought up children in 'militarie affaires', so much so that 'they seeke the warres'.[87] It was one of his most central contentions, which recurred in most of Scott's pamphlets, that war was justified and that it often proved highly beneficial to the community. There was a close link between corruption, the pursuit of private profit and the promotion of peace. As 'in the microcosme of private estates', so 'in the megacosme of publique wealths' there was nothing which made 'an estate' more secure 'then to have an enemy' and nothing which more corrupted 'a state, then security and peace'. A long period of peace 'softneth, and make's effeminate the heart of men, with immoderate pleasure'. In effect, every state which allowed itself to degenerate through long peace presented 'it selfe to subjection, with all the opportunity, and advantage, that may wooe any lustfull enemy to attempt'.[88]

[84] [Scott], *Vox regis*, p. 7.
[85] [Scott], *Vox Dei*, p. 42.
[86] [Scott], *The Belgicke pismire*, pp. 36–7; Bacon, *Essaies* (1612), in *Works*, VI, p. 675. Cf. Sutton, *The serpent anatomized*, p. 30.
[87] [Scott], *The Belgicke pismire*, pp. 30–1.
[88] [Scott], *Vox Dei*, p. 48, cf. pp. 48–9; *The Belgicke pismire*, p. 51. Cf. Hale 1971, p. 376.

When Scott placed so much emphasis on the merits of martial valour and on the corrupting nature of peace respectively, it is apparent that he had a specific target in mind. Those who advocated the Spanish match and therefore a peaceful foreign policy could follow the royal line of argument in their public remarks. In 1618 a tract, *The peace-maker: or Great Brittaines blessing*, bearing the royal arms and voicing James's opinion, strongly argued for peace. The purpose of the publication was to continue 'that mightie Happinesse wherein this Kingdome excells manie Empires'. England was referred to as 'the Land of Peace, under the King of Peace' and the British people, living 'in Beth-salem the house of Peace', sang 'this song of peace, Beati pacifici'.[89] Similar opinions were expressed throughout the period. John Denison had preached before the king in 1611 that 'no man knowes thorowly the benefit of Peace, but hee that hath seene the dolefull face of warre'. The sermon was published in 1620 to 'stirre men up to a serious consideration, and correspondent thankefulnesse for these blessed daies of Peace'.[90] In 1622 Robert Willan contrasted the 'Halcion dayes' of England with 'tumultuarie times' of other parts of the Christian world.[91] And in 1623 these opinions became louder and more voluminous.[92]

Yet the Bohemian crisis prompted several authors to compose treatises upon warfare. Abraham Gibson argued in traditional rhetoric

---

[89] Anon., *The peace-maker: or Great Brittaines blessing* (London, 1619), sigs. A4^r, B1^v–2^r. According to Gardiner 1863–84, III, p. 183, a view which Willson 1956, p. 271 endorses, the tract was mostly written by Lancelot Andrewes. It should be noted that at least the argument that warfare without a just cause was an 'Apparition of Honour' and its contrast, 'Honourable Services, publike Merits, good Causes, and Noble Adventures', (sig. D2^v–3^r) were taken almost verbatim from Francis Bacon's *The charge touching duells* (1614), in *Letters*, IV, pp. 399–409, at p. 401.

[90] John Denison, *Beati pacifici: the blessednes of peace-makers: and the advancement of Gods children: in two sermons preached before the king* (London, 1620), pp. 12, 14–15, sig. A2^{r-v}.

[91] R[obert] Willan, *Conspiracie against kings, heavens scorne: a sermon preached at Westminster-Abbey before the iudges, vpon the fifth of Novemb. 1622* (London, 1622), pp. 1–3; Walter Curll, *A sermon preached at White-hall, on the 28. of April, 1622* (London, 1622), pp. 1–4, 7–8, 10–13, 17–23; Thomas Adams, *Eirenopolis: the citie of peace* (1622), in *The workes of Tho: Adams* (London, 1630), pp. 993–1015. Cf. however idem, *The souldiers honovr* (London, 1617).

[92] See e.g. John Stradling, *Beati pacifici: a divine poem* (London, 1623), pp. 6, 24, see also pp. 7–10, 22–4, 33–5, 48–50; Nehemiah Rogers, *A strange vineyard in Palaestina: in an exposition of Isaiahs parabolical song of the beloued, discouered: to which Gods vineyard in this our land is paralleld* (London, 1623), especially pp. 15, 258–62; idem, *Christian curtesie: or St Pavls vltimum vale: deliuered in two semons ... at St Margarets on Fish-street hill in London* (London, 1621), pp. 62–5; Edmund Garrard, *The covntrie gentleman moderator* (London, 1624), pp. 50–1; G[eorge] Warburton, *King Melchizedech: a sermon preached at the court, at East-Hampsted, in ... the second of September. 1623* (London, 1623), sig. A3^{r-v}, pp. 33–5, 49–53; P[attenson], *The image of bothe chvrches*, p. 2; Joseph Hall, *The true peace-maker: laid forth in a sermon before his maiesty at Theobalds. September 19, 1624* (London, 1624), p. 43.

that it was partly because of his friends' admonitions that in 1619 he finally published his sermon on the preparations for war, preached in April 1618. But he hastened to add that he also did it because of 'these late rumours of warres'. Recommending his military treatise to the potential reader, Thomas Trussell wrote: 'Let the example of forraine evils warne England to awaken it selfe out of securitie.'[93] Many of these war-manuals repudiated the all-embracing blessedness of peace; 'these Halcion dayes, wherein Peace and Plentie lull us asleepe in the lap of Securitie', as one author put it.[94] It is arguable, however, that they were justifying their own enterprises rather than expressing apprehensions about James's foreign policy. But when we come to Edward Davies's *The art of war*, published in 1619, the target becomes somewhat more definite. Promising to make 'the many unexpert traine-men of this Kingdome' 'absolute Souldiers', Davies readily confessed that he was facing an uphill struggle since the would-be soldiers had 'reaped a large harvest of peace under the most peacefull Monarch in Europe'.[95] As early as 1618 John Everard had preached that 'the name of a Souldier' was 'at this time ridiculous among secure fooles, and contemptible among such birds of peace, as cannot abide the Drumme, saving in a Morris-dance' and that 'wee have turned *Memento mori*, the meditation of death, into *Viue hodie*, an Epicurean and sensuall life'.[96] As James endeavoured to solve the mounting crisis peacefully, the advocacy of war became more blatant. In early 1622, one author wrote that although peace was the most praiseworthy blessing of heaven, 'a man may have too much of his Fathers blessing'. He expressed his fear that 'wee have too much cause to complaine of your Majesties

93 Gibson, *Christiana-polemica*, sig. A5^r-v; Thomas Trussell, *The souldier pleading his owne cause*, 2nd impression (London, 1619), sig. A3^r. Pierre Du Moulin, *A preparation to suffer for the Gospell of Iesus Christ* (London, 1623), pp. 1–3, 42–4, amply evoked forbearance and patience.

94 J. T., *The ABC of armes, or an introduction directorie; whereby the order of militarie exercises may easily bee vnderstood, and readily practised, where, when, and howsoeuer occasion is offered* (London, 1616), sig. A4^r. Cf. e.g. Jeremy Leech, *The trayne souldier: a sermon preached befor the worthy Societie of the captaynes and gentlemen that exercise armes in the Artillery garden* (London, 1619), pp. 60–1; Trussell, *The souldier*, pp. 31–2; Gibson, *Christiana-polemica*, pp. 1–2, where the argument is conventionally directed against the Anabaptists. For this, see e.g. [Leighton], *Speculum belli sacri*, p. 6. Cf. Croft 1986, p. 14.

95 Edward Davies, *The art of war, and Englands traynings* (London, 1619), sig. ¶2^v. Cf. idem, *Military directions, or the art of trayning* (London, 1618).

96 John Everard, *The arriereban*, pp. 25, 27–8, 56, 73–4, 87–9, 91–2, 101–2. See in general Hunt 1990, pp. 226–8.

unlimited Peace' because the excess of peace 'hath long since turned vertue, into Vice, and health into sicknes'.[97]

The fact that John Reynolds's *Votivae Angliae* was published in 1624 might serve to explain the absence of any lavish description of corruption, but Reynolds was careful to warn the king about the shameful consequences of an overlong period of peace. 'And although your Majestie', he wrote, 'delight and glorie to be tearmed, A Prince of Peace; yet lett your Peace live and flourish in Honnor, and not wyther dye in Contempt and shame.' He was not 'a true Subject' and 'a faithfull and loyall-harted Britton' who was not ready to sacrifice his life for the good of his country.[98]

In his denunciation of peace and his exhortation to martial enter-prises, Scott was concerned to uphold the same set of values. It was his firm opinion that England ought to renounce James's peaceful foreign policy, denounce every possible treaty with Spain (including of course the marriage treaty) and adopt a more aggressive role in international politics. As early as 1621, when the truce between Spain and the Netherlands was due to expire, Scott insisted that 'all Treaties of Peace and Truce to be made with the King of Spaine, are wholly unprofi-table' for the Dutch. Since a permanent peace was 'impossible' and the 'Truce hurtfull', 'what resteth onely to bee expected but warre?'[99] Two years later, he repeated that although peace was in principle a valuable thing, in practice it turned out to be ruinous because 'the time agreeing with the necessity, we are in regard of the feare of the Spanish greatnesse'.[100] This kind of rhetoric became especially powerful and explicit in 1624 when Charles and Buckingham decided to campaign for war. Scott dedicated his tract *The Belgick sovldier*, subtitled 'warre was a blessing', to parliament, and promised to prove 'that Warre hath

---

[97] Anon., *Tom tell troath*, p. 7, cf. pp. 10–11, 27. Cf. e.g. Sutton, *The serpent anatomized*, p. 8; Francis Markham, *Five decades of epistles of warre* (London, 1622), especially sig. A3ᵛ, p. 9; Samuel Buggs, *Miles mediterraneus: the Mid-land souldier: a sermon* (London, 1622), p. 17; Richard Bernard, *The seaven golden candlestickes: Englands honour* (London, 1621), sig. A4ʳ. It was opinions such as these that Thomas Adams sought to answer in his *Eirenopolis*, when he pointed out that it was not simply prosperity which destroyed our peace; it was 'the prosperitie of fooles' alone which brought about the violation of peace, *The workes*, p. 1012.

[98] R[eynold]s, *Votivae Angliae*, sig. E1ᵛ, *4ʳ; idem, *Vox coeli*, pp. 31, 34, for corruption see pp. 35, 36; [Leighton], *Speculum belli sacri*, pp. 7–8, 42. Cf. the views expressed by the prince's chaplain, Isaac Bargrave, *A sermon preached before … the lower house of parliament: February the last 1623* (London, 1624), pp. 25–6, 35–6; idem, *A sermon against selfe policy*, pp. 30–4. Later in the 1620s those who criticized Charles saw James's foreign policy as an epitome of England's corruption; see e.g. J. R., *The spy discovering the danger of Arminian heresie and Spanish trecherie* (Strasburg, 1628), sig. B2ʳ⁻ᵛ.

[99] [Scott], *A relation of Holland*, sig. A2ʳ, p. 11.

[100] [Scott], *An experimentall discoverie*, pp. 1–2, 6–7.

been better than peace, and that the Commonwealth and Religion of England have had their glory and propagation by opposing Antichrist, and in plaine termes reputing Spaine'.[101] Using the earl of Essex as his spokesman, Scott insisted that James was being seriously misled 'by (some) false hearted Counsellours' and that the king had himself been 'a peaceable King from his Cradle', so much so that 'BEATI PACIFICI is his happy destined Motto'. Although it was a good thing to be at peace, it was 'an unhappy and dangerous a thing to have league or amity with Romane-Catholique Kings'.[102]

Although in arguing against effeminate peace and for a valorous war Scott had the possible misfortune or success of his native country in mind, he employed specific vocabularies in support of his case. First, the pursuit of a martial policy could be justified on the basis of religious arguments alone. Scott claimed that 'I will onely deale with the Church of God, and cause of Religion.' But he also ridiculed the earlier Christian humanists for extolling the blessings of the peace with Cicero. 'He that pleaded for peace', he expounded, 'and cried out in an insulting bravery, *Cedant arme* [sic] *togae, concedat laurea linguae* [sic], that maintained the morrall precepts of Philosophy, that an unjust peace was to be preferred before a just warre' singlemindedly forgot that Cicero had also set down 'in his lib. I. *De officij*' that '*Suscipienda quidem bella sunt ob eam causam, vt sine iniuria in pace Vivatur* [War could only be justified that we may live in peace without harm]'.[103]

Nevertheless, elsewhere Scott was inclined to use a somewhat different vocabulary. In denouncing sloth and idleness and exhorting his countrymen to action, Scott proclaimed that continual exercise was of vital importance since otherwise men would become weak and wholly 'unfit for any imployment'. Hence, Scott wrote, 'an army is termed *Exercitus, quod exercitando fit melior*, because it is much bettered by exercise'. The truth of this was most easily discerned from the examples of the Romans, who had known it well and who had therefore been 'not only carefull to exercise their owne persons and the people at home, but their armies abroad'.[104] In his prefatory verses to Samuel Bachiler's *Miles christianvs* in 1625, Scott rhymed:

---

101 [Scott], *The Belgick sovldier*, pp. 2–3; cf. e.g. *A second part*, sig. c4^r; [Thomas Scott?], *Certaine reasons and arguments of policie* (n.p., 1624), sig. B2^v, B4^v.

102 [Thomas Scott], *Robert earle of Essex his ghost, sent from Elizian: to the nobility, gentry, and commvnaltie of England* (Paradise [i.e. London], 1624), pp. 2, 4.

103 [Scott], *The Belgick sovldier*, pp. 4–5; cf. in general *Digitvs Dei*; Cicero, *De officiis*, 1.35.

104 [Scott], *The Belgicke pismire*, pp. 12–13; cf. *A tongve-combat*, p. 61.

> The Campe's a Court, where all heroick seedes
> Of Courage, freedome, Noblesse, vertue breedes,
> Where native comelynes is man-like brave,
> And inward worth may unbought honour have.[105]

He compared England ('so base a State') unfavourably to Rome ('so brave a State') and posed a question to his countrymen: 'Can you exceede all Nations in Christendome in wastfull vanities; And can you not arme your selves against one Nation, (which you have ever beaten) for your necessary defence?'

Underlying Scott's reasoning was the old Roman idea of the citizen bearing arms. In order to survive in the hostile world and to uphold liberty, it was vital to arm the people. To illustrate his point further, Scott proclaimed that perhaps he was living in 'so degenerate an Age' that 'you will not be able to defend your owne Land'. But he sincerely hoped that 'there is yet left some seed of that auncient vertue' which had enabled other nations to defend their fatherland. Scott's most instructive example was Publius Valerius Publicola, who had played a crucial role in the expulsion of Tarquinius Superbus from Rome, who at his death had been hailed as the greatest soldier and statesman of his day and who had therefore been buried at public expense, for inspite of his renown he had been so poor that his resources had not been enough to allow for the funeral.[106] Invoking the memory of the Roman hero, Scott wrote: 'And doubtlesse there will ever be found some VALERII, who (so the State may stand and flourish) will not care thogh they leave not where with to bury themselves, though other some bury their money, not caring in what estate they leave the State.'[107]

This background to Scott's arguments serves to explain why he sometimes regarded war as a way of achieving civic greatness. His point of departure was the belief that, to some extent, the end justified the means. He saw the world in the almost Machiavellian terms of continuous warfare. Where 'the preservation of Kingdomes' was at stake, it would be a misguided policy to have 'too much fidelity to others', for this had proved to be the destruction of 'great and potent Kingdomes, Provinces and Townes'. The safest rule of conduct for

---

[105] Samuel Bachiler, *Miles christianvs: or the campe royal* (Amsterdam, 1625), sig. B1ʳ.
[106] *Livy*, 2.17.
[107] [Thomas Scott], *Robert earle of Essex his ghost*, pp. 14–15; R[eynolds], *Vox coeli*, sig. B2ᵛ. Cf. Anon., *The military discipline* (n.p., 1623), where the basic argument was directed against the relevance of ancient examples to modern warfare. See also [Scott], *Vox Dei*, p. 20. Cf. Gibson, *Christiana-polemica*, pp. 23–4.

'private men or publique States' was, therefore, 'mistrust'.[108] Scott drew two conclusions from this argument. First, he insisted that a preventive war was a just war. More importantly, commonwealths always had to be ready to fight a war, and hence the best general policy was one of aggression. Urging James to make an about-turn in his foreign policy, Scott reminded him that 'the desire of honour to advance States, and enlarge Kingdomes, is naturally grafted in the hearts of all Princes of noble spirits; and there was never any King, of a worthy and high courage, but desired to leave to his posterity the memorie of some noble and worthy action'.[109] And to prove that it was above all by martial enterprises that greatness could be achieved, Scott claimed that Henry IV of France acquired fame and 'greatnesse' whilst 'the warres lasted' but that as soon as 'peace was contracted, his honour was distracted'. But the Low Countries furnished more conclusive proof still that it was war which brought about civic glory, and Scott asked his readers to judge the matter for themselves. The Dutch people had 'augmented their fame and renown abroad, and increased their wealth and territories at home'. When England had fought Spain in Elizabeth's times, 'we were', Scott boldly claimed, 'beholding to the warres and such Martiall spirits: who tooke example from ancient Patriots, to be indulgent over their Countries renowne and enriching'.[110]

Of all the advocates of a martial foreign policy it was Francis Bacon who made the most daring use of civic greatness in his arguments. After his impeachment in May 1621, Bacon never gave up the hope of being able to return to the court and to politics. In 1622, during the period of rapprochement with Spain, he wrote the incomplete *An advertisement touching an holy warre*, where he discussed the possibility of a common attack of Christians against the Ottomans.[111] But the main way in which he attempted his political comeback was by promoting a more martial foreign policy. He returned, in other words, to the issue which had been prominent in his political statements during the first years of James's reign – civic greatness. Bacon's somewhat ambivalent position is well described by John Reynolds in *Vox coeli*, a dialogue between the Tudors and the Stuarts. 'Sir Nicholas Bacon my Chan-

---

[108] [Scott], *An experimentall discoverie*, pp 3–4. For a similar notion, see R[eynolds], *Votivae Angliae*, sig. B3ʳ.

[109] [Scott], *An experimentall discoverie*, p. 33.

[110] [Scott], *The Belgick sovldier*, pp. 28, 29, 31, 36–7, 39; *The proiector*, p. 1. Cf. Anon., *Tom tell troath*, p. 2.

[111] Bacon, *Works*, VII, pp. 3–36; Cogswell 1989a, pp. 38–9. Cf. Patrick 1971.

cellor on his Death-bed', Queen Elizabeth remarked, 'wrote me a letter, that the Glory and Conservation of England consisted in holding Spaine at Rapiers point; and will not his sonne Sir Francis, the now [sic] Chancellor tell his Maister so much?' But Prince Henry quickly replied: 'O no, he is otherwise imployed.'[112] The issue of civic greatness surfaced afresh in *The historie of the raigne of king Henry the seventh* which was written as an advisory book for Prince Charles immediately after Bacon's impeachment and published early in 1622. In 1622 he also received a Latin translation of the *Advancement of learning*[113] and it was finally published in 1623 in a greatly expanded form bearing the title *De dignitate et augmentis scientiarum*. The only issue of the art of government which he discussed in the treatise was the extension of the empire. When Charles and Buckingham returned from Madrid, Bacon was actively involved in offering advice to Buckingham about a possible war against Spain, noting that 'the King will put a hook in the nostrils of Spain, and lay a foundation of greatness here to his children in these west parts'.[114] His final verdict upon the greatness of states was the expanded essay 'Of the true greatnesse of kingdomes and estates', published in the final edition of his *Essayes* in 1625, which was almost a verbatim translation of the treatise in *De augmentis*.

Again Bacon opened his account by vehemently arguing that the right touchstone of greatness was an undertaking of the greatest difficulty. Hence he emphasized not only the danger of miscalculation but also the difference between seeking longevity and greatness of states. There were many counsellors and statesmen who were able 'to mannage Affaires, and to keepe them from Precipices, and manifest Inconveniences', but these qualities were far removed from 'the Abilitie' or '*virtus*', as Bacon put it in the *De augmentis*, of amplifying a commonwealth.[115] The difficulty of measuring greatness notwithstanding, Bacon was convinced that he himself was fully qualified to perform the task of advising on the subject, since, as he explained, he had 'long-continued experience in business of estate, and much conversation in books of policy and history'.[116] In 1623 he wrote to Buckingham to recommend his services: 'My good Lord, somewhat I

---

[112] R[eynold]s, *Vox coeli*, p. 34.
[113] See Bacon to Father Redemptus Baranzano, 30 June 1622, in *Letters*, VIII, pp. 375–7.
[114] Ibid., VII, p. 445.
[115] Bacon, *Essayes*, p. 90; *De augmentis*, in *Works*, I, p. 793.
[116] Bacon, 'Considerations touching a war with Spain', in *Letters*, VII, p. 469.

have been, and much have I read; so that few things which concern states or greatness, are new cases unto me.'[117]

Bacon strongly emphasized that the only way to attain civic greatness lay in the possession of arms. 'But above all', he insisted vigorously, 'for Empire and Greatnesse [*ad Imperii Magnitudinem*], it importeth most; That a nation doe professe Armes, as their principall Honour, Study, and Occupation.'[118] To enhance the military valour of the people, it was essential to have 'just causes' or 'pretexts' for waging a war.[119] Following this principle, Bacon carefully pointed out that a war against Spain was a preventive war and thus justifiable. 'Howsoever', he argued, 'some schoolmen (otherwise reverend men, yet fitter to guide penknives than swords) seem' to insist, they were of no 'authority to judge this question against all the precedents of time.' 'For certainly,' he went on, 'as long as men are men ... and as long as reason is reason, a just fear will be a just cause of a preventive war.'[120]

Although Bacon expressed his admiration for the Spanish veteran army which was 'alwaies on Foot', nonetheless reason and experience told him that Spain could scarcely match England. Spain lacked both men and valour. It was a country 'thin sown of people'. Even more importantly, 'the Spaniard's valour lieth in the eye of the looker on' while 'the English valour lieth about the soldier's heart'.[121] But the most ruinous weakness of Spanish politics was that the greatness of their empire was not grounded on arms but on money. In his earlier papers on civic greatness, Bacon had, of course, rejected the idea that money contributed to civic greatness and warlike valour, and the same idea continued to occupy a prominent place in his later writings on the same issue. In October 1620, Bacon introduced a draft of a proclamation to summon a parliament and wrote that for 'moneys being the sinews of war' 'no man is so ignorant' as to think that a successful war could be waged without 'some large and bountiful help of treasure'.[122] But in the *De augmentis* as well as in 'Of the true greatnesse of kingdomes

---

[117]   Bacon to Buckingham 18 April 1623, in *Letters*, VII, p. 424.
[118]   Bacon, *De augmentis*, in *Works*, I, pp. 794–5, 799–800; *Essayes*, pp. 91–2, 95–7.
[119]   Bacon, *De augmentis*, in *Works*, I, p. 800; *Essayes*, pp. 96–7.
[120]   Bacon, 'Considerations touching a war with Spain', in *Letters*, VII, p. 477. Cf. Secretary Conway's justification, Cogswell 1989a, p. 70; Walter Ralegh, 'A discourse of the original and fundamental cause of natural, arbitrary, necessary, and unnatural war' (1614–16), in *Works*, VIII, pp. 253–97, p. 259. For Ralegh's tract in general, see Luciani 1948.
[121]   Bacon, *De augmentis*, in *Works*, I, p. 801; *Essayes*, p. 97; 'Considerations touching a war with Spain', in *Letters*, VII, p. 499. Cf. in general Roger Williams, *The actions of the Lowe Countries* (London, 1618).
[122]   Bacon, *Letters*, VII, p. 126.

and estates', Bacon squarely denied this and maintained: 'Neither is Money the Sinewes of Warre, (as it is trivially said) where the Sinewes of mens Armes, in base and Effeminate People, are failing.'[123] Instead of being based on valorous people, the greatness of Spain ultimately hinged on the treasures and riches she had obtained from America. 'For Money', Bacon wrote, 'no doubt it is the principal part of greatness of Spain.' Spanish 'greatness', he added, 'consisteth in their treasure; their treasure in their Indies; and their Indies (if it be well weighed) are indeed but an accession to such as are masters by sea'.[124]

One of the main aims of Scott's public statements was to effect a dramatic change in English foreign policy, and to insist, therefore, that she was quite capable of adopting a more militant role. But he never limited the scope of his discussion to warfare alone. The people's martial deeds did not comprise the only domain of their active role. Their virtuous character was not limited to courage but also included prudence. Similarly, the children of true nobility ought to be trained not merely in warlike discipline but also 'in counsell'. True nobles, Scott wrote, are not 'accomplished, till they are able both to advise, and execute in matters of State'.[125] As Scott saw it, it was above all the role of counsellor which recommended itself to the active subject. On the one hand, he was most emphatic that it was unfaithful counsel which had misled James into adopting the ruinous foreign policy of peace. On the other hand, the solution was not to disregard counsellors and to establish an absolute monarchy, but rather to give sincere advice. Scott had the earl of Essex admonish the nobility, gentry and commons 'seriously and yet submissively to dehort and dissawade your King, to leave off and absolutely dissolve all Treaties of Matches' with Spain.[126] Counselling called for prudence or 'humane and politique providence' which enabled one to 'foresee that which in our actions and dealings is fit to be foreseene and prevented'.[127]

Scott stressed that a man ought to participate on his own initiative in both the military and the political arenas. Advising the king in 1623 to

---

[123] Bacon, *De augmentis*, in *Works*, I, pp. 794–5; *Essayes*, pp. 91–2. Cf. Everard, *The arriereban*, p. 7.
[124] Bacon, 'Considerations touching a war with Spain', in *Letters*, VII, pp. 499–500; 'Notes of a speech concerning a war with Spain', in *Letters*, VII, p. 464; *De augmentis*, in *Works*, I, pp. 795, 801; *Essayes*, p. 91, 97–8. Cf. [Leighton], *Speculum belli sacri*, pp. 31–2; R[eynold]s, *Vox coeli*, p. 32. It is probable that Buckingham was following Bacon's advice when he told his strategic plans to the parliament on 3 March; see Ruigh 1971, 191–2; Cogswell 1989a, 181–2.
[125] [Scott], *The Belgicke pismire*, pp. 30–1. Cf. Leech, *Trayne souldier*, pp. 62–3; [Leighton], *Speculum belli sacri*, p. 91.
[126] [Scott], *Robert earle of Essex his ghost*, p. 13.
[127] [Scott], *A relation of Holland*, p. 1.

abandon 'this mischievous and poysonous peace with Spaine', Scott took some pains to point out that 'though I be not called, yet considering I am your subject ... I cannot but presume to speake of such things, which I thinke now fit to be considered'.[128] Obviously he was much preoccupied with this justification of political action, since in *Vox regis* he claimed that 'the generall grievances of the Church and State' justified the writing of his book. 'This', Scott wrote, 'I might well see, being a Member of the Multitude: my Office also being to see, to watch, to speake, to blowe the Trumpet, to give warning.' The common people best knew 'where the disorders of a State, & the mischiefes [were] approching', and it was therefore from this source that kings could gather 'the best and most certaine intelligence of their Domesticke affaires'.[129]

Parliament, however, dominated Scott's concept of the *vita activa*. There was nothing exceptional in this. A number of writers pointed out that parliament was the place where grave political problems could be remedied.[130] But as Lake has perceptively pointed out, for Scott parliament had 'an almost mystical significance as the ultimate source of unity and concord'.[131] Making use of James's argument against the claims of the pope, Scott contended that the king could not give away his crown without his 'Peeres & peoples consent'. It followed that the Lords, the Commons, and through them the whole commonwealth took part in the public life of parliament. As Scott himself put it, 'the Parliament makes free-Denizens, and incorporates members into the State by publike Acts, and not the King alone'.[132] In Scott's schemes, there was a sharp contrast between a timeserver who thought of nothing else but his own private gain and a freely elected parliament which held the common good as its chief aim.[133] The fact that the law – the king's highway – was established by the king together with the Lords and the Commons made 'every Freeholder' 'a way-maker'.[134]

---

[128] [Scott], *An experimentall discoverie*, p. 45, see also p. 46. Cf. Anon., *Tom tell troath*, pp. 1, 5; Randol, *A sermon*, pp. 1–2.

[129] [Scott], *Vox regis*, p. 18. According to John Randol, it was important to grasp the point that 'there is a division that makes for the good of the whole'. It was as 'in pursuit of deliberative argument' where 'Disputants' were often divided and yet in the end there was 'the unitie of the same conclusion'. It was, Randol told his listeners, 'not onely lawfull, but most necessary to be divided for the publicke good'; *A sermon*, pp. 25–6.

[130] Anon., *Tom tell troath*, pp. 13, 6; Rous, *Oile of scorpions*, pp. 36–7; R[eynolds], *Vox coeli*, sig. B1ᵛ– 2ʳ.

[131] Lake 1982, p. 818, see also pp. 814, 815.

[132] [Scott], *Vox regis*, p. 12; *Robert earl of Essex his ghost*, pp. 15–16; cf. *Englands ioy*, pp. 4, 6.

[133] [Scott], *Vox popvli*, sig. B3ᵛ–4ʳ. Cf. [Leighton?], *The interpreter*, p. 5.

[134] [Scott], *The high-waies of God*, p. 86.

But parliament also took part in more general matters of policy. The chief grievance of England – the Spanish match – had been caused by disregarding the normal procedure of decision-making. The prince was 'a publike and private person'. Both aspects had to be respected when his consort was chosen. 'As a private person,' Scott argued, 'he may chuse for his private affection, and match where he list; provided he neglect not the publike part, which is the principall.' The prince, in other words, ought to listen to popular opinion about his spouse. And this opinion was aired by 'the State representative (that is, the Parliament) . . . wherein the consent of everie Subject is included'.[135]

Most importantly, Scott saw parliament as both discussing and deciding on the central issues of foreign policy. In 1624 he offered parliament a long list of detailed issues for discussion. 'First, whether we have sufficient occasion or no to fall out with Spaine? Secondly, how shall a warre be maintained? Thirdly, where the seate of this warre shall be? Fourthly, who shall be called to our assistance? And last of all, whether the Country be willing to such a designement?' Scott did not answer these questions but told the MPs that they were summoned to a parliament 'to decide these things'.[136]

So far we have seen that in Scott's vision a healthy commonwealth was represented by a community where everyone would be willing to practise his virtues to its benefit. It is clear, however, that Scott was not completely satisfied with this rather platitudinous view. Although he espoused the idea that the reform of corruption was, to a great extent, a matter of morality, it is obvious that he never thought that corruption and servility could be nipped in the bud by simple moral inducements. This was so because moral decay had a striking parallel in the social domain.

When Bacon turned to the issues of civic greatness anew in the early 1620s, he developed his former discussion of the material basis of a truly great state. Although he now placed a somewhat stronger emphasis on the commanding of the seas, he did not abandon his former conviction that the infantry formed the backbone of an army.[137] To ensure that a state which aimed at greatness had a proper infantry, it was of crucial importance to look after its social organization. Since free and sturdy farmers made a good infantry, the nobility

[135] [Scott], *Vox regis*, p. 14.
[136] [Scott], *The Belgick souldier*, p. 4; cf. [Scott], *Second part*, p. 24.
[137] Bacon, *De augmentis*, in *Works*, I, p. 796; *Essayes*, pp. 92–3. Cf. Everard, *The arriereban*, p. 7; Markham, *Five decades*, p. 43.

should under no circumstances expand too rapidly. To this familiar argument Bacon now added his example of Henry VII's land policy. It first appeared in his *History of the raigne of Henry the seventh* and was taken up in *De augmentis* and in the *Essayes*. Whereas Italy and particularly France had a good cavalry but no real infantry because there were only either 'noblesse or peasantry', in England, due to Henry's prudent land policy, the plough was kept in the hands of the owner and she consequently had a proper infantry. Henry had realized that landlords had been turning arable land into pasture with the effect that yeomen had been replaced by 'a few herdsmen'. As Bacon carefully explained, to change the course of this development, Henry in consultation with parliament had decided that all farms of twenty acres or more, 'should be maintained and kept up for ever'. This measure had guaranteed that the farmer had not become 'a beggar or cottager', but had remained 'a man of some substance, that might keep hinds and servants, and set the plough on going'. As Bacon put it in the 'Of the true greatnesse of kingdomes and estates', he could 'live in Convenient Plenty'. Most of the land was thus held and occupied by 'the yeomanry or middle people' which, according to 'the true principles of war and the examples of other kingdoms', yielded the best soldiers. As he made clear in *De augmentis*, Bacon mainly emphasized that the farmer could either be the owner of the land or at least have its *usufruct*, but under no circumstances should he be a hireling (*conductius, mercenarius*).[138] The reason was obvious. As soon as the farmer became a hireling, he would lose his independence and by losing this he would lose sight of the common good.

As we saw in the previous chapter, Bacon coupled this idea of free and sturdy farmers with a further social argument to the effect that sedentary and indoor arts were not conducive to a great state. As a result, the majority of the people should abstain from direct involvement in economic life. In the early 1620s, Bacon repeated the same argument noting that 'the principall Bulke of the vulgar Natives' ought to be 'Tillers of the Ground; Free Servants; and Handy-Crafts-Men, of

<hr/>

[138] Bacon, *The history of the raigne of Henry the seventh*, in *Works*, VI, pp. 93–5; *De augmentis*, in *Works*, I, pp. 796–7; *Essayes*, pp. 92–3. Cf. Markham, *Five decades*, p. 17; Trussell, *The souldier*, p. 30. According to Trussell, soldiers should be 'neither servant nor hireling ... but home-keepers of good worth and ability'. In 1623 John Bingham published his translation of Xenophon and appended to it portions from Justus Lipsius' *De militia Romana* where it was argued that militia suited only a 'Free-estate' and that princes ought to follow 'what the Turke doth in his Ianizar'; *The historie of Xenophon: contaning the ascent of Cyrus into the higher countries*, translated by John Bingham (London, 1623), sig. v2$^{\text{r-v}}$.

Strong, and manly Arts, as Smiths, Masons, Carpenters', but not, as Bacon diligently remembered to add, 'Professed Souldiers'. Although this list of manly professions with a martial inclination was commonplace, Bacon's argument carried with it an ideological dimension of great importance. For if the majority of the people should avoid taking part in economic acitivities, the question of how these activities were looked after could be raised. With a view to answering this question, Bacon pointed out that it had been a 'great Advantage, in the Ancient States of Sparta, Athens, Rome, and others, that they had the use of Slaves, which commonly did rid those Manufactures'. The success of the ancient commonwealths was thus based on the extensive exploitation of slavery. But this solution was not applicable in the Europe of his own times since 'the Christian Law' had mostly abolished slavery. The only way open was to leave sedentary occupations 'chiefly to Strangers'.[139]

Scott's discussion of the material basis of a commonwealth is in some respects similar to Bacon's. But it bears even more striking similarity to John Mair's earlier analysis of the ways in which the nobility could be checked in Scotland.[140] Scott began with the juxtaposition of a corrupted and a healthy commonwealth. The former was dominated by a peasantry which had lost its independence and freedom and had become subjected to landlords. And by losing their liberty, the peasants had lost their care for the common good which they now identified as nothing but 'the Leavie burthen that presseth them'.[141]

Although the material basis of the commonwealth could degenerate because of the people's lack of moral vigilance, it occurred most often because of the corruption of the nobility. Scott claimed that he had witnessed this degeneration taking place in Scotland, where he had seen 'the miserable Cottages of the poore Hindes; and I wondered awhile at the cause'. According to his own testimony, he had first thought, significantly, that this unhappy state of affairs was due to 'the barrennesse of the soyle'. Then he had surmised that the unhealthy state of the Scottish peasants should be attributed to their own moral degeneration – to 'the lazie disposition of the Commons'. Nonetheless, when he had 'looked up higher, and inquired diligently into the true cause', he had found out that the land had been fertile and 'the poore men painfull'. The true cause of their social decline was to be found in

[139] Bacon, *De augmentis*, in *Works*, I, pp. 798–9; *Essayes*, p. 95.
[140] Williamson 1979, p. 100.
[141] [Scott], *The Belgicke pismire*, pp. 31–2.

the actions of their social superiors; 'the lordly Owner', Scott argued, 'is in all the fault'. The primary objective of the nobility had been 'to live at Court (not for action, but idlenesse)' and in order to be able to afford a sumptuous courtly life, they had had to raise their rents 'to the extreamest racke'. To increase his profits, the noble 'never lets out Lease but from yeere to yeere; and he that gives most is the next new Farmer for my next new master'. The situation had become worse because the nobles' idle course of life had forced them on many occasions to sell their lands to 'the diligent tradesman' who was even more prone to maximize his profit. The fact that the peasant was often driven from his farm gravely impoverished the country. But it also prompted the farmer himself to fall 'to theft as well as beggerie' and thereby to a 'lazie kinde of life' and, in a way, to imitate his former landlord. Having reached this ultimate state of corruption, the peasant no longer cared for the common good, since 'such as have nothing are without care and fear', and instead he became the stuff from which those desirous of 'theft, ryot, or rebellion' were made.[142]

This most unhappy state of affairs contrasted sharply with a healthy commonwealth. The date of *The Belgicke pismire* (1622) might account for the fact that Scott depicted a similarly disastrous development taking place in England. 'And whilst I speake of Scotland,' he carefully emphasized, 'because it is there a generall practise, I except not England, as if this sinne were a stranger in any part of Brittaine.' The partial corruption of the English nobility could precipitate a similar development amongst the common people. But in England there were both 'some long Leases yet unexpired' and 'some good men yet left'. By and large, the English commonwealth was chiefly based on 'the Yeomandrie'. They were 'one of the chiefe glories of our Nation, and the principal base and foundation of the Common-wealth, at least of the strength and libertie thereof'.[143] The only way to keep the external corruption at bay and to uphold liberty was to secure the economic position of the yeomen so that they would be willing to fight for their country.

But as well as constituting the military strength of the commonwealth, 'the ancient English yeomandrie' also helped to sustain its political well-being. In politics corruption occurred when the active people lost their freedom and thereby their dedication to the commonwealth, and instead became dependent on others. It was exactly this

[142] Ibid., pp. 32–3.
[143] Ibid., pp. 28, 34.

kind of decay which was infecting England. It occurred, in the first place, at court. Scott opened his analysis by pointing out that men thought that they 'must goe into the Countrey to heare the newes of the Court: because in the Court men dare not speake what they know'. At court men could not speak nor advise freely for fear that they would lose their 'preferment'. Courtiers, in other words, had lost their freedom and become the retainers of their superiors. 'And thus', Scott wrote, 'there is such a generall conspiracie against Plainenesse in such places, by reason of the necessarie dependancie that one man hath of another; the Inferiour of his Superiour, and all of the highest, that it is impossible, that Truth which is knowne to the lowest, should ever arrive at the eares of the highest, though the knowledge of all, concernes him above all.'[144]

Even more importantly, the same kind of degeneration loomed large in parliamentary elections. In addition to favouring Spain and to crying 'the lawes down' and crying 'up the prerogative', the corrupt politician tried to make sure that freeholders 'shal never choose their sheere Knights and Burgesses freely' when summoned to parliament. This is what often happened as landlords pressurized their tenants into doing what they had been told. The freeholders lost their freedom, and their voice was no longer theirs but their lord's; they no longer cared for the common good but placed their own interest and particularly that of their lord before everything else. The elections, as Scott wrote in 1620, 'are caried which way the great persons who have lands in those countries please, who by their letters command their tenants, followers and friends to nominate such as adhere to them, and for the most part are of one faction, and respect their owne benefit or grace rather then their countries good, yea the country people themselves will every one stand for the great man their Lord, or neighbour, or master, without regard of his honesty, wisdome, or religion'.[145]

In a sermon preached at Thetford in 1620, Scott told his listeners: 'Bee therefore wary, when you heare a Parliament summoned by his Majestie, whom you choose Knights of the Shire, and Burgesses of Corporations; that is, whom you constitute in your places to repaire or make these high-wayes of the King, wherein you are bounde to walke obediently for conscience sake.' In cases such as these it was important that 'the Ministers prepare the people, and warne them of the worke in hand'. But it was of even greater importance that freeholders consulted

---

[144] [Scott], *Vox regis*, pp. 31–2.
[145] [Scott], *Vox popvli*, sig. B3ᵛ. See in general Sacks 1992, pp. 116–17.

with each other about the best choice. Their choice, Scott argued, ought to fall upon such who sought no 'change of the State, Lawes, and Religion' and not upon such who were 'ambitiously' looking for 'place, honor, and preferment'. Most importantly, freeholders should neglect 'both their landlords, or great neighbours, or the Lord Liftenants themselves'. As freeholders they ought, in other words, to assert their concomitant freedom from their superiors. They ought to 'looke upon the wisest, stoutest, and most religious persons; and be carefull to choose such as have no dependancie upon Greatnes'.[146]

The final measure for preventing the decay of the commonwealth and for restoring the community to its efflorescence involved its political institutions. Corruption and slavery could infiltrate most insidiously, we recall, when those in authority abused their position to the point of becoming tyrannous. Although this menace was partly solved by reorientating people's morality, it was also essential to look to it that the political institutions of the commonwealth were such that they stunted the growth of tyranny whilst at the same time securing the people's and the nobility's role in virtuous public life. To restore 'a decayed estate', Scott wrote in *The Belgicke pismire*, required not only morality but also 'rule by vertuous Lawes'.[147] When Scott discussed this issue of institutions, he put forward arguments for the mixed republican form of government in general and for the Dutch version in particular. His stubborn insistence that one should advise and act on one's own initiative, his idea of the preeminent role of parliament in decision-making and his scathing criticism of the court as a place of subjection where genuine counsel is impossible; all point to republican concepts of equality and of people themselves being the governors of their commonwealth. His use of the ant as an example of 'a good Commonwealths man' points in the same direction, for the anthill was commonly seen as a republic.[148] In *The Belgicke pismire*, he roundly declared that the pismire's 'waies in the Politickes' taught us among other things that 'what shee doth, is freely of herselfe without coaction, or instruction, having no guide, governour, nor ruler'.[149]

---

[146] Scott, *The high-waies of God*, pp. 86–7. Cf. R[eynolds], *Vox coeli*, p. 40. This is not to imply that Scott aimed at contested elections; cf. Kishlansky 1986, pp. 11, 62, 71–2. Cf. Hirst 1975, pp. 65–89.

[147] [Scott], *The Belgicke pismire*, p. 39.

[148] [Richard Brathwait], *A strange metamorphosis of man, transformed into a wildernesse* (London, 1634), sigs. FII^v–GI^r. Brathwait argued that ants 'have no King, because they will have none ... They like better of the Republiques, then of Monarchies, for so they may come happily to shuffle their owne cards themselves.'

[149] [Scott], *The Belgicke pismire*, p. 25. Cf. however, *Vox regis*, pp. 68, 6, sig. [..]2^r.

This tendency to set great store by republicanism had already appeared in Alexander Leighton's as well as in Bacon's writings. Pondering the qualities of counsellors, Leighton remarked that 'the Romane Senate were pickt out as men of sufficiencie for counsell'. The importance of counsel was so great that, as Leighton put it, 'it is a question amongst Humanists and Statesmen, Whether a weak Prince, and a wise Councel, or a weak Councel and a wise King be better'. For Leighton there was little doubt that 'both reason and experience doe prove the former to be the better'. Many wise men, he argued in a familiar manner, could guide a weak man better than one wise man could guide many weak. Directing his words to parliament, he also pointed out that 'you are the Eyes and Armes of our Sovereign, the Body of the land, the Councell and Strength for warre, the Sword and Shield of Gods distressed cause ... and in a word the very Helm of the State'. Because of their preponderant role, it was of overriding importance that MPs discarded their private interest and determined to serve the common good. As Leighton told them, 'as you look to have honour here, and glory hereafter, Stand fast, and quit your selves like men for God and your Country'. And to be able to perform their tasks, they ought to be like 'the Greek Ephori, the Roman Senators, and the States of Venice to this day'. They ought to 'lay down themselves, and all private passions of fear, flattery, and the rest, before they enter the Senate house, *Vt Reipub. serviant*'. 'So you', Leighton wrote, spelling out the moral of his examples, 'must be all the Common-wealths, and none of your own.'[150]

It might occasion some surprise to find similarities between Francis Bacon's ideas and the arguments of such puritans as Thomas Scott and Alexander Leighton. Yet we have already seen in previous chapters that Bacon's major political ideas formed an integral part of the English humanist tradition, that republics earned his sincere respect and that there were some similarities between him and George Wither. In the early 1620s, in the *De augmentis* and in 'Of the true greatnesse of kingdomes and estates', Bacon repeated the idea, first put forward in 'Of the greatnesse of kingdomes' in 1612, that people overburdened with taxes could not rise to civic greatness, since tributes diminished the prowess and valour of the people. But he added that this degeneration could be curbed, if taxes were 'levied by Consent of the Estate'. This was evident in 'the Subsidies of England', but the instance of 'the Excises of

[150] [Leighton], *Speculum belli sacri*, pp. 90–1, 93, 97, sig. B2ᵛ–3ʳ. Cf. P[attenson], *The image of bothe chvrches*, p. 107, who denied the association of peers with 'Ephori'.

the Low Countries' was most conspicuous.[151] Furthermore, in the final edition of the *Essayes*, Bacon made an important addition to the essay 'Of nobility'. Speaking of the nobility as 'a Portion of an Estate', he pointed out that a monarchy without a nobility was 'a pure, and absolute Tyranny', since the nobility tempered the monarchy. This was reminiscent of the more general argument for the mixed constitution that the middle element of the nobility kept the monarchical element in check so that it could not degenerate into tyranny. But the nobility themselves posed a threat, since they were always prone to organize factions. This was the reason why democracies, which did not need the nobility, were 'more quiet, and lesse subject to Sedition'. There were, however, even more noteworthy advantages to democracies. Since they did not have the nobility as 'a Portion of an Estate', the idea of a meritocracy could easily materialize in republics. Counsellors were not selected on the basis of lineage but on merit. 'For mens Eyes', Bacon wrote, 'are upon the Businesse, and not upon the Persons: Or if upon the Persons, it is for the Businesse sake, as fittest, and not for Flags and Pedegree.' This could already be seen in Switzerland; 'the Switzers last well', because 'Utility is their Bond, and not Respects'. But for Bacon, as for Scott, the advantages of a meritocracy were even more manifest in 'the united Provinces of the Low Countries'. In 'Government', they 'excell', since 'there is an Equality' and hence 'the Consultations are more indifferent, and the Payments and tributes more cheerfull'.[152]

The claim for the special merits of the Dutch government was, however, most forcefully advanced by Scott. It is of course true that this has not been lost on historians. Nevertheless, the claim has been almost exclusively linked with religion; the Dutch commonwealth was 'the very model of a godly commonwealth'.[153] There is little doubt that the strong religious element pervading Scott's writings was also prevalent in his esteem for the Netherlands. But it is arguable that to see Scott's admiration for the Dutch in purely religious terms is an oversimplification; it is to overlook a quite different set of values which Scott attributed to the Dutch commonwealth. Scott expressed his admiration for more commonwealths than the United Provinces alone. He referred to Roman examples, argued that in their frugality the

---

[151] Bacon, *De augmentis*, in *Works*, I, p. 795; *Essayes*, p. 92. For a similar remark, see Croft 1986, p. 167; Rabb 1981, pp. 63–4. Cf. John Yates, *Ibid ad caesarem: or a svbmissive appearance before Caesar* (London, 1626), pp. 39–40.

[152] Bacon, 'Of nobility', in *Essayes*, p. 41.

[153] Lake 1982, p. 811.

Dutch were imitating 'the renowned Spartans'[154] and occasionally used Athens and Venice as cases in point.[155] More importantly, religion alone did not account for the excellence of the Netherlands. According to Scott, the whole Dutch commonwealth was so prosperous that it was difficult to decide whether to attribute this 'to the good disposition of the people, and their care of posteritie, or to the wisedome and diligence of the Magistrates, executing good lawes strictly and impartially which tend and respect publique utility; or to the people and Magistrates joyntly concurring and consenting in one for the common good'.[156]

The most conspicuous feature of the Dutch commonwealth was, however, its form of government. Scott opened his account of the Dutch commonwealth in *The Belgicke pismire* as follows: 'I should conclude all with a touch of their Councel, and politique Government in point of State, but that the businesse is too deepe and private for my inquisition.' These scruples did not, however, restrain him from making a few observations. In the Netherlands there was 'a generall freedom' which Scott took to amount to a constitution which allowed every free man to take part in the government of the commonwealth. The general freedom, Scott wrote, was permitted and used 'where generall actions which concerned all, and are maintained by all, are generally debated, argued, sifted and censured by all men without contradiction'. This system yielded the best counsel. Scott believed that the aim of the Dutch system was 'that ... the best and worst may bee seene or heard, and all danger and advantages discovered which are subject to the common eye'. Everyone was permitted 'freely to do all the good they can with their tongues, without feare of punishment'. Despite this extended system of counsel, the final power to decide remained in the hands of a more exclusive council. When it was time to decide matters, 'the resolution and conclusion is silent and sodaine' and 'whilst they give all men libertie to informe, they themselves only direct and dispose of the businesse'. The aim of the system, Scott emphasized, was not to seek 'the satisfaction of their owne wils so much, as the generall satisfaction of all, where in may be with the good of all'. Scott conscientiously added that all this meant that the Low Countries were 'a Common-wealth' and hence they did not have

---

[154] [Scott], *The Belgicke pismire*, p. 81.
[155] [Scott], *An experimentall discoverie*, pp. 25–6, see also pp. 3–4, 6–7; *The Belgicke pismire*, pp. 51, 87–8.
[156] [Scott], *The Belgicke pismire*, pp. 73–4, cf. p. 82.

'that absolute power over their members, which Monarchies have and may use'.[157]

In *A tongve-combat* Scott presented a somewhat more detailed account of the Dutch form of government. His advocate for the United Provinces argued: 'I will briefly as I may, satisfie all your demands, shewing first the true and naturall constitution of that mixed Governement *ab initio*.' He stressed that the Dutch 'first possest the Land which they now hold'. This served as an important argument to prove that the Low Countries had always been free. Explaining what he took the freedom of a commonwealth to be, Scott wrote: 'Thus originally they are free without forraine tenure for the place, or complaint of any person for elbow-roome or intrusion.' But to be a free commonwealth implied internal as well as external freedom. 'Their Government also', Scott added, 'was as free as governement could possibly be.' This meant that the people themselves were in charge of their government. First of all, 'they chose their Governours themselves'. They were also most careful to look to it that 'their Liberties and welfare should not rest in the bosome or disposition of one man onely'. They imposed such strict limits upon their governor that he was unable to ruin the commonwealth irrespective of his personal qualities. The Dutch people controlled the movements of their governor to the extent that he could only 'profit them' but could not 'ruine them himselfe, or betray them to be ruined by the Tyrannie of others'. To accomplish their aim, the Dutch had a council; 'they chose', as Scott put it, 'a certaine mixed number of the Nobles and Commons to sit in Councell, whom they called States Generall'. It was this body which was invested with the chief authority; 'these consisted a great part of the Soveraingtie'. 'States Generall' had the power to curb 'the over-swelling torrent of Tyrannie in the Superiour', but at the same time they made sure that the popular element did not grow excessively. In this way 'States Generall' acted 'as a Moderator betwixt Prince and people'. Just as in *The Belgicke pismire*, Scott's mouthpiece in *A tongve-combat* argued that 'in these States united, together with their Prince ... was the Soveraigne Power included'. The people completed this picture of the 'mixed Governement'. It was again as advisers that they could actively participate. 'States Generall' and the prince 'had reference in all great affaires to the people also'. This enabled Scott's spokesman to boast that in the United Provinces the people 'were not shut out, (like beastes by

---

[157] Ibid., pp. 89–91.

Butchers against the day of slaughter) but called to counsell, if the
businesse concerned them, and the generall welfare'.[158]

Even though Scott had carefully presented this ideal mixed constitution as the Dutch form of government, there is no doubt that he took it
to be an example for other commonwealths. In *The Belgicke pismire* he
hinted that it was highly desirable for every commonwealth to seek to
imitate the Netherlands at least in this respect.[159] For England this was
relatively easy since there were striking similarities between the Dutch
and the English forms of government. England should simply look to
Norwich, which 'may be a mirror to all the Kingdome besides'.
According to Scott, 'the order and good governement of the Magistrates' and 'the diligence of the Citizens' in Norwich was 'principally
occasioned by the example of the Dutch' and had been brought about
'by a kinde of vertuous emulation, to which the English are excited by
their diligence'. Although England could perfect its government by
following the example of Norwich, which had imitated the Dutch,
Scott believed that it did not have to do so in every respect. There was
an English institution which already equalled that of the Dutch system.
If the 'States Generall' curbed the potentially tyrannous dispositions of
the prince as well as the subversive inclinations of the people, in
England this task could be accomplished by 'our Parliaments'.[160] Scott
was fully convinced that imitating the United Provinces provided all
the answers and that it rendered the search 'for *Plato his communitie*, or
Sir *Thomas More* his *Utopia*' unnecessary since 'the realitie of their wishes
and best conceptions are brought into action; and the best of what they
fancied might bee, is' in the Low Countries 'seene truly to bee'.[161]
Surely, the ideal commonwealths as depicted by Plato or More and
embodied in the United Provinces are not merely godly commonwealths.

It is undoubtedly true to say that there was a pervasive religious
element in Scott's pamphlet campaign. But religious motives cannot
completely account for Scott's purposes. At the heart of his campaign
lay an unmistakable classical republican analysis of the English com-

---

[158] [Scott], *A tongve-combat*, pp. 12–14; cf. in general *The proiector*, pp. 9–10. See also *A tongve-combat*,
p. 88; *Vox Dei*, pp. 80–1.
[159] [Scott], *The Belgicke pismire*, p. 90.
[160] [Scott], *A tongve-combat*, p. 13.
[161] [Scott], *The Belgicke pismire*, p. 90. It was of course commonplace to argue that Plato's
commonwealth and More's utopia were of no real value, because of their imaginary nature.
See e.g. [William Vaughan], *The golden fleece diuided into three parts* (London, 1626), i, p. 148.
Francis Markham, *The booke of honovr: or five decads of epistles of honovr* (London, 1625), pp. 198–9;
Howell, *Dodona's grove*, p. 28.

monwealth. The well-being of the English commonwealth was jeopardized both from within and without. Scott stubbornly insisted that the first way to avert this imminent danger was to remould the people's morality so that they would be willing to pursue the common good and to uphold their liberty. Their moral qualities were partly safeguarded by maintaining their social independence. But the moral basis of the commonwealth was also guaranteed by the retention of the classical mixed constitution. In Scott's analysis, these were the essential characteristics England needed to possess if it was to survive the crisis of the early 1620s.

CHAPTER 6

The continuity of the humanist tradition in early Caroline England

After more than twenty years of peace, England finally entered the European war in 1625. But the ensuing campaigns – Mansfeld's expedition, the Cadiz, Ré and La Rochelle expeditions – resulted in a series of infamous defeats which do not rank particularly high in the list of English martial achievements. As a result, England negotiated peace with France and Spain in 1629 and 1630 respectively and this marked the end of England's active involvement in the Thirty Years War, to the dismay of many protestant subjects who were willing to support the protestant cause, especially when Gustavus II Adolphus scored his victories.

War demands money, and Charles's war policy led to numerous parliaments and heated disputes over supply. In 1625 it was mainly the distrust and suspicion towards Buckingham that prompted the Commons to decline the traditional lifelong grant of Tonnage and Poundage. Charles summoned another parliament early in 1626 in order to finance a renewed war effort. Although the Commons was willing to contribute, it was resolved in its attempt to impeach Buckingham. The king refused to abandon his favourite and instead dissolved parliament. By 1626 Charles had radically altered his former favourable view of parliament and sought to gain money by extra-parliamentary means, of which the Forced Loan was the most successful and notorious. Although he was still disinclined to summon a parliament, his ministers managed to persuade him to do so in 1628. One of his aims seems to have been to achieve a reconciliation with his subjects, but the outcome was quite the contrary, as the session ended with the famous Petition of Right. The second session of the same parliament met in January 1629 and although a major obstacle to a more cooperative session, Buckingham, had been removed, the session ended in a serious deadlock and the king refused to summon another parliament for more than a decade.[1]

---

[1]   Russell, 1979; Lockyer 1989, pp. 217–31, 325–51; Cust 1987; Reeve 1989.

These years have naturally aroused keen interest and they have provided abundant material for studies in political history and the history of political thought alike.[2] Although scholarly attention has mostly focused on the absolutist, contractarian and juristic arguments, it is of some interest to ask whether the vocabulary of the humanist tradition was at all employed in these debates. There is indeed some evidence that this was the case.

To begin with, Roman historians and moralists were used to level criticism at the king and his politics. It is perhaps not without significance that an edition of Sallust's histories was published in English in 1629. In a prefatory poem addressed to the translator, Francis Wortley sharply contrasted the virtue of the Romans with that of his own times: 'Twas native love durst such a Genius raise, / To tell Romes vertue in our Sluggish dayes.' By reading Sallust one could see 'the horrid plots of faithlesse Kings, / Whose jealous feares ne'r wanted Instrument'.[3] One author argued that though the emulation of Demosthenes' and Cicero's speeches against tyrants 'would better fit the times', he must imitate Solon 'and write rimes'. For such was 'the malice of the age' that opinions voiced 'in presse, or pulpit' were always censured although they aimed 'at the common good' and strictly avoided 'blame'. The author was encouraged in his attempt by the 'Councels, of old ... Who boldly would, for publiq; safety utter / What, now, the best, in private, dare not mutter'.[4] He assured his readers that he was himself one of the 'true Patriots' who sought 'publiq; preservation'. By carefully studying 'the monuments of former ages', one could easily learn that 'No State, or Kingdome ever did sustaine / Such fatall downfalls, gene'rall devastations, / Finall subversions, and depopulations,' prompted either 'by open foes' or 'by intestine civill broyles'. 'The Greacian Monarchy' and the Roman 'greatnes' had been destroyed by internal discord.[5] The modern 'Catilines' were those who favoured 'Spaines designes'. They had been corrupted by 'Indian gold' and they had, therefore, lost their proper sense of the common good. These 'abused statesmen' made England lose 'honour' and incur the 'contempt and hate' of 'all nations', as was obvious for everyone to see in the case of 'Rochell' and 'th' Ile of Re'.[6]

---

2   E.g. Judson 1949; Sommerville 1986; Cust 1987.
3   *The workes of Caius Crispus Salustius*, translated by William Crosse (London, 1629), sig. A4ʳ⁻ᵛ.
4   J. R., *The spy discovering the danger of Arminian heresie and Spanish trecherie* (Strasburg, 1628), sig. A1ʳ.
5   J. R., *The spy*, sigs. A2ʳ, C2ʳ⁻ᵇ.
6   Ibid., sigs. D2ʳ, D3ᵛ, E1ʳ⁻ᵛ.

The foolhardy foreign policy was thus an index of the total degeneration of the English commonwealth:

> Thus is our land made weake, our treasure wasted,
> Our court corrupted, and our honour blasted,
> Our lawes are broke, our justice sold: and they
> That should reforme these mischiefes, give them way.
> All symptomes of a Kingdome, that hath beene
>   Declining long, may be in England seene:
> Our strength's decayd, the flow're of all the land
> Have perish'd under Buckinghams command.
> Those that their lives, have ventur'd for their King,
> Home, nought but labour for their paines can bring.[7]

Moreover, there is some evidence that the orthodox Ciceronian
ideals of true nobility and the *vita activa* were embraced in order to
assail Charles and his court. In their attempt to impeach Buckingham
in 1626, the Commons argued that the duke had perverted the ways in
which honour was bestowed. 'Titles of honor of the kingdom',
Christopher Sherland asserted, 'were not to be put upon such as are
rich, but upon such industrious persons as should merit them by its
services.' The Commons declared in their article of impeachment
against Buckingham that honour should be conferred 'as great rewards
upon such virtuous and industrious persons as has merited them by
their faithful service'.[8] One author reiterated in 1628 that 'honour is
not to be valued according to the vulgar opinion of men, but priz'd
and esteemed, as the surname of virtue, ingendered in the mind'.
Arguing against 'the base and mercenary' system of selling titles, the
author claimed that if striving 'to be more honourable than others',
man 'ought to abandon passion, pride, and arrogancy, that so his
virtue may shine above others; for honour consists not in the title of a
lord, but in the opinion people have of his virtue; for it is a much more
honour to deserve and not to have it, than to have it and not deserve
it'.[9] Advocating an honourable war, Ralph Knevet wrote the following
verse in 1628:

---

[7] Ibid., sig. E4ʳ. Later, in sigs. E4ᵛ–F1ʳ, the author hinted that Buckingham was ultimately
     aiming at becoming a king with the help of Spain. Cf. A. Ar., *The practise of princes* (n.p., 1630),
     pp. 5–8.

[8] Peck 1993a, pp. 194–5; *PP1626*, I, p. 469, cf. pp. 446–7. Cf. P[ierre] M[atthieu], *The powerfull
     favorite: or the life of Aelius Seianus* (Paris, 1628), pp. 29–30; Giovanni Manzini, *Political observations:
     upon the fall of Seianus*, translated by T[homas] H[awkins] (London, 1634), pp. 3, 42–4.

[9] 'A letter written to the Lower House of Parliament' [1628?], in *Somers tracts*, IV, pp. 105–15,
     especially pp. 108–9.

And by his proper actions doth descrive;
A Gentleman: for Fortune can't inherit
(By right) those graces, which pertaine to merit:
    And wretched is that Gentrie, which is gotten
    From their deedes, that long since be dead and rotten.
The favour of the Prince, and Fortune, arts,
And Ancestrie, are but the outward parts
Of true Nobilitie, for her soule is,
An harmonie, of vert'ous qualities.[10]

In the autumn of 1628, Alexander Leighton urged MPs to adopt a more decisive role when parliament would be reassembled. He dedicated his tract to parliament, calling MPs 'Right Honourable and High Senators'. In order to emphasize his point, Leighton invoked the idea of the *vita activa*. This mode of life was particularly pertinent to MPs since, as Leighton told them, 'your choyce and place requireth you to bee men of activitie'. This amounted to the knowledge as well as the practice of virtues; a man of *negotium* was 'inwardly and outwardly compleate with prudence, prowesse, valour and diligence'. The purpose of this virtuous mode of life was, moreover, to act for the common good. According to Leighton, 'hee is an unworthy man that preferreth his own particular safetie to the saveinge of the common weale'. Leighton again turned to the lesson of ancient history for an example: 'Wee neede not tell you of the Roman Patriots, or the Athenian Kings; who were willinge to dye that the glorie of their nation might live.'[11]

Leighton's espousal of the idea of *negotium* enabled him to highlight the political role of parliament. He argued that, according to 'the late Lord Verulam', the 'office and place' of 'the howse of commons' was 'to vendicate the Soveraigne power, the good of State-government, and the glorie of Gods worship from pollution, ruine, & Indignitie'.[12] Paraphrasing Thomas Smith, he wrote: 'The Parliament hath in it the power of the whole Kingdome, yea both of the head and of the body.' In effect, parliament must assume the concomitant responsibilities and be ready to exercise its authority. 'You', as Leighton addressed the MPs, 'are the Elders of Israell; you are an armie of Generals; that supream Court, that may call any place, or person to an account,

10   Ralph Knevet, *Stratiotikon: or a discourse of militarie discipline* (n.p., 1628), sig. F2ᵛ.
11   [Leighton], *An appeal to the parliament: or Sions plea against the prelacie* (n.p., n.d. [1628]), the epistle
     dedicatory.
12   Ibid., p. 211, in general pp. 211–20; Bacon, *Advancement of learning*, in *Works*, III, p. 345; *Essayes*,
     p. 48.

whether they be for the glorie of God, the good of the King and State, or no.' Leighton's argument implied that it was ultimately parliament's duty to reform the ills of the English commonwealth; MPs were 'the Physitians of State'. By placing his utmost emphasis on the importance of parliament, Leighton was seriously curtailing the power of the king. 'In a word it were happie for our King and us, if you knew your power practicallie.'[13]

More open evidence that classical history in general and Tacitus in particular were used to bear out the excellence of the republican form of government is to be found in the famous lectures in December 1627 by Isaac Dorislaus, the first incumbent of the history lectureship in Cambridge founded by Fulke Greville. Greville had first endeavoured to establish the history lectureship in 1615 but after a few years of vacillation he abandoned the plan. He renewed his attempt in 1624 and this time the whole project materialized. It was Greville's idea that Dorislaus should lecture on Tacitus' *Annals*. In his first lecture, delivered on 7 December 1627, Dorislaus discussed the different types of monarchies and argued that in some cases a tyrant could legitimately be resisted. Five days later he continued and used Tarquinius Superbus' tyrannical rule and Lucius Junius Brutus' liberation of his country from this tyranny as his examples. At the instigation of Matthew Wren, Master of Peterhouse, who thought that Dorislaus had made statements which were 'applicable to the expectation of these villainous times', the matter was investigated. Nothing was found, but an order from the king prohibited Dorislaus from lecturing. It is probable that Greville, who had suggested the topic of the lectures, also approved of their contents. Although it remains uncertain whether the lectures were intended, as Wren perhaps suspected, to criticize the Forced Loan, it seems clear that Greville's ultimate aim had been to remind his contemporaries of the centrality of virtuous public service to the reform of the commonwealth.[14]

In the course of 1627 Thomas May, the future official historian of the Long Parliament, published his well-known translation of Lucan's *Pharsalia* (the first three books had already appeared in 1626). The

---

[13] [Leighton], *An appeal to the parliament*, p. 174, cf. p. 170. Attorney-general Robert Heath detected this strand of Leighton's argument. In his speech against Leighton in the Star Chamber, Heath reminded his listeners that although 'the Parliament is a great Court, a great Counsell, the great Counsell of the Kinge', its members were 'but his Counsell, not his governours', Robert Heath, 'Speech in the case of Alexander Leighton, in the Star Chamber, June 4, 1630', ed. S. R. Gardiner, Camden Society, XIV, n.s., *Camden miscellany*, 7 (1875), p. 9.

[14] This paragraph is based on Sharpe 1989, pp. 218–29.

whole volume was dedicated to the earl of Devonshire and separate
books to such magnates as the earls of Pembroke, Essex, Lindsey,
Lincoln and Warwick. Many of them, as David Norbrook has recently
observed, were widely seen as 'men of patriotic independence, which
had driven several of them into opposition to royal policies'.[15] May
claimed that Rome's 'transcendent greatnes will admit no comparison
with other States'. Civic greatness had coincided with the period of
liberty and popular government, but the 'unhappy height' of Rome
had brought about luxury and pride, which had commenced deterior-
ating 'the Roman Vertue'. Consequently, the people had lost
'fredome', whereas Caesar had assumed 'too absolute and undeter-
mined a power'. Caesar was, in other words, the villain of the story,
and May was reluctant to call Pompey a 'head of a faction'. He
would rather call him 'the true servant of the publike State'.[16]
Pompey was identified with 'Romes vast power, her liberty &
Lawes'.[17] If May was so impressed by Pompey, he felt equal admiration for two other republican heroes – Cato and Brutus. They had
joined Pompey, but May carefully emphasized that they had 'favour'd
neither side' and that they had not 'engaged by a private cause': 'For
Rome, her state, her freedome, and her laws pride, / Their loyall
virtue stood.' For May, Cato was an embodiment of virtuous 'true
Nobility'.[18] May had no qualms about applying these ideas to
contemporary politics. Dedicating the seventh book to Horace Vere,
May identified Vere with Pompey, extolling his eagerness to fight for
Dutch liberty and English fame. But it was the earl of Pembroke who
earned the most fulsome praise. He was not merely 'Free from
ambition, free from faction', he was also 'An honest Lord, a noble
Patriot', matching both Cato and Brutus.[19]

Perhaps the most extensive application of humanist notions to the
politics of the late 1620s is to be found in George Wither's long
commentary, *Britains remembrancer* published in 1628.[20] In 1613 Wither
had found a solution to the political problems of the day in the

15   Norbrook 1994, pp. 58–60. My indebtness to this admirable analysis is obvious.
16   M. A. Lucan, *Pharsalia: or the civill warres of Rome, betweene Pompey the Great, and Ivlivs Caesar: ten
     bookes*, translated by Thomas May (London, 1627), sig. a2ᵛ–a4ᵛ.
17   Ibid., sig. M1ʳ; see also o1ʳ.
18   Ibid., sig. B6ʳ; see also Q2ʳ.
19   Ibid., sig. B6ʳ.
20   George Wither, *Britains remembrancer containing a narration of the plague lately past* (n.p., 1628).
     Although the work was published in 1628, Wither claimed that 'it is above two yeares since I
     laboured to get this Booke printed, fo. [14ᵃ]. Yet, he referred to the Ré expedition, which
     sailed in June 1627, fo. 220ᵛ.

humanist concepts of *negotium* and *vera nobilitas*. In the 1620s the political situation was much more serious, but many of the themes which we have encountered in his *Abuses stript, and whipt*, also figured largely in his *Britains remembrancer*. But Wither's analysis also bears a close resemblance to Thomas Scott's arguments. The main theme of Wither's *Britains remembrancer* was a familiar one: to reveal the sickness – 'the Pestilence' or 'the Plague' – ravaging England and to prescribe remedies for it. In his dedication to the king, Wither revealed his intentions:

> Here, view you may (before too far they steale)
> The sicknesses of Church and Commonweale
> What brings upon your Person, and the State,
> Such care, and so much trouble as of late:
> What marres your Counsels, and what undermines
> Your most approved, and most wise designes.[21]

Later in the treatise Wither broadened his audience and addressed the whole realm: 'I tell thee therefore, Britaine, thou art sick.'[22] This decay manifested itself in religion, foreign policy and trade: treaties, alliances, 'forraine enterprizes' and even naval expeditions had failed to produce the desired results.[23] Foreign trade depended on ships, 'which are the walls, / By which thy temp'rall greatnesse, stands, or falls'. But now most of the ships 'begin to sinke, for want of trade'.[24]

The main reasons for corruption were hardly less familiar. First, Wither endorsed the long-standing view that the corruption of the court and the nobility had contaminated the whole commonwealth. 'The Court is fraught with bribery, with hate, / With envie, lust, ambition, and debate.' Wither was convinced that 'True Vertue's almost quite exiled thence.'[25] Although there still were 'Some Courtiers, and some Nobles' who had retained 'their True Nobility', most of them 'live luxuriously' and despise those who 'might advance the publike weale'. The greatest favours were bestowed on those who knew 'how to ride a horse, or take the Ring, / Or hunt, or hawk, or caper'. Offices were sold, but the king's coffers remained empty as long as the luxurious habits of these 'Parasites' and 'Buffoones' were subsidized.[26]

Wither also endorsed the equally traditional belief that decay was

21 Ibid., fo. 8ᵛ.
22 Ibid., 216ᵛ; see in general fos. 9ʳ, 39ʳ, 65ʳ–66ʳ, 102ᵛ, 109ᵛ–110ʳ, 222ʳ.
23 Ibid., fos. 218ᵛ–220ᵛ. For religion see e.g. fos. 169ᵛ–173ᵛ.
24 Ibid., fos. 216ᵛ–218ʳ, 198ʳ.
25 Ibid., fo. 196ʳ⁻ᵛ, in general, fos. 196ʳ–198ʳ.
26 Ibid., fos. 180ᵛ–189ᵛ.

caused by a more general lack of virtue and a universal pursuit of one's own private good.[27] Finally, he believed that corruption manifested itself in the arena of politics, which had turned into 'The Closet-Counsels, and the Chamber work'. No news spread any longer from St Paul's Cathedral; there was 'scarce a Walker in her middle Ile', as Wither put it.[28]

The remedies which Wither prescribed to this sickness were also largely dependent on traditional arguments. But before embarking on the project of suggesting his remedies, he pointed out that decay and corruption were to an extent inescapable:

> I saw how Cities, Common-wealths, and Men,
> Did rise and fall, and rise and fall agen.
> I saw the reason, why all Times and States,
> Have such vicissitudes, and various fates.
> I saw what doth occasion War, and Peace;
> What causeth Dearth, and what doth bring Encrease.
> I saw what hardens, and what mollifies.[29]

First of all, Wither's withering criticism the private life implied an unqualified endorsement of *negotium*. 'Prejudicate opinions, faction, pride' should be laid aside, and everyone should 'serve the Publike'.[30] Virtuous *vera nobilitas* was another time-honoured remedy to which Wither resorted. In the first canto, he exhorted the king to abandon 'base Officer' and advance men of 'true Honor'.[31] The same issue emerged even more clearly in the sixth canto, where Wither reproved 'The course in which our Nobles move'. The only way to change the course of events was to dispense with 'Parasites' and 'Buffoones' and to promote those who exhibited 'ancient Vertues'.[32] Wither's argument implied that virtue was to be found amongst ancient families, but in the next canto he reminded his readers that true virtue could also repose amongst merchants.[33] He strongly supported the anti-Spanish foreign policy, extolling England's maritime position, and praised Queen Elizabeth and the heroes of her reign, including again Walter Ralegh.[34]

27 Ibid., fos. 114^{r-v}, 222^r–233^v.
28 Ibid., fos. 107^v–108^v.
29 Ibid., fo. 152^v.
30 Ibid., fos. 234^v, 67^r–71^r.
31 Ibid., fo. 28^v.
32 Ibid., fos. 168^r, 180^v–198^r, quotations 184^r, 185^v. Cf. George Wither, *A collection of emblemes, ancient and moderne* (London, 1635), p. 5.
33 Wither, *Britains remembrancer*, fo. 209^v.
34 Ibid., fos. 218^v–220^v, 168^v, 165^v–166^r, 120^v–121^v, 182^v. For a balanced account of the queen's memory, see Woolf 1985.

According to Wither, parliament played an important role in repairing the decay of the commonwealth. It was above all in parliament that men should lay aside their private thoughts and focus on serving the public good.[35] In order to ensure this, meticulous care should be exercised in parliamentary elections. First, too many people thought that

> The Common-wealth would surely come to nought,
> Unlesse his knowledge, or his vertues, were
> Elected, to be exercised there.

Moreover, too many elections were 'out of order' (i.e. contested). In such cases MPs were inclined to serve 'meere private ends' of their 'Chusers', rather than the good of the whole community. Most importantly, however, people should make their choices free:

> they that should have past
> A free election, have their voices cast
> By force, constraint, or for some by-respect,
> On those, whom others, for their ends elect.
> There be in Court, and bordring round about
> Thy Burroughs, many wiser men, no doubt,
> Then some that in Elections have their voice;
> And, by their ayd, there is sometime a choice
> Of good and able men: yet, best it were,
> That all men left to their just freedomes were.[36]

Given Wither's belief in the crucial importance of the virtuous active life, it comes as no surprise that he criticized the king in an only thinly veiled manner, that he believed the Council could control the king and that he was inclined to give the people a significant role in the political life of the commonwealth.

> A King is for a blessing, or a curse:
> And therefore (though a Foole he were, or worse,
> A Tyrant, or an Ethnick) no man may
> So much as in their private clossets, pray
> Against his person; though they may petition
> Against the wickednesse of his condition.

Wither called the Council 'An Aristocracy', claiming that sometimes 'they over-rule' the King 'in ev'rything'. But 'the pop'lar voice' did

[35] Wither, *Britains remembrancer*, fo. 234^v.
[36] Ibid., fos. 230^r–231^v.

sometimes 'awe the Counsell', so much so that God often made 'much alteration / in formes of Government'.[37]

There is thus little doubt that humanist parlance was used to level criticism at the king and his government: the present state of the realm was depicted in terms of corruption, the court was seen as a place devoid of true nobility and it was possible to seek the solution in the qualities of *negotium* and *vera nobilitas*. Nevertheless, it seems to be the case that no extensive analysis of England as a virtuous commonwealth, let alone as a mixed state, was developed in the late 1620s. The importance of parliament and of more effective parliamentary control was often stressed but without any reference to a humanist vocabulary.[38] There seemed to be, in other words, a partial decline in the popularity of Ciceronian humanist concepts in the English political discourse of the 1620s.[39]

If Ciceronian ideals were receding, Tacitean values were, to an extent, taking their place, though again they often appeared together. As is well known, Buckingham's opponents invoked Tacitus' analysis of imperial Rome in their accusations against the duke. John Eliot compared Buckingham with Tiberius' corrupt favourite L. Aelius Sejanus in the 1626 parliament when the Commons endeavoured to impeach the duke.[40] Writing immediately after Buckingham's assassination in 1628, Alexander Leighton went even further and claimed that 'Sejanus' had never been as 'ungratefull, nor perfidious to his Master' as Buckingham.[41] In 1628 too, two separate translations of Pierre Matthieu's *The powerfull favorite, or the life of Aelius Seianus* were published as an attack on Buckingham. Matthieu did not confine himself to a mere description of Sejanus' infamous life; he claimed that

[37]   Ibid., fo. 265[r–v].

[38]   See e.g. Henry Burton, *Israels fast: or, a meditation vpon the seuenth chapter of Joshuah; a faire precedent for these times* (London, 1628), sigs. A4[r–v], B1[r]–4[r], p. 13; and especially idem, *An apology of an appeale: also an epistle to the true-hearted nobility* (n.p., 1636), pp. 20–3; idem, *A plea to an appeale: trauersed dialogue wise* (London, 1626), p. 2. See Cust 1987, pp. 302–3. For examples of non-puritan views, see e.g. [Robert Cotton], *The danger wherein the kingdom, now standeth & the remedie* (n.p., 1628), pp. 7–12; [Ralph Starkey], *The priuiledges and practice of parliaments in England: collected out of the common lawes of this land* (n.p., 1628). For the prevalent tendency to contrast the corruption of one's own time with the healthy commonwealth of Elizabeth's reign, see e.g. Thomas Gataker, *An anniuersarie memoriall of Englands delivery from the Spanish inuasion: deliuered in a sermon on Psal. 48.7,8* (London, 1626); Walter Cary, *The present state of England* (London, 1627). Cf. in general Lake 1982, pp. 815–18; Cust and Lake 1981, pp. 44–8; Cust 1987, p. 181; Cust 1986; Clark 1978; Fielding 1988; Hughes 1986; Cope 1987, pp. 116–17, 120; Thompson 1972; Zaller 1983.

[39]   This has been suggested by Mendle 1989a, pp. 116–17.

[40]   *PP1626*, I, p. 462; Tenney 1941, p. 160. See in general Butler 1985, pp. 143–6.

[41]   [Alexander Leighton], *An appeal to the parliament*, pp. 160–2.

the whole age had been 'so corrupted' that it had been 'then a vertue to doe no evill, and piety not to be impious'. An absolute ruler's court was full of obsequiousness and flattery. It was sheer madness to oppose 'the will of the Prince', for when the prince said 'I will have it so, he renders reason enough of his actions'.[42] Autocracy had abandoned both the commonwealth and the court to Fortune. It was ultimately her fickle nature which had caused Sejanus' ruin. He had been 'a prodigious example of extreame insolencie and unfortunate ambi-tion'.[43] Matthieu was careful to point out that some people who had been accustomed to live in the court had in the end found 'no other defence against the violence of the time then a solitary life' and had withdrawn to the country. 'The solitary life', he announced, 'was the most assured, the civill more perillous, and the Country more pleasing.'[44]

A new version of Matthieu's tract was published in 1632 (reprinted in 1639),[45] and the same story was retold in the translation of Giovanni Manzini's *Politicall observations: upon the fall of Seianvs* in 1634. Sejanus' tragic end was rehearsed 'rather for example then delight'. 'Let the Courtier', Manzini pointed out, 'learne true politike arts, from the History of this wretched forlorne creature', for he 'who studieth prudence on anothers bookes' would be happy. Manzini's was also a story about the unsteady and fickle nature of Fortune especially in princely courts. The reader learned how little man 'should confide in the vanity of that Fortune, which knowes not how to be stable, even in marble'.[46] Explaining the courtier's rules, Manzini emphasized that he ought to ascribe nothing to his own abilities but 'all to the vertue, to merit, to the fortune of the Prince'. Disaster was around the corner when 'the prince hath given all' favours to the courtier, since as soon as 'the Favorite can desire no more', he and the prince 'quickly grow weary one of another'.[47] Stoic forbearance was the best defence, for although the courtier

---

[42] M[atthieu], *The powerfvll favorite*, pp. 30–1, for flattery, see especially pp. 40–1, 48; Sommerville 1986, p. 58.

[43] M[atthieu], *The powerfvl favorite*, pp. 61–2; in general pp. 43–4, 48; for autocracy and fortune, see p. 26.

[44] Ibid., pp. 25–6.

[45] P[ierre] Matthieu, *Vnhappy prosperitie expressed in the histories of Aelius Seianus and Philipppa the Catanian*, translated by T[homas] Hawkins (n.p., [London], 1632).

[46] Manzini, *Politicall observations*, pp. 2, 36, 1, 14.

[47] Ibid., pp. 37–8. Cf. T[homas] Powell, *The art of thriving: or the plaine path-way to preferment* (London, 1635), sig. A5^{r-v}; Anon., *Satyrae seriae: or, the secrets of things* (London, 1640), pp. 13–15, 22–3, 47–8, 94–133: John Saltmarsh, *The patience of policie in a christian life* (London, 1639).

could never be 'free from the effects' of fortune, yet he could 'exempt from the occasions'.[48]

Thomas May's interpretation of the Roman republic was also highly ambivalent. In addition to Lucan's *Pharsalia*, he translated Virgil's *Georgics* and Martial's *Epigrams*.[49] In his two Roman tragedies *Cleopatra* (acted in 1626) and *Julia Agrippina* (acted in 1628), May again depicted the corruption of late republican and early imperial Rome. But whereas his translation of Lucan's *Pharsalia* contained glowing tributes to the virtues of republican Rome, in his Roman tragedies of the same period liberty has been lost for ever:

> A show of liberty
> When wee have lost the substance, is best kept
> By seeming not to understand those faults
> Which wee want power to mend.[50]

Cato is now presented as a point of contrast rather than identification.[51] The thoroughness of corruption is graphically illustrated by the fact that the hope of recovering freedom was placed in *Cleopatra* on Antonius, for whom politics disturbed the pleasures of love (the epitome of the private life), and who was most easily defeated.[52] Similarly, *The tragedy of Julia Agrippina* presents the imperial court as a place of wholesale decay: 'Let Vertue lurke among the rurall Swaines, / Whilest Vice in Romes Imperiall Palace reignes.'[53] The only remedy available was to withdraw from the public life, to 'tast the sweetes of privaty' and to 'Enjoy our lives free from the glorious noise, / And troubles of a Court'.[54]

In 1630 May published his well-known continuation of Lucan's *Pharsalia*, the tone of which is markedly different from the comments in the translation. Brutus is still called 'The vindicatour of lost libertie' and Caesar's 'power' is described as 'Distastfull' 'to Cities borne free'. But the Romans are now said to have been happy to forgive the loss

48 Manzini, *Politicall observations*, pp. 43–4. Cf. Arthur Warwick, *Spare-minutes: or, resolved meditations and premeditated resolvtions*, 2nd edn (London, 1634), sigs. F3ᵛ–5ʳ, G8ʳ–9ᵛ; Enrico Gaetani, *Instrvctions for yovng gentlemen*, translated by anon. (Oxford, 1633), pp. 23–4; N[icolas] C[aussin], *The unfortunate politique*, translated by G. P. (London, 1638).
49 For May's outlook, see Norbrook 1994, pp. 60–3.
50 Thomas May, *The tragoedy of Cleopatra queene of Aegypt*, ed. Denzell S. Smith (New York: Garland, 1979), I.i.113–16.
51 Ibid., I.ii.166–71.
52 Ibid., I.ii.153–6, 162–5.
53 Thomas May, *The tragedy of Julia Agrippina; empresse of Rome*, ed. F. Ernst Schmid, Materialen zur Kunde des älteren Englischen Dramas, 43 (1914), p. 5.
54 May, *Julia Agrippina*, II.151–6; IV.84–5, 121–2.

of their liberty and glad to adore 'A safe and peacefull Scepter', for the real 'substance' of their freedom had been overthrown long time ago. Peace was the most fervent hope of 'plebeians' and 'the weary'd Senate' alike. Their allegiance to Caesar's absolute power was unswerving: 'Making his power so great, there's nothing now / But he himselfe may on himselfe bestow.'[55] And when May published a 'corrected' translation of Lucan's poem in 1631, the praises of the republican heroes had become weaker, and the identifications of May's contemporaries with the Roman republican heroes had disappeared altogether.[56] May's novel interpretation bore fruit – Charles commissioned him to write historical poems on the reigns of Henry II and Edward III.[57]

Tacitean themes and stoic forbearance were thus supplanting Ciceronian ideals. In 1624 John Reynolds had published two tracts, in which he advocated an aggressive foreign policy in no uncertain terms. Five years later, however, he published a translation of Léonard de Marandé's *The ivdgement of humane actions* which was permeated by values of tranquillity and endurance. De Marandé had endorsed scepticism, regarded virtues as the battery against passions and preferred, at least to an extent, the contemplative life.[58] In his dedication to the earl of Dorset, Reynolds wrote that although France was now an enemy of England, he did not renounce his translation, 'considering that Peace is the gift and blessing of God'. He, therefore, wished for a permanent peace in 'the whole Christian

---

[55] Thomas May, *A continvation of Lucan's historicall poem till the death of Ivlivs Caesar* (London, 1630), sigs. 18^{r-v}, 15^r–6^v, K3^r.

[56] M. A. Lucan, *Pharsalia: or the civill warre of Rome, betweene Pompey the Great, and Ivlivs Caesar: ten bookes: the second edition, corrected, and the annotations inlarged*, translated by Thomas May (London 1631). The dedication to the earl of Devonshire was the same, but all the dedications of the individual books had been withdrawn. According to Norbrook (1994, p. 60), the dedications of the individual books in most surviving copies of the 1627 edition had already been tampered with. It should be noted that May's translation of John Barclay's *Icon animorum* (originally printed in 1614) was published in 1631. Barclay not only argued for a strong monarchy but also pointed out that 'those people, who subject themselves to no Scepter, though they abhorre the name of servitude, yet doe not enjoy true liberty. For they must needs elect Magistrates, to whom they give jurisdiction over themselves; and the publike power, which they glory to be in the whole Nations, is adorned in a few men; so that in those Countries, where you would think all did reigne, the greatest part are Servants'; John Barclay, *The mirrour of mindes: or Barclays Icon animorum*, translated by Thomas May (1614) (London, 1631), sig. Ee2^{r-v}; in general sig. Ee2^r–10^r.

[57] Norbrook 1994, p. 61.

[58] Léonard de Marandé, *The ivdgement of humane actions*, translated by John Reynolds (London, 1629), pp. 38–9, 44–67, 114–22, 193–4, 232–49, 196–8.

world', because 'Learning is universally to be cherished'. He placed the aims of the *otium* before those of *negotium*.[59]

The same idea emerged even more forcefully in John Eliot's case. Scholars have mostly been preoccupied with the possible inconsistency between Eliot's parliamentary practice and his theoretical works written during his final imprisonment, on the one hand, and with the possible incongruity between *De jure majestatis* and *The monarchie of man*, on the other.[60] Much less attention has been given to the tension within his own work – *The monarchie of man*. The tract starts off as a treatise on the nature of monarchy. Eliot first assumed that the king exercised authority alone, but reached the crux of his argument when he pointed out that the prince was always liable to become corrupt. In order to protect the commonwealth from this, laws had been established.[61] Although it was nowadays common 'to make Monarchie unlimited, an absolutenes of government without rule', Eliot gave a staggering list of classical authors to prove that 'lawes have an influence on kings'.[62]

So far Eliot had employed a juristic vocabulary, but changing his theme, he also changed his vocabulary. The chief way in which the king could foster the common good was to embrace the cardinal virtues. Again, however, the king's virtuous character was always susceptible to moral decline. This time, though, Eliot did not seek the solution in laws but claimed instead that the only conceivable way of solving the inadequacies of one-man rule was to be found in counsel.[63] Although 'many arguments' had been put forward in order to prove that 'to admitt this authorittie of this Senate' was to make 'a competition for the government' and 'to divide the State', it was beyond doubt that virtuous counsellors provided the best safeguard against tyranny, as the example of Tarquinius Superbus made plain.[64] In England the chief arena where counselling took place was parliament. Alongside the humanist line of argument Eliot thus maintained that the only possible means of bringing about the common good was not to leave the

---

59   de Marandé, *The iudgement*, sig. A3ʳ⁻ᵛ, cf. sig. A6ʳ⁻ᵛ. Cf. Reynolds's preface to his translation of Eustache Du Refuge, *A treatise of the court: or instruction for courtiers* (London, 1622), where he advocated a virtuous public service.

60   See e.g. Ball 1985; Sommerville 1986, pp. 157–8. For a brief discussion, see Hulme 1957, pp. 369–74.

61   John Eliot, *The monarchie of man* 2 vols., ed. A. B. Grossart (London: privately printed, 1879), II, pp. 41–4.

62   Ibid., II, pp. 44–52; cf. pp. 58–9, where he referred to John Fortescue.

63   Ibid., II, pp. 65–70.

64   Ibid., II, pp. 75–7, 81–3.

governance of the commonwealth solely to the king but to assert the values of the *vita activa*.

He firmly proclaimed that 'to the publike both our words & actions must first move without respect, without retraction for our private, they must first intend the common good and benefitt'.[65] Virtues must 'be profytable to many: not to our selves alone, not to the advancement of our families, not to our friends & allies ... but generally to all for the common benefitt & commoditie, the publike utilitie & good'. Cicero had called those 'optimates & nobles' who, irrespective of their birth, 'defend their Contrey to the utmost of their powers, those that are ready to rescue from all dangers the Commonwealth'.[66] Eliot enquired, moreover, whether we should be ready to forsake the sweetness of tranquillity and quietness and to adopt *negotium* which necessarily involved 'troubles & perplexities'. 'Shall wee neglect', he asked, 'that fattnes of our peace ... for the publicke use & service; for the profitt & comodity of others?' His immediate and unconditional answer was: 'yes, noe difficulties may retard us, no troubles may divert us, noe exception is admitted to this rule, but where the greater good is extant, the duty & office there is absolute, without caution or respect.'[67]

Eliot's account was essentially stoic. He invoked Cicero's and Seneca's authority and drew the stoic conclusion that 'vertue', which was 'the reward of her selfe', was the *'summum bonum'*.[68] His definition of virtue as 'agreeable to nature' was equally stoic. And when he explained the qualities of virtue, he began by saying that there were four cardinal virtues, but proceeded to point out that 'each must participate of all to make a true vertue'. All of them must 'be contemperate', they 'must be compounded' so that in the end they were but one.[69] True honour came 'by vertue'; it was 'the crowne of vertue' and was attained by being 'a servant unto vertue'.[70] In a completely stoic argument, Eliot further maintained that the cardinal virtues would eradicate the 'impediments & corruptions' of felicity – passions. These were four in number: 'feare, hope, joy, & sorrow', and a great part of Eliot's treatise was devoted to explaining the ways in which virtues could eliminate these passions.[71]

---

[65] Ibid., II, pp. 207–8.
[66] Ibid., II, pp. 182–4.
[67] Ibid., II, pp. 208–11.
[68] Ibid., II, p. 100; in general pp. 95–105.
[69] Ibid., II, pp. 108–9, 64.
[70] Ibid., II, pp. 176–86.
[71] Ibid., II, pp. 107–8, 138–205.

Contradicting his analysis of *negotium*, Eliot maintained that, as virtue eradicated passions, it enabled the mind to build 'a tranquilitie, & calm-nes free from all trouble & distemper in the contemplation of all accidents'. To live 'in privacie and leisure' was more 'pleasant than any dignitie'. When a man's life was 'vacant of busines & imployment', it was 'the freer from distractions'.[72] Contemplation was wholly dependent on wisdom but this was 'not that wisedome of the vertues, that wisedome which wee reckon'd in our lawes, but another wisedome'. Defining the difference between prudence and sapience, Eliot claimed that the latter was 'a wisedome of more excellence, of more excellencie in the facultie; of more excellence in the object'.[73] Sapience surpassed prudence on the grounds that whereas 'men & actions onely are the entertainement of the other', sapience 'ha's it's conversation in the Heavens, & is verst in the high misteries of Divinity'. This contemplation was commended not solely by divines but also 'by the Ethicks'.[74]

The question which Eliot thus addressed was whether action or contemplation was of greater weight. 'But here', he wrote, 'a question may arise, whether of these is chiefe, whither is more principle in the vertue.' He admitted that this issue had 'bene frequently discust' and that 'with varietie of arguments on both sides'. However, he had no hesitation in maintaining that 'contemplation is the chiefe'. It was Marsilio Ficino from whom Eliot derived his argument at this point. Contemplation was more valuable than action because it provided the latter both with the end and with the beginning. Action was 'but a derivative from' contemplation and, moreover, as soon as action came to its end, contemplation began again.[75] Although Eliot could assert the central values of Ciceronian humanism, in the final analysis he abandoned them and wholeheartedly embraced the idea of *otium*. He confessed that, in principle, the virtuous active life in public service was most precious, but the verdict which he gave from his confinement was that the noblest way of life must be one of contemplative leisure. During his imprisonment Eliot obtained a copy of Lipsius' *De constantia*.[76]

The conclusion that the humanist tradition did not have as strong an ideological significance in the latter part of the 1620s as in the late

---

72 Ibid., II, pp. 102, 104–5.
73 Ibid., II, p. 216.
74 Ibid., II, pp. 216–221.
75 Ibid., II, pp. 222–3. Cf. William Jeffray, *The picture of patience: or, direction to perfection* (London, 1629), pp. 1–2, 9. For Ficino, see e.g. Rice 1958, pp. 58–68.
76 Sharpe 1979, p. 106.

sixteenth century and the first two decades of the seventeenth might appear, at first glance, somewhat surprising. One might have thought that the turbulent and politically troubled years of the late 1620s would have created the right circumstances for a fully developed ideology of the mixed state, of true nobility and of the active life. As we have seen, this had happened several times during an acute crisis. And although some of these humanist concepts were employed in the late 1620s, no-one formulated or advanced a full-blooded humanist theory of a virtuous commonwealth. This can partly be explained, as Margo Todd has pointed out, by the growing Anglican and Laudian reaction against puritanism and its social ethics based mainly on Christian humanism.[77] More importantly, a sense of frustration with politics, so obvious in Eliot's case, had something to do with this decline. Alexander Leighton wrote: 'When all things were so farre out of frame, that we are becom the prey of our enimies, the mockerie of our friends, a shame to our selves, and the fotestoole of a favourite: then nothing but a Parliament, Oh! a Parliament would men all; But Parliament we had after Parliament, and what was amended?'[78] Similar expressions of frustration can be found from George Wither's writings of the 1620s. As early as 1621 Wither said that he was not interested in 'the Bohemian state' or 'The Palatinate', nor in 'Eighty-eight', 'the Powder-plot, or any thing of Spaines'. He was 'not much inquisitive to know' about 'newes from France, or Spaine', or about 'For what brave Action our last Fleet did go'. He claimed that he could 'accord' 'with a Jewe, or Spaniard' as long as they had 'a Vertuous, and Heroicke minde'.[79] In 1625 parliament had two sessions, but to Wither it looked 'That all the time, the labour, and the cost, / Which had bestowed beene, was wholly lost'.

> We wisht for Parliaments; and them we made
> Our God: for, all the hope that many had
> To remedy the publike discontent,
> Was by the wisdome of a Parliament
> Well; Parliaments we had; and what in being,
> Succeedeth yet, but greater disagreeing,
> With greater grievances then heretofore?[80]

---

[77] Todd 1987, pp. 206–60; cf. Reeve 1989, pp. 62–71.
[78] Cf. Reeve 1989, pp. 209–10; Leighton, *An appeal to the parliament*, pp. 172–3.
[79] George Wither, *Wither's motto: nec habeo, nec careo, nec curo* (n.p. [London], 1621), sigs. A6ᵛ, D2ʳ⁻ᵛ, B4ᵛ.
[80] Wither, *Britains remembrancer*, fo. 106ʳ⁻ᵛ, sig. z8ʳ.

A frustration with politics might to some extent account for the partial submergence of a humanist vocabulary, but there is little doubt that the main reason for this lies in the precise nature of the issues involved. Although criticism of the court offered ample opportunities for the development of the concept of corruption, the real issues at stake – religion, taxation, the Forced Loan, arbitrary imprisonment and the conduct of war – were such that a juristic vocabulary and more particularly one of the ancient constitution proved perhaps more efficacious in countering the king's policy. The lofty yet somewhat general ideal of the active life and true nobility had few answers to the practical problems of warfare or to the constitutional or legal disputes over taxation and the Forced Loan. Appeals to the reason of state and the claims of the divine rights of kings made in favour of the Forced Loan, were answered by arguments based on the common law or to a lesser extent on the resistance theories developed within the natural law tradition.[81] Edward Coke's proposed solution to the problems engendered by the Forced Loan – the Petition of Right – was a question of rights and the law rather than of virtue, true nobility and the *vita activa*.[82] For George Wither, parliament had proved unable to solve the pressing problems, and his belief in the humanist concepts had markedly abated. Instead, he turned to the language of body politic, emphasizing the 'blessed union' of the people and the king 'as the Body and the Head'. As to 'the Infringement of our lawfull Liberties', they were secured by the principles of the ancient constitution, which guaranteed both the king's authority and 'all just freedomes of the Land'. Although Wither asserted that they who claim that 'no law doth bound' the king were making him 'a Tyrant', he also admitted that the king could in certain cases flout the law.

> They, who deny the King free pow'r to do
> What his Republikes weale conduceth to,
> Because some Law gainsayes; ev'n those deprive
> Their Soveraigne of a due prerogative;
> Since, for the common good, it just may be,
> That some injustice may be done to me.[83]

[81] Cust 1987, pp. 157–85.
[82] The same seems to be true in so far as the circumstances leading to the Bishops' war are concerned, see e.g. John Corbet, *The vngirding of the Scottish armour: or, an answer to the informations for defensive armes against the kings majestie* (Dublin, 1639); Henry Valentine, *God save the king: a sermon preached in St Pavls church the 27th. of March. 1639* (London, 1639).
[83] Wither, *Britains remembrancer*, fos. 29ʳ, 227ᵛ–228ʳ, 234ᵛ–235ʳ, 236ᵛ–237ʳ. Cf. idem, *Wither's motto*, sig. B1ᵛ, where the argument is directed against any use of the reason of state.

The partial decline of the classical humanist tradition does not mean, however, that it disappeared altogether during the late 1620s and the 1630s. At the beginning of the 1630s Thomas May may have described Rome's liberty as irrevocably lost, but by the time he published his continuation of Lucan's *Pharsalia* in Latin in 1640, he had again strengthened the republican emphases of the work: Caesar appears now more arbitrary; the problems caused by freedom have disappeared, as has the eulogy of Augustus.[84] The political disputes of the late 1620s may have lacked a fully fledged humanist response, but three distinct themes of humanist tradition were continuously restated during the 1630s. The first one was the issue of the militia. Although the northern humanists – mainly following Cicero – had opposed the use of brute force, we have seen that the idea of the citizen carrying arms, so central in Italian republican humanism, had also made a lasting impact in England. Essentially similar arguments, often based on Bacon's pioneering analysis, were already rehearsed in the late 1620s but also in the 1630s.

As soon as Charles ascended the throne, he was committed to reforming the English militia and to leading England into the European war. Where the reformation of the English army was concerned, it was Charles's aim to create a perfect militia. Early in 1626 he recalled some English sergeants from the Netherlands to train it. A general assessment is difficult to give because of the great variation between counties, but it seems plausible to say that Charles's efforts improved the quality of the militia although it failed to provide Charles with strong troops when he needed them in 1638.[85]

Partly because of Charles's attempts to create a disciplined militia but mainly because of the adoption of a more belligerent policy, the later years of the 1620s witnessed the publication of a number of tracts and treatises about warfare.[86] The idea of professional and mercenary soldiers received occasional endorsement. John Hagthorpe argued in 1625 that 'he that hath coyne shal have strangers to fight for him, but he that hath none though peradventure he number

---

[84] Bruère 1949; Norbrook 1994, p. 63.

[85] Boynton 1967, pp. 244–97; Fletcher 1986, pp. 286–316.

[86] E.g. W[illiam] N[eade], *The double-armed man, by the new inuention: briefly shewing some famous exploits atchieued by our Brittish bowmen* (n.p., [London], 1625); W. C., *The Dutch suruay* (London, 1625); John Roberts, *Compendium belli: or the touchstone of martiall discipline* (London, 1626); E[dward] C[ooke], *The prospectiue glasse of warre* (London, 1628); Thomas Taylor, *The valew of true valour: or, the probation and approbation of a right military man* (London, 1629); [George] Lauder, *The Scottish souldier* (Edinburgh, 1629).

many subjects, yet in his need hee shall finde but few souldiers'.[87] Richard Bernard, a puritan cleric from Somerset, discussed 'souldiers honoureable calling and imployment' and asserted that 'the profession of armes' had raised many from mean conditions to great honour.[88] The new armies of the Netherlands and especially Sweden commanded admiration. The Swedish defence was partly based, as one author put it, on the fact that 'the maritane parts not of Swethland onlye, but of Finland also, are for the most part environed with high and steepe rocky hils & Ilands', which made it difficult for strangers 'to saile neere their shore'. But it derived its main strength from military organization. 'The military forces' of Sweden were not 'forreine mercenary forces' but were 'culled and pickt out from among the choicest youth of the kingdome, by decimation, or taking every tenth man'. Becoming soldiers radically changed the status of Swedes, since as soon as they were enrolled 'they are not onely freed from all subsidies, impositions, or other payments whatsoever, but have also a yeerely stipend allowed them of the king'. That is to say, they were professional soldiers, exempt from taxation, constantly employed and paid by the king.[89]

But the traditional idea of the citizen militia received the widest acceptance. Robert Cotton insisted that 'for a safetie of a Common-wealth, the wisedome of all times did never interesse the publique cause to any other, then such as have a portion in the publique adventure',[90] whilst William Gouge maintained that 'Freemen, Freeborne, Native Subjects, Naturall Citizens' were also true soldiers. According to John Davenport, soldiers must not be like 'Hannibals Army, gathered of riff-raff, the reffuse, and dregs of the

---

87   John Hagthorpe, *Englands-Exchequer: or a discourse of the sea and navigation* (London, 1625), p. 7, cf. pp. 13–14, 21. Cf. William Hampton's sermon in favour of the benevolence, *A proclamation of warre from the lord of hosts … a sermon at Pauls Crosse Iuly the 23. 1626* (London, 1627), p. 36. According to Hampton, money was the '*nervus Belli*, without which Warre cannot subsist'; it was the subject's duty to 'part with a penny to enioy a pound'.

88   Richard Bernard, *The Bible-battells: or the sacred art military* (n.p. [London], 1629), pp. 31–7, see also pp. 63–5, 69–71, 152. Cf. e.g. Thomas Barnes, *Vox belli: or, an alarvm to warre* (London, 1626), p. 33; Edward Cooke, *The character of warre* (London, 1626), sig. B2^r–3^r.

89   Anon., *A short survey of the kingdome of Sweden* (London, 1632), pp. 6, 36–8, 50–3. It was as early as 1627 that the English first took interest in Sweden's success. Anon., *A trumpet to call souldiers on to noble actions* (London, 1627); [Alexander Gil], *The new starr of the north shining vpon the victorious king of Sweden* (1631) (London, 1632), pp. 25–9; John Russell, *The two famous pitcht battels of Lypsich and Lutzen* (Cambridge, 1634), pp. 11–12, 23; and especially Anon., *The Swedish discipline, religious, civile, and military* (London, 1632); Henry Hexham, *The principles of the art militarie* (n.p. 1637); idem, *The second part of the principle of the art militarie* (London, 1638); idem, *The third part of the principle of the art militarie* (The Hague, 1640).

90   [Cotton], *The danger*, p. 7; Burton, *Israels fast*, p. 3.

people, but a Company of worthy Cittizens'. Moreover, warfare should not become a separate trade or occupation. 'Whereas in other places, some are for Armes, some Artizans, some labourers,' in Switzerland 'all are Souldiers.' Men must not forget their 'particular callings' although they spend some time in training: 'So minde the exercises in the field, that you forget not necessary businesse in your shop.'[91]

The idea of the citizen militia was treated even more fully in Walter Ralegh's *The prerogatives of parliaments in England*, first published 'in these distracted Times' in 1628. If the king was not content with parliamentary subsidies, he might, like the French king, have to face numerous rebellions and would need foreign mercenary troops to suppress them. But imitating France implied giving up a strong army since 'the strength of England doth consist of the People and Yeomanry'. The fact that English yeomen owned their land and that their property could not be alienated without their consent rendered them economically independent. Although this made it somewhat more difficult for the king to raise taxes, at the same time it made Englishmen able soldiers.[92] The same argument was used in the 1628 parliament to criticize the Forced Loan. Nathaniel Rich said that if the subject did not have his property, there would be neither 'industry' nor 'valor'. For Dudley Digges, 'that king that is not limited rules slaves that cannot serve him' and he claimed in his famous example that because of their arbitrary government 'Muscovites' were no match for Englishmen. 'Let us', Edward Kirton asserted, 'be free Englishmen at home and valorous abroad.'[93]

When Charles informed the House of Commons on 4 June 1628 that he was determined to stick to his former answer to the Petition of Right, which the House had found unacceptable, and that he was going to dissolve parliament within a week, the king stung the MPs into an outburst.[94] On 5 June, John Eliot expressed fears of employing foreign mercenaries. 'We are weakened not only in our friends abroad but at home also. And there are drawn hither

---

[91] William Gouge, *Gods three arrowes: plague, famine, sword, in three treatises* (London, 1631), pp. 410–11; John Davenport, *A royall edict for military exercises: published in a sermon preached ... in Saint Andrewes Vndershaft, in London, Iune 23. 1629* (London, 1629), pp. 13–18; Knevet, *Stratiotikon*, sig. E4ʳ.

[92] Walter Ralegh, *The prerogatives of parliaments in England* (Middelburg, 1628), pp. 6–7. Cf. Thomas Overbury, *His observations in his travailes vpon the state of the XVII provinces as they stood anno dom. 1609* (n.p., 1626), pp. 12–16.

[93] *CD1628*, II, pp. 124, 66, 71, 299; cf. p. 334, III, pp. 187, 193. See e.g. Guy 1982; Reeve 1986; Cust 1987, pp. 4, 331–3; Reeve 1989, pp. 16–19.

[94] Cf. Russell 1979, p. 378.

praetorian bands and placed amongst us, and are drawn near this city.'[95] Although Eliot refrained from spelling out the implications of his speech, he was arguing that foreign mercenaries could become a dangerous weapon of arbitrary government. Next day John Strange-ways expressed the same fear and told the Commons that scattering billeted soldiers and importing 'troops of Germany horse' would not contribute to the defence of the kingdom since 'England is not so weak as to need such succor.' He was backed by many of his colleagues. According to Eliot, 'the drawing on of foreign horses' was utterly useless since 'our English are not of so poor heart and courage but that we are able to make our King great at home and abroad'. When Sir Humphrey May told the Commons that 'the Germany horses were not for England' but 'for a foreign service', Eliot bluntly replied that 'no man doubts of his Majesty. But our fear is that, contrary to his good thoughts, the horses may be brought to his prejudice and the prejudice of the kingdom.'[96] The defence of the kingdom could only be entrusted to her citizens.

This way of thinking about the militia and mercenaries emerges clearly when Sir John Maynard, who had close relations with Buck-ingham, spoke on 7 June. Relying on Machiavelli, 'an author in fashion', he said that all armies were composed either of countrymen or strangers. In the former case there were two possibilities: they were either 'trained bands' or 'mercenary' and, as he said, according to Machiavelli it was 'absolutely a destruction of a country to entertain mercenaries'. This rule also applied to foreign troops in general since they were useless regardless of whether they were 'valiant or coward'. If they were cowards, 'all is lost' and if they were valiant, the prince would become their 'prisoner'. Maynard drew the conclusion that 'this nation [is] never happy to employ strangers: the King has brave soldiers of his own subjects'.[97]

The same idea found its way into the Commons' Remonstrance – a report of the present state of the realm addressed to the king in case he had been systematically misled. Most menacing, the Commons told Charles, was 'the report of the strange and dangerous purpose of bringing in German horse and riders'. Although the Commons grate-

---

[95] *CD1628*, IV, p. 117; II, 62. Cf. in general 'A letter', in *Somers tracts*, IV, pp. 111–12. See also M[atthieu], *The powerfull favorite*, p. 2; Virgilio Malvezzi, *Romulus and Tarquin*, translated by [Henry Carey] (London, 1637), pp. 160–1, where the 'Guard' is linked with tyranny. Cf. Schoewerer 1974, pp. 19–32.

[96] *CD1628*, IV, 145–9, 244; Reeve 1989, p. 27.

[97] *CD1628*, IV, pp. 188–9.

fully acknowledged the king's assurances that these foreign troops were not intended for use in England, they wanted to point out that the very idea of employing foreign troops was totally at odds with the freedom of the English people. It was not easy to 'be ignorant that the bringing in of strangers for aid has been pernicious to most states where they have been admitted, but to England fatal'. The only way to defend the kingdom was to have an army of countrymen. 'We', the Commons told the king, 'are bold to declare to your Majesty and the whole world that we hold it far beneath the heart of any free Englishman to think that this victorious nation should now stand in need of German soldiers to defend their own King and kingdom.'[98]

In Thomas May's *The tragedy of Julia Agrippina*, acted in 1628, the praetorian guard, 'The German souldiers', played a central role in the corrupt intrigues of the imperial court.[99] Later in autumn 1628, Alexander Leighton asked: 'Why are the strangers within us gott up above us ... a sort of rude, Barbarous, needlesse, and uselesse souldiers (without Example in a free nation?).'[100]

England's withdrawal from the European war in 1630 did not terminate the furious debate over the issues of war and militia.[101] Robert Johnson argued against Bacon when he noted in his 1630 edition of Botero's *Relations* that 'although some men will not suffer money to be called the sinewes of warre', there were cases where money alone would carry the day.[102] But he also appended to his account (though without acknowledgement) several passages from Bacon's essay on the greatness of states. Most importantly, he cited Bacon to the effect that a warlike disposition required freedom and a light burden of taxes. Moreover, the strength of the Englishman was grounded on Henry VII's prudent land policy.[103]

A similar argument was presented by George Tooke in *The legend of*

---

[98] Ibid., IV, pp. 314–15.

[99] May, *Julia Agrippina*, I, 12–13, 537–9; IV, 294–7, 305–12, 789–94; V, 5–10.

[100] Leighton, *An appeal to the parliament*, pp. 146–7.

[101] E.g. G[ervase] M[arkham], 'The muster-master' [1630?], ed. Charles L. Hamilton, Camden Society, 4th ser., XIV *Camden miscellany*, 26 (1975); Xenophon, *Cyropaedia: the institution and life of Cyrus*, translated by Philemon Holland (London, 1632), the dedication to the king by Henry Holland, sig. PP8ʳ; Gerratt Barry, *A discourse of military discipline, devided into three bookes* (Brussels, 1634); William Barriffe, *Military discipline: or, the yong artillery man* (London, 1635); idem, *Mars his triumph: or, the description of an exercise performed the xvii. of October, 1638 in Merchant-Taylors Hall* (London, 1639); Gervase Markham, *The souldiers accidence: or an introduction into military discipline* (London, 1635); see also Henry Hexham's treatises mentioned above in n.52.

[102] Giovanni Botero, *Relations of the most famous kingdomes and common-wealths thorowout the world*, translated by R[obert] J[ohnson], (London, 1630), p. 34.

[103] Botero, *Relations*, pp. 28–9; see pp. 21, 25–6, 27, 29, 30, 39–41.

Brita-mart published in 1635. Tooke began the tract, organized as a dialogue, by asserting that the soldier was a central 'complexion' in the 'body politicke', as the example of 'illustrious Sparta' and the accounts of 'our moderne critickes' easily proved. If one examined 'the facility and open site of our present England; respecting her want of fatnesse, or fortification', it was easy to decide that she did not have an 'other refuge' than 'the Souldiers brest'. It was useless and fatal to assume that 'ambition and the thirst of Empire' had become 'extinct' or that it had been 'transplanted farre away to the Antipodes'. The urgent need for soldiers was due to the profound imperial aspirations of states and the only method of adapting oneself to these conditions was to have a powerful army. 'Are wee not', Tooke wrote, 'daily surrounded with a further accesse of power, and more compact then formerly?' If the state did not want to 'lie at the devotion of every hungry pretender', the only solution was to rely 'rather upon our owne abilities'.[104]

The importance of one's own army was put across by two arguments. First, it was extremely dangerous to rely on foreign help.[105] But in England it was equally fatal to rely on the sea and the navy alone. Tooke confessed that it was possible to argue that 'the sea' was 'our moate' and that 'our armado' had been 'such a wall as hitherto has bin invincible'.[106] But this argument, he was convinced, did not stand up to scrutiny. Bacon had demonstrated that 'the foot-combatant' was superior in comparison with 'the horseman' and to the navy. The navy in particular was vulnerable to the blind forces of fortune. As Tooke put it in a rhetorical question, 'must our maine rest be set up, I say, upon such uncertainties'? Since the 'wooden wall' was 'so tickle' it was much more 'expedient' to place trust in 'our yron one, our infantery'.[107] The infantry should consist of free farmers. According to Tooke, 'my Lord of S. Alban' had convincingly demonstrated the warlike capacities of 'this midle people, betweene Cottagers and gentlemen'.[108]

It is of some importance to note that Tooke was at pains to refute the central role of the navy in the defence of England just at the time when a propaganda campaign for the navy and the

---

104 George Tooke, *The legend of Brita-mart* (London, 1635), sig. B2^r–v.
105 Ibid., sigs. B4^v–5^r, B7^r–C1^v.
106 Ibid., sig. B3^r.
107 Ibid., sig. B3^r–v, B6^v.
108 Ibid., sig. C3^v. See also Robert Powell, *Depopulation arraigned, convicted and condemned, by the lawes of God and man* (London, 1636), pp. 6–8, 20–30, 32, 35, 40–6, 60–1, 96, 104–5; Thomas Nash, *Qvaternio: or a fovrefold way to a happie life* (London, 1633), pp. 4–6.

urgent need of maritime supremacy was launched in support of ship money.[109] According to Henry Valentine, 'shipping is the very nerves, and sinewes, the strength and security of a nation' and particularly 'our ships are (and so they may well be) called the walls of our Kingdome'. Thomas Powell pointed out that since England was an island, 'a Sea-Soldier' was 'more usefull to his Country' than 'a Land Soldier'.[110] Preaching in Bristol in 1635, Thomas Palmer told his listeners that 'it is lawfull for a prince to defend the Title and Jurisdiction of his Seas: and offend those who would intrench upon them'. This was of particular importance to England not only since 'the sea is our Wall' but also since 'our best (though wooden) Battlements is our navy'. As a result, it was 'a provident care of our gratious Soveraigne to incircle our Iland with a stately Royall Navy', and it was the subject's duty to be 'thankfull unto him in our Loyal and liberall asisstance'. Repeating the old commonplace that treasures were 'the sinewes of war', Palmer exhorted his countrymen as follows: 'Let not our purse bee narrow, because our seas are so.'[111]

Although the ideas of the citizen militia and its social foundation were thus elaborated with occasional reference to the republican tradition, a word of caution is in place here. For all the insistence on the free husbandman carrying arms, it is clear that these accounts stopped short of a fully fledged republican argument. This becomes clear in the authors' willingness to employ a conspicuously different repertoire of instances.[112] An English militia, Tooke wrote, had already appeared in Saxon times when King Etheldred had been 'miserably harassed by the Dane'. He had, therefore, decided that 'every eight

---

[109] John Boroughs, *The sovereignty of the British seas* (1633), ed. T. C. Wade (Edinburgh, 1920), pp. 41, 454–6, 49, 76–7; John Selden, *Mare clausum seu de dominio maris* (London, 1635), sig. b2ʳ, pp. 185–6; see the translation, *Of the dominion, or, ownership of the sea*, translated by Marchamont Nedham (London, 1652), sig. e2ᵛ, pp. 128–9; cf. Barrett 1964. See also S. R. Gardiner, *The constitutional documents of the Puritan Revolution 1628–1660* (Oxford: Clarendon Press, 1889), pp. 37–9; Giovanni Botero, *The cause of the greatness of cities: with certain observations concerning the sea*, translated by Sir T. H. (London, 1635), pp. 179–236; Marcotte 1975, p. 164, n.3; Adams 1983, pp. 84, 100; Loomie 1986, pp. 39–42; Swales 1977; Gordon 1910; Andrews 1991, pp. 128–59; Woolf 1990, p. 244. For the opposition, see Rowe 1962; Bard 1977.

[110] Henry Valentine, *Fovre sea-sermons, preached at the annuall meeting of the Trinitie Companie, in the parish church of Deptford* (London, 1635), p. 9. Powell, *The art of thriving*, p. 101.

[111] Thomas Palmer, *Bristolls military garden: a sermon preached unto the worthy company of practisers in the military garden of the well governed citie of Bristoll* (London, 1635), pp. 15–16; Thomas Heywood, *A true description of his majesties royall ship, built this yere 1637 at Wolwitch* (London, 1637), especially pp. 24–5.

[112] Schwoerer 1974, pp. 12–15.

hides of land throughout the Kingdome' should provide 'a corselet'.[113]
Bacon had strongly emphasized the value of free and sturdy farmers,
but even he had readily argued that 'Servants and Attendants upon
Noblemen and Gentlemen' were 'no waies inferiour, unto the Yeomanry', in so far as they were 'Free'.[114] Robert Johnson quoted this
passage from Bacon, pointing out that when 'the Lord of the Mannor'
had been called 'to serve the King', he had taken 'his Tenants' with
him.[115] Englishmen blended, in other words, the classical republican
tradition with their indigenous medieval and feudal inheritance.

The second way in which the humanist tradition still exercised some
influence on the early Caroline England of the 1630s was in the terms
of the *vita activa*. To Daniel Tuvill, 'Contemplation' was 'but a glorious
title invented onely, to set a glosse uppon a base and idle disposition'. It
was in 'action' alone that 'a man doth better him-selfe, and benefite
others'. Whereas philosophers' labours were mostly useless 'sophisticall
Elenches' (i.e. sophisms) tending 'to outward pompe and ostentation',
truly wise was only he 'whose Knowledge is more for Profit, them for
Show'.[116] William Gouge wondered whether it was the same man he
saw in a forenoon 'sitting, and giving advice among the wise Senators
of our City, and in an afternoone marching before the Martiall
Gentlemen'. But before long he recalled that the best amongst the
Romans, such as Brutus and Scipio, had been 'both *Togati and Armati*,
prudent Consuls, potent Captaines'.[117]

A particular form of presenting the values of the active life and true
nobility had been the highly polished manuals for a gentleman's
education. Although this genre had a long history, it was particularly
popular in England from Thomas Elyot to Henry Peacham. In the
early Caroline period, this tradition was vigorously continued by
Richard Brathwait. He first treated these issues in his long but popular
The English gentleman, published in 1630 and reprinted three years later.

---

[113] Tooke, *The legend of Brita-mart*, sig. B5ᵛ. It should be noted that ship money was associated with
Etheldred's Danegeld; Boroughs, *The sovereingty*, pp. 50–2; Selden, *Of the dominion*, pp. 260,
262–3, 296–7. Cf. [William Prynne], *An humble remonstrance to his maiesty, against the tax of ship-
money* (n.p., 1641), pp. 35–46; John Rusworth, *Historicall collections* (London, 1682), I, p. 362.

[114] Bacon, 'Of the true greatnesse of kingdomes and estates', in *Essayes*, p. 93.

[115] Botero, *Relations*, p. 29.

[116] Daniel Tuvill, *Vade mecum: a manuall of essayes morrall, theologicall* (London, 1629), pp. 4–5, 10–11,
22–3. Cf. e.g. John Taylor, *An armado, or nauye, of 103 ships & other vessels* (London, 1627), sig.
A7ʳ⁻ᵛ; Bartenio Holyday, *Philosophiae polito-barbarae specimen* (Oxford, 1633), pp. 170–3, 137–42;
Anon., *Vertues reward wherein the living are incouraged unto good workes* (n.p. [Amsterdam], 1639), pp.
2–3, 4–5, 6; Anon., *Satyrae seriae*, pp. 16–17, 45–7. William Pemble, *A summe of morall philosophy*
(Oxford, 1632), pp. 1–2, 5–7.

[117] William Gouge, *Gods three arrowes*, pp. 406–7.

The same set of values was further endorsed in his enlarged edition of the *The schollers medley*, entitled *A survey of history: or, a nursery for gentry*, which appeared in 1638.

Brathwait's avowed intention in *The English gentleman* was to explain what belonged 'to the making up of an Accomplish'd Gentleman'. This goal was of great significance, since 'the Gentry of this age' was effeminate and depraved.[118] Brathwait opened the treatise with a definition: 'vertue the greatest Signall and Symbol of Gentry: is rather expressed by goodnesse of Person, than greatnesse of Place'. He contrasted true nobility with the perverted idea of nobility maintained by 'the bleere-ey'd vulgar'. Whilst the latter was based on 'the purple', 'descent' and 'title', true nobility consisted of 'the person', 'desert' and 'merit'.[119] It was virtue alone which led the way 'to the true sight and light of glory'.[120]

The same conclusion also emerged in *A survey of history*. In *The schollers medley*, we recall, Brathwait gave an account of virtue in which he emphasized the values of patience, moderation and forbearance. He continued in *A survey of history* to offer an essentially stoic account, maintaining that a man ought to learn 'to be a Soveraigne over his owne passions: and to restraine the surging billowes of an over-flowing will, to the command of Reason'. He lamented, moreover, that it was 'the misery' of his times that due respect was not always fixed 'upon Merit', that singularly equipped persons 'sleepe many times in silence, unregarded, at least unrewarded: while more sterile Conceipts receive advancement'. But he still repeated the conviction, already put forward in *The schollers medley*, that true honour derived from one's own meritorous deeds and added that honour was only won 'by passing through Vertues Temple'.[121] Perusing 'the Lives of many of those eminent Orators, Athenian & Roman pleaders', it was easy to see that 'their beginnings [had been] obscure; their Meanes of rising small; and for their outward parts' they had been 'weakely promised' but yet 'their inward abilities' had been

118 Richard Brathwait, *The English gentleman* (London, 1630), sig. ¶2ʳ. It is of some significance to note that Brathwait explicitly compared his own treatise with that of Henry Peacham and found Peacham's account much wanting, sig. ¶2ᵛ.
119 Ibid., the epistle dedicatory. Cf. e.g. Anthony Stafford, *Honour and vertue, triumphing over the grave* (London, 1640), pp. 9–11, 15–16, 18; R[ichard] H[erne], *Ros coeli: or a miscellany of ejaculations, divine, morall, &c* (London, 1640), pp. 185–6.
120 Brathwait, *The English gentleman*, p. 113.
121 Richard Brathwait, *A survey of history: or, a nursery for gentry* (London, 1638), pp. 63, 96, 257–8, 119; cf. *The English gentleman*, pp. 110–13.

such that they had soon become 'a glory to their Countrey; a renowne to themselves and their surviving posterity'.[122]

This notion of true nobility was closely linked with another familiar concept – the active life. It is perhaps fair to say that a central theme in *The English gentleman* was the exposition of this idea. Brathwait opened his assessment in the customary way, by extolling the merits of contemplation. 'It is', he assured his readers, 'rare and wonderfull to observe what admirable Contemplations the Heathen Philosophers enjoyed.' But the chief benefits of *otium* were closely associated with Christianity. If the heathens could enjoy contemplation without being 'partakers of the least glimpse of that glorious light which is to us revealed', it was almost impossible to describe the happiness of Christian contemplation. In order to be free from the hindrances of 'any wordly objects', it was best 'to with-draw our eye from the Creature, and fix it wholly upon our Creator'.[123]

Pursuing the topic further, Brathwait adopted quintessentially 'civic' humanist tactics and quickly changed his priorities. There was little doubt that *otium* was 'sweet and delightfull' for its practioners; but 'in respect of humanity' it was 'too unsociable'.[124] Although it had sometimes been regarded more valuable than action by virtue of its difficulty, Brathwait was fully convinced that as a matter of fact this was not the case. For as he pointed out, things are 'easier to discourse of than to finde: for men naturally have a desire to know all things, but to doe nothing; so easie is the Contemplative in respect of the Active, so hard the Practicke in respect of the Speculative'. We do not attain our perfection 'by knowledge only, or Contemplation', but mainly 'by seconding or making good our knowledge by Action'. 'Wee are therefore', Brathwait reiterated a little later, 'not only to know, but to doe' and he added that 'it is little or to no purpose, that wee know, conceive, or apprehend, unlesse we make a fruitfull use of that knowledge by serious practice, to the benefit of our selves and others'.[125] It was his principal aim to demonstrate that although 'those, who continued in a Contemplative and solitary life, sequestring themselves from the cares and company of this world doubtlesly conceived ineffable comfort in that sweet

122 Brathwait, *A survey of history*, pp. 259–61, see also pp. 23, 67–8, 381–2, 297–8; *The English gentleman*, p. 70.
123 Brathwait, *The English gentleman*, pp. 382–6.
124 Ibid., p. 387. Cf. however, idem, *Essaies vpon the five senses, revived by a new supplement*, 2nd edn (London, 1635), p. 157; idem, *Whimzies: or, a new cast of characters* (London, 1631), pp. 98–104.
125 Brathwait, *The English gentleman*, pp. 391–2, 400; cf. pp. 135, 403, 91–3.

retirement: yet in regard they lived not in the world, the world was not bettered by their example'.[126]

Brathwait singled out three reasons for the superiority of the active life. On the most general level, he argued that since the ultimate aim of man's pursuits was virtue, this had immediate bearing upon his choice between *otium* and *negotium*. This was so because 'vertue consisteth in Action'. It was hence impossible 'to be favourers, followers, or furtherers of vertue', as long as 'wee surcease from Action, which is the life, light, and subsistence of vertue'.[127] Secondly, the active life enabled men to avoid idleness and to embrace labour and diligence. Whereas idleness was the cause of 'all vices', labour was the 'supporter of all vertues'.[128]

Finally and most importantly, *negotium* made it possible to be of benefit to one's fellow men. The man of *negotium* could be a *homo faber* but he was still chiefly a *homo politicus*. Whereas 'a private or retired life estranged [a man] from humane societie' and 'deprived others of the benefit', an active life tended 'to the common good' and the 'benefit or utilitie of humane societie'.[129] It was man's highest duty – the point of perfection in his life – to act in a way which profited the public good. The solitary life of the *otium*, Brathwait pointed out, was 'fitter for a Cell then a Court'. He would have young gentlemen become not 'Hermits' but active members of their community; he wanted them to address themselves 'to those studies, exercises and labours, which may benefit the Church or Common-wealth'.[130] It followed that the *vita activa* was mainly associated with political activities. The gentleman's public vocation was employment 'in affaires of State, either at home or abroad'.[131] His duty was to minister matters 'unto others' and he needed to be well versed in rhetoric, in order to be able to perform his duty 'in publike assemblies'.[132] The Athenian and Roman orators, as Brathwait wrote in *A survey of history*, had been most steadfast 'in their Opposition to the greatest Enemies of State, they [had] stood constant for the liberty of their Countrey, and suppressing all such ... as [had] fished in troubled Waters, or [had] inclined to mutiny'. This meant

---

[126] Ibid., p. 407. For a different interpretation, see Wright 1958, pp. 126–8, where Brathwait's ideas are accounted for puritanism. Cf. Walzer 1965, pp. 250–3.
[127] Brathwait, *The English gentleman*, p. 400.
[128] Ibid., pp. 103–7, cf. pp. 46–7; *A survey of history*, pp. 165–6. Cf. e.g. Nash, *Qvaternio*, sig.)(3ʳ.
[129] Brathwait, *The English gentleman*, pp. 407–9.
[130] Ibid., pp. 388–9, 397.
[131] Ibid., pp. 136, 47.
[132] Ibid., pp. 397, 88.

that it was 'Merit' which had held sway 'in the Court of Justice' and that 'Corruption' had been 'a stranger to the hand or heart of a Counsellour'. In their undertakings, Brathwait emphasized, they had aimed 'neither at publique fame, nor private safety' but had geared all their actions and 'the whole bent of their Councels to the improvement and security of their Countrey'.[133] Cicero, 'that Prince of Oratory', had given a preeminent place to 'The Gowne', to those who excelled 'in Elegancy of Speech, mannaging of judiciall Causes, and steering State-affaires'.[134]

Faithful to the tradition, Brathwait argued in both *The English gentleman* and *A survey of history* that the chief means of inculcating the young with a proper sense of virtue, honour and the common good was to pay close attention to their education. *The English gentleman* was, of course, cast in the form of an educational treatise and a central chapter dealt with these issues in more detail. In youth a man was like 'the Philosophers *rasa tabula*', he was like clay in the hands of his tutor. This pointed, in the first place, to the idea of meritocracy. For if men were like *tabulae rasae* in their youth, it followed, of course, that it was not so much their lineage or ancient wealth as their ensuing life which determined their place in the commonwealth. Secondly, and more importantly, the conviction that a man's mind was like an empty canvas at birth demonstrated the overriding importance of education; the mind was 'apt to receive any good impressure'.[135] As a result, it was relatively easy to demonstrate the 'absolute power' of education. 'For shall wee not see some,' Brathwait wrote, 'whose faire outsides promise assured arguments of singular worth, for want of breeding meere painted Trunks, glorious features, yet shallow Creatures? and whence commeth this, but through want of that which makes man accomplished, seconding nature with such exquisite ornaments, as they enable him for all managements publike or private?'[136] The chief aim of education was not merely to impart knowledge but also to teach how to put this knowledge into action. Knowledge gained in education was but 'barren, fruitlesse and livelesse', if it was not 'reduced to Action'.[137]

Although Brathwait claimed in *The English gentleman* in a somewhat

---

133 Brathwait, *A survey of history*, pp. 260–2.
134 Ibid., pp. 259, 263–6.
135 Brathwait, *The English gentleman*, p. 4.
136 Ibid., p. 92.
137 Ibid., pp. 99–101.

platitudinous and stereotyped manner that peace, plenty and ambition endangered the pursuit of virtues and the public good,[138] it ought to be remembered that the treatise appeared just after the serious deadlock between the king and parliament in the spring of 1629 and just when Charles was leading England away from the European war.[139] If we interpret Brathwait's treatise, to a certain extent, as a response to the political events and circumstances of the early years of Charles's reign, it would be possible to say that his solution to the internal problems of England was a vigorous defence of the traditional humanist idea of implanting virtues in the political nation which would enable its serious involvement in a virtuous *negotium* for the good of the commonwealth.

A survey of history, with its strong emphasis on the values of the active life, was likewise published after a decade of personal rule. Brathwait declared that 'even those Republicks' which 'promised to themselves most security, were enforced to runne into other channels' and had ultimately met their destruction. To provide a more tangible instance, Brathwait resorted to the history of the Roman republic. Before the destruction of Carthage, the republic had been almost like 'a brave Platonicke Common-weale'. At that time, Rome had 'both quietly and modestly govern'd her affaires'. This amounted, according to Brathwait, to a state of affairs, where 'there was no contending nor contesting for glory nor command amongst her Citizens; they guided all things peaceably, and succeeded in all things prosperously'. These blissful circumstances had, however, been destroyed as soon as the 'antient Kings-evill', ambition, or the 'desire of raigning and invading' had begun to hold sway. The point he stressed was that these ancient instances were applicable to 'these present times', but apart from briefly mentioning the ills of private property, he did not elaborate on this point.[140]

In addition to the idea of the militia and the virtuous civic life, it is possible to find traces of a more distinctively republican outlook in the 1630s.[141] It is of course true that a number of continental treatises

---

[138] Ibid., pp. 30–2, 34–9.

[139] See e.g. Reeve 1989, pp. 99–117.

[140] Brathwait, *A survey of history*, pp. 4, 336; cf. pp. 44–5, 166–7, pp. 274–7, where Brathwait censured 'vicious Pamphletters' who advanced anything 'noxious or malignant' 'to the State', 'our Statizing Pamphletters' who 'under borrowed names have strucke at high Personages' and those who condemned 'Recreations of indifferency, for no other cause, but because they are countenanc'd by Majesty'. See Butler 1984, for Brathwait's career in the early 1640s.

[141] For the American puritan colonies, see Kupperman 1989.

emphasizing monarchical authority were translated into English in the 1630s,[142] but to concentrate exclusively upon these is to overlook a different series of translations.[143] Polybius was translated into English in 1633 and was twice reprinted during the next two years.[144] Edward Dacres's well-known translation of Machiavelli's *Discorsi* appeared in 1636 and a year later Henry Carey published his translation of Virgilio Malvezzi's somewhat more aristocratic and sceptical treatises *Il Romvlo* and *Il Tarqvinio svperbo*.[145]

Dacres had no difficulty in tracing the central argument of the *Discorsi*. Machiavelli had aimed, he wrote, at discovering 'the first foundations' and 'the very grounds, upon which the Romane Commonwealth was built, and afterwards rose to such glory and power, that neither before nor after all the ages of the world ever afforded the like example'.[146] Dacres claimed that the *Discorsi* would present the duke of Lennox, to whom he dedicated the translation, with 'a good seacard' and would make him fully equipped to assume an active role 'neare the helme' 'in this our ship of State'. In times of peace and quiet, it was mainly 'allyance, bloud, and favour' which counted when it came to preferments; 'yet when the times grow perplex'd with perills and difficulties, true worth and experience are sought after'. And since 'no climate is so benigne, as to afford a perpetuall calme', it was safest to be prepared for more stormy weather. Dacres thus wanted to remind the duke that more 'turbulent times' were ahead and that Machiavelli would teach him how to provide for them.[147] Dacres was not, however, unaware of the weaknesses and even outright errors of the *Discorsi*. He wrote: 'Nothwithstanding however my Author in what he hath done well, hath farre excell'd others, yet is he not without his blemishes and errours too.' In consequence, to make

142 Philippe de Béthune, *The covnsellor of estate: contayning the greatest and most remarkeable considerations serving for the managing of publicke affaires*, translated by E[dward] G[rimeston] (London, 1634); Etienne Molinier, *A mirrovr for christian states: or, a table of politick vertues considerable amongst christians*, translated by William Tyrwhit (London, 1635); Juan de Santa Maria, *Christian policie: or, the christian common-wealth*, translated by [Edward Blount] (London, 1632), pp. 6–7; Nicholas Faret, *The honest man: or the art to please in court*, translated by Edward Grimestone (London, 1632).

143 Sharpe 1989, pp. 17–18.

144 Polybius, *The history of Polybivs the Megalopolitan*, translated from French by Edward Grimeston (London, 1634). Cf. Worden 1991a, p. 445.

145 Malvezzi, *Romvlvs and Tarqvin.*

146 Niccolo Machiavelli, *Discovrses upon the first decade of T. Livius*, translated by Edward Dacres (London, 1636), sig. A4[r–v].

147 Ibid., sig. A4[v]–6[r].

the *Discorsi* even better, Dacres noted all Machiavelli's 'notorious errors' and 'added some observations'.[148]

Not surprisingly, the bulk of Dacres's misgivings concerned the role of religion in the *Discorsi*. It had been Machiavelli's error to bring 'the mistresse to serve the handmaid, religion to serve policy'.[149] Dacres also criticized Machiavelli for having discarded the cardinal virtue of justice. He had erroneously stated that promises need not be kept and that a prince must have 'guile', using both the lion's force and the fox's craft. These convictions could easily be countered, Dacres believed, on the authority of Cicero.[150] Moreover, Dacres did not accept Machiavelli's contention that whereas persuasiveness could easily reduce 'a licentious and tumultuous people' 'to reason', 'a mischeivous Prince' could be remedied by 'the sword' alone. Dacres saw this as an attempt to justify resistance for which he found 'no warrant from divine or humane lawes'.[151]

Dacres's final scruple concerned Machiavelli's argument that the good of the community and that of the prince were often irreconcilable. In his own conception, grounded on the hierarchic view of society, the prince and the people made 'onely one politique body' and their aims, in most cases, overlapped. For Dacres, problems arose not because the king had a wholly different set of goals from that of the people, but because of a possible disequilibrium in the balance of the body politic, as in the case when 'a Princes exchequer ... excessively abounds' and in the end 'beggers the whole country'.[152] Dacres did not disagree with Machiavelli as much about the danger of the prince's possible greed as about the way to conceptualize this.

There are two conclusions to be drawn from Dacres's commentary on Machiavelli. Firstly, in 1636 he was willing to endorse the view that the prince's covetousness could ultimately ruin the whole country. Secondly and more importantly, he did not censure Machiavelli's republicanism. Even when Dacres commented on those chapters where Machiavelli had stated his republicanism most openly, he was totally silent about this and instead concentrated on minor points of detail. Despite Dacres's reticence, some theorists argued that far from being disastrous, the republican form of government could in fact turn out to

---

[148] Ibid., sig. A6ʳ⁻ᵛ.
[149] Ibid., pp. 567–8; 1.12, 11.2, 5, 11.30, pp. 66–8, 265–6, 284–5, 581–3.
[150] Ibid., pp. 318–19; 11.13, cf. pp. 48–50; 1.19, 18.
[151] Ibid., pp. 234–6; 1.58.
[152] Ibid., pp. 260–2.

be, to some extent, highly beneficial. One author pointed out that the excellence of Sweden was based not simply on her system of forming a professional army but also on the peculiar fact that in the Swedish parliament the peasants had their own estate; coming somewhat inadvertently to the crux of the idea of Nordic liberty, an anonymous author wrote: 'the countrye people' had 'a voyce as well as any of the others' in their 'Parliaments'. It was mainly because of this that the idea of meritocracy had flourished in Sweden; 'the meanest or lowest degree is not neglected, nor no well deserving subject hindered to climbe to as high a pitch of honour, as his vertues can attaine unto'.[153]

Even more relevant to the English context was Francis Rous's use of republican examples in his description of the government of England in the _Archaeologiae Atticae_ in 1637. He not only described the Polybian cycles of governments, but he also argued that the English form of government matched those of Athens and Venice. Rous began by giving a detailed account of the Athenian great council. 'The authority of this Councel', he explained, 'was great, for it handled causes of war, tributes making of Lawes, civill businesses and events, affaires of confederates, collections of money, performance of sacred rites' and a number of minor tasks. This council was reminiscent, in the first place, of 'the Venetian Gran Consiglio, or Senate' as portrayed by Contarini. But it no less resembled the way in which England was governed. Resorting to the authority of Thomas Smith, Rous asserted that by the consent of 'our Court of Parliament in England' 'all Lawes are abrogated, new made, right and possessions of private men changed, formes of religion established, Subsidies, Tailes, Taxes, and impositions appointed, waights and measures altered, &c'.[154]

At one point in _A survey of history_ Brathwait maintained that, whereas under the 'Democratick Government or headlesse Monster' merits were not properly rewarded, a knowing Prince' could measure 'the value of mens actions' and was, therefore, capable of offering just rewards.[155] But in his exposition of the merits and honours of the ancient orators he drew an opposite conclusion. Like a number of Englishmen before him, we recall, Brathwait argued

[153] Anon., _A short survey_, p. 41, in general see pp. 34–46.
[154] Francis Rous [Jr], _Archaeologiae Atticae libri tres: three bookes of the Attick antiquities_ (Oxford, 1637), pp. 28–35, 104–9. Cf. in general John Randol, _Noble Blastus: the honor of a Lord Chamberlaine: and of a good bedchamber-man: a sermon preacht the 27. of March, 1631_ (London, 1633), p. 19.
[155] Brathwait, _A survey of history_, p. 54.

that the idea of true nobility had materialized most successfully in republics. 'The Athenians' had conferred the greatest amount of honour 'upon their Consuls, Orators and Philosophers'. Similarly, in Sparta 'the Ephori', who were equivalent to the Roman tribunes, 'were elected not in respect of their descent but of their desert: which made a flourishing State; seeing, there was none, were he never so ignoble by birth, but he received grace, if his inward abilities deserved such respect'. But the most remarkable example was provided by Rome. Discoursing 'of the Civill government of the Romans', Brathwait observed that the Romans had reached the pinnacle of greatness 'during their Democracy', and they 'delighted in nothing more then advancing such, who employed their tongues or penns in defence of the publique liberty', for 'that victorious State' was most grateful 'to deserving men'.[156]

Perhaps a proper conclusion to this chapter is, however, a note of caution. Although the prevalent ways of speaking about politics in absolutist circles were to emphasize the divine nature of the king's earthly authority, to point to the necessity of the king's undertakings and to belittle the role of the subject,[157] the humanist vocabulary could also be manipulated for strongly absolutist ends. In his Tacitean treatise, *Augustus*, which was similar to Joseph Wybarne's account as well as to 'A discourse upon the beginning of Tacitus' in the *Horae subseciuae*, Peter Heylyn examined 'those meanes and counsels, whereby the common-wealth of Rome was altered, and reduced unto a monarchy'. He depicted the constitutional history of Rome essentially in terms of Polybian cycles. But he did not draw the Polybian conclusion about the merits of the mixed constitution. In theory it was possible to argue that if the people had acquired their proper share in government, the commonwealth would have become immortal. But in practice it had turned out to be impossible to achieve an 'equall mixture of Plebeians and Patritians'. Confusion had, in effect, continued to hold sway, until the Roman commonwealth had regressed to a monarchy.[158] The bulk of Heylyn's treatise was devoted to demonstrating the methods which Octavian had employed to consolidate his

---

[156] Ibid., p. 263.
[157] Robert Sibthorpe, *Apostolike obedience: shewing the duty of subiects to pay tribute and taxes to their princes ... a sermon preached at Northampton, at the assises, for the countie, Feb. 22. 1626* (London, 1627), sig. A2^v, pp. 9–15; John Featley, *Obedience and submission: a sermon preached at St Saviours-church in South-warke, at a visitation, on Tuesday, the eight day of December: anno dom. 1635* (London, 1636). Cf. in general Hampton, *A proclamation of warre*, especially p. 36; Mendle 1989b.
[158] Peter Heylyn, *Augustus* (London, 1632), pp. 7–10, 13–22.

authority. By and large, he had done this partly by force and partly with guile.[159] Octavian had 'assumed to himselfe the Imperiall, Censoriall, and Tribunitian authority together with the Sacerdotall dignity'. Since he had made himself 'Emperor and Generall of the men of Warre', he had been in a position to 'presse Soldiers, raise Taxes, proclaime wars, make peace; yea and put to death the very best and stoutest of the Senators'. But in order to establish and secure his power, Octavian had organized Rome as a mixed state. The consuls had continued to discuss 'Matters of State' and the commons had 'assembled in Comitia, to enact Lawes, and elect Magistrates'. Nevertheless, Heylyn made it clear that the purpose of these arrangements had been to sweeten the pill of Octavian's absolute authority. Nothing had been done without his consent and he had prescribed 'Lawes and Orders as himselfe [had] listed'.[160]

A more openly political use of similar issues can be found in Henry Peacham's *The dvty of all trve svbiects to their king*, published in the spring of 1639. In the epistle to the reader, Peacham claimed that, according to Plato, the ideal commonwealth included three elements: the king, the nobility and the commons. The most precious value of commonwealths was thus unity; 'every Common-wealth is in hazard to be ruined, when of a third joyned with a first are made two severall or disagreeing harmonies'. The unity of 'those three Estates' was essential for the subsistence of the commonwealth.[161] Peacham also referred to the 'glorious acts and noble atchievements' of the ancients both 'for the preservation and defence' and 'for the enlargement' of their countries, such as those of Marcus Brutus who had risked his life 'to set his Countrie at libertie' and 'Junius Brutus' who had defended the commonwealth against his own sons and witnessed their beheading.[162] He invoked the most cherished exponents of the Roman republic so as to argue that the subject's crucial duties were loyalty and obedience.[163] Everyone should be most willing to defend their country against 'forreigne enemies or domesticke, and homebred Traytors and Rebels',

---

[159] Ibid., see especially pp. 35–8, 40–1, 49–51, 89–90, 93, 107–9, 111, 112–16, 157–60, 163.

[160] Ibid., pp. 116–19, 120–4, 142, 147, 150. Woolf 1990, pp. 183–6. See also Mendle 1985, p. 112, and more generally Smuts 1987, pp. 258–60.

[161] H[enry] P[eacham], *The dvty of all trve svbiects to their king: as also to their native countrey, in time of extremity and danger* (London, 1639), sig. *3ʳ–4ʳ. Cf. Lord Ellesmere's use of a similar vocabulary against the enlargement of 'the Popular state' in 1611: Thomas Egerton, 'Speciall observacions touching all the sessions of the last parlement' (1611), in Louis A. Knafla, *Law and politics in Jacobean England* (Cambridge University Press, 1977), p. 254.

[162] Peacham, *The dvty of all trve subiects*, pp. 7–8, 39–40, 55. See in general also pp. 27–48.

[163] Ibid., pp. 4, 8.

and the best way to contribute was 'to open our purses, with the widest, for the common good', not 'coldly' but 'freely and cheerefully'.[164] Whereas the idea of the mixed state testified to the necessity of unity, the two greatest heroes of the Roman republic, Lucius Junius Brutus and Marcus Brutus were used to demonstrate that Englishmen should fight for their monarch against the rebellious Scots.

[164] Ibid., pp. 33, 62. Cf. in general idem, *The truth of our times: revealed out of one mans experience, by way of essay* (London, 1638), pp. 42–9; idem, *The valley of varietie: or, discourse fitting for the times* (London, 1638), pp. 107–28. Cf. Robert Ward, *Anima'dversions of warre: or, a militarie magazine of the truest and ablest instruction, for the managing of warre* (London, 1639), the epistle dedicatory, pp. 28, 161–4, 167; Miles Sandys, *The first part of a small worke* (London, 1634), pp. 3–5, 119–20; James Howell, *Dendrologia: Dodona's grove, or the focall forest* (n.p. [London], 1640), pp. 5–6, 209–12.

Epilogue

Sixty years separated the treatises of Roger Baynes, John Barston and John Foord from Richard Brathwait's *A survey of history*. It would be wrong to deny the numerous differences between them, but it would be equally misleading to dispute their striking similarities. There is little doubt that humanism as political parlance was not completely overshadowed by other vocabularies in the mid sixteenth century. On the contrary, its central convictions were forcefully rehearsed throughout the late sixteenth and early seventeenth centuries. The English showed complete familiarity with such deeply entrenched notions of the humanist tradition as the virtuous civic life and *vera nobilitas*. These notions enabled them to portray themselves as citizens and to characterize their life as one of participation rather than subjection. From Thomas Rogers to Richard Brathwait it was argued that, before everything else, a virtuous *negotium* made an Englishman capable of acting as a magistrate of his local community or of the community of the whole realm and of performing his duty in public assemblies whether local or national in composition. And to lead such a life guaranteed the well-being of the whole commonwealth.

As well as subscribing to the notions of the *vita activa* and *vera nobilitas* in their attempt to conceive of themselves as active citizens, early modern Englishmen many a time resorted to more openly republican themes. Ancient and contemporary republics not merely aroused curiosity and captured attention; they also commanded sincere admiration. This is not to say that those who expressed their admiration were republicans. Nevertheless, as we have seen, Englishmen were perfectly capable of employing at least three central characteristics of classical republicanism. In the first place, it was often maintained that a republican form of government implemented in a highly successful manner the idea of meritocracy. Such was the view shared by Robert Ashley, Francis Bacon, Alexander Leighton and Richard Brathwait.

They all argued that republics had succeeded in securing the rule of the most virtuous men.

The second and more important aspect of the republican tradition to exert profound influence was the classical idea of the mixed constitution. Although historians have generally claimed that this concept played no positive role in the political debate of the late sixteenth and early seventeenth centuries, it is clear that the English never lost sight of this republican notion. It loomed large in numerous republican translations. Even more importantly, it was voiced every now and then in treatises composed by the English themselves. This happened both in the context of urban communities and in that of the situation in Ireland. But the idea of the mixed constitution was also developed in the context of English politics: together with the notion of virtuous citizenship it enabled the English to promote an image of the centrality of parliament for the English commonwealth.

Thirdly, and most importantly, some of the theorists we have examined in this study felt no qualms about employing the central notion of republicanism – that governors should be elected rather than inherited. John Foord stated succinctly that the princely office should be elective. But even more to the point of English politics in the early 1580s, he espoused the view that in the case of the sudden demise of the prince, a regent should be elected by parliament. John Barston, Richard Beacon and the author of the *Organon reipvblicae* put forward an even more genuinely republican argument. They all maintained that power and authority had the unavoidable tendency to corrupt their possessor(s). It followed that this corruption could only be held at bay by setting certain limits on those in authority. One of the most effective checks was to restrict the duration of the governor's term in office. That is to say, the republican device that governors and magistrates should continuously be rotated was taken to be the most effective solution to the looming problem of corruption.

A central aim of this study has also been to locate the uses of these arguments in their proper historical circumstances. We have seen that the humanist and republican vocabularies were used in numerous different contexts and with numerous different intentions. When humanist and republican arguments were strongly reiterated in the 1570s and 1580s, one of the aims which their proponents endeavoured to achieve was to remind the English of the importance of a virtuous *negotium* in preventing the political turmoils of the continent from reaching England. At the same time John Barston articulated the civic nature of local community in his *Safegarde of societie* and sought to criticize the oligarchy of Tewkesbury. Towards the end of the sixteenth century foreign republican treatises were translated with a view to suggesting that they had an important lesson to teach. The ideas of civic life and the mixed constitution were used by Jacobeans to argue for a limited kingship.

Another aim of this study has been to trace the reception of Machiavelli's republicanism in England. It first caught serious attention in England in the 1580s, when Alberico Gentili argued that the Florentine had been 'a eulogist of democracy' and when John Wolfe printed *Il principe* as well as the *Discorsi* in London and drew a similar conclusion to Gentili's from the *Discorsi*. Nevertheless, these brief remarks were a far cry from an extensive use of Machiavellian republicanism. This occurred in 1594, when Richard Beacon system-atically employed Machiavelli's republican concepts in his attempt to lay new foundations for the Irish commonwealth. Some central Machiavellian notions were also embraced by Walter Ralegh and even more so by Francis Bacon. Both of them evinced a profound interest in republican and aristocratic forms of government and sometimes even showed a sincere respect for them. Likewise, they both displayed even greater enthusiasm for the distinctively Machiavellian issue of civic greatness. In particular, Bacon invoked Machiavellian notions of *grand-ezza* in his defence of the Anglo-Scottish union and in his attempt to demonstrate the means by which Britain would become a truly great state. Ralegh was more willing to endorse some of the doctrines of the newer theory of civic greatness put forward by Justus Lipsius and Giovanni Botero, but even he readily acknowledged (with a direct reference to Bacon) the crucial importance of civic virtue as well as 'the moderate use of sovereigne power' in the attainment of *grandezza*. The idea of the armed citizen, so central in Bacon's concept of civic greatness, was further developed by Thomas Hedley (who borrowed it from Bacon), when he argued in 1610 against the new impositions. A number of theorists also used the concept of the armed citizen in the political debates of the late 1620s and the 1630s, with similar intentions, and often invoking the authority of Bacon.

One of the most common ways in which humanist and republican notions were articulated was to show how a decayed commonwealth could be reformed. This line of argument is clearly discernible in the writings of the 1570s and 1580s and becomes more prominent in John Barston's analysis and especially in Richard Beacon's reform programme for the Irish commonwealth. But the most forceful use of the humanist and republican vocabularies against corruption emerges in Thomas Scott's pamphlet campaign in the early 1620s. A distinctively classical republican argument runs through his whole attempt to stave off any corruption – be it internal or external – of the English commonwealth.

Although classical humanist and republican arguments were voiced throughout the period from the 1570s to the 1630s, there is little doubt that, with the passage of time, the tradition lost some of its force. The first signs of exhaustion could perhaps be discerned already at the turn of the century, as neostoic and Tacitean ideas made their appearance, although this did not mean, as some scholars have claimed, that Ciceronian humanism was totally displaced. These signs of erosion of the humanist tradition became somewhat clearer during the 1620s and 1630s, but some of the foremost values of the tradition were still repeated in the 1630s when Machiavelli's *Discorsi* was published in English for the first time.

At about the time the classical humanist tradition was drawing to a close, England faced a crisis of unprecedented seriousness. Although it took a decade before republican concepts were stated afresh, it was above all the Civil War and its aftermath which prompted this revival of classical republicanism. It is essential to an understanding of the classical republicanism of the 1650s, however, to recognize that John Milton, James Harrington, Algernon Sidney and their *epigoni* did not invent the republican tradition completely anew. There are of course marked dissimilarities between their arguments and those of the late-sixteenth- and early-seventeenth-century exponents of classical humanism and republicanism. But it would be strange indeed if there had been none after the upheavals of the 1640s. Nonetheless, these differences should not completely overshadow the fact that Harrington, Milton and Sidney were, to some extent, direct followers of the earlier generations of humanist and republican writers. George Wither and Thomas May, who had used humanist parlance and demonstrated a keen interest in republican issues, became avowed republicans during the Civil War and form thus a direct link between our period and the mid-century.[1] It is a well-known fact that James Harrington cited Francis Bacon's *Essays* several times in his *Oceana*, but the striking similarities between Bacon and Harrington have not been adequately

---

[1] Worden 1981, pp. 191–2.

appreciated. They both agreed with Machiavelli that the pursuit of civic greatness was a principal duty of every state.[2] And they claimed that the greatness of a state depended on its military strength, which in turn hinged on the people's virtuous character rather than on the treasure of the state.[3] Furthermore, both contended that the Roman method of establishing colonies and of forming 'unequal leagues', as Harrington put it, should be imitated. And they also agreed that the new inhabitants acquired by these Roman methods should be naturalized.[4] It is of course true that, whereas Harrington was an avowed republican, Bacon's respect for the republican form of government was much more restricted. Nevertheless, they both insisted that democracies were 'lesse subject to sedition', as Bacon put it.[5] Most importantly, Harrington grounded the social analysis of his republican theory on Bacon's account of the social conditions of a great state,[6] and Bacon's 'Of the true greatnesse of kingdomes and estates' provided together with Machiavelli the whole point of departure of his book. It is thus arguable that the commonwealth of Oceana was Bacon's Great Britain writ large. The unearthing of the predecessors of the mid-century classical republicans helps us understand both how the English articulated their civic nature before the Civil War and why the classical republicans of the 1650s could expect that their arguments would be understood as well as adopted.

2   James Harrington, *The common-wealth of Oceana* (London, 1656), p. 266.
3   Ibid., pp. 81, 308, 44.
4   Ibid., *Oceana*, pp. 261–2.
5   Bacon, 'Of nobility', in *Essays*, p. 41; Harrington, *Oceana*, pp. 21–2.
6   Harrington, *Oceana*, sig. B1^{r-v}, pp. 39–40.

Bibliography

PRIMARY SOURCES

Dates in brackets following titles indicate the date of first publication.

Adams, Thomas, *The sovldiers honovr*, London, 1617.
  The workes of Tho: Adams, London, 1630.
Anton, Robert, *The philosophers satyrs*, London, 1616.
A. Ar., *The practise of princes*, n.p., 1630.
Aristotle, *Politiqves: or discourse of government*, translated by I. D., London, 1598.
Ascham, Roger, *English works*, ed. W. A. Wright, Cambridge University Press,
  1904.
Ashley, Robert, *Of honour*, ed. Virgil B. Heltzel, San Marino: Huntington
  Library, 1947.
d'Avity, Pierre, *The estates, empires, & principallities of the world*, translated by
  Edward Grimeston, London, 1615.
[Aylmer, John], *An harborowe for faithfull and trew svbiectes*, Strasburg, 1559.
A. D. B., *The covrt of the most illvstrious and most magnificent James, the first; king of
  Great Britaine, France, and Ireland: &c*, London, 1619.
Bachiler, Samuel, *Miles christianvs: or the campe royal*, Amsterdam, 1625.
Barclay, John, *The mirrovr of mindes: or Barclays Icon animorum*, translated by
  Thomas May (1614), London, 1631.
Bargrave, Isaac, *A sermon against selfe policy*, London, 1624.
  *A sermon preached before king Charles, March 27. 1627: being the anniuersary of his
  maiesties inauguration*, London, 1627.
  A sermon preached before ... the lower house of parliament: February the last 1623,
  London, 1624.
Barnes, Barnabe, *Fovre bookes of offices: enabling private persons for the speciall seruice of
  all good princes and policies*, London, 1606.
Barnes, Thomas, *Vox belli: or, an alarvm to warre*, London, 1626.
  The wise-mans forecast against the evill time, London, 1624.
Barriffe, William, *Mars his trivmph: or, the description of an exercise performed the xvii.
  of October, 1638 in Merchant-Taylors Hall*, London, 1639.
  Military discipline: or, the yong artillery man, London, 1635.
Barry, Gerratt, *A discourse of military discipline, devided into three bookes*, Brussels, 1634.

Barston, John, *Safegarde of societie: describing the institution of lawes and policies, to preserue euery felowship of people by degrees of ciuil gouernment; gathered of the moralls and policies of philosophie*, London, 1576.

Baynes, Roger, *The praise of solitarinesse, set down in the form of a dialogue, wherein is conteyned, a discourse philosophical, of the lyfe actiue and contemplatiue*, London, 1577.

Beacon, Richard, *Solon his follie: or a politiqve discovrse, tovching the reformation of common-weales conquered, declined or corrupted*, Oxford, 1594.

Bernard, Richard, *The Bible-battells: or the sacred art military*, n.p. [London], 1629.
The seauen golden candlestickes: Englands honour, London, 1621.

de Béthune, Philippe, *The covnsellor of estate: contayning the greatest and most remarkeable considerations seruing for the managing of publicke affaires*, translated by E[dward] G[rimeston], London, 1634.

Blandy, William, *The castle or picture of pollicy, shewing forth most liuely, the face, body and partes of a commonwealth*, London, 1581.

Blenerhasset, Thomas, *A direction for the plantation in Vlster*, London, 1610.

Blundeville, Thomas, *The true order and methode of wryting and reading hystories*, London, 1574.

Boccalini, Trajano, *The new-found politicke, disclosing the secret natvres and dispositions as well of priuate persons as of statesmen and courtiers*, translated by J. Florio, T. Scott and W. Vaughan, London, 1626.

Bodin, Jean, *The six bookes of a commonweale*, translated by Richard Knolles, London, 1606.

Boroughs, John, *The sovereignty of the British seas* (1633), ed. T. C. Wade, Edinburgh: W. Green & Son, 1920.

Bosswell, John, *Workes of armorie, deuyded into three bookes*, n.p., 1572.

Botero, Giovanni, *The cavse of the greatnesse of cities: with certaine obseruations concerning the sea*, translated by Sir T. H., London, 1635.
Delle relationi vniversali: parte seconda, Rome, 1592.
The reason of state, translated by P. J. and D. P. Waley, London: Routledge, 1956.
Relations of the most famovs kingdoms and common-weales thorovgh the world, translated by R[obert] J[ohnson], London, 1608.
Relations of the most famous kingdomes and common-wealths thorowout the world, translated by R[obert] J[ohnson], London, 1630.
The travellers breviat: or an historicall description of the most famous kingdomes in the world, translated by R[obert] J[ohnson], London, 1601.
A treatise, concerning the causes of the magnificencie and greatnes of citie, translated by Robert Peterson, London, 1606.
The worlde: or an historicall description of the most famous kingdomes and common-weales therein, translated by R[obert] J[ohnson], London: Routledge, 1601.

[Botero, Giovanni,], *Observations vpon the liues of Alexander, Caesar, Scipio*, translated by anon., London, 1602.

Anon., *A breefe, declaring and approuing the necessarie and inuiolable maintenance of the laudable customes of London*, London, 1584.

[Braham, Humfrey,], *The institucion of a gentleman*, London, 1555.

Brathwait, Richard, *The English gentleman*, London, 1630.

Essaies vpon five senses, London, 1620.

Essaies vpon the five senses, revived by a new supplement, 2nd edn, London, 1635.

The golden fleece, London, 1611.

The schollers medley: or an intermixt discovrse vpon historicall and poeticall relations, London, 1614.

A strange metamorphosis of man, transformed into a wildernesse, London, 1634.

A svrvey of history: or, a nursery for gentry, London, 1638.

Times curtaine drawne: or the anatomie of vanitie, London, 1621.

Whimzies: or, a new cast of characters, London, 1631.

Bryskett, Lodovick, *A discovrse of civill life: containing the ethike part of morall philosophie*, London, 1606.

Buckeridge, John, *A sermon preached at Hampton Court before the kings maiestie, on Tuesday the 23 of September, anno 1606*, London, 1606.

Buggs, Samuel, *Miles mediterranevs: the Mid-land souldier: a sermon*, London, 1622.

Burton, Henry, *An apology of an appeale: also an epistle to the true-hearted nobility*, n.p., 1636.

Israels fast: or, a meditation vpon the seuenth chapter of Joshuah; a faire precedent for these times, London, 1628.

A plea to an appeale: trauersed dialogue wise, London, 1626.

W. C., *The Dvtch svrvay*, London, 1625.

[Carew, George], 'Relation of the state of Polonia' (1598), ed. Carolus H. Talbot, Elementa ad fontium editiones, 13 Rome, 1965.

Cary, Walter, *The present state of England*, London, 1627.

C[aussin], N[icolas], *The unfortunate politique*, translated by G. P., London, 1638.

Chappell, Bartholomew, *The garden of prudence*, London, 1595.

Churchyard, Thomas, *A generall rehearsall of warres, wherein is fiue hundred seuerall seruices of land and sea*, London, 1579.

A pleasant discourse of court and wars, London, 1596.

Cicero, M. T., *The first book of Tullies Offices*, translated by John Brinsley, London, 1616.

The thre bookes of Tullyes offyces, translated by Robert Whittinton, London, 1534.

Thre bokes of duties to marcus his sonne, translated by Nicolas Grimalde, London, 1556.

Cleland, James, *Propaideia: or the institution of a young noble man*, Oxford, 1607.

[Clichtove, Josse], *The boke of noblenes: that sheweth how many sortes & kyndes there is*, translated from French by John Larke, n.p. [London], n.d. [1550?].

Contarini, Gasparo, *The commonwealth and gouernment of Venice*, translated by Lewes Lewkenor, London, 1599.

Cooke, Edward, *The character of warre*, London, 1626.

C[ooke], E[dward], *The prospectiue glasse of warre*, London, 1628.

Corbet, John, *The vngirding of the Scottish armour: or, an answer to the informations for defensive armes against the kings majestie*, Dublin, 1639.

Cornwallis, William, *Discovrses vpon Seneca the tragedian*, London, 1601.

    Essayes (1606–10), ed. Don Cameron Allen, Baltimore: John Hopkins University Press, 1946.

[Cornwallis William,], *The miracvlovs and happie vnion of England and Scotland*, London, 1604.

Cotton, Robert, *An answer to such motives as were offer'd by certain military-men to prince Henry*, London, 1675.

[Cotton Robert,], *The danger wherein the kingdom, now standeth & the remedie*, n.p., 1628.

Covell, William, *Polimanteia: or, the meanes lawfull and vnlawfull, to ivdge of the fall of a common-wealth*, Cambridge, 1595.

Cowell, John, *The interpreter: or booke containing the signification of words*, Cambridge, 1607.

[Cox Leonard,], *The arte or crafte of rhethoryke*, London, n.d. [1532?].

Craig, Thomas, *The right of succession to the kingdom of England*, London, 1703.

    De unione Britanniae tractatus, ed. C. Sanford Terry, Edinburgh: T. & A. Constable, 1909.

Crashaw, W[illiam], *A sermon preached in London before the right honorable the Lord Lawarre, Lord Gouernour and Captaine Generall of Virginea*, London, 1610.

Crewe, Thomas, *The nosegay of morall philosophie*, London, 1580.

Crompton, Richard, *The mansion of magnanimitie*, London, 1599.

Crosse, Henry, *Vertues common-wealth: or the high-way to honovr*, London, 1603.

Crowley, Robert, *A sermon made in the chappel at the Gylde Halle in London, the xxix. day of September, 1574*, London, 1575.

    The way to wealth, wherein is plainly taught a most present remedy for sedicion, n.p. [London], 1550.

Curll, Walter, *A sermon preached at White-hall, on the 28. of April, 1622*, London, 1622.

Anon., *Cyuile and vncyuile life*, London, 1579.

Dallington, Robert, *Aphorismes civill and militarie: amplified with authorities, and exemplified with historie, out of the first quarterne of Fr Guicciardine*, London, 1613.

    A svrvey of the great dvkes state of Tvscany: in the yeare of our Lord 1596, London, 1605.

Davenport, John, *A royall edict for military exercises: published in a sermon preached ... in Saint Andrewes vndershaft, in London, Iune 23. 1629*, London, 1629.

Davies, Edward, *The art of war, and Englands traynings*, London, 1619.

    Military directions: or the art of trayning, London, 1618.

Davies, John, *A discoverie of the trve cavses why Ireland was neuer entirely subdued, nor brought vnder obedience of the crowne of England, vntill the beginning of his maiesties happie raigne*, n.p. [London], 1612.

    Le primer report des cases & matters en ley resolues & adiudges en les courts del roy en Ireland, Dublin, 1615.

Davies, John, *Microcosmos: the discovery of the little world, with the government thereof*, Oxford, 1603.

Dee, John, *General and rare memorials pertayning to the perfect arte of navigation*, London, 1577.

Denison, John, *Beati pacifici: the blessednes of peace-makers: and the advancement of Gods children: in two sermons preached before the king*, London, 1620.

Anon., *A description of the prosperitie, strength, and wise government of the vnited Prouinces of the Netherlands*, London, 1615.

Dickinson, William, *The kings right, briefely set downe in a sermon preached before the reuerend iudges at the assizes held in Reading for the county of Berks. Iune 28. 1619*, London, 1619.

Digges, Leonard and Thomas, *An arithmeticall militare treatise, named Stratioticos*, London, 1579.

Anon., *A discourse of the commonweal of this realm of England*, (1581), ed. Mary Dewar, Charlottesville: University of Virginia Press, 1969.

Ducci, Leonardo, *Ars avlica or the courtiers arte*, translated by [Edmund Blount] London, 1607.

Du Moulin, Pierre, *A preparation to svffer for the Gospell of Iesvs Christ*, London, 1623.

Dunster, John, *Caesars penny: or a sermon of obedience … preached at St Maries in Oxford at the assies the 24 of Iuly 1610*, Oxford, 1610.

Du Refuge, Eustache, *A treatise of the court: or instructions for courtiers*, translated by John Reynolds, London, 1622.

Du Vair, Guillaume, *A bvckler against adversitie: or a treatise of constancie*, translated by Andrew Court, London, 1622.

The moral philosophie of the stoicks, translated by T[homas] J[ames], London, 1598.

Egerton, Thomas, 'Speciall obseruacions touching all the sessions of the last parlement anno 7 regis and etc' (1611), in Louis A. Knafla, *Law and politics in Jacobean England: the tracts of Lord Chancellor Ellesmere*, Cambridge University Press, 1977, pp. 254–62.

Eliot, John, *The monarchie of man*, 2 vols., ed. A. B. Grossart, London: privately printed, 1879.

Evans, William, *A translation of the booke of nature, into the vse of grace*, Oxford, 1633.

Everard, John, *The arriereban: a sermon preached to the company of the Military Yarde*, London, 1618.

Faret, Nicholas, *The honest man: or the art to please in court*, translated by Edward Grimestone, London, 1632.

Featley, John, *Obedience and submission: a sermon preached at St Saviours-church in South-warke, at a visitation, on Tuesday, the eight day of December: anno dom. 1635*, London, 1636.

Felippe, Bartolome, *The covnseller: a treatise of counsels and counsellers of princes*, translated by J[ohn] T[horius], London, 1589.

Felltham, Owen, *Resolues diuine, morall, politicall*, London, [1623].

Fenton, Geffrey, *A forme of christian pollicie gathered out of French*, London, 1574.

Golden epistles, conteyning varietie of discourse, both morall, philosophicall, and diuine, London, 1577.

Ferne, John, *The blazon of gentrie: deuided into two parts*, London, 1586.

Floyd, Thomas, *The picture of a perfit common wealth*, London, 1600.

Foord, John, *Synopsis politica*, London, 1582.

Ford, John, *A line of life: pointing at the immortalitie of a vertuous name*, [London], 1620.

Forset, Edward, *A comparative discovrse of the bodies natvral and politiqve*, London, 1606.

A defence of the right of kings, London, 1624.

Fougasses, Thomas de, *The generall historie of the magnificent state of Venice*, translated by W. Shute, London, 1612.

Fulbecke, William, *An historicall collection of the continvall factions, tvmvlts, and massacres of the Romans and Italians*, London, 1601.

The pandectes of the law of nations, London, 1602.

Fullwood, William, *The enemie of idlenesse teaching the manner and stile how to endite, compose, and wryte all sortes of epistles and letters*, (1568), London, 1571.

Furió [Ceriol], Federico, *A very briefe and profitable treatise declaring howe many counsells, and what maner of counselers a prince that will gouerne well ought to haue*, abridged and translated by Thomas Blundeville, London, 1570.

Gaetani, Enrico, *Instrvctions for yovng gentlemen*, translated by anon., Oxford, 1633.

[Gainsford, Thomas], *The rich cabinet furnished with varietie of excellent discriptions*, London, 1616.

G[ainsford], T[homas], *The vision and discovrse of Henry the seuenth: concerning the vnitie of Great Brittaine*, London, 1610.

Gardiner, S. R. (ed.), *The constitutional documents of the Puritan Revolution 1628–1660*, Oxford: Clarendon Press, 1889.

Garey, Samuel, *Great Brittans little calendar: or, triple diarie*, London, 1618.

Garrard, Edmund, *The covntrie gentleman moderator*, London, 1624.

Gataker, Thomas, *An anniuersarie memoriall of Englands delivery from the Spanish inuasion: deliuered in a sermon on Psal. 48.7,8*, London, 1626.

Gates, Geoffrey, *The defence of militarie profession*, London, 1579.

Anon., 'The genealogie of vertue', in *The anathomie of sinne, briefely discovering the braunches thereof*, London, 1603.

Gentili, Alberico, *De legationibus libri tres*, (1594), 2 vols., translated by Gordon J. Laing, New York: Oxord University Press, 1924.

Regales disputationes tres: id est, de potestate regis absoluta: de vnione regnorvm Britanniae: de vi ciuium in regem semper iniusta, London, 1605.

Anon., *The gentlemans academie: or, the booke of S. Albans … reduced into a better method, by G. M[arkham]*, London, 1595.

Gibbon, Charles, *The order of eqvalitie: contriued and diuulged as a generall directorie for common sessements*, Cambridge, 1604.

The praise of a good name, London, 1594.

Gibson, Abraham, *Christiana-polemica: or a preparatiue to warre … a sermon*, London, 1619.

Gibson, Thomas, *The blessing of a good king: deliuered in eight sermons*, London, 1614.

[Gil, Alexander], *The new starr of the north shining vpon the victorious king of Sweden*, (1631), London, 1632.

Gordon, John, *Enotikon: or a sermon of the vnion of Great Brittannie, in antiquitie of language, name, religion, and kingdome*, London, 1604.
The vnion of Great Brittaine, London, 1604).

[Goslicius], Laurentius Grimalius, *The covnsellor: exactly pourtraited in two bookes*, translated by anon., London, 1598.

Gouge, William, *Gods three arrowes: plague, famine, sword, in three treatises*, London, 1631.

Greene, Robert, *The royal exchange: contayning sundry aphorismes of phylosophie, and golden principles of morrall and naturall quadruplicities*, London, 1590.

Guazzo, Stefano, *The ciuile conuersation ... diuided into foure bookes*, the first three translated from French by G[eorge] Pettie, the fourth translated from Italian by Barth. Young, London, 1586.

Hagthorpe, John, *Englands-Exchequer: or a discovrse of the sea and navigation*, London, 1625.

[Hall, Arthur], 'An admonition to the father of F. A.', appendix to *A letter sent by F. A. touchyng the proceedings in a priuate quarell ... betweene Arthur Hall, and Melchisedech Mallerie gentlemen, to his very friende L. B. being in Italie*, n.p., n.d. [1579].

Hall, Joseph, *The works of Joseph Hall*, London, 1647.
Characters of vertves and vices: in two bookes, London 1608.
The true peace-maker: laid forth in a sermon before his maiesty at Theobalds. September 19, 1624, London, 1624.

Hampton, William, *A proclamation of warre from the lord of hosts ... a sermon at Pauls Crosse Iuly the 23. 1626*, London, 1627.

Harington, John, *A tract on the succession to the crown* (1602), ed. C. R. Markham London: Roxburghe Club, 1880.

Harrington, James, *The common-wealth of Oceana*, London, 1656.

Harvey, Gabriel, *Ciceronianus* (1577), ed. Harold S. Wilson, translated by Clarence A. Forbes, University of Nebraska Studies in the Humanities, no. 4, 1965.
Letter-book, AD 1573–1580, ed. E. J. L. Scott. Camden Society, 2nd ser., XXXIII, 1884.
Marginalia, ed. G. C. Moore Smith, Stratford: Shakespeare Head Press, 1913.
Rhetor, vel duorum dierum oratio, de natura, arte, & exercitatione rhetorica, London, 1577.
The works, 3 vols., ed. Alexander B. Grosart, London: Huth Library, 1884.

Hayward, John, *An answer to the first part of a certaine conference, concerning svccession*, London, 1603.
The first part of the life and raigne of king Henrie the IIII, London, 1599.
A treatise of vnion of the two realmes of England and Scotland, London, 1604.

Heath, Robert, 'Speech in the case of Alexander Leighton, in the Star Chamber, June 4, 1630', ed. S. R. Gardiner, Camden Society, 2nd ser., XIV, *Camden miscellany*, 7, 1875.

Herbert, William, *Croftus, sive de Hibernia liber*, (1588/9), ed. W. E. Buckley, London: Roxburghe Club, 1887.

H[erne], R[ichard], *Ros coeli: or a miscellany of ejaculations, divine, morall, &c*, London, 1640.

Heron, Haly, *A newe discourse of morall philosophie, entituled the kayes of counsaile*, London, 1579.

Hexham, Henry, *The principles of the art militarie*, n.p. 1637.
The second part of the principle of the art militarie, London, 1638.
The third part of the principle of the art militarie, The Hague, 1640.

Heylyn, Peter, *Augustus*, London, 1632.

Heywood, Thomas, *A true description of his majesties royall ship, built this yere 1637 at Wolwitch*, London, 1637.

Hitchcock, John, *A sanctvary for honest men: or an abstract of humane wisdome*, London, 1617.

Hobbes, Thomas, *Leviathan*, (1651), ed. C. B. Macpherson, Harmondsworth: Penguin, 1968.

Holyday, Bartenio, *Philosophiae polito-barbarae specimen*, Oxford, 1633.

Anon., *Horae subseciuae: observations and discovrses*, London, 1620.

Horne, Robert, *The christian gouernour, in the common-wealth, and priuate families*, London, 1614.

Howell, James, *Dendrologia: Dodona's grove, or the focall forest*, n.p. [London], 1640.

Hull, William, *The mirrovr of maiestie ... set forth in fiue sermons*, London, 1615.

Hume, David, *De vnione insvlae Britannicae tractatus*, London, 1605.

Jacobean union, The six tracts of 1604, ed. Bruce R. Galloway and Brian P. Levack, Edinburgh: Scottish History Society, 1985.

Jeffray, William, *The picture of patience: or, direction to perfection*, London, 1629.

Jerome, Stephen, *Englands ivbilee: or Irelands ioyes io-paean, for king Charles his welcome*, Dublin, 1625.

Johnson, Robert, *Essaies: or rather imperfect offers*, London, 1607.

J[ohnson], R[obert], *The new life of Virginea: declaring the former svccesse and present estate of that plantation being the second part of Noua Britannia*, London, 1612.
Nova Britannia: offring most excellent fruites by planting in Virginia, London, 1609.

Jonson, Ben, *The complete plays*, 4 vols., ed. G. A. Wilkes, Oxford University Press, 1981.

K[empe], W[illiam], *The education of children in learning: declared by the dignitie, vtilitie, and method thereof*, London, 1588.

[Keymer, John?], 'Observations touching trade and commerce with the Hollander, and other nations', in Walter Ralegh, *Works*, 8 vols., ed. W. Oldys, Oxford University Press, 1829, vol. VIII, pp. 351–76.

Knevet, Ralph, *Stratiotikon: or a discourse of militarie discipline*, n.p., 1628.

[La Place, Pierre de], *Politiqve discourses, treating of the differences and inequalities of vocations, as well publique, as priuate*, translated by Aegremont Ratcliffe, London, 1578.

La Primaudaye, Pierre de, *The French academie*, translated by T. B[owes?] London, 1586.

Lauder, [George], *The Scottish sovldier*, Edinburgh, 1629.

Leech, Jeremy, *The trayne souldier: a sermon preached befor the worthy Societie of the captaynes and gentle-men that exercise armes in the Artillery garden*, London, 1619.

[Leighton, Alexander], *An appeal to the parliament: or Sions plea against the prelacie*, n.p., n.d. [1628].

Speculum belli sacri: or the looking-glasse of the holy war, n.p., 1624.

[Leighton, Alexander?] *The interpreter wherin three principall termes of state: much mistaken by the vulgar are clearely unfolded*, n.p., 1624.

Leighton, William, *Vertve trivmphant: or a lively description of the fovre vertves cardinall*, London, 1603.

Le Roy, Louis, *Of the interchangeable covrse: or variety of things in the whole world*, translated by Robert Ashley, London, 1594.

Lever, Christopher, *Heauen and earth, religion and policy: or, the maine difference betweene religion and policy*, London, 1608.

Lipsius, Justus, *Admiranda, siue, de magnitudine Romana libri quattour*, Paris, 1598.

Sixe bookes of politickes or civil doctrine, translated by William Jones, London, 1594.

Two bookes of constancie, (1594), translated by John Stradling, ed. Rudolf Kirk New Brunswick: Rutgers University Press, 1939.

Loe, William, *Vox clamantis: Mark 1.3: a stil voice, to the three thrice-honourable estates of parliament*, n.p., 1621.

Lucan, M. A., *Pharsalia: or the civill warres of Rome, between Pompey the Great and Ivlivs Caesar: ten bookes*, translated by Thomas May, London, 1627.

Pharsalia: or the civill warres of Rome, between Pompey the Great Ivlivs Caesar: ten books: the second edition corrected, and the annotations inlarged, translated by Thomas May, London, 1631.

Lucinge, René de, *The beginning, continvance, and decay of estates: wherein are handled many notable questions concerning the establishment of empires and monarchies*, translated by John Finet, London, 1606.

Lyly, John, *Euphues: the anatomy of wit*, (1579), ed. Edward Arber, London, 1868.

Euphues and his England, (1580), ed. Edward Arber, London, 1868.

Machiavelli, Niccolò, *The arte of warre*, translated by Peter Withorne, London, 1588.

Discovrses upon the first decade of T. Livius, translated by Edward Dacres, London, 1636.

The Florentine historie, translated by Thomas Bedingfield, London, 1595.

Il principe e Discorsi, ed. Sergio Bertelli, Milan: Fettrinelli, 1960.

Malvezzi, Virgilio, *Romvlvs and Tarqvin*, translated by [Henry Carey], London, 1637.

Malynes, Gerard de, *The maintenance of free trade, according to the three essentiall parts of traffique*, London, 1622.

Manzini, Giovanni, *Politicall observations: upon the fall of Seianvs*, translated by T[homas] H[awkins], London, 1634.

Marandé, Léonard de, *The ivdgement of humane actions*, translated by John Reynolds, London, 1629.

Markham, Francis, *The booke of honovr: or five decads of epistles of honovr*, London, 1625. *Five decades of epistles of warre*, London, 1622.

Markham, Gervase, *The sovldiers accidence: or an introduction into military discipline*, London, 1635.

M[arkham], G[ervase], 'The muster-master' [1630?], ed. Charles L. Hamilton, Camden Society, 4th ser., XIV, *Camden miscellany*, 26, 1975.

Martyn, William, *Youths instruction*, London, 1612.

Matthieu, P[ierre], *Vnhappy prosperitie expressed in the histories of Aelius Seianus and Philipppa the Catanian*, translated by T[homas] Hawkins, n.p., [London], 1632.

M[atthieu], P[ierre], *The powerfvll favorite: or the life of Aelius Seianus*, Paris, 1628.

May, Thomas, *A continvation of Lucan's historicall poem till the death of Ivlivs Caesar*, London, 1630.

The tragedy of Cleopatra queene of Aegypt, ed. Denzell S. Smith, New York: Garland, 1979.

The tragedy of Julia Agrippina; empresse of Rome, ed. F. Ernest Schmid, Materialen zur Kunde des älteren Englischen Dramas, 43, 1914.

Melton, John, *A sixe-folde politician: together with a sixe-folde precept of policy*, London, 1609.

Merbury, Charles, *A briefe discovrse of royall monarchie, as of the best common weale*, London, 1581.

Meriton, George, *A sermon of nobilitie: preached at White-hall, before the king in February 1606*, London, 1607.

Middleton, Richard, *The carde and compasse of life: containing many passages, fit for these times*, London, 1613.

Anon., *The military discipline*, n.p., 1623.

Moffet, Thomas, *Nobilis: or a view of the life and death of a Sidney*, (1593), ed. and translated by Virgil B. Heltzel and Hoyt H. Hudson, San Marino: Huntington Library, 1940.

Molinier, Etienne, *A mirrovr for christian states: or, a table of politick vertues considerable amongst christians*, translated by William Tyrwhit, London, 1635.

More, George, *Principles for yong princes: collected out of sundry authors*, London, 1611.

Morrice, Thomas, *An apology for schoolemasters, tending to the aduauncement of learning, and to the vertuous education of children*, London, 1619.

Mulcaster, Richard, *Positions wherin those primitive circvmstances be examined, which are necessarie for the training vp of children*, London 1581.

Nannini, Remigio, *Civill considerations vpon many and svndrie histories*, translated from French by W. T[raheron], London, 1601.

Nash, Thomas, *Qvaternio: or a fovrefold way to a happie life*, London, 1633.

N[eade], W[illiam], *The double-armed man, by the new invention: briefly shewing some famous exploits atchieued by our Brittish bowmen*, n.p., [London], 1625.

Nenna, Giovanni, *Nennio, or a treatise of nobility*, translated by William Iones, n.p., [London], 1595.

N[esbit], E., *Caesars dialogue: or a familiar communication containing the first institution of a subiect, in allegiance to his soveraigne*, London, 1601.

Nixon, Anthony, *The dignitie of man, both in the perfections of his sovle and bodie*, London, 1612.

[Nixon, Anthony], *In the royall entertainement of his moste excellent maiestie, the queene, and the prince: the 27. of August last; 1605*, London, 1605.

Anon., *Of affectation: a morall discourse, of some delight, and of much vse for these times*, London, 1607.

Osorio de Fonseca, Jeronimo, *The five bookes ... contayninge a discourse of ciuill, and christian nobilitie*, translated by William Blandie, London, 1576.

Overbury, Thomas, *His observations in his travailes vpon the state of the XVII provinces as they stood anno dom. 1609*, n.p., 1626.

Palmer, Thomas, *Bristolls military garden: a sermon preached unto the worthy company of practisers in the military garden of the well governed citie of Bristoll*, London, 1635.

    An essay of the meanes how to make our trauailes, into forraine countries, the more profitable and honourable, London, 1606.

Parsons, Bartholomew, *The magistrates charter examined, or his duty and dignity opened: in a sermon preached at an assises, held at Sarum in the county of Wiltes, on the ninth day of March, last past, 1614*, London, 1616.

[Parsons, Robert], *A conference abovt the next svccession to the crowne of Ingland*, n.p., 1594.

Patrizi, Francesco, *A moral methode of ciuile policie*, translated by Richard Robinson, London, 1576.

P[attenson], M[atthew], *The image of bothe chvrches, Hiervsalem and Babel, vnitie and confvsion: obedience and sedition*, Tornay, 1623.

Anon., *The peace-maker: or Great Brittaines blessing*, London, 1619.

Peacham, Henry, *The compleat gentleman*, London, 1622.

    Minerva Britanna: or a garden of heroical deuises, furnished, and adorned with emblemes and impresa's of sundry natures, London, 1612.

    The truth of our times: revealed out of one mans experience, by way of essay, London, 1638.

    The valley of varietie: or, discourse fitting for the times, London, 1638.

P[eacham], H[enry], *The dvty of all trve svbiects to their king: as also to their native countrey, in time of extremity and danger*, London, 1639.

Pemble, William, *A svmme of morall philosophy*, Oxford, 1632.

Perrott, James, *The first part of the consideration of hvmane condition*, Oxford, 1600.

Plutarch, *The lives of the noble Grecians and Romanes*, translated from French by Thomas North, London, 1579.

Polybius, *The history of Polybivs the Megalopolitan*, translated from French by Edward Grimeston, London, 1634.

P[onet], J[ohn], *A shorte treatise of politike power*, n.p. [Strasburg?], 1556.

Pont, Robert, 'Of the union of Britayne', in *The Jacobean union: six tracts of 1604*, ed. Bruce R. Galloway and Brian P. Levack, Edinburgh: Scottish History Society, 1985.

Powell, Robert, *Depopvlation arraigned, convicted and condemned, by the lawes of God and man*, London, 1636.

Powell, T[homas], *The art of thriving: or the plaine path-way to preferment*, London, 1635.

Anon., *The prayse and commendacion of suche as sought comen welthes*, London, n.d. [1549].

Pricke, Robert, *The doctrine of svperioritie, and of subiection*, London, 1609.

Pritchard, Thomas, *The schoole of honest and vertuous lyfe profitable and necessary for all estates and degrees*, London, n.d. [1579].

P[rocter], T[homas], *Of the knowledge and conducts of warres, two bookes*, n.p., 1578.

Proctor, Thomas, *The right of kings: conteyning a defence of their supremacy*, n.p. [Amsterdam], 1621.

[Prynne, William], *An hvmble remonstrance to his maiesty, against the tax of ship-money*, n.p., 1641.

[I. R.], *Organon reipvblicae*, London, 1605.

   Organon reipvblicae: or the north starre of pollicie, by which the course of a common-wealth may be directed, London, 1605.

J. R., *The spy discovering the danger of Arminian heresie and Spanish trecherie*, Strasburg, 1628.

Rainolds, John, *Oxford lectures on Aristotle's 'Rhetoric'*, ed. Lawrence D. Green, Newark: University of Delaware Press, 1986.

Ralegh, Walter, *The historie of the world*, London, 1614.

   'Of the art of warre by sea' (1608–9), in Pierre Lefranc, *Sir Walter Ralegh écrivain: l'œuvre et les idées*, Paris: Librairie Armand Colin, 1968, pp. 597–601.

   '[On the conduct of war]' (1596–7), ed. Pierre Lefranc, *Etudes Anglaises*, 8 (1955), 193–211.

   '[On the succession]', 23 February 1593, ed. Pierre Lefranc, *Etudes Anglaises*, 13 (1960), 38–46.

   The prerogatives of parliaments in England, Middelburg, 1628.

   'The present state of thinges as they now stand betweene the three great kingdomes' (1608), in Pierre Lefranc (ed.), *Sir Walter Ralegh écrivain: l'œuvre et les idées*, Paris: Librairie Armand Colin, 1968, pp. 590–5.

Randol, John, *Noble Blastus: the honor of a Lord Chamberlaine: and of a good bedchamber-man: a sermon preacht the 27. of March, 1631*, London, 1633.

   A sermon preacht at St Maries in Oxford, the 5. of August: 1624: concerning the kingdomes peace, Oxford, 1624.

Reeve, Thomas, *Mephibosheths hearts ioy vpon his soveraignes safetie: deliuered in a sermon in the church of Great Yarmouth in Norfolke, the 19. day of October. 1623*, London, 1624.

Register of the University of Oxford, vol. II (1571–1622), pt 1, ed. Andrew Clark, Oxford Historical Society, 1887.

R[eynolds], J[ohn], *Votivae Angliae: or the desires and wishes of England*, Utrecht, 1624.

   Vox coeli: or, newes from heaven, Elesium [i.e. London], 1624.

Rich, Barnaby, *Allarme to England foreshewing what perilles are procured, where the people liue without regarde of martiall lawe*, London, 1578.

   A new description of Ireland, London, 1610.

   Opinion diefied: discouering the ingins, traps, and traynes, that are set in this age, whereby to catch opinion, London, 1613.

Roberts, John, *Compendium belli: or the tovchstone of martiall discipline*, London, 1626.

Robinson, Richard, *The vineyarde of vertue collected, composed, and digested into a tripartite order*, London, n.d. [1579].

Rogers, Nehemiah, *Christian curtesie: or St Pavls vltimum vale: deliuered in two sermons ... at St Margarets on Fish-street hill in London*, London, 1621.

    A strange vineyard in Palaestina: in an exposition of Isaiahs parabolical song of the beloued, discouered: to which Gods vineyard in this our land is paralleld, London, 1623.

Rogers, Thomas, *A philosophicall discourse, entituled, the anatomie of the minde*, London, 1576.

Rous, Francis, *The arte of happines*, London, 1619.

    Diseases of the time, attended by their remedies, London, 1622.

    Meditations of instrvction, of exhortation, of reprofe: indeavovring the edification and reparation of the house of God, London, 1616.

    Oile of scorpions: the miseries of these times turned into medicines and curing themselues, London, 1623.

    The onely remedy, that can cvre a people when all other remedies faile, London, 1627.

Rous, Francis [Jr], *Archaologiae Atticae libri tres: three bookes of the Attick antiquities*, Oxford, 1637.

Rushworth, John, *Historical collections*, London, 1682.

Russell, John, 'A treatise of the happie and blissed union', in *The Jacobean union: six tracts of 1604*, ed. Bruce R. Galloway and Brian P. Levack, Edinburgh: Scottish History Society, 1985.

    The two famous pitcht battels of Lypsich and Lutzen, Cambridge, 1634.

E. C. S., *The government of Ireland vnder the honorable, ivst, and wise gouernour sir John Perrot*, London, 1626.

Sallust, C. C., *The workes of Caius Crispus Salustius*, translated by William Crosse, London, 1629.

Saltmarsh, John, *The patience of policie in a christian life*, London, 1639.

Sandys, Miles, *The first part of a small worke*, London, 1634.

Sansovino, Francesco, *The quintesence of wit*, translated by Robert Hitchcock, London, 1590.

Santa Maria, Juan de, *Christian policie: or, the christian common-wealth*, translated by [Edward Blount], London, 1632.

Anon., *Satyrae seriae: or, the secrets of things*, London, 1640.

Scot, Patrick, *A table-booke for princes: containing short remembrances for the gouernment of themselues and their empire*, London, 1621.

[Scott, Michael], *The philosophers banqvet: newly furnished and decked forth*, 2nd edn, London, 1614.

Scott, Thomas, [of Canterbury], *A discourse of polletique and civill honour*, in G. D. Scull, *Dorothea Scott*, Oxford: Parker & Co, 1883.

Scott, Thomas, *The high-waies of God and the king: wherein all men ovght to walke in holinesse here, to happinesse hereafter: deliuered in two sermons preached at Thetford in Norfolke, anno 1620*, London, 1623.

Newes from Pernassvs: the politicall touchstone, taken from Mount Pernassus, Helicon, 1622.

The proiector: teaching a direct svre, and ready way to restore the decayes of the Church and state both in honour and revenue. Delivered in a sermon before the iudges in Norwich, at summer Assises there holden, anno 1620, London, 1623.

The Spaniards perpetvall designes to an vniversall monarchie, n.p., 1624.

[Scott, Thomas], *Aphorismes of state*, Utrecht, 1624.

The Belgicke pismire: or stinging the slothfull sleeper, London, 1622.

The Belgick sovldier: dedicated to the parliament: or, warre was a blessing, Dort, 1624.

Boanerges: or the hvmble svpplication of the ministers of Scotland, to the high covrt of parliament in England, Edinburgh, 1624.

A briefe information of the affaires of the Palatinate, n.p., 1624.

Digitvs Dei, n.p., n.d., [1623].

Englands ioy, for svppressing the papists, and banishing the priests and iesuites, n.p., 1624.

An experimentall discoverie of Spanish practises or the covnsell of a well-wishing souldier, for the good of his prince and state, n.p., 1623.

A relation of some speciall points concerning the state of Holland, The Hague, 1621.

Robert earle of Essex his ghost, sent from Elizian: to the nobility, gentry, and commvnaltie of England, Paradise [i.e. London], 1624.

The second part of Vox popvli: or Gondomar appearing in the likenes of Mathiauell in a Spanish parliament, Goricom [i.e. London], 1624.

Sir Walter Rawleighs ghost: or Englands forewarner, Utrecht, 1626.

Synmachia: or, a trve-loves knot, n.p., n.d., [1624].

A tongve-combat, lately happening betweene two English souldiers in the tilt-boat of Gravesend, London, 1623.

Vox Dei, n.p, n.d., [1623?].

Vox popvli: or newes from Spaine, n.p., 1620.

Vox regis, n.p., [Utrecht], n.d., [1624].

[Scott, Thomas?], *Certaine reasons and argvments of policie*, n.p., 1624.

Selden, John, *Mare clausum seu de dominio maris*, London, 1635.

Of the dominion, or, ownership of the sea, translated by Marchamont Nedham, London, 1652.

Seneca, L. A., *The workes of Lvcius Annaevs Seneca, both morrall and naturall*, translated by Thomas Lodge, London, 1614.

Anon., *A short svrvey of the kingdome of Sweden*, London, 1632.

Sibthorpe, Robert, *Apostolike obedience: shewing the duty of subiects to pay tribute and taxes to their princes ... a sermon preached at Northampton, at the assises, for the countie, Feb. 22. 1626*, London, 1627.

Sidney, Algernon, *Discourses concerning government*, (1698), ed. Thomas G. West, Indianapolis: Liberty Fund, 1990.

Sidney, Philip, *The complete works*, 4 vols., ed. Albert Feuillerat, Cambridge University Press, 1922–6.

The Countess of Pembroke's Arcadia (The old Arcadia), ed. Katherine Duncan-Jones, Oxford University Press, 1985.

Smith, Thomas, *De republica Anglorum*, (1583), ed. Mary Dewar, Cambridge University Press, 1982.

Smythe, John, *Instroctions, obseruations, and orders mylitarie*, London, 1595.

Spelman, Henry, 'Of the union', in *The Jacobean union: six tracts of 1604*, ed. Bruce R. Galloway and Brian P. Levack, Edinburgh: Scottish History Society, 1985.

Spenser, Edmund, *A view of the present state of Ireland*, (1596), ed. W. L. Renwick, Oxford University Press, 1970.

Stafford, Anthony, *Staffords heauenly dogge: or the life, and death of that great cynicke Diogenes*, London, 1615.

Honour and vertue, triumphing over the grave, London, 1640.

Staffords Niobe: or his age of teares, London, 1611.

[Starkey, Ralph], *The priuiledges and practice of parliaments in England: collected out of the common lawes of this land*, n.p., 1628.

Starkey, Thomas, *A dialogue between Pole and Lupset*, ed. T. F. Mayer, Camden Society, 4th ser. xxxvii, 1989.

Stephens, John, *Essayes and characters ironicall, and instroctive*, 2nd impression, London, 1615.

[Stoughton, William], *An assertion for true and christian church-policie*, n.p., 1604.

Stradling, John, *Beati pacifici: a divine poem*, London, 1623.

Stubbes, Philip, *The anatomie of abuses*, London, 1583.

Sturmius, Joannes, *A ritch storehouse or treasurie for nobilitye and gentleman, which in Latine is called nobilitas literata*, translated by T[homas] B[rowne], London, 1570.

Styward, Thomas, *The pathwaie to martiall discipline, deuided into two bookes*, London, 1581.

Sutcliffe, Matthew, *The practice, proceedings, and lawes of armes*, London, 1593.

Sutton, Edward, *The serpent anatomized: a morall discourse*, (1623), London, 1626.

Sutton, Thomas, *The good fight of faith: a sermon preached at Saint Mary-acts in London, vnto the gentlemen of the Artilley Garden, the 19. of Iune, 1623*, London, 1624.

Iethroes covnsell to Moses: or a direction for magistrates: a sermon preached at St. Saviours in Southwarke. March 5. 1621, London, 1631.

Anon., *The Swedish discipline, religiovs, civile, and military*, London, 1632.

Swetnam, Joseph, *The schoole of the noble and worthy science of defence*, London, 1617.

J. T., *The ABC of armes: or an introduction directorie: whereby the order of militarie exercises may easily bee vnderstood, and readily practised, where, when, and howsoeuer occasion is offered*, London, 1616.

Tacitus, C., *The annales*, translated by Richard Greneway, London, 1598.

Tanner, J. R., *Constitutional documents of the reign of James I AD 1603–1625*, Cambridge University Press, 1930.

Taylor, John, *An armado, or nauye, of 103 ships & other vessels*, London, 1627.

An English-mans love to Bohemia, Dort, 1620.

Taylor, Thomas, *Circumspect walking describing the seuerall rules, as so many seuerall steps in the way of wisedome*, (1619), London, 1631.

The valew of trve valovr: or, the probation and approbation of a right military man, London, 1629.

Thornborough, John, *A discovrse plainely proving the euident vtilitie and vrgent necessitie of the desired happie vnion of the two famous kingdomes of England and Scotland,* London, 1604.

The ioiefvll and blessed revniting the two mighty & famous kingdomes, England & Scotland into their ancient name of great Brittaine, Oxford, n.d., [1605].

Anon., *Tom tell troath: or a free discourse touching the manners of the tyme,* n.p., n.d., [1622?].

Tooke, George, *The legend of Brita-mart,* London, 1635.

Topsell, Edward, *The house-holder: or, perfect man: preached in three sermons lately at Hartfield in Svssex,* n.p., 1609.

Anon., *The treasvre of tranquillity: or a manvall of morall discourses, tending to the tranquillity of mindes,* translated by James Maxwell, London, 1611.

Anon., ['A treatise about the union of England and Scotland'] in *The Jacobean union: six tracts of 1604,* ed. Bruce R. Galloway and Brian P. Levack, Edinburgh: Scottish History Society, 1985.

Trigge, Francis, *To the kings most excellent maiestie: the hvmble petition of two sisters; the chvrch and common-wealth,* London, 1604.

Anon., *A trvmpet to call sovldiers on to noble actions,* London, 1627.

Trussell, Thomas, *The sovldier pleading his owne cause,* 2nd impression, London, 1619.

Tuvill, Daniel, *Essaies politicke, and morall,* London, 1608.

Vade mecum: a manuall of essayes morrall, theologicall, London, 1629.

T[uvill], D[aniel], *The dove and the serpent,* London, 1614.

Essayes, morall and theologicall, London, 1609.

Anon., *A twofold treatise, the one decyphering the worth of specvlation, and of a retired life: the other containing a discoverie of youth and old age,* Oxford, 1612.

Valentine, Henry, *Fovre sea-sermons, preached at the annuall meeting of the Trinitie Companie, in the parish church of Deptford,* London, 1635.

God save the king: a sermon preached in St Pavls chvrch the 27th. of March. 1639, London, 1639.

Valerius, Conrad, *The casket of iewels: contaynynge a playne description of morall philosophie,* translated by J[ohn] C[harlton], London, 1571.

[Vaughan, William], *The golden fleece diuided into three parts,* London, 1626.

Vegetius, Fl. R., *The fovre bookes contayninge a plaine forme and perfect knowledge of martiall policye,* translated by John Sadler, London, 1572.

Anon., *Vertves reward wherein the living are incouraged unto good workes,* n.p. [Amsterdam], 1639.

Vowell alias Hooker, John, *The order and usage of the keeping of a parlement in England,* (1572) in Vernon F. Snow, *Parliament in Elizabethan England. John Hooker's order and usage,* New Haven: Yale University Press, 1977.

Orders enacted for orphans and their portions within the citie of Excester, London, [1575].

A pamphlet of the offices and duties of euerie particular sworned officer, of the citie of Excester, London, 1584.

Wake, Isaac, *Rex Platonicus: sive de potentissimi principis Iacobi Britanniarvm regis, ad illustrissimam Academiam Oxoniensem, adventu, Aug. 27. anno 1605*, Oxford, 1607.

Walshe, Edward, 'Conjectures concerning the state of Ireland' (1552), ed. D. B. Quinn, *Irish Historical Studies*, 5 (1947), pp. 315–21.

Warburton, G[eorge], *King Melchizedech: a sermon preached at the court, at East-Hampsted, in ... the second of September. 1623*, London, 1623.

Ward, Robert, *Anima'dversions of warre: or, a militarie magazine of the trvest and ablest instrvction, for the managing of warre*, London, 1639.

Warwick, Arthur, *Spare-minutes: or, resolved meditations and premeditated resolvtions*, 2nd edn, London, 1634.

Webbe, George, *The path-way to honor*, London, 1612.

The practice of qvietnes or a direction how to liue quietly, London, 1608.

Wentworth, Peter, *A pithie exhortation to her maiestie for establishing her svccessor to the crowne*, n.p., 1598.

[West, Richard], *The schoole of vertve, the second part: or, the young schollers paradice*, London, 1619.

Wits ABC: or a centurie of epigrams, London, n.d. [1608].

Wheeler, John, *A treatise of commerce*, London, 1601.

Whetstone, George, *The English myrror: a regard wherein al estates may behold the conquests of enuy*, London, 1586.

An heptameron of ciuill discourses, London, 1582.

The honovrable repvtation of a sovldier, Leyden, 1586.

A mirovr for magestrates of cyties, London, 1584.

White, Christopher, *A sermon preached in Christ-church in Oxford, the 12. day of May 1622*, London, 1622.

White, Rowland, 'Discors touching Ireland' (c.1569), ed. Nicholas Canny, *Irish Historical Studies*, 20 (1977), pp. 446–63.

Wilkes, William, *Obedience or ecclesiasticall vnion*, London, 1605.

Willan, R[obert], *Conspiracie against kings, heavens scorne: a sermon preached at Westminster-Abbey before the iudges, vpon the fifth of Novemb. 1622*, London, 1622.

Williams, Roger, *The actions of the Lowe Countries*, London, 1618.

Willymat, William, *A loyal svbiects looking-glasse: or a good subiects direction*, London, 1604.

Wilson, Thomas, 'The state of England anno Dom. 1600', ed. F. J. Fisher, Camden Society, 3rd ser., LII, *Camden miscellany*, 16, 1936.

Wither, George, *Abvses stript and whipt: or satirical essaies, diuided into two bookes*, London, 1613.

Britains remembrancer containing a narration of the plague lately past, n.p., 1628.

A collection of emblemes, ancient and moderne, London, 1635.

A satyre written to the kings most excellent maiestie, (1614), in George Wither, *Ivvenalia a collection of those poems*, London, 1622, sigs. cc7–Ff1.

Wither's motto: nec habeo, nec careo, nec curo, n.p. [London], 1621.

Wright, Henry, *The first part of the disqvisition of trvth concerning political affaires*, London, 1616.

Wright, Leonard, *A display of dvty, deckt with sage sayings, pithy sentences, and proper similies* (1589), London, 1616.

Wybarne, Joseph, *The new age of old names*, London, 1609.

Xenophon, *Cyrvpaedia: the institvtion and life of Cyrvs*, translated by Philemon Holland, London, 1632.

The historie of Xenophon: contaning the ascent of Cyrus into the higher covntries, translated by John Bingham, London, 1623.

Yates, John, *Ibid ad caesarem: or a svbmissive appearance before Caesar*, London, 1626.

SECONDARY SOURCES

Adams, John C. 1989, 'Alexander Richardson's philosophy of art and the sources of the puritan social ethic', *Journal of the History of Ideas*, 50, 227–47.

1990, 'Gabriel Harvey's Ciceronianus and the place of Peter Ramus' Dialecticae libri duo in the curriculum', *Renaissance Quarterly*, 43, 551–69.

Adams, S. L. 1973, 'The protestant cause: religious alliance with the West European Calvinist communities as a political issue in England 1585–1630'. Unpublished D Phil. diss., Oxford University.

1976, 'Captain Thomas Gainsford, the "Vox spiritus" and the Vox populi', *Bulletin of the Institute of Historical Research*, 49, 141–4.

1983, 'Spain or the Netherlands? The dilemmas of early Stuart foreign policy', in Howard Tomlinson (ed.), *Before the English Civil War: essays on early Stuart politics and government*. Basingstoke: Macmillan, pp. 79–101.

1984, 'Eliza enthroned? The court and its politics', in Christopher Haigh (ed.), *The reign of Elizabeth I*. Basingstoke: Macmillan, pp. 55–77.

1985, 'Foreign policy and the parliaments of 1621 and 1624', in Kevin Sharpe (ed.), *Faction and parliament: essays on early Stuart history*. London: Methuen, pp. 139–71 (first published 1978).

Allen, J. W. 1938, *English political thought 1603–1644*. London: Methuen.

Andrews, Kenneth R. 1991, *Ships, money and politics: seafaring and naval enterprise in the reign of Charles I*. Cambridge University Press.

Anglo, Sydney 1966, 'The reception of Machiavelli in Tudor England: a re-assessment', *Il Politico*, 31, 127–38.

1990, 'A Machiavellian solution to the Irish problem: Richard Beacon's Solon his follie (1594)', in Edward Chaney and Peter Mack (eds.), *England and the continental renaissance: essays in honour of J. B. Trapp*. Woodbridge: Boydell Press, pp. 153–64.

d'Avack, Lorenzo 1975, 'La teoria della monarchia mista nell'Inghilterra del cinque e del seicento', *Rivista Internazionale di Filosofia del Diritto*, 4th series, 52, 574–617.

Axton, Marie 1977, *The queen's two bodies: drama and the Elizabethan succession.* London: Royal Historical Society.

Baldwin, T. W. 1944, *William Shakspere's small Latine & lesse Greeke.* 2 vols. Urbana: University of Illinois Press.

Ball, J. N. 1985, 'Sir John Eliot and parliament, 1624–1629', in Kevin Sharpe (ed.), *Faction and parliament: essays on early Stuart history.* London: Methuen, pp. 173–207 (first published 1978).

Baluk-Ulewiczowa, Teresa 1988, 'The Senator of Wawrzyniec Goslicki and the Elizabethan counsellor', in Samuel Fiszman (ed.), *The Polish renaissance in its European context.* Bloomington: Indiana University Press, pp. 258–77.

Bard, Nelson P. 1977, 'The ship money case and William Fiennes, Viscount Saye and Sele', *Bulletin of the Institute of Historical Research,* 50, 177–84.

Baron, Hans 1966, *The crisis of the early Italian renaissance.* Princeton University Press (first published 1955).

Barratt, D. M. 1964, 'The publication of John Selden's Mare clausum', *Bodleian Library Record,* 7, 204–5.

Barry, Jonathan 1990, Introduction, in Jonathan Barry (ed.), *The Tudor and Stuart town: a reader in English urban history.* Harlow: Longman, pp. 1–34.

Bayley, C. C. 1961, *War and society in renaissance Florence: the De Militia of Leonardo Bruni.* University of Toronto Press.

Beck, Hans 1935, *Machiavellismus in der englischen Renaissance.* Duisburg: Dietrich & Hermann.

Benjamin, Edwin B. 1965, 'Bacon and Tacitus', *Classical Philology,* 60, 102–10.

Bennett, James 1830, *The history of Tewkesbury.* Tewkesbury: privately printed.

Berkowitz, D. S. 1984, *Humanist scholarship and public order: two tracts against the Pilgrimage of Grace by Sir Richard Morison.* Washington: Folger Shakespeare Library.

Berry, Edward I. 1971, 'History and rhetoric in Bacon's Henry VII', in Stanley E. Fish (ed.), *Seventeenth-century prose: modern essays in criticism.* New York and Oxford: Oxford University Press, pp. 281–308.

Binns, J. W. 1990, *Intellectual culture in Elizabethan and Jacobean England: the Latin writings of the age.* ARCA no 24.

Bock, Hellmut 1937, *Staat und Gesellschaft bei Francis Bacon: ein Beitrag zur politischen Ideologie der Tudorzeit.* Berlin: Junker und Dunnhaupt.

Boutcher, Warren 1991, 'Florio's Montaigne: translation and pragmatic humanism in the sixteenth century'. Unpublished Ph.D diss., Cambridge University.

Bouwsma, William J. 1968, *Venice and the defense of republican liberty.* Berkeley: University of California Press.

Bowler, Gerald 1981, 'English Protestants and resistance theory, 1553–1603'. Unpublished Ph.D diss., London University.

1984, ' "An axe or an acte": the parliament of 1572 and resistance theory in early Elizabethan England', *Canadian Journal of History,* 19, 349–59.

Box, Ian 1982, 'Bacon's essays: from political science to political prudence', *History of Political Thought*, 3, 31–49.

Boynton, Lindsay 1967, *The Elizabethan militia 1558–1603*. London: Routledge.

Bradford, Alan T. 1983, 'Stuart absolutism and the "utility" of Tacitus', *Huntington Library Quarterly*, 46, 127–55.

Bradshaw, Brendan 1978, 'Sword, word and strategy in the reformation in Ireland', *Historical Journal*, 21, 475–502.

1981, 'More on utopia', *Historical Journal*, 24, 1–27.

1988, 'Robe and sword in the conquest of Ireland', in Claire Cross, David Loades and J. J. Scarisbrick (eds.), *Law and government under the Tudors*. Cambridge University Press, pp. 139–62.

1991, 'Transalpine humanism', in J. H. Burns (ed.), *The Cambridge history of political thought 1450–1700*. Cambridge University Press, pp. 95–131.

Brady, Ciaran 1986a, 'Court, castle and country: the framework of government in Tudor Ireland', in Ciaran Brady and Raymond Gillespie (eds.), *Natives and newcomers: essays on the making of Irish colonial society, 1534–1641*. Dublin: Irish Academic Press, pp. 22–49.

1986b, 'Spenser's Irish crisis: humanism and experience in the 1590s', *Past and Present*, no. 111, 17–49.

1988, 'Reply', *Past and Present*, no. 120, 210–15.

Bruère, R. T. 1949, 'The Latin and English version of Thomas May's *Supplementum Lucani*', *Classical Philology*, 44, 145–63.

Burke, Peter 1966, 'A survey of the popularity of ancient historians, 1450–1700', *History and Theory*, 5, 135–52.

1969, 'Tacitism', in T. A. Dorey (ed.), *Tacitus*. London: Routledge, pp. 149–71.

1990, 'The spread of Italian humanism', in Anthony Goodman and Angus MacKay (eds.), *The impact of humanism on Western Europe*. Harlow: Longman, pp. 1–22.

1991, 'Tacitism, scepticism and reason of state', in J. H. Burns (ed.), *The Cambridge history of political thought 1450–1700*. Cambridge University Press, pp. 479–98.

Bush, Douglas 1939, *The renaissance and English humanism*. University of Toronto Press.

Butler, Martin 1984, 'A case study in Caroline political theatre: Brathwaite's "Mercurius Britannicus" (1641)', *Historical Journal*, 27, 947–53.

1985, 'Romans in Britain: *The Roman actor* and the early Stuart classical plays', in Douglas Howard (ed.), *Philip Massinger: a critical reassessment*. Cambridge University Press, pp. 139–70.

Canny, Nicholas P. 1973, 'The ideology of English colonization: from Ireland to America', *William and Mary Quarterly*, 3rd ser., 30, 575–98.

1976, *The Elizabethan conquest of Ireland: a pattern established 1565–1576*. Hassocks: Harvester Press.

1978, 'The permissive frontier: the problem of social control in English settlements in Ireland and Virginia 1550–1650', in K. R. Andrews, N. P.

Canny and P. E. H. Hair (eds.), *The westward enterprise: English activities in Ireland, the Atlantic and America 1480–1650*. Liverpool University Press, pp. 17–54.

1983, 'Edmund Spenser and the development of an Anglo-Irish identity', *The Yearbook of English Studies*, 13, 1–19.

1987, 'Identity formation in Ireland: the emergence of the Anglo Irish', in Nicholas Canny and Anthony Pagden (eds.), *Colonial identity in the Atlantic world, 1500–1800*. Princeton University Press, pp. 159–212.

1988a, *Kingdom and colony: Ireland in the Atlantic world 1560–1800*. Baltimore: Johns Hopkins University Press.

1988b, 'Spenser's Irish crisis: humanism and experience in the 1590s', *Past and Present*, no. 120, 201–9.

Caspari, Fritz 1954, *Humanism and the social order in Tudor England*. University of Chicago Press.

Cavanagh, Shiela T. 1986, '"Such was Irena's countenance": Ireland in Spenser's prose and poetry', *Texas Studies in Literature and Language*, 28, 24–50.

Charlton, Kenneth 1965, *Education in renaissance England*. London: Routledge.

Christianson, Paul 1991, 'Royal and parliamentary voices on the ancient constitution, c. 1604–1621', in Linda Levy Peck (ed.), *The mental world of the Jacobean court*. Cambridge University Press, pp. 71–95.

Chwalewik, Witold 1968, Introduction, in Witold Chwalewik (ed.), *Anglo-Polish renaissance texts*. Warszawa: Pan'stwowe Wydawnictwo Naukowe, pp. 7–42.

Clark, Peter 1977, *English provincial society from the reformation to the revolution: religion, politics and society in Kent 1500–1640*. Hassocks: Harvester Press.

1978, 'Thomas Scott and the growth of urban opposition to the early Stuart regime', *Historical Journal*, 21, 1–26.

1979, '"The Ramoth-Gilead of the good": urban change and political radicalism at Gloucester 1540–1640', in Peter Clark, Alan G. R. Smith and Nicholas Tyacke (eds.), *The English commonwealth 1547–1649: essays in politics and society*. Leicester University Press, pp. 167–87.

1988, 'Early modern Gloucester, 1547–1720', in N. M. Herbert (ed.), *A history of the county of Gloucester*, vol. IV. Oxford University Press, pp. 73–123 (*The Victoria history of the counties of England*).

Clark, Peter and Slack, Paul 1976, *English towns in transition 1500–1700*. Oxford University Press.

Clark, Stuart 1970. 'Francis Bacon: the study of history and the science of man'. Unpublished Ph.D diss., Cambridge University.

Cochrane, Eric 1976, 'Science and humanism in the Italian renaissance', *American Historical Review*, 81, 1039–57.

Cochrane, Rexmond C. 1958, 'Francis Bacon and the architect of fortune', *Studies in the Renaissance*, 5, 176–95.

Cogswell, Thomas 1989a, *The blessed revolution: English politics and the coming of war, 1621–1624*. Cambridge University Press.

1989b, 'England and the Spanish match', in Richard Cust and Ann Hughes (eds.), *Conflict in early Stuart England: studies in religion and politics 1603–1642*. Harlow: Longman, pp. 107–33.

Collins, Stephen L. 1989, *From divine cosmos to sovereign state: an intellectual history of consciousness and the idea of order in renaissance England*. New York and Oxford: Oxford University Press.

Collinson, Patrick 1987, 'The monarchical republic of queen Elizabeth I', *Bulletin of the John Rylands Library*, 69, 394–424.

1990, *De republica Anglorum: or, history with the politics put back*. Inaugural lecture delivered 9 November 1989. Cambridge University Press.

Condick, Frances 1982, 'The self-revelation of a puritan: Dr Alexander Leighton in the sixteen-twenties', *Bulletin of the Institute of Historical Research*, 55, 196–203.

Conley, C. H. 1927, *The first English translators of the classics*. New Haven: Yale University Press.

Cope, Esther S. 1987, *Politics without parliaments, 1629–1640*. London: Allen & Unwin.

Costello, William 1958, *The scholastic curriculum at early seventeenth-century Cambridge*. Cambridge, Mass.: Harvard University Press.

Cressy, David 1982, 'Binding the nation: the Bonds of Association 1584 and 1696', in Delloyd J. Guth and John W. McKenna (eds.), *Tudor rule and revolution: essays for G. R. Elton from his American friends*. Cambridge University Press, pp. 217–34.

Croft, Pauline 1986, 'Annual parliaments and the Long Parliament', *Bulletin of the Institute of Historical Research*, 59, 155–71.

Croll, Morrice W. 1971, 'Attic prose: Lipsius, Montaigne, Bacon', in Stanley E. Fish (ed.), *Seventeenth-century prose: modern essays in criticism*. New York and Oxford: Oxford University Press, pp. 3–25.

Cunningham, Bernadette 1984, 'The composition of Connacht in the lordships of Clanricard and Thomond, 1577–1641', *Irish Historical Studies*, 24, 1–14.

Curtis, Mark H. 1959, *Oxford and Cambridge in transition 1558–1642*. Oxford University Press.

1962, 'The alienated intellectuals of early Stuart England', *Past and Present*, no. 23, 25–43.

Cust, Richard 1986, 'News and politics in early seventeenth-century England', *Past and Present*, no. 112, 60–90.

1987, *The forced loan and English politics 1626–1628*. Oxford University Press.

Cust, Richard and Hughes, Ann 1989, 'Introduction: after revisionism', in Richard Cust and Ann Hughes (eds.), *Conflict in early Stuart England: studies in religion and politics, 1603–1642*. Harlow: Longman, pp. 1–46.

Cust, Richard and Lake, Peter G. 1981, 'Sir Richard Grosvenor and the rhetoric of magistracy', *Bulletin of the Institute of Historical Research*, 54, 42–53.

Davis, J. C. 1991, 'Utopianism', in J. H. Burns (ed.), *The Cambridge history of political thought 1450–1700*. Cambridge University Press, pp. 329–44.

[Day, P.] 1991, *They used to live in Tewkesbury*. Stroud: privately printed.

Dean, Leonard F. 1941, 'Sir Francis Bacon's theory of civil history-writing', *English Literary History*, 8, 161–83.

Dewar, Mary 1964, *Sir Thomas Smith: a Tudor intellectual in office*. London: Athlone Press.

Donaldson, Peter S. 1988, *Machiavelli and mystery of state*. Cambridge University Press.

Dowling, Maria 1986, *Humanism in the age of Henry VIII*. London: Croom Helm.

Eccles, Mark 1933, 'Barnabe Barnes', in Charles J. Sisson (ed.), *Thomas Lodge and other Elizabethans*. Cambridge, Mass.: Harvard University Press, pp. 165–241.

Eccleshall, Robert 1978, *Order and reason in politics: theories of absolute and limited monarchy in early modern England*. Oxford University Press.

Edwards, R. Dudley 1961, 'Ireland, Elizabeth I and the counter-reformation', in S. T. Bindoff, J. Hurstfield and C. H. Williams (eds.), *Elizabethan government and society*. London: Athlone Press, pp. 315–39.

Eerde, Katherine S. van 1968, 'The Spanish match through an English Protestant's eyes', *Huntington Library Quarterly*, 32, 59–75.

Eiseley, Loren 1962, *Francis Bacon and the modern dilemma*. Lincoln: University of Nebraska.

Ellis, Steven G. 1985, *Tudor Ireland: crown, community and the conflict of cultures 1479–1603*. Harlow: Longman.

Elrington, C. R. (ed.) 1968, *A history of the county of Gloucester*, vol VIII. Oxford University Press (*The Victoria history of the counties of England*).

Elton, G. R. 1979, 'Reform and the "commonwealth-men" of Edward VI's reign', in Peter Clark, Alan G. R. Smith and Nicholas Tyacke (eds.), *The English commonwealth 1547–1640: essays in politics and society*. Leicester University Press, pp. 23–38.

    1981, 'Arthur Hall, Lord Burghley and the antiquity of parliament', in Hugh Lloyd-Jones, Valerie Pearl and Blair Worden (eds.), *History and imagination: essays in honour of H. R. Trevor-Roper*. London: Duckworth, pp. 83–103.

    1990, 'Humanism in England', in Anthony Goodman and Angus MacKay (eds.), *The impact of humanism on Western Europe*. Harlow: Longman, pp. 259–78.

Ennis, Lambert 1940. 'Anthony Nixon: Jacobean plagiarist and hack', *Huntington Library Quarterly*, 3, 377–401.

Epstein, Joel J. 1977, *Francis Bacon: a political biography*. Athens: Ohio University Press.

Farrington, Benjamin 1964, *The philosophy of Francis Bacon*. Liverpool University Press.

Ferguson, Arthur 1963, 'The Tudor commonweal and the sense of change', *Journal of British Studies*, 3, 11–35.

    1965, *The articulate citizen and the English renaissance*. Durham, NC: Duke University Press.

1986, *The chivalric tradition in renaissance England*. Washington: Folger Shakespeare Library.

Fielding, John 1988, 'Opposition to the personal rule of Charles I: the diary of Robert Woodford, 1637–1641', *Historical Journal*, 31, 769–88.

Fink, Zera S. 1945, *The classical republicans: an essay in the recovery of a pattern of thought in seventeenth-century England*. Evanston: Northwestern University.

Fischer, Kuno 1857, *Francis Bacon of Verulam: realistic philosophy and its age*. London: Longman.

Fletcher, Anthony 1986, *Reform in the provinces: the government of Stuart England*. New Haven: Yale University Press.

Fox, Alistair and Guy, John 1986, *Reassessing the Henrician age: humanism, politics and reform 1500–1550*. Oxford: Basil Blackwell.

Fussner, F. Smith 1962, *The historical revolution: English historical writing and thought 1580–1640*. London: Routledge.

Galloway, Bruce R. 1986, *The union of England and Scotland, 1603–1608*. Edinburgh: John Donald.

Gardiner, Samuel R. 1863–84, *History of England from the accession of James I to the outbreak of the Civil War*. 10 vols. London: Longman.

Gelderen, Martin van 1990, 'The Machiavellian moment and the Dutch Revolt: the rise of Neostoicism and Dutch republicanism', in Gisela Bock, Quentin Skinner and Maurizio Viroli (eds.), *Machiavelli and republicanism*. Cambridge University Press, pp. 205–23.

Goldberg, S. L. 1955, 'Sir John Hayward, "politic" historian', *Review of English Studies*, n.s., 6, 233–44.

Goldsmith, M. M. 1987, 'Liberty, luxury and the pursuit of happiness', in Anthony Pagden (ed.), *The languages of political theory in early-modern England*. Cambridge University Press, pp. 225–51.

Gollancz, I. 1914, 'The name Polonius', *Archiv für das Studium der neueren Sprachen und Literaturen*, 68, 141–4.

Gordon, M. D. 1910, 'The collection of ship-money in the reign of Charles I', *Transactions of the Royal Historical Society*, 3rd ser., 4, 141–62.

Grafton, Anthony 1991, 'Humanism and political theory', in J. H. Burns (ed.), *The Cambridge history of political thought 1450–1700*. Cambridge University Press, pp. 9–29.

Grafton, Anthony and Jardine, Lisa 1986, *From humanism to the humanities: education and the liberal arts in fifteenth- and sixteenth-century Europe*. London: Duckworth.

Greenleaf, W. H. 1964, *Order, empiricism and politics: two traditions of English political thought 1500–1700*. London: Oxford University Press.

Guy, J. A. 1982, 'The origins of the Petition of Right reconsidered', *Historical Journal*, 25, 289–312.

1988, *Tudor England*. Oxford University Press.

1993, 'The Henrician age', in J. G. A. Pocock (ed.), *The varieties of British political thought, 1500–1800*. Cambridge University Press, pp. 13–46.

Hale, J. R. 1960, 'War and public opinion in renaissance Italy', in E. F. Jacob (ed.), *Italian renaissance studies*. London: Faber and Faber, pp. 359–87.

1971, 'Incitement to violence? English divines on the theme of war, 1578 to 1631', in J. G. Rowe and W. H. Stockdale (eds.), *Florilegium historiale: essays presented to Wallace K. Ferguson*. University of Toronto Press, pp. 369–99.

1975, 'To fortify or not to fortify? Machiavelli's contribution to a renaissance debate', in H. C. Davis et al. (eds.), *Essays in honour of John Humphreys Whitfield*. London: St George's Press, pp. 99–119.

Hanson, Donald W. 1970, *From kingdom to commonwealth: the development of civic consciousness in English political thought*. Cambridge, Mass.: Harvard University Press.

Heltzel, Virgil B. 1952, 'Haly Heron: Elizabethan essayist and Euphust', *Huntington Library Quarterly*, 16, 1–21.

Hexter, J. H. 1950, 'The education of the aristocracy in the renaissance', *The Journal of Modern History*, 22, 1–20.

Hill, Christopher 1965, *Intellectual origins of the English revolution*. Oxford University Press.

1972, *The world turned upside down: radical ideas during the English revolution*. Harmondsworth: Penguin.

1986a, *Puritanism and revolution: studies in interpretation of the English revolution of the 17th century*. Harmondsworth: Penguin (first published 1958).

1986b, *Society and puritanism in pre-revolutionary England*. Harmondsworth: Penguin (first published 1964).

Hinton, R. W. K. 1960, 'English constitutional theories from Sir John Fortescue to Sir John Eliot', *English Historical Review*, 75, 410–25.

Hirst, Derek 1975, *The representative of the people? Voters and voting in England under the early Stuarts*. Cambridge University Press.

1981, 'The place of principle', *Past and Present*, no. 92, 79–99.

Hughes, Ann 1986, 'Thomas Dugard and his circle in the 1630s: a "parliamentary–puritan" connexion?', *Historical Journal*, 29, 771–93.

1991, *The causes of the English Civil War*. Basingstoke: Macmillan.

Hulme, Harold 1957, *The life of Sir John Eliot 1592 to 1632: struggle for parliamentary freedom*. New York University Press.

Hunt, William 1990, 'Civic chivalry and the English Civil War', in Anthony Grafton and Ann Blair (eds.), *The transmission of culture in early modern Europe*. Philadelphia: University of Pennsylvania Press, pp. 204–37.

Hurstfield, Joel 1961, 'The succession struggle in late Elizabethan England', in S. T. Bindoff, J. Hurstfield and C. H. Williams (eds.), *Elizabethan government and society*. London: Athlone Press, pp. 369–96.

James, Mervyn 1986, *Society, politics and culture: studies in early modern England*. Cambridge University Press.

Jardine, Lisa 1974, *Francis Bacon: discovery and the art of discourse*. Cambridge University Press.

338   *Bibliography*

1990, 'Mastering the uncouth: Gabriel Harvey, Edmund Spenser and the English experience in Ireland', in John Henry and Sarah Hutton (eds.), *New perspectives on renaissance thought: essays in the history of science, education and philosophy: in memory of Charles B. Schmitt.* London: Duckworth, pp. 68–82.

Jorgensen, Paul A. 1956, *Shakespeare's military world.* Berkeley: University of California Press.

Judson, Alexander C. 1947, 'Spenser and the Munster officials', *Studies in Philology*, 44, 157–73.

Judson, Margaret Atwood 1949, *The crisis of the constitution: an essay in constitutional and political thought in England 1603–1645.* New Brunswick: Rutgers University Press.

Kanerva, Jukka 1985, *Matkaan! Tutkimus Francis Baconin poliittisesta ajattelusta.* Jyväskylän yliopisto, Valtio-opin laitos, julkaisuja no. 49.

Kearney, Hugh 1970, *Scholars and gentlemen: universities and society in pre-industrial Britain 1500–1700.* London: Faber and Faber.

Kelso, Ruth 1929, 'The doctrine of the English gentleman in the sixteenth century', *University of Illinois Studies in Language and Literature*, 14, 1–288.

Keohane, Nannerl O. 1980, *Philosophy and the state in France: the renaissance to the enlightenment.* Princeton University Press.

Kishlansky, Mark A. 1986, *Parliamentary selection: social and political choice in early modern England.* Cambridge University Press.

Klein, Jürgen 1987, *Francis Bacon oder die Modernisierung Englands.* Anglistische und Amerikanistische Texte und Studien, vol. 4.

Klein, William E. 1987, 'Parliament, liberty and the continent in the early seventeenth century: the perception', *Parliamentary History*, 6, 209–20.

Kraus, Oskar 1926, *Der Machtgedanke und die Friedensidee in der Philosophie der Engländer. Bacon und Bentham.* Zeitfrage aus dem Gebiete der Soziologie, 3rd ser., issue 1.

Kristeller, Paul Oskar 1988, 'Humanism and moral philosophy', in Albert Rabil, Jr (ed.), *Renaissance humanism: foundations, forms, and legacy.* 3 vols. Philadelphia: University of Pennsylvania Press, vol. III, pp. 271–309.

Kupperman, Karen Ordahl 1989, 'Definitions of liberty on the eve of Civil War: Lord Saye and Sele, Lord Brooke, and the American puritan colonies', *Historical Journal*, 32, 17–33.

Lake, P. G. 1982, 'Constitutional consensus and puritan opposition in the 1620s: Thomas Scott and the Spanish match', *Historical Journal*, 25, 805–25.

1987, '[review]', *Parliamentary History*, 6, 335–6.

1989, 'Anti-popery: the structure of prejudice', in Richard Cust and Ann Hughes (eds.), *Conflict in early Stuart England: studies in religion and politics, 1603–1642.* Harlow: Longman, pp. 72–106.

Larmine, V. M. 1982, 'The godly magistrate: the private philosophy and public life of Sir John Newdigate 1571–1610', *Dugdale Society Occasional Papers*, no. 28.

Lathrop, H. B. 1933, *Translations from the classics into English from Caxton to Chapman 1477–1620*. University of Wisconsin studies in language and literature, no. 35.

Lefranc, Pierre 1968, *Sir Walter Ralegh écrivan: l'œuvre et les idées*. Paris: Libraire Armand Colin.

Lehmberg, Stanford E. 1960, *Sir Thomas Elyot, Tudor humanist*. Austin: University of Texas Press.

Levack, Brian P. 1987, *The formation of the British state: England, Scotland, and the union 1603–1707*. Oxford University Press.

Levy, F. J. 1967, *Tudor historical thought*. San Marino: Huntington Library.

1986, 'Francis Bacon and the style of politics', *English Literary Renaissance*, 16, 101–22.

1987, 'Hayward, Daniel, and the beginnings of politic history in England', *Huntington Library Quarterly*, 50, 1–34.

Lievsay, John Leon 1961, *Stefano Guazzo and the English renaissance 1575–1675*. Chapel Hill: University of North Carolina Press.

Liljeqvist, Efraim 1894, *Om Francis Bacons filosofi med särskild hänsyn till det etiska problemet*. Uppsala: Almqvist & Wiksell.

Limon, Jerzy 1986, *Dangerous matter: English drama and politics in 1623/4*. Cambridge University Press.

Lindenbaum, Peter 1990, 'Sidney and the active life', in M. J. B. Allen et al. (eds.), *Sir Philip Sidney's achievements*. New York: AMS Press, pp. 177–93.

Lockyer, Andrew 1979, '"Traditions" as context in the history of political theory', *Political Studies*, 27, 201–17.

Lockyer, Roger 1989, *The early Stuarts: a political history of England, 1603–1642*. Harlow: Longman.

Logan, George M. 1977, 'Substance and form in renaissance humanism', *Journal of Medieval and Renaissance Studies*, 7, 1–34.

Loomie, Albert J. 1986, 'The Spanish faction at the court of Charles I, 1630–8', *Bulletin of the Institute of Historical Research*, 59, 37–49.

Luciani, Vincent 1947, 'Bacon and Machiavelli', *Italica*, 24, 26–40.

1948, 'Ralegh's *Discourse of war* and Machiavelli's *Discorsi*', *Modern Philology*, 46, 122–31.

MacCaffery, W. T. 1961, 'Place and patronage in Elizabethan politics', in S. T. Bindoff, J. Hurstfield and C. H. Williams (eds.), *Elizabethan government and society*. London: Athlone Press, pp. 95–126.

McConica, James Kelsey 1965, *English humanists and reformation politics under Henry VIII and Edward VI*. Oxford University Press.

MacCulloch, Diarmaid 1986, *Suffolk and the Tudors: politics and religion in an English county 1500–1600*. Oxford University Press.

McNamee, Maurice B. 1971, 'Bacon's inductive method and humanistic grammar', *Studies in the Literary Imagination*, 4, 81–106.

Malcolm, Noel 1981, 'Hobbes, Sandys, and the Virginia Company', *Historical Journal*, 24, 297–321.

Marcotte, Elaine 1975, 'Shrieval administration of ship money in Cheshire, 1637: limitations of early Stuart governance', *Bulletin of the John Rylands Library*, 58, 137–72.

Martin, Julian 1988, ' "Knowledge is power": Francis Bacon, the state, and the reform of natural philosophy'. Unpublished Ph.D diss., Cambridge University.

Marwil, Jonathan 1976, *The trials of counsel: Francis Bacon in 1621*. Detroit: Wayne State University Press.

Mason, Roger A. [s.a.], '*Rex stoicus*: George Buchanan, James VI and the Scottish polity', in John Dwyer et al. (eds.), *New perspectives on the politics and culture of Early modern Scotland*. Edinburgh: John Donald, pp. 9–33.

Matthiessen, F. O. 1931, *Translation, an Elizabethan art*. Cambridge, Mass.: Harvard University Press.

Maus, Katherine Eiseman 1984, *Ben Jonson and the Roman frame of mind*. Princeton University Press.

Mayer, Thomas F. 1985, 'Faction and ideology: Thomas Starkey's dialogue', *Historical Journal*, 28, 1–25.

1986, 'Thomas Starkey's aristocratic reform programme', *History of Political Thought*, 7, pp. 439–61.

1989, *Thomas Starkey and the commonweal: humanist politics and religion in the reign of Henry VIII*. Cambridge University Press.

Mendle, Michael 1973, 'Politics and political thought 1640–42', in Conrad Russell (ed.), *The origins of the English civil war*. London: Macmillan, pp. 219–45.

1985, *Dangerous positions: mixed government, the estates of the realm, and the making of the Answer to the XIX propositions*. The University of Alabama Press.

1989a, 'A Machiavellian in the Long Parliament before the Civil War', *Parliamentary History*, 8, 116–24.

1989b, 'The ship money case, *The case of shipmoney*, and the development of Henry Parker's parliamentary absolutism', *Historical Journal*, 32, 513–36.

Miller, Peter, N. 1994, *Defining the common good: empire, religion and philosophy in eighteenth-century Britain*. Cambridge University Press.

Mitchell, R. J. 1938, *John Tiptoft (1427–1470)*. London: Longman.

Monsarrat, Gilles D. 1984, *Light from the porch: stoicism and English renaissance literature*. Collection Etudes Anglaises, no. 86.

Morris, Christopher 1953, *Political thought in England: Tyndale to Hooker*. London and Oxford: Oxford University Press.

1969, 'Machiavelli's reputation in Tudor England', *Il Pensiero Politico*, 2, 416–33.

Mosse, George L. 1957, *The holy pretence: a study in christianity and reason of state from William Perkins to John Winthrop*. Oxford: Basil Blackwell.

Neale, J. E. 1924, 'Peter Wentworth', *English Historical Review*, 39, 36–54, 175–205.

1953–7, *Elizabeth I and her parliaments*. 2 vols. London: Jonathan Cape.

1963, *The age of Catherine de Medici and essays in Elizabethan history*. London: Jonathan Cape.

Nederman, Cary J. 1993, 'Humanism and empire: Aeneas Sylvius Piccolomini, Cicero and the imperial ideal', *Historical Journal*, 36, 499–515.

Neustadt, Mark S. 1987, 'The making of the instauration: science, politics, and law in the career of Francis Bacon'. Unpublished Ph.D diss., the John Hopkins University.

Nippel, Wilfried 1980, *Mischverfassungstheorie und Verfassungsrealität in Antike und früher Neuzeit.* Stuttgart: Klett-Cotta.

1988, 'Bürgerideal und Oligarchie. "Klassischer Republikanismus" aus althistorischer Sicht', in Helmut G. Koenigsberger (ed.), *Republiken und Republikanismus im Europa der Frühen Neuzeit.* Munich: R. Oldenbourg, pp. 1–18.

Norbrook, David 1984, *Poetry and politics in the English renaissance.* London: Routledge.

1987, '*Macbeth* and the politics of historiography', in Kevin Sharpe and Steven Zwicker (eds.), *Politics of discourse: the literature and history of seventeenth-century England.* Berkeley: University of California Press, pp. 78–116.

1994, 'Lucan, Thomas May, and the creation of a republican literary culture', in Kevin Sharpe and Peter Lake (eds.), *Culture and politics in early Stuart England.* Basingstoke: Macmillan, pp. 45–66.

Notestein, Wallace 1971, *The House of Commons 1604–1610.* New Haven: Yale University Press.

Oestreich, Gerhard 1982, *Neostoicism and the early modern state*, ed. Birgitta Oestreich and H. G. Koenigsberger, translated by David McLintock. Cambridge University Press.

Orsini, Napoleone 1936, *Bacone e Machiavelli.* Genoa: Emiliano degli Orfini.

Outhwaite, R. B. 1985, 'Dearth, the English crown and the "crisis of the 1590s"', in Peter Clark (ed.), *The European crisis of the 1590s.* London: George Allen & Unwin, pp. 23–43.

Panizza, Diego 1969, 'Machiavelli e Alberico Gentili', *Il Pensiero Politico*, 2, 476–83.

1981, *Alberico Gentili, giurista ideologo nell'Inghilterra elisabettiana.* Padua: privately printed.

Patrick, J. Max 1971, 'Hawk versus dove: Francis Bacon's advocacy of a holy war by James I against the Turks', *Studies in the Literary Imagination*, 4, 159–71.

Peardon, Barbara 1982, 'The politics of polemics: John Ponet's *Short treatise of politic power* and contemporary circumstance 1553–1556', *Journal of British Studies*, 22, 35–49.

Peck, Linda Levy 1993a, *Court patronage and corruption in early Stuart England.* London: Routledge (first published 1990).

1993b, 'Kingship, counsel and law in early Stuart Britain', in J. G. A. Pocock (ed.), *The varieties of British political thought, 1500–1800.* Cambridge University Press, pp. 80–115.

Penrose, S. B. L. 1934, *The reputation and influence of Francis Bacon in the seventeenth century.* New York: Columbia University.

Pocock, J. G. A. 1966, ' "The onely politician": Machiavelli, Harrington and Felix Raab', *Historical Studies. Australia and New Zealand*, 12, 265–96.

1970, 'James Harrington and the Good Old Cause: a study of the ideological context of his writings', *Journal of British Studies*, 10, 30–48.

1971, *Politics, language and time: essays on political thought and history*. London: Methuen.

1975a, 'England', in Orest Ranum (ed.), *National consciousness, history and political culture in early modern Europe*. Baltimore: John Hopkins University Press, pp. 98–117.

1975b, *The Machiavellian moment: Florentine political thought and the Atlantic republican tradition*. Princeton University Press.

1977, 'Historical introduction', in J. G. A. Pocock (ed.), *The political works of James Harrington*. Cambridge University Press, pp. 1–152.

1981a, 'The Machiavellian moment revisited: a study in history and ideology', *Journal of Modern History*, 53, 49–72.

1981b, 'Virtues, rights and manners: a model for historians of political thought', *Political Theory*, 9, 353–68.

1985a, 'The history of British political thought: the creation of a center', *Journal of British Studies*, 24, 283–310.

1985b, 'The sense of history in renaissance England', in John F. Andrews (ed.), *William Shakespeare: his world, his work, his influence*. Vol. 1. New York: Charles Scribner's Sons, pp. 143–57.

1985c, *Virtue, commerce, and history: essays on political thought and history, chiefly in the eighteenth century*. Cambridge University Press.

1987a, *The ancient constitution and the feudal law: a study of English historical thought in the seventeenth century. A reissue with a retrospect*. Cambridge University Press.

1987b, 'The concept of a language and the métier d'historien: some considerations on practice', in Anthony Pagden (ed.), *The languages of political theory in early-modern Europe*. Cambridge University Press, pp. 19–38.

Power, M. J. 1985, 'London and the control of the "crisis" of the 1590s', *History*, 70, 371–85.

Praz, Mario 1928, 'Machiavelli and the Elizabethans', *Proceedings of the British Academy*, 49–97.

Pritchard, Allan 1963 *'Abuses stript and whipt* and Wither's imprisonment', *Review of English Studies*, n.s., 14, 337–45.

Quinn, D. B. 1945, 'Sir Thomas Smith (1513–1577) and the beginning of English colonial theory', *Proceedings of the American Philosophical Society*, 89, 543–60.

1947, 'Edward Walshe's "Conjectures" concerning the state of Ireland [1552]', *Irish Historical Studies*, 5, 303–14.

1976, 'Renaissance influences in English colonization', *Transactions of the Royal Historical Society*, 26, 73–93.

Raab, Felix 1964, *The English face of Machiavelli: a changing interpretation 1500–1700*. London: Routledge.

Rabb, Theodore K. 1969, 'Francis Bacon and the reform of society', in Theodore K. Rabb and Jerrold E. Seigel (eds.), *Action and conviction in early modern Europe*. Princeton University Press, pp. 163–93.

Rabb, Theodore K. 1981, 'The role of the Commons', *Past and Present*, no. 92, 55–78.

Rabil, Jr, Albert 1988, 'The significance of "civic humanism" in the interpretation of the Italian renaissance', in Albert Rabil, Jr (ed.), *Renaissance humanism: foundations, forms and legacy*. 3 vols. Philadelphia: University of Pennsylvania Press, vol. i, pp. 141–74.

Rawson, Elizabeth 1969, *The Spartan tradition in European thought*. Oxford University Press.

Reeve, L. J. 1986, 'Sir Robert Heath's advice for Charles I in 1629', *Bulletin of the Institute of Historical Research*, 59, 215–24.

1989, *Charles I and the road to personal rule*. Cambridge University Press.

Reynolds, N. B. and Hilton J. L. 1993, 'Thomas Hobbes and authority of the *Horae subsecivae*', *History of Political Thought*, 14, 361–80.

Reynolds, Susan 1977, *An introduction to the history of English medieval towns*. Oxford University Press.

1982, 'Medieval urban history and the history of political thought', *Urban History Yearbook*, 14–23.

Rice, Eugene F. 1958, *The renaissance idea of wisdom*. Cambridge, Mass.: Harvard University Press.

Rice, Lawrence H. 1963, 'The ecclesiastical polity of Francis Bacon'. Unpublished Ph.D diss., Michigan State University.

Rossi, Paolo 1968, *Francis Bacon: from magic to science*. London: Routledge.

Rowe, V. A. 1962, 'Robert, second earl of Warwick and the payment of ship-money in Essex', *Transactions of the Essex Archaeological Society*, 3rd. ser., i, 160–3.

Roy, Ian 1988, 'The English Republic, 1649–1660: the view from the Town Hall', in Helmut G. Koenigsberger (ed.), *Republiken und Republikanismus im Europa der Frühen Neuzeit*. Munich: R. Oldenbourg, pp. 213–37.

Ruigh, Robert E. 1971, *The parliament of 1624: politics and foreign policy*. Cambridge, Mass.: Harvard University Press.

Russell, Conrad 1971, *The crisis of parliaments: English history 1509–1660*. London and Oxford: Oxford University Press.

1979, *Parliaments and English politics 1621–1629*. Oxford University Press.

1990, *The causes of the English civil war*. Oxford University Press.

Sacks, David Harris 1992, 'Parliament, privilege, and the liberties of the subject', in J. H. Hexter (ed.), *Parliament and liberty from the reign of Elizabeth to the English Civil War*. Stanford University Press, pp. 84–121.

Salmon, J. H. M. 1959, *The French religious wars in English political thought*. Oxford University Press.

1980, 'Cicero and Tacitus in sixteenth-century France', *American Historical Review*, 85, 307–31.

1989, 'Stoicism and Roman example: Seneca and Tacitus in Jacobean England', *Journal of the History of Ideas*, 50, 199–225.

Saxonhouse, Arlene W. 1981, 'Hobbes & the *Horae subsecivae*', *Polity*, 13, 541–67.

Schellhase, Kenneth C. 1976, *Tacitus in renaissance political thought*. University of Chicago Press.

Schmitt, Charles, B. 1983, *John Case and Aristotelianism in renaissance England*. Kingston: McGill–Queen's University Press.

Schoeck, Richard J. 1988, 'Humanism in England', in Albert Rabil, Jr (ed.), *Renaissance humanism. Foundations, forms, and legacy.* 3 vols. Philadelphia: University of Pennsylvania Press, vol. II, pp. 5–38.

Schwoerer, Lois G. 1974, *"No standing army!" The antiarmy ideology in seventeenth-century England*. Baltimore: John Hopkins University Press.

Scott, Jonathan 1988, *Algernon Sidney and the English republic 1623–1677*. Cambridge University Press.

Shapiro, Barbara J. 1983, *Probability and certainty in seventeenth-century England: a study of the relationship between natural science, religion, history, law and literature*. Princeton University Press.

Sharpe, Kevin 1979, *Sir Robert Cotton 1586–1631: history and politics in early modern England*. Oxford University Press.

1985, 'Introduction: parliamentary history 1603–1629: in or out of perspective?', in Kevin Sharpe (ed.), *Faction and parliament: essays on early Stuart history*. London: Methuen, pp. 1–42 (first published 1978).

1989, *Politics and ideas in early Stuart England: essays and studies*. London: Pinter.

Sherman, William H. 1990, 'John Dee's Brytannicae reipublicae synopsis: a reader's guide to the Elizabethan commonwealth', *Journal of Medieval and Renaissance Studies*, 20, 293–315.

Shutte, Anne Jacobson 1983, 'An early Stuart critique of Machiavelli as historiographer: Thomas Jackson and the Discorsi', *Albion*, 15, 1–18.

Simon, Joan 1966, *Education and society in Tudor England*. Cambridge University Press.

Skinner, Quentin 1978, *The foundations of modern political thought*. 2 vols. Cambridge University Press.

1987, 'Sir Thomas More's Utopia and the language of renaissance humanism', in Anthony Pagden (ed.), *The languages of political theory in early-modern Europe*. Cambridge University Press, pp. 123–57.

1988, 'Political philosophy', in Charles B. Schmitt and Quentin Skinner (eds.), *The Cambridge history of renaissance philosophy*. Cambridge University Press, pp. 387–452.

1990a, 'Machiavelli's Discorsi and the pre-humanist origins of republican ideas', in Gisela Bock, Quentin Skinner, Maurizio Viroli (eds.), *Machiavelli and republicanism*. Cambridge University Press, pp. 121–41.

1990b, 'The republican idea of political liberty', in Gisela Bock, Quentin Skinner and Maurizio Viroli (eds.), *Machiavelli and republicanism*. Cambridge University Press, pp. 293–309.

1990c, 'Thomas Hobbes: rhetoric and the construction of morality', *Proceedings of the British Academy*, 76, 1–61.

Smith, Alan G. R. 1973, 'Constitutional ideas and parliamentary developments in England 1603–1625', in Alan G. R. Smith (ed.), *The reign of James VI and I*. London: Macmillan, pp. 160–76.

Smuts, R. Malcolm 1987, *Court culture and the origins of a royalist tradition in early Stuart England*. Philadelphia: University of Pennsylvania Press.

1994, 'Court-centred politics and the uses of Roman historians, c.1590–1630', in Kevin Sharpe and Peter Lake (eds.), *Culture and politics in early Stuart England*. Basingstoke: Macmillan, pp. 21–43.

Snow, Vernon F. 1977, *Parliament in Elizabethan England: John Hooker's order and usage*. New Haven: Yale University Press.

Sommerville, J. P. 1986, *Politics and ideology in England, 1603–1640*. Harlow: Longman.

1989, 'Ideology, property and the constitution', in Richard Cust and Ann Hughes (eds.), *Conflict in early Stuart England: studies in religion and politics, 1603–1642*. London: Longman, pp. 47–71.

1991, 'James I and the divine right of kings: English politics and continental theory', in Linda Levy Peck (ed.), *The mental world of the Jacobean court*. Cambridge University Press, pp. 55–70.

Stern, Virginia F. 1979, *Gabriel Harvey: his life, marginalia and library*. Oxford University Press.

Stone, Lawrence 1964, 'The educational revolution in England, 1560–1649', *Past and Present*, no. 28, 41–80.

1986, *The causes of the English revolution 1529–1642*. London: Routledge (first published 1972).

Swales, Robin J. W. 1977, 'The ship money levy of 1628', *Bulletin of the Institute of Historical Research*, 50, 164–76.

Tenney, Mary F. 1941, 'Tacitus in the politics of early Stuart England', *Classical Journal*, 37, 151–63.

Thompson, Christopher 1972, 'The origins of the politics of the parliamentary middle group, 1625–1629', *Transactions of the Royal Historical Society*, 5th ser., 22, 71–86.

Tittler, Robert 1989, 'Elizabethan towns and the "points of contact": parliament', *Parliamentary history*, 8, 275–88.

Todd, Margo 1983, 'Seneca and the protestant mind: the influence of stoicism in puritan ethics', *Archiv für Reformationsgeschichte*, 75, 182–99.

1987, *Christian humanism and the puritan social order*. Cambridge University Press.

Trevor-Roper, H. R. 1945, 'Five letters of Sir Thomas Bodley', *Bodleian Library Record*, 2, 134–9.

Trinkaus, Charles 1990, 'Renaissance ideas and the idea of renaissance', *Journal of the History of Ideas*, 51, 667–84.

Tuck, Richard 1979, *Natural rights theories: their origin and development*. Cambridge University Press.

1983, 'Grotius, Carneades and Hobbes', *Grotiana*, n.s., 4, 43–62.

1987, 'The "modern" theory of natural law', in Anthony Pagden (ed.), *The languages of political theory in early-modern Europe*. Cambridge University Press, pp. 99–119.

1989, *Hobbes*. Oxford University Press.

1990, 'Humanism and political thought', in Anthony Goodman and Angus Mackay (eds.), *The impact of humanism on Western Europe*. London: Longman, pp. 43–65.

1993, *Philosophy and government 1572–1651*. Cambridge University Press.

Underdown, David 1985, *Revel, riot, and rebellion: popular politics and culture in England 1603–1660*. Oxford University Press.

Venn, John and Venn, J. A. 1927, *Alumni Cantabrigienses*. Cambridge University Press.

Vickers, Brian 1984, 'Bacon's so-called "utilitarianism": sources and influence', in Marta Fattori (ed.), *Francis Bacon: terminologia e fortune nel xvii secolo*. Rome: Edizioni dell' Ateno, pp. 281–314.

Walzer, Michael 1965, *The revolution of the saints: a study in the origins of radical politics*. Cambridge, Mass.: Harvard University Press.

Warhaft, Sidney 1971, 'The providential order in Bacon's new philosophy', *Studies in the Literary Imagination*, 4, 49–64.

Webster, Charles 1975, *The great instauration: science, medicine, and reform 1626–1660*. London: Duckworth.

Weinbaum, Martin 1943, *British borough charters 1307–1660*. Cambridge University Press.

Weinberger, Jerry 1980, Introduction, in Francis Bacon, *The great instauration and New Atlantis*, ed. Jerry Weinberger. Arlington Heights: AHM Publishing Corporation, pp. vii–xxix.

1985, *Science, faith, and politics: Francis Bacon and the utopian roots of the modern age*. Ithaca: Cornell University Press.

Weiss, Roberto 1957, *Humanism in England during the fifteenth century*. Oxford: Basil Blackwell (first published 1941).

Weston, C. C. 1960, 'The theory of mixed monarchy under Charles I and after', *English Historical Review*, 75, 426–43.

Weston, C. C. and Greenberg, J. R. 1981, *Subjects and sovereigns: the grand controversy over legal sovereignty in Stuart England*. Cambridge University Press.

Wheeler, Harvey 1956, 'The constitutional ideas of Francis Bacon', *Western Political Quarterly*, 9, 927–36.

Whitaker, Virgil K. 1970, 'Bacon's doctrine of forms: a study of seventeenth-century eclecticism', *Huntington Library Quarterly*, 33, 209–16.

White, Howard B. 1958, 'Bacon's imperialism', *American Political Science*, 52, 470–89.

1968, *Peace among the willows: the political philosophy of Francis Bacon*. The Hague: Martinus Nijhoff.

Whitney, Charles 1986, *Francis Bacon and modernity*. New Haven: Yale University Press.

Willcox, William Bradford 1940, *Gloucestershire: a study in local government 1590–1640*. New Haven: Yale University Press.

Williams, Penry 1984, 'The crown and the communities', in Christopher Haigh (ed.), *The reign of Elizabeth I*. Basingstoke: Macmillan, pp. 125–46.

Williamson, Arthur H. 1979, *Scottish national consciousness in the age of James VI*. Edinburgh: John Donald.

Willson, David Harris 1956, *King James VI and I*. London: Jonathan Cape.

Wolff, Emil 1910–13, *Francis Bacon und seine Quellen*. Literarhistorische Forschungen, issues XL, LII.

Womersley, David 1991, 'Sir Henry Savile's translation of Tacitus and the political interpretation of Elizabethan texts', *The Review of English Studies* n.s., 42, 313–42.

Woolf, D. R. 1985, 'Two Elizabethans? James I and the late queen's famous memory', *Canadian Journal of History*, 20, 167–91.

1990, *The idea of history in early Stuart England*. University of Toronto Press.

Wootton, David 1986, Introduction, in David Wootton (ed.), *Divine right and democracy: an anthology of political writing in Stuart England*. Harmondsworth: Penguin, pp. 21–86.

Worden, Blair 1981, 'Classical republicanism and the puritan revolution', in Hugh Lloyd-Jones, Valerie Pearl and Blair Worden (eds.), *History and imagination: essays in honour of H. R. Trevor-Roper*. London: Duckworth, pp. 182–200.

1990, 'Milton's republicanism and the tyranny of heaven', in Gisela Bock, Quentin Skinner and Maurizio Viroli (eds.), *Machiavelli and republicanism*. Cambridge University Press, pp. 225–45.

1991a, 'English republicanism', in J. H. Burns (ed.), *The Cambridge history of political thought 1450–1700*. Cambridge University Press, pp. 443–75.

1991b, 'The Revolution of 1688–89 and the English republican tradition', in Jonathan I. Israel (ed.), *The Anglo-Dutch moment: essays on the Glorious Revolution and its world impact*. Cambridge University Press, pp. 241–77.

1994, 'Ben Jonson among the historians', in Kevin Sharpe and Peter Lake (eds.), *Culture and politics in early Stuart England*. Basingstoke: Macmillan, pp. 67–89.

Wright, Louis B. 1943, 'Propaganda against James I's "appeasement" of Spain', *Huntington Library Quarterly*, 6, 149–72.

1958, *Middle-class culture in Elizabethan England*. Ithaca: Cornell University Press (first published 1935).

Young, Michael B. 1985, 'Buckingham, war, and parliament: revisionism gone too far', *Parliamentary History*, 4, 45–69.

Zagorin, Perez 1954, *A history of political thought in the English revolution*. London: Routledge.

Zaller, Robert 1983, 'Edward Alford and the making of country radicalism', *Journal of British Studies*, 22, 59–79.

Zeeveld, W. Gordon 1969, *Foundations of Tudor policy*. London: Methuen (first published 1948).

Index

IDEAS IN CONTEXT

Edited by Quentin Skinner (general editor), Lorraine Daston, Wolf Lepenies, Richard Rorty and J. B. Schneewind

Series list

Titles marked with an asterisk are also available in paperback

Printed in the United States
130489LV00002B/318/A